A VERY CAPITALIST CONDITION
A History and Politics of Disability

Roddy Slorach

CW01497734

Roddy Slorach is a longstanding socialist based in east London who works as a disability adviser in Higher Education.

A VERY CAPITALIST CONDITION

A History and Politics of Disability

Roddy Slorach

Bookmarks Publications

A Very Capitalist Condition: A History and Politics of Disability
By Roddy Slorach
First published 2016 by Bookmarks Publications
This edition published 2024 by Bookmarks Publications
c/o 1 Bloomsbury Street, London WC1B 3QE
© Bookmarks Publications
Typeset by Peter Robinson
Cover by Esther Neslen
Printed by Halstan Limited
ISBN 978 1 914143 98 4 (pbk)

Contents

Acknowledgements

I owe a debt to many people for their help in writing this book. It would certainly not have been possible without Mike Oliver and Vic Finkelstein, whose development of the "social model" comprised the first Marxist understanding of disability. Any criticisms I have of their work has benefited from the several decades of wide-ranging debate it inspired.

Some research was particularly helpful in turning a vague idea into a clearer plan, particularly Martha Rose's book on ancient Greece and Irina Metzler's work on feudalism. Chris Stringer suggested key sources on the earliest human societies. Thanks to Martin Empson for comments on an early draft of Chapter 4, and to Graham Mustin for advice on Chapter 5. John Parrington and Lee Humber were a great help in writing Chapter 7. Thanks to Jacqui Freeman for translating a lengthy article as part of my research for Chapter 8 (which I unfortunately could not use). Daniela Manske and Felix Peter translated and identified German sources for Chapter 9, while Jenny Chan and Hsiao-Hung Pai helped me find material on China. Thanks to Nicky Evans and Geraldine O'Halloran for help with Chapter 10—and also to two Deaf women I met in Glasgow's Laurieston Bar in April 2015, whose names I am sorry to say I cannot recall. Chapter 11 was hugely improved with help from Andrew Brammer, Beth Greenhill, Iain Ferguson and Sue Kelly. Richard Rieser, Mike Harker, Keir McKechnie and especially Shirley Franklin all helped improve the individual sections of Chapter 12.

More generally, several sections of the book benefited from discussion with Nicki Martin, Rob Murthwaite and Ellen Clifford. I owe greatest thanks to Lee Humber, who gave me sound advice on the book's content and structure, and to Sheila McGregor and

Gareth Jenkins, who both provided invaluable comments on an advanced draft. Thanks too to Esther Neslen for the great cover design, and to Peter Robinson, Carol Williams, Eileen Short and Lina Nicolli for their work on the production.

Last but certainly not least, thanks to Daniela for all her patience and support.

Responsibility for the final text, including any mistakes or wrong judgments or arguments, is of course mine alone, particularly as I did not always follow the advice offered.

I dedicate this book to my mother.

Introduction to the 2024 edition

First published in 2016, this book documents the ways in which disability is hardwired into a society based on competitive accumulation – the pursuit of profit at all costs. The remorseless and ruinous drive for profit under capitalism inhibits, disfigures and disables human capacities. The book's central argument is that to unleash these capacities requires fundamental change; in short, revolution. The working class, as the most diverse part of our society, contains within it both the power and the potential to uproot the source of all inequality and exploitation. Disabled people, for so long marginalised and excluded, must be among the leaders of such a movement – not least to demonstrate to ourselves and to those who struggle alongside us that we are capable.

Much has changed since the book was first published. Mainstream politics, not least in the US and in the UK, is increasingly dominated by the agenda of the far right. Government policies target migrants in particular but also "woke" policies in general which are held to favour minorities at the expense of the "left behind". Comparisons between our current "age of catastrophe" and that of the 1930s are increasingly apposite:

> Many of the factors that made the world so volatile, crisis-prone, and dangerous during the inter-war period – mounting inequality, widespread civil strife, rising populism and xenophobia, growing economic nationalism and pressures to deglobalise, resurgent authoritarianism, backsliding democracy, escalating great power rivalry, American retreat, brittle international institutions, and a free world in disarray – were *already* re-emerging in our own time during

the years before the coronavirus pandemic struck... COVID and the shockwaves flowing from it have made all these problems worse.[1]

Climate chaos is another major factor in this "polycrisis", making life for the vast majority of the world's population harder, poorer and shorter. In this new introduction I explore what these changes have meant for disabled people.

Disabling the world

The growth in the world's population of disabled people has prompted new research by international agencies. In December 2022, the World Health Organisation (WHO) reported that the "number of persons with significant disabilities worldwide is approximately 1.3 billion and represents 16% of the world's population".[2] This social group "die earlier, have poorer health and functioning, and are more affected by health emergencies than persons without disabilities".[3] The WHO lists several causes: first, "the very broad socioeconomic and political context, and the mechanisms that generate social stratification"; second, "the social determinants of health (the conditions in which people are born, grow, live, work and age)"; third, "noncommunicable diseases, including tobacco use, diet, alcohol consumption and amount of exercise, as well as environmental factors such as air pollution"; and fourth, the quality and inclusivity of available health services.[4]

War and other forms of violence are also major causes: "For every child killed in warfare, three are injured and acquire a permanent form of disability. In some countries, up to a quarter of disabilities result from injuries and violence".[5] Another major report found that people who are disabled are likely to die on average 10-20 years before those who are not.[6]

These reports confirm that the root cause of much impairment and disability is poverty itself. "Poor people are...forced to live and work in unsafe environments with poor sanitation, crowded living conditions, and with little access to education, clean water, or enough good food. This makes diseases such as tuberculosis and polio...much more common".[7]

Social factors also govern which impairments meet a given definition of disability. In China's census of 2011, "about one in 16 of the population...were classified as disabled. This compares with one in five in Britain and one in eight in America. Unlike in the West, China's definition of disabled does not cover those with chronic illnesses. It also excludes many people who have use of their limbs but struggle with routine tasks".[8] Nevertheless, China is not an exception. The US definition of disability is more restrictive than that used in the UK, while the proportion of those classified as disabled in European Union countries ranges from 11 percent in Malta at one extreme to 39.5 percent in Latvia at the other".[9]

Another feature common to these reports by international agencies is their conflation of two very different things. They describe causes of impairment – limitations in how our bodies, minds or senses work – but routinely use the term disability to do so. It is not, however, a lack of function in our bodies, minds or senses which cause people with impairments to be systematically excluded or marginalised from society. To disable something or someone is to *prevent* them from functioning or working. Taking the social model of disability as its starting point (see Chapter 3), this book explains how capitalism by its very nature generates both impairment and disability on an immense scale. Treating these terms as interchangeable – focusing on perceived deficits in the individual – is to effectively disguise the ways in which our society oppresses disabled people.

Leading the world backwards

Some things have improved. In many countries, especially in the Global North, cinemas, theatres and restaurants have become accessible, as has much of public transport. More recently, disability has become more visible in arts and culture, with disabled characters no longer simply a token presence in mainstream TV programmes.[10] Nonetheless, these improvements have been partial, piecemeal, and painfully slow in coming. Moreover, in countries such as the US and the UK, life for most disabled people has over recent years become much harder.

In 2021, around 25 percent of disabled people in the US were defined as living in poverty, compared to 12 percent of non-disabled people.[11] In that year, pay for disabled adults was on average less than two-thirds of that for those who were not disabled.[12] Disabled workers in the US can legally be paid less than a dollar an hour and are exempted by law from (very low) minimum-wage standards "if the worker's disability reduces his or her ability to do the job".[13]

The US social security system shares many similarities with the UK, not least a complex and bureaucratic claims process designed to exclude claimants. Of around two million Disability Insurance claims made annually, two-thirds are initially denied and nine-tenths of review applications rejected – although over half of claims pursued to appeal courts are successful.[14] As the government states, the parallel Social Security Income programme is "barely enough to keep a beneficiary above the 2018 poverty level".[15] In granting the majority of appeals, judges have condemned errors all too familiar to UK claimants; "inaccurate assessments of whether claimants can work, failures to consider medical evidence and factual mistakes".[16] In addition – despite its legal obligations – "the federal government is currently paying less than half of its originally promised per-pupil funding",[17] leaving millions of disabled children without vital support.

Big business has profited handsomely from this misery. In March 2022, the Sackler family was fined $6 billion (£4.5 billion) for its role in the US opioid epidemic. Its company Purdue Pharma promoted sales of the painkiller OxyContin despite knowing it was addictive. OxyContin killed nearly half a million (overwhelmingly working class) people between 1999 and 2019.[18] Some took the drug to ease the pain of physical labour in order to keep working, then became addicted. The crisis was worst "in states where industry has been smashed. Here, opioid addiction is linked to what in the US have been called 'deaths of despair'—suicide, alcohol and drug-related deaths".[19]

What of the UK? Over 25 years after the introduction of the Disability Discrimination Act by a previous Conservative government, Boris Johnson published a foreword to his government's

National Disability Strategy. The then Prime Minister stated "a disabled person with a degree is no more likely to have a job than a non-disabled person who left school at 16", and spoke of a need to address "countless instances of unfairness that plague daily life in everything from grocery shopping to the accessibility of courtrooms". Johnson also wrote of the need to bridge a "gaping chasm of education, skills and employment".[20] A House of Lords committee report found it "an affront to Parliament" that "parts of the Equality Act, now over 10 years old, are still not in force".[21]

Nonetheless, reporting only this woeful lack of progress is to deliberately misrepresent the progressive immiseration caused by the UK's ongoing "war on disabled people".[22] As the government itself reported:

> In 2016 the UK was investigated under the Optional Protocol of the UN CRPD following a formal request from several disability organisations. The UN Committee…found that "grave or systematic violations" of disabled persons' rights had taken place because of welfare reforms in the UK since 2010… [which] had "disproportionally and adversely" affected the rights of people with disabilities, citing changes to Housing Benefit entitlement, eligibility criteria for Personal Independence Payment (PIP) and social care, and the ending of the Independent Living Fund.[23]

An alternative submission to the UN by disabled people's organisations in August 2023 found that, "benefits in the UK are comparatively low by international standards with one of the lowest benefit rates relative to earnings", and that the "real terms value of the standard benefit payment" was over ten percent lower than in 2010.[24] According to disability charity Scope, the average disabled household in the UK (including at least one disabled adult or child) faces extra costs of £1,122 per month (a rise of £147 over the three years to 2023).[25] This makes disabled people "almost three times as likely to live in material deprivation than the rest of the population".[26]

Despite the UN's findings, the current UK government plans to scrap the work capability assessment (WCA), a change which is likely to cost one million incapacity benefit claimants about £350 a month.[27] The WCA, which assesses capacity for work, will be replaced by the personal independence payment (PIP) test, which measures only the extra living costs of disability. PIP tests – no more trusted by disabled people's organisations than the WCA – currently take 14 weeks to process. Many disabled people with conditions deemed to prevent them working will no longer receive extra support.

Not every assault has been successful. The government's long-established plans to close 1,000 ticket offices, threatening access to the rail network, were abandoned in October 2023. A campaign led by the RMT rail union and disabled people's organisations included 750,000 participants – "the biggest ever response to a public consultation".[28]

Little wonder that, in August 2023, the government refused to participate in a meeting at the UN to assess the UK's progress on disability rights since the 2016 report.[29] Ministers may well have decided they could not defend their record.

COVID-19

As documented by Oxfam in June 2022, the global coronavirus pandemic dramatically exposed and exacerbated existing social inequalities:

> The incomes of 99% of humanity are worse off because of COVID-19. Widening economic, gender, and racial inequalities – as well as the inequality that exists between countries – are tearing our world apart... The world's 10 richest men have doubled their fortunes, while over 160 million people are projected to have been pushed into poverty. Meanwhile, an estimated 17 million people have died from COVID-19 – a scale of loss not seen since the Second World War.[30]

The terrible toll of COVID-19 was partly due to competition between rival nation-states. Modern science made it possible to develop a vaccine in less than a year, but its distribution was overwhelmingly concentrated in the richer countries of the Global North, making the emergence of new variants more likely.[31]

Meanwhile, studies suggest that "at least 65 million people" globally have long COVID, with symptoms that impair functional and cognitive capacity".[32]

The COVID-19 death toll was also "concentrated mainly outside the wealthy 'core' of the system, with the main exception of the United States, where the residents of Republican controlled southern states paid a high price".[33] There was, of course, another outlier. "Among comparator high-income countries (other than the US), only Spain and Italy had higher rates of excess mortality in the pandemic to mid-2021 than the UK".[34] The record of the UK, which entered the pandemic with social care and health services already overstretched and at full capacity, provides further proof that some lives are less valued than others.

Data published by the UK's Office for National Statistics (ONS) shows that disabled people accounted for 60 percent of all deaths from the disease in 2020.[35] A later study found that in England those with learning difficulties were eight times more likely to die from the virus, and that "discrimination, exclusion and living in residential care homes probably added to the risk".[36]

In early 2020, the government's decision to discharge hospital patients infected with COVID-19 to care homes in England and Wales led directly to the death of 20,000 elderly or disabled people.[37] Throughout the lockdown, Boris Johnson's government refused to provide British Sign Language interpreters for its live COVID-19 briefings.[38] Both decisions were subsequently ruled to be illegal.

The experience of lockdown was not universally negative. Some disabled people welcomed a new solitude and control over their routine, combined with the absence of unwanted social contact and the stresses this involves. For most of those placed on furlough or working from home, however, lockdown meant overcrowding, a lack of space and facilities, and intensified pressures on households – including increased domestic violence.[39] On the other hand, "key workers" forced to go out to work, often to provide essential services, faced greater exposure to the risk of illness and death.

For the rich minority (statistically those least at risk) the pandemic provided new opportunities to enrich themselves further. The UK Parliament's Public Accounts Committee reported in June 2022 that:

> The Department for Health & Social Care lost 75% of the £12 billion it spent on personal protective equipment (PPE) in the first year of the pandemic to inflated prices...24% of the PPE contracts awarded are now in dispute – including contracts for products that were not fit for purpose and one contract for 3.5 billion gloves where there are allegations of modern slavery against the manufacturer.[40]

Anti-corruption watchdog Transparency International UK identified COVID-19 contracts worth more than £3.7 billion which were awarded during 2020, including the existence of a "VIP lane" which was "used to fast track offers of PPE from companies referred by MPs, peers and senior officials".[41]

The interests of profit came first at every turn – and the government partied as people died.

Climate chaos and war

The climate crisis intensifies the difficulties already endured by those living in poverty. Disabled people in low and middle-income countries are highly "climate vulnerable":

> For example, 54.3% and 27% of the adult populations of Afghanistan and Syria respectively have a disability (including physical, intellectual, psychosocial, sensory or other impairments). Climate change may lead to a higher risk of forced displacement through an increased frequency and intensity of extreme weather events, such as cyclones and drought, as well as environmental degradation that impacts livelihoods and survival. People with disabilities face heightened protection risks and barriers to inclusion and are likely to have specific, additional needs related to forced displacement in the context of disasters and climate change.[42]

In addition to Afghanistan and Syria, more recent wars in Sudan and Ukraine have added to this global refugee crisis. The number of refugees is now over 100 million for the first time on record, and around one-tenth of them are disabled.[43] Governments have typically responded by adopting racist policies on migration previously associated only with the far right. "Having once denounced Donald Trump's plans to build a wall on the US border with Mexico as morally unacceptable, the European Union now has…steel walls or razor-wire fences, running to a combined length of nearly 2,000km".[44]

It is too early to say at the time of writing just how many Palestinians will be killed, displaced or traumatised by the Israeli state's onslaught against Gaza that began in October 2023. Several months earlier, an authoritative report found that over half the adult population of Gaza and the West Bank screened positively for depression, with the rate in Gaza specifically at 71 percent. In addition, "more than a quarter of survey respondents reported… conflict-related trauma".[45]

Like many of their non-disabled peers, "many forcibly displaced people settle in camps and in slums, where infrastructure and services are weak and inaccessible", and "face barriers accessing safe water for drinking, sanitation and hygiene".[46] Among those "most adversely affected in an emergency, sustaining disproportionately higher rates of morbidity and mortality, [they are also] among those least able to access emergency support".[47] Disabled people are particularly badly impacted by "sea-level rise, human mobility, flooding, natural disasters, water scarcity, the loss of agricultural land and impacts on health and livelihoods".[48]

Huge wildfires, record-breaking heatwaves and widespread flooding are now common in the wealthier states of the Global North. A landmark report in September 2023 found that the UK has lost over half its biodiversity, with one in six species at risk of extinction. Climate change, combined with intensive farming and fishing, is the major contributing factor.[49] Here, as elsewhere, the dismantling of regulatory mechanisms puts lives at risk. Satellite data shows that 98 percent of people across Europe face air pollution above limits recommended by the WHO,[50] impacting on birth and early life, as well as mental health and dementia.[51]

The climate emergency is also damaging people's mental health. An authoritative study by the Grantham Institute at Imperial College found "clear evidence for severe distress following extreme weather events such as floods", that people "who already meet the criteria for mental illness are more vulnerable to the effects of climate change on physical as well as mental health", and that climate change "exacerbates mental distress, particularly among young people, even for individuals who are not directly affected (eg, eco-anxiety')".[52]

The politics of identity

One of the themes explored in these pages is the specific nature of disability as a form of oppression. Impairments and identities alike are shaped by social, economic and political forces.

The intensified discrimination described above has led some disabled people to reject what they perceive to be a "stigmatised identity". New terms emphasise the abilities of people rather than their perceived deficits. Some, for example, advocate an "affirmative model" in place of the social model of disability, others that we should replace the term specific learning "difficulty" with the word "difference". In similar vein, others suggest we talk of "differently abled" in preference to disabled people. Autistic people are often referred to as "thinking differently" due to brains which are "differently wired",[53] or as "neurodiverse" as opposed to the "neurotypical" norm.[54]

These approaches, given a common intention to tackle stigma and to empower people, are not without merit but are in my view mistaken. The use of euphemisms such as "differently abled" firstly "suggests that the term disability *should* be uncomfortable and therefore should be avoided", in effect "discouraging discussion about disability and what it means to be disabled".[55] The implication in all these terms is "that there is in fact a correct or right way to be 'able'. It supports the false idea of the normal body/mind, which is what 'differently abled' is supposed to undermine".[56] Crucially, the use of such terms reduces social and economic marginalisation and discrimination to an individual problem. Adopting these terms (or having them imposed by others) does not leave individuals any less likely to experience discrimination than others who do not.

If the terms discussed above sidestep the issue of discrimination, another popularised in recent years – the concept of "allyship" – is based on an explicit recognition of that reality. According to disability charity Scope, "A disability ally supports disabled people and uses their privilege to make change".[57] This concept of "privilege", however, is problematic.[58] Why should people who do not face disability discrimination oppose it if they have a material interest in maintaining that oppression?

If all non-disabled people benefit from the oppression of disabled people and so are inherently stained by prejudice, then oppression can never be ended. Allyship focuses on individual relations but, as this book shows, disability is rooted in the structures and institutions of our society. As with other forms of oppression, disability discrimination is built on notions of superior and inferior, normal and abnormal. It functions as a means of divide and rule, breaking the working class and the poor into competing groups. Governments and employers who pay lip service to diversity maintain a hierarchy where some lives – as demonstrated by the experience of the COVID-19 pandemic – are seen as less important than others. Building solidarity, in contrast to allyship, is based on the idea that all those who resist discrimination have a vested interest in the success of the struggle.[59]

Identity can unite and mobilise people around a powerful sense of unity against a shared injustice to demand change. At the height of the Black Lives Matter movement in the summer of 2020, a poll in *The Economist* found that 67 percent of people in the developed world expressed support for its aims.[60] This raised vital questions, not only for black people who previously thought they had to fight racism alone but also for the many white people who joined the protests and wanted to know what role they could play in ending racism. Other movements, from #MeToo to the struggles for trans rights, can shape or change people's sense of identity, instilling a sense of dignity and pride.

Organising based on identity also raises difficult questions. Can those who don't suffer a particular form of discrimination be part of the fight against it? Who is in and who is out? Who decides what individual experience is valid or authentic? Is Elon Musk's autistic identity as relevant as that of autistic people who are not multi-billionaires? Who chooses representatives and community leaders?[61]

Tom Shakespeare, whose earlier writings on disability are discussed in these pages, argues on the one hand that identities can be powerful and give people a sense of belonging but that on the other they risk "reinforcing our separateness" and carry a danger of fragmentation. Shakespeare cites Lennard Davis: "The list of identities will only grow larger, tied to an ever-expanding idea of inclusiveness. After all, when all identities are finally included, there will be no identity".[62]

Neither is it a given that all members of one oppressed group will support or identify with others. In recent years, for example, some feminists have opposed or even campaigned against transgender rights. In 2019, several board members of the UK-based academic journal *Disability & Society* resigned in protest at chief editor Michele Moore's claims that "transgender ideology is inherently dangerous to children and young people".[63]

The key difficulty with organising on the basis of a common disability identity, however, is that disabled people as a group are divided by class.

Class and the return of class struggle

Relentless media headlines and political rhetoric about "benefit cheats" have helped to intensify the already common perception that all "deserving" or "genuine" disabled people are jobless. Certainly, unemployment rates among disabled people in the UK remain stubbornly high.[64] Some impairment groups are particularly badly affected, with just 16 percent of autistic people and less than 6 percent of people with "learning disabilities" in full-time work.[65]

Disgraceful though these figures are, around half of all disabled people of working age – 1 in 7 of the total UK workforce[66] – have jobs. They are more likely to be in lower-skilled roles, to be self-employed and to be working part-time (with less hours).[67] Like their non-disabled counterparts, low pay forces many disabled workers to rely on tax credits and housing benefits.[68]

The fact that so many disabled workers are concentrated in lower-paid and often precarious employment has led many activists and commentators to argue that disabled people as a whole form what Karl Marx referred to as a reserve army of labour, "identified by the mass of unemployed *and underemployed* individuals".[69] Nonetheless, this description does not apply to a significant proportion of disabled people.

UK reports show that disabled people are most likely to work in health, retail or education,[70] but not what kind of jobs they have. We do know that more disabled people are studying in higher education, comprising almost 16 percent of all university students in 2021/22 compared to less than 9 percent in 2011/12.[71] Of those disabled people with a degree, 73 percent work, many of them in skilled or professional jobs.[72] These figures strongly suggest that many of the 5 million disabled people in employment do not belong to the reserve army of labour and, instead, form a permanent part of the British workforce.

Promoting a series of articles on disability in the *Financial Times*, the blind Labour peer and former home secretary David Blunkett argued that "perversely, the higher you climb in any form of employment, the more support you get".[73] "Perverse" may well be an appropriate term, as disabled people are rarely found in senior roles. "According to 2020 annual reports, there are no executives or senior managers who have disclosed a disability, at any of the FTSE 100 companies".[74]

The evidence from elsewhere, however, suggests that more "new faces in high places" does little to advance equality. The ethnic identity of UK politicians such as Kemi Badenoch and Suella Braverman, for example, has allowed them to promote overtly racist policies in a way that white politicians would find harder. As Angela Davis put it in relation to the record of black politicians in the US, "When people call for diversity and link it to justice and equality, that's fine. But there's a model of diversity as the difference that makes no difference, the change that makes no change".[75]

A recent US study found that workers "who disclose [disability/impairment] are more content (65% versus 27%) and less isolated (8% versus 37%) at work than employees who do not disclose".[76]

Challenging discrimination by workmates can help to undermine stereotypes and assumptions. As one delegate at the 2022 Trades Union Congress Disabled Workers' Conference explained, "My reasonable adjustments made me visible, and my hope would be for all disabled workers who need them, to have the right to them, to have the confidence to request them and to work in workplaces where they are seen as standard and not an afterthought".[77]

Every major UK trade union offers training for activists on campaigning for reasonable adjustments at work, and several have dedicated sections for disabled members. Many disabled people work in areas where there is greater trade union density such as education and local government. Not only are disabled workers "significantly more likely" than others to join a trade union,[78] but studies show that "equality rights are more likely to be secured in workplaces where unions are present".[79]

Class is not based on how we feel or on our identity; nor is it based on what we eat or how we dress. It is instead based on our economic relation to capital, in which the vast majority are exploited by a small minority. Class influences who is likely to be *born* disabled, who is likely to *become* disabled and what it is like to *be* disabled. The rich are unlikely to be cannon fodder in wars or to contract illnesses from polluted water or damp housing. Wealthy disabled people are unlikely to be excluded from society by underfunded social and health services, benefit cuts or inaccessible public transport. They are unlikely to see disability as a class issue but instead as one of misfortune or individual circumstance, which at best involves securing civil rights that are compatible with the status quo.

This brings us to Keir Starmer's Labour Party, which promises to be a government for big business, spending restraint and law and order. Shadow health and social care secretary Wes Streeting has already ruled out an immediate end to charges for adult social care in favour of a more gradual move towards "affordability".[80] Starmer used a column in *The Sun* newspaper to denounce critics of Labour's hard-line stance on immigration as "un-British".[81] Such an approach threatens to repeat the failures of Labour-type parties across Europe, where broken hopes have laid the basis for far-right and explicitly fascist parties to join or even dominate the political mainstream.

We live in a world polarised between hope and despair. In both the US and the UK – the two countries central to much of the above discussion – media headlines were at the time of writing dominated by industrial disputes notable for both their impact and high degree of public support.[82]

Class politics returned to the agenda in the UK in the summer of 2022. The months which followed saw the highest number of strikes for over 30 years, involving many thousands of workers, from NHS staff to rail workers and civil servants. Disabled people have been a visible presence on picket lines at schools and universities. Strike action on such a scale can lead to a wider questioning of identity, where participants see their status as workers as more significant than their professional role. As Donna, a disabled activist in the University and College Union, recently explained, "being part of strike organising has massively boosted my networks, communication ability and self-worth".[83]

All forms of oppression are rooted in a society which forces humans to compete with each other from the nursery to the grave – in exams, jobs, housing and every sphere of life – for the sake of profit. This book shows that disability is a very recent invention in human history. It is a form of discrimination which arose with and is inseparable from a society based on grading and valuing people according to their suitability for profit extraction.

The experience of injustice often demoralises its victims. When it leads to resistance, however – as shown by the rich history of struggle outlined in these pages – it can rapidly embolden and politicise those who participate. We who wish to save humanity from barbarism must do all we can to fan these flames of resistance, and to fight for a vision of a different world based on interdependence and solidarity.

- Roddy Slorach, 14 November 2023

1.
Introduction

Disability in contemporary society is a complex and widely misunderstood issue. Two contradictory trends in recent years illustrate this well.

The first global report on disability, published by the World Health Organisation in 2011, identified 1 billion disabled people—15 percent of the global population. As a proportion of the total, this figure is expected to continue rising for the foreseeable future. Since its adoption in December 2006, over 150 countries have ratified the United Nations (UN) Convention on Rights for People with Disabilities. Thanks largely to pressure from the world's most influential disability movements, Britain and the US adopted anti-discrimination laws championed by the UN as models of best practice. Many other states have adopted similar legislation, with others likely to follow in the near future. As an international political issue, the profile of disability rights has in many respects never been higher.

Another side to disability, however, is better known to many more people. Today, the media and governments in Britain and the US routinely allege fraud by benefit "scroungers" or "fakers" to justify drastic cuts in disability-related benefits and services. In a climate of escalating austerity and protracted economic crisis, this pattern is increasingly being emulated elsewhere. In Britain, definitions have been altered to reduce the number of those deemed to be "genuinely disabled", and therefore (supposedly) deserving of support. The drastic nature of these "welfare reforms" is perhaps best illustrated by the fact that, in the summer of 2015, disabled activists succeeded in persuading the United Nations Committee on the Rights of Persons with Disabilities to investigate alleged violations of disabled people's human rights in the UK; the findings of the confidential investigation are due to be published in 2017. Another aspect of this more negative side to disability is the remarkable fact that the vast majority of those still officially classified as disabled neither disclose this to employers nor identify as such to anyone else.

What explains these contradictory trends? What, indeed, is disability in the first place? This book sets out to answer these questions by examining the social and historical roots of the nature of disability discrimination.

Disability was first identified as a particular form of discrimination at the end of the 19th century. The modern disability movement, however, only emerged in the decades after the Second World War. Referred to by one author as "the last civil rights movement",[1] disability activism only began to peak after others, such as those of women, black people and gays and lesbians had already passed into decline. In Britain the disability movement has recently revived after an absence of almost 20 years in response to government cuts in disability-related benefits and services.

Most writing about disability falls into one of three categories. First, there are personal stories, mainly of "overcoming adversity" or the "tragedy" of living with impairment. Although tending to reinforce stereotypical notions of heroic "superhumans", these may often provide important insights into the lives of individual disabled people. Second, there are accounts by and for health care or social service professionals. Finally, most discussion in the academic discipline of Disability Studies takes place in expensive specialist journals, the language of which is often impenetrable and the content of questionable relevance. The aim of this book is to build on the scattered handful of historical accounts of disability and disabled people, to provide a wider history that is also accessible to a broader audience.

The book locates the emergence of disability in the wider history of class society in general and capitalist society in particular. It takes the view that understanding its development, roots and nature as a particular form of oppression is key to the wider project of human emancipation.

Asking the question "what is disability?" prompts a range of different answers. For most people the term refers to a range of limitations in the mental or physical functioning of individuals—an approach reflected in most of the current disability-related legislation in Britain and elsewhere. The first chapter of this book therefore traces the development of the term and its associated meanings, addressing in addition the related and often thorny question of terminology.

One set of ideas has had more influence among disability activists and those working in the disability field than any other. With its origins in a tiny and obscure group of socialist wheelchair users, and with an avowedly materialist perspective, the social model of disability has been a political and ideological battleground since its development in the 1980s. What does this conception of disability have to say about impairment, or other forms of oppression? Chapter 2 makes a critical defence of the social model, finding the alternatives offered by its many critics deficient in several important respects, most crucially in terms of their relative utility as a vehicle for change. Unlike the social model, however, this account is unequivocal in seeing impairment and disability alike as for the most part social in origin.

Having established a framework within which to discuss disability, the following three chapters discuss its historical development. Recent research has provided further evidence that people with impairments have not always been marginalised or discriminated against. It is clear that social attitudes varied depending on the nature of a given society. Despite the many difficulties inherent in looking back at ancient societies, it is evident that the development of class distinctions had a negative impact on the fortunes of people with impairments. If pre-class societies did not exclude or marginalise such people, then this must be possible for an alternative future society.

Although early origins can be found in the late feudal period, the evidence demonstrates it was the rise of industrial capitalism that created disability as a distinct form of oppression. Successive innovations in medicine, science and technology led on the one hand to more disabled people surviving and living more independent lives, while at the same time marginalising them on the grounds that their labour was less productive. The Marxist concepts of alienation and exploitation have been either too crudely applied or completely neglected in existing accounts. They are, however, vital to understanding the nature of disability in contemporary capitalist society.

The drive for profit and the cyclical but chaotic disruption of economic booms and slumps have led to the marginalisation or exclusion of disabled people from the workforce. The most advanced economies of the late 19th and early 20th centuries—particularly Germany, Britain and the US—were home to eugenicist movements that saw different physical and mental impairments as evidence of degeneracy and/or imperial decline. Rooted in concepts of racial and genetic superiority, these ideas were taken to their extreme and logical conclusion in Nazi Germany with the mass murder of certain groups of disabled people demonised as an economic burden. Until the evidence of Nazi genocide began to emerge, versions of eugenic ideas were more widely shared, even among some socialists of the period, and have since then reappeared in different forms. Chapter 7 looks at the main principles involved in this issue.

As capitalist production assumes a bigger and more global scale, so the wars it generates have led to ever greater and more widespread destruction. Ironically, such wars have often proved to be drivers of social and economic change. As the First World War ended in revolutions and mass unrest, injured soldiers, particularly in Germany, played a direct role in winning social gains. Chapter 8 looks at the history of disabled war veterans and their relationship to wider social movements.

Chapter 9 looks at the history of disability movements and highlights some lesser-known events involving groups of disabled people, which predate the modern disability movement, and considers other countries where such movements have not developed. Finally, it discusses the disability charities and their constant and contradictory role in the lives of many people.

Disability movements have sometimes excluded certain groups, either because they disagree that they were indeed disabled or for more complex reasons. People experiencing mental health difficulties comprise the largest group of disabled people and also perhaps the most misunderstood. On a global scale, depression alone is projected to become the single biggest cause of impairment by 2030.[2] Of all areas of disability, mental health arouses the greatest fear, ignorance and discrimination—including among other disabled people. Chapter 10 argues that mental distress is best understood as a form of disability and therefore also as a social problem demanding a social solution.

Another social group has historically remained separate from the disability movement, in large part because their representatives have not considered themselves to be disabled. Many deaf people see themselves instead as a linguistic minority with a distinct history and culture. Chapter 11 discusses this disputed area along with the varying fortunes of sign language. Part of the following chapter develops this debate on the nature and perceptions of impairment and disability, this time in relation to learning difficulties and neurodiversity. This chapter also goes on to tackle perhaps the most controversial issues in the book—disability hate crime and assisted suicide. The latter in particular raises further and more complex issues of disability rights in contemporary society.

This brings us to the nature and place of disability discrimination in contemporary capitalist society. Far from the 21st century signalling new progress for humanity, global austerity, wars and environmental and climate chaos threaten to thrust us dramatically backwards. Chapter 13 brings together the previous strands discussed to analyse the particularities of disability as a form of oppression, examining in addition the reasons for the greater prominence of disability as a political issue in recent years.

The final chapter asks whether science is an ally or enemy of progress. It then goes on to address the key question implicit throughout the book: is it possible to build a genuinely inclusive society for the many disabled people who work and the many others who do not? Could a future society completely abolish disability as a form of discrimination?

While considerable effort has been made to provide a more global analysis, the bulk of the literature, research and statistical material currently available is from US or UK sources. This reflects the fact that these are respectively the most powerful and oldest of the advanced capitalist nation states, where disability movements have also had the greatest influence or had the greatest influence on the introduction and development of relevant legislation and services. The UK is also, of course, where both the social model of disability and the academic discipline of Disability Studies first developed.

Finally, as the title implies, this book is written from a Marxist perspective. The scale and severity of the current economic crisis have helped prompt renewed interest in such ideas. The popular view remains, however, that such an approach offers little to an understanding of social oppression. I hope this account demonstrates that, on the contrary, only Marxism offers the necessary tools to explain the roots and nature of disability as a form of discrimination, as well as offering a vision as to how it can be overcome.

2.
What is disability?
Definitions and terminology

For most people familiar with the term, disability refers in Western societies to limitations in an individual's mental or physical functions. Disabled people themselves, however, disagree on what exactly disability refers to.

The first area of difficulty concerns impairment itself. The term "disability" applies to people with a diverse range of impairments, the majority of which are invisible to others. Second, many people who meet the legal definition of disability do not define themselves as disabled, although others with an identical impairment may well do so. A third complication is that some impairments fluctuate or become progressively more incapacitating while others which are more constant in their effects vary in their levels of severity.

There are nevertheless compelling political reasons for preferring particular terms—for instance, "disabled person" or "person with a disability" rather than older terms such as "handicapped" or (particularly in the US) "retarded". It is largely due to campaigns by disabled people and their supporters that both of the latter came to be seen as offensive and associated with helplessness or inferior human status. This led UK charity The Spastics Society, for example, to change its name to Scope in 1995.

Any serious discussion of the history and politics of disability requires as a starting point a clear and consistent approach to definitions and terminology. The use of particular terms can advance or undermine understanding, depending on the specific historical context. Those who believe disability has always existed, for example, apply the term uncritically to societies and historical periods where the term or concept was unknown. This approach is fundamentally mistaken. Even today, the majority of the world's population living in the Global South[3] may refer to blind or "slow" people or those with walking difficulties, but have no general term equivalent to "disability" or "disabled people" in their language or culture.[4]

The most important issue concerning definitions is the way in which modern society constantly confuses or conflates the distinct concepts of impairment and disability, often treating them as interchangeable terms. In order to fully address this we need to begin by asking how disability is defined in the relevant existing legislation.

Official definitions of disability

The Americans with Disabilities Act of 1990 states: "The term 'disability' means, with respect to an individual: (A) a physical or mental impairment that substantially limits one or more of the major life activities of an individual; (B) a record of such an impairment; or (C) being regarded as having such an impairment".[5] The UK Equality Act (2010) takes a slightly different approach, defining disability as "a long-term impairment which has a significant adverse effect on his/her ability to carry out day-to-day functions." Both legal definitions embody a contradiction; disability is defined in individual and medical terms—in other words as the property of the individual—but is simultaneously treated as equivalent to other forms of discrimination.

This confusion over terminology is not new. In 2006 an article in the medical journal *The Lancet* attempted to grapple with an earlier definition:

> The current draft of the UN Convention does not define disability but rather people with disabilities. Unfortunately, this definition fails to acknowledge that disability is a central health issue that plays out in all areas of individual and social life. The definition in the Convention of people with disabilities is solely medical and restricts the concept of disability to only those with long-term impairments irrespective of their level of participation... Proposed replacement—"Disability is a difficulty in functioning at the body, person, or societal levels, in one

or more life domains, as experienced by an individual with a health condition in interaction with contextual factors.[6]

The WHO's definition makes a clearer distinction between the terms:

Disabilities is an umbrella term, covering impairments, activity limitations, and participation restrictions. An impairment is a problem in body function or structure; an activity limitation is a difficulty encountered by an individual in executing a task or action; while a participation restriction is a problem experienced by an individual in involvement in life situations. Thus disability is a complex phenomenon, reflecting an interaction between features of a person's body and features of the society in which he or she lives.[7]

In Britain disability has recently become strongly associated with incapacity and benefits dependency. On the eve of the London 2012 Games, Paralympics Committee President Philip Craven (himself a wheelchair user) went so far as to argue that the word "disabled" should be dropped from all media coverage altogether. As he put it: "How could these athletes be viewed as anything other than 'able'?"[8]

These examples demand some political and historical context. On the one hand, they reflect the social progress made by disabled people since they were referred to officially as spastics, imbeciles or worse. However, they also obscure the vital distinction established by the disability movement between individual impairment and disability as social discrimination.

The social model of disability[9]

The nature and heterogeneity of impairment is one aspect of disability which distinguishes it from other forms of oppression. Impairments may be physical or mental (or both), single or multiple, temporary or permanent, and acquired before or after birth. Most are hidden or invisible but may be severely disfiguring or incapacitating, painful or even terminal. As Tom Shakespeare observes in *Disability Rights and Wrongs*:

[T]he limitations which individual bodies or minds impose...vary from the trivial to the profound... The majority of disabled people do not have stable, congenital impairments...or sudden traumatic lesions (such as spinal cord injury), but instead have rheumatism or cardio-vascular disease or other chronic degenerative conditions associated with ageing.[10]

Most people don't fit into neat binary categories of disabled on the one hand or non-disabled on the other. People with slight visual or hearing defects can render these almost irrelevant with the use of spectacles or hearing aids (although these may not be free).[11] Those defined as blind or deaf, however, face far greater obstacles to social integration. In addition, people with the most severe impairments may be highly dependent on care or support provided by others (such as the 6 million carers in the UK alone).

A related problem is that disabled people "constantly fear that they may become associated with those that they see as less employable and more dependent. By trying to distance themselves from groups that they see as more disabled than themselves they can hope to maintain their claim to economic independence and an acceptable status in the community".[12] One recent British study shows that "[both] disabled and non-disabled people regard those with a learning disability or a mental illness as the least desirable groups".[13]

According to government research, a large majority of disabled people, in the UK at least, do not actually consider themselves to be disabled.[14] Deaf people pose a particular problem in these terms. Many whose first language is sign see themselves as a linguistic minority and regard integration as a threat to a history and culture which is at least 250 years old.[15]

A final consideration here is that by far the greatest proportion of impairments are acquired during an individual's lifetime rather than at birth, most commonly as a result of disease, injury or some other trauma. The sudden change involved can be an immense challenge. It may even trigger a wholesale reassessment of one's life, priorities and political perspective. Vic Finkelstein and Mike Oliver, who became leading figures in the disability movement, were both paralysed from the neck down after accidents they had as young adults.

All this points to the importance of the pioneering distinction between impairment and disability. This was first made explicit by a tiny group of disabled socialists in 1975. The Union of the Physically Impaired Against Segregation (UPIAS) declared that disability, far from being biologically determined, was a social creation and as such could be challenged and eliminated.

> In our view, it is society which disables physically impaired people. Disability is something imposed on top of our impairments by the way we are unnecessarily isolated and excluded from full participation in society. Disabled people are therefore an oppressed group in society.
>
> Thus we define impairment as lacking all or part of a limb, organ or mechanism of the body; and disability as the disadvantage or restriction of activity caused by a contemporary social organisation which takes little or no account of people who have physical impairments and thus excludes them from the mainstream of social activities.[16]

These "Fundamental Principles" formed the basis for what became known as the social model of disability. As Mike Oliver put it:

> [If disability] is seen as a tragedy, then disabled people will be treated as if they are the victims of some tragic happening or circumstance. This treatment will...be translated into social policies which will attempt to compensate these victims for the tragedies that have befallen them... [I]f disability is defined as social oppression, then disabled people will be seen as the collective victims of an uncaring or unknowing society... Such a view will be translated into social policies geared towards alleviating oppression rather than compensating individuals.[17]

The social model of disability (discussed in more detail in the next chapter) became hugely influential, particularly in the UK. It helped shape the disability movement of the late 1980s and 1990s, was key to the foundation of the academic field of Disability Studies and informed (albeit to a very limited degree) the subsequent anti-discrimination legislation. This fundamental distinction between disability and impairment informs the approach taken throughout this book.

How many disabled people are there? Global estimates of impairment

Defining disability is not only a matter of policy. More fundamental, at least to those who run and control the economy, is the issue of numbers and therefore of cost. *The Economist*, Britain's leading business magazine, recently articulated these concerns:

> Measuring pain and misery is hard. Over 1 billion people—one in seven—have some kind of disability, according to the World Health Organisation. But that may be on the high side. America's Census Bureau, which has been counting the disabled since 1830, found 57m in a survey of economic status in 2012. That was nearly one in five, of whom half said their disability was severe. A national housing survey counted a mere 22m, whereas a health survey tallied 62m. Ireland's 2006 census found a disability rate of 9.3 percent. The 2011 round also asked about pain and breathing troubles; it reported a rate 40 percent higher... Some count dyslexia and autism as a disability. Others, including many with these conditions, fiercely contest what they see as a negative label.
>
> The effect of a disability also depends on what means are available to cope with it. A survey in Zambia found that more than four out of five disabled people lacked the devices and aids they needed. What may be a nuisance in a rich country can be truly crippling in a poor one.
>
> This makes it hard to decide the threshold at which disadvantage or woe merits recognition or special treatment.[18]

Such worries are widely shared among the world's rulers. The proportion of disabled people rose from an estimated 10 percent of the global population in the 1970s to 15 percent in 2011, due mainly to an ageing population and a rise in chronic health conditions such as cardiovascular and respiratory diseases. The same WHO report concludes that disabled people remain second-class citizens, with one in five experiencing "significant difficulties".

In the advanced economies of Organisation for Economic Co-operation and Development (OECD) countries, disabled people are three times more likely to be denied healthcare than other people and disabled children are less likely to start or stay in school. In OECD countries the comparative employment rates for disabled and non-disabled people are 44 percent and 75 percent respectively. The WHO report identified barriers such as discrimination, inadequate healthcare and rehabilitation services, and inaccessible transport, buildings and information.

Higher living costs (for example, transport, support services and assistive technology) also mean that disabled people have a 50 percent greater risk of incurring "catastrophic health costs"—so high that they push them under the poverty line.[19]

The WHO survey, conducted across 51 countries, gives employment rates of 52.8 percent for men with disability and 19.6 percent for women with disability, compared with 64.9 percent for non-disabled men, and 29.9 percent for non-disabled women. It also found that individuals with mental health difficulties or intellectual impairments experience the lowest employment rates and are more likely to be employed in segregated settings.

In the countries of the Global South, the picture is even worse. According to the 2011 WHO survey, 20 percent of the world's poorest people are disabled, with nearly 80 percent living in low-income countries.[20] Figures from the World Bank in 2009 showed that in Latin America and the Caribbean (LAC) the incidence of impairment:

is especially high in post-conflict countries and in areas of natural disasters. About 80-90 percent of disabled people in LAC are unemployed or outside the work force. Most of those who have jobs receive little or no pay... In Argentina, the unemployment rate of disabled people is estimated to be close to 91 percent... In countries for which data is available, less than 20 percent of disabled people receive insurance benefits.[21]

Leaving aside its terminology for the moment, an earlier 2008 WHO report provides a picture of the most common causes of impairment globally:

Hearing loss, vision problems and mental disorders are the most common causes of disability... A significant proportion of disabilities are caused by traffic crashes, falls, burns, and acts of violence such as child abuse, youth violence, intimate partner violence, and war...up to one quarter of disabilities may result from injuries and violence. [These] include: physical and/or cognitive limitations due to neurotrauma; paralysis due to spinal cord trauma; partial or complete amputation of limbs; physical limb deformation resulting in mobility impairments; psychological trauma; sensory disability such as blindness and deafness.[22]

The WHO's 2008 Report also highlights mental "disorders" as among the 20 leading causes of disability worldwide, with depression alone affecting around 120 million people. Fewer than 25 percent of those affected have access to adequate treatment and health care.

These statistics prove three things above all. Firstly, a large proportion of the world's population are disabled. Secondly, many of their impairments are socially caused. And thirdly, a large majority of disabled people are poor.

Words as weapons

The Economist article quoted above points out that the UN Convention on the Rights of Persons with Disabilities calls disability an "evolving concept", and also that in the US, those labelled as "imbeciles" and "defectives" were segregated and sterilised until the 1960s. It could be added that homosexuality was listed in the American *Diagnostic and Statistical Manual of Mental Disorders* (*DSM*) as a psychiatric disorder until 1973.[23]

Sometimes differences in terms are merely just that. For example, "paralysis of the legs and some trunk muscles is known in the UK as paraplegia, and in the US as quadriplegia".[24] But while this may be true for many medical terms, in other fields the language used is revealing. The word "idiot", for example, was once a legal term to describe someone with a mental impairment and featured in the 1901 UK census. The UK's Electoral Administration Bill was amended only in May 2006 to abolish rules stipulating that "idiots" could not vote and that "lunatics" could do so only during their lucid intervals. Laws using these terms date back to the 17th century, but most have been replaced or repealed in the last 40 years or so.[25] The US Congress replaced the term "mental retardation" with "intellectual disabilities" as recently as 2010.[26] Few complained about "political correctness" when the Education for All Handicapped Children Act (1975) was replaced in 1990 by the Individuals with Disabilities Education Act.

Matters are not always so straightforward. One writer recently discussed the difficulties in using appropriate terminology in the area of mental health:

> I used the term service users because I wanted to avoid imposing a label on people. I didn't want to use the term "mentally ill" because I know there are plenty of people using mental health services who do not consider themselves to be mentally ill. Referring to "people with mental health problems" or "difficulties" or "issues" also leaves me slightly uneasy because it seems to me to draw a line where I don't believe one exists... "Patients", "clients" and "consumers" all have a slightly Orwellian ring, especially when referring to "clients" being detained against their will... But language is also what links individuals. And however precarious the bridge, we have to keep striving to cross it.[27]

The problem with the term "service user", of course, is that it excludes anyone who does not use mental health services.

In the UK, school pupils diagnosed with specific learning difficulties such as dyslexia are commonly described as having "special needs", but this term is never used in higher education where it is (correctly in my view) considered an anachronism.

One other example will suffice to illustrate the complexity of this area. The word "handicap" is largely no longer used, partly due to the widespread belief that its origin derives from begging, as in "cap in hand". In fact the term was first used in the Middle Ages and referred to games or sport:

The 17th Century diarist Samuel Pepys enjoyed a game of Handicap... The word 'handicap' in connection to people with impairments can only be traced back to the beginnings of the 20th Century and then derived from a sense of disadvantage, in the sense of inequalities of race or gender, in horse racing and the game of golf. And even then it has no historical association with begging.[28]

It is, however, the meanings commonly associated with words that matter most. The term "handicapped" became so strongly associated with charity and paternalistic attitudes to disabled people that its real origins became irrelevant. The term "disability," in contrast, understood as referring to discrimination against people with mental and physical impairments, became a political expression of the fight for rights.

The situation today could be described as "free market civil rights".[29] In 2010, the UK Coalition government launched its historic assault on the NHS by stating that its "guiding principle" was "No decision about me without me"—a clear reference to the famous slogan of the disability rights movement, "nothing about us without us".[30] Politicians have become adept at "turning rebellion into money"[31]—in this case, using the language of disability rights to further their removal in practice.

Most of us would prefer genuine support from people unfamiliar with the right terminology to brusque, dismissive or plain insulting attitudes from someone careful to use the correct language. There is a qualitative difference between someone using the term "confined to a wheelchair" while supporting equal access to transport, and a coach company which trains its staff in the use of more acceptable terms such as "wheelchair user" while still refusing to provide accessible vehicles on cost grounds. What is true for individuals, in other words, applies to a far greater degree to the actions of governments and big business.

Use of terms in the book

All this is of course a political argument and language is itself a political battleground. This book uses the term "disabled people" rather than "people with disabilities". The latter term, occasionally used in Britain, is that used in the US (and favoured by the US disability movement). Both terms have much to commend them in comparison to their predecessors, but there is good reason for the preference.

"People with disabilities" is sometimes described as a "people first" term, because it starts with the fact that a person with an impairment is first and foremost a human being, as opposed to an object of pity or charity. However, it still implies that disability is the property of the person.

"Disabled people" is the term campaigned for and popularised by the UK disability movement. It refers to disadvantage, inequality and discrimination primarily as a social phenomenon, something caused by society rather than directly arising from each individual's impairment. If it is possible to show that people are disabled by society not by their impairments, then a society that treats impairment differently must also be possible.

Others argue that we should use the term "differently abled" in preference to disabled. This approach confuses acceptable language with social context, as if the issue of discrimination can simply be wished away or ignored altogether. In a similar vein, this book avoids using the term "specific learning differences."

The case of Deaf people is slightly different. The use of the capital "D" signifies membership of and identification with a community whose preferred and sole form of communication (in place of speech) is sign language and who perceive themselves to have a shared history and culture. Although this book discusses some of the difficulties of such an approach, it uses the capital "D" because this is the format preferred by most Deaf people.

Mental health is a more complex area where meanings and labels are even more contested, including in respect of mental illnesses themselves. As the British Psychological Society put it, seeing "experiences as symptoms of illnesses is only one way of seeing them, and one that not everyone finds helpful".[32] People who experience mental health difficulties are often called "patients" or "sufferers," although they may not see themselves as being ill. This book—unavoidably—uses specific diagnostic terms, while recognising that these are controversial and contested. Terms such as "patient", "disorder" or "condition" are therefore used here only in the appropriate context. Even the more neutral formulation "service users" ignores the very large numbers of people with mental health difficulties who never use mental health services. As the least value-laden term available, I have therefore opted to use the term "mental distress," even if it may seem too trivial to cover the most serious categories of mental ill health.

The final issue here concerns tautology. This book argues not only that disability is a distinct form of oppression, but also that this social understanding of disability is little known or only partially understood. I have therefore at various points felt the need to add "discrimination" after the word disability in order to ensure this meaning is clearly conveyed. The contradiction here is one that exists in society, which is why the real meaning of this "very capitalist condition" will remain contested until that reality is itself altered.

3.
The social model and its critics

In themselves, handicaps are nowise tragic, but through the eyes of others, through their voices and their actions, we are constantly made aware that it is, and the sea of these 'white missionaries' is so great that they make converts of us—some falling rapidly into their concepts of our conditions, and some of us, less fortunate, struggling against this lie of tragedy.[33]

The issue of what disability "really is" has been debated for the past half century. The first disability activists drew parallels with other oppressed groups while grappling with the distinctive features of disability. Where and how to draw a line between limitations imposed on individuals by particular impairments on the one hand and their widely varying experiences of social discrimination on the other remains a complex issue. This chapter critically assesses what is by far the most important and successful attempt to meet this challenge—the social model of disability.

The rise of the social model of disability

The Union of Physically Impaired Against Segregation (UPIAS) was one of many small groups of radical socialists in Britain during the early 1970s. UPIAS members felt that a "new interpretation" of disability was necessary "to challenge the traditional 'tragedy' view of disability." Their discussions were to lead to the British disability movement's "big idea."

UPIAS began with an initiative by Paul Hunt, a resident at Le Court, a Leonard Cheshire Foundation Home. He had already written about the segregation characterising the lives of many disabled people in Britain, at a time when the struggle against racism in the US had reached its peak. *Stigma: The Experience of Disability*, a series of essays by disabled men and women, was one of the first books focusing on social rather than biological factors in understanding disability. Hunt's piece argued that:

> We do not enjoy many of the 'goods' that people in our society are accustomed to... Employers turn away qualified and competent workers simply because they are disabled. Restaurants and pubs give transparent excuses for refusing our custom. Landladies reject disabled lodgers. Parents and relations fight the marriage of a cripple into their family—perhaps with more reason than with a black African, but with many of the same arguments. And it's not hard to see the analogy between a racial ghetto and the institutions where disabled people are put away and given enough care to salve society's conscience.[34]

Hunt went on to lead a rebellion by residents to secure representation on Le Court's board of management, gaining for the first time a say in how the home was run.[35] In September 1972 he wrote a letter to the *Guardian* newspaper, calling for a new organisation of disabled people to campaign against segregation in institutions.[36] Among those who responded was Vic Finkelstein, who had moved to Britain after being banished from South Africa for involvement in the anti-apartheid movement. Until his exchanges with Hunt, Finkelstein had not thought of his experiences as a wheelchair user as discrimination (ironically, the apartheid regime had freed him early from a prison sentence because he was "a cripple"). He began to draw parallels between the systematic racism in his homeland and the experience of disabled people. Hunt in turn generalised his earlier insights into a wider understanding of disability discrimination.[37]

UPIAS founding members, Finkelstein wrote later, withdrew "in practice if not intention, from the public arena and engaged in private discussion about the meaning of disability. We spent about two or three years exchanging ideas in an internal circular, because of the practical difficulties in meeting".[38] The most important issue to be resolved was the relationship between impairment and disability:

Having an impairment is a prerequisite for being a disabled person but having an impairment cannot cause a person to become disabled. Even losing an arm and an eye does not make a disabled person. The national culture would have to attribute certain characteristics to such impairments before designating the person as being disabled. Once these attributes are embedded in the national culture, and accepted as defining features of disability, then impairments such as missing an arm and eye would not only formally become disabilities but they would be seen as the dominant characteristics of the individual (ie the person would be 'labelled disabled'). In such a society acquiring certain culturally identifiable impairments transforms the individual at the same time into a person with a disability. Both 'impairment' and 'disability', then, become attributes located within the individual. Thereafter the two conditions can be awfully difficult to disentangle.[39]

In 1975, UPIAS were invited by the newly formed Disability Alliance to join their campaign for a comprehensive income scheme for all disabled people. Their subsequent discussions formed the text of the UPIAS *Fundamental Principles*. Hunt and his allies saw the Alliance (and its predecessor, the Disablement Income Group) as being too vague on the meaning and causes of disability. Whereas the Alliance was a coalition of disability groups and non-disabled academics, UPIAS wanted to create a mass grassroots organisation comprising only disabled people. For them, poverty was a "symptom of our oppression, but it is not the cause…it is absolutely vital that we get this question of the cause of disability quite straight, because on the answer depends the crucial matter of where we direct our main energies in the struggle for change".[40] To quote their perspective at greater length:

[I]f disability is a social condition then an analysis of the ways in which society actually disables physically impaired people is obviously required before the condition can be eliminated… In our view, it is society which disables physically impaired people. Disability is something imposed on top of our impairments by the way we are unnecessarily isolated and excluded from full participation in society. Disabled people are therefore an oppressed group in society.

To understand this it is necessary to grasp the distinction between the physical impairment and the social situation, called 'disability', of people with such impairment. Thus we define impairment as lacking part of or all of a limb, or having a defective limb, organ or mechanism of the body; and disability as the disadvantage or restriction of activity caused by a contemporary social organisation which takes no or little account of people who have physical impairments and thus excludes them from participation in the mainstream of social activities. Physical disability is therefore a particular form of social oppression...

It is clear that our social organisation does not discriminate equally against all physical impairments and hence there arises the appearance of degrees of exclusion (degrees of disability). For example, people having mild visual impairments (wearing glasses) are doubtless not more impoverished than their visually unimpaired peers. Our social organisation does not exclude people using glasses to the same extent that it excludes people who are blind, or deaf, or cannot speak, or who have brain damage, or who use wheelchairs. Nevertheless, it is the same society which disables people whatever their type, or degree of physical impairment, and therefore there is a single cause within the organisation of society that is responsible for the creation of the disability of physically impaired people.[41]

At this stage, then, UPIAS had identified disability as a specific type of discrimination in modern society. They saw this "social understanding of disability" as the key political basis for a future "independent, democratic organisation of disabled people...which is increasingly clear about the cause of disability and about the changes required to overcome it".[42]

Another wheelchair user, Mike Oliver (along with others such as Finkelstein) developed this crucial distinction between impairment and disability into the social model of disability during the course of the 1980s, particularly in his influential book, *The Politics of Disablement*, which first appeared in 1990. His conception of two contrasting models of disability, as he later explained, "was taken quite simply and explicitly from the distinction originally made" by UPIAS:

I originally conceptualised models of disability as the binary distinction between what I chose to call the individual and social models of disability. This was no amazing new insight on my part dreamed up in some ivory tower but was really an attempt to enable me to make sense of the world for the social work students and other professionals who I was teaching at the time...the social model was received much more enthusiastically by disabled people because it made an immediate connection to their own experiences. It quickly became the basis for disability awareness and later disability equality training. It was adopted by democratic disability organisations all over the world including Disabled Peoples International (DPI) and the British Council of Organisations of Disabled People (BCODP).[43]

Oliver also developed the social model as a response to his own experiences as a disabled activist:

When we were trying to build a sort of coalition across impairments I started meeting blind people and deaf people. We spent the first couple of years trying to imagine what it would be like to be someone else. I would say to a blind person, 'Cor, I am glad I am not blind.' And they would say, 'I would rather be blind than in a wheelchair like you.' We realized...it was not about trying to understand how we felt about each other... It was about trying to understand why we all had crappy lives.[44]

This new concept was a direct political challenge to the way disability was commonly understood. Oliver, who broke his neck in a diving accident at the age of 17, later explained this with reference to his own experience of impairment:

I don't see myself as a person with a disability. Black people don't want to be seen as people with a different coloured skin, women as people with a different genital arrangement. You have to find ways of recognising, valuing and respecting difference rather than ignoring it. I don't want you to understand what it is like to have no control over bladder or bowel. I want you to understand that I need a job, to use the same public spaces and facilities as you, that I need a decent education and a house with a front door I own, and to control who comes in. I want you to understand these things. I don't need you to understand that I sit in this wheelchair from the neck down without feeling anything, and what it feels like, because I don't know what it's like to have a period. In order to be sensitive about it, I don't need to know about it.[45]

The social model was not, in other words, about the particularities of each individual's impairment(s). It was instead a way of illustrating the nature of disability as a specific form of discrimination, which was "ultimately due to our continued exclusion from the processes of production... [T]he social model of disability is concerned with the personal and collective experiences of disabling social barriers and how its application might influence professional practice and shape political action".[46] The social model, therefore, was above all intended as a practical tool.

This new way of looking at disability turned received wisdom on its head and had a hugely liberating impact on many disabled individuals. It helped many activists, particularly in Britain, understand and challenge discrimination. It won widespread acceptance as the disability movement grew under Margaret Thatcher's Tory governments of the 1980s. It also led to the establishment of a new academic discipline, Disability Studies, and was used to train social services professionals. The social model's influence was evident (albeit in highly diluted form) in the Disability Discrimination Act, its subsequent amendments in 2005, as well as the Equality Act of 2010. As Colin Barnes explained:

The 'social model' of disability's emphasis on disabling social and environmental barriers was contrasted with the current orthodoxy that viewed disability as a 'personal tragedy', and disabled people as in need of 'care'. Oliver drew on contemporary debates in the social sciences to explain this individualised approach to disability as a social creation of industrial capitalism. Moreover, the 'social model' approach pointed to areas where political action might bring about the social changes necessary to overturn the social exclusion of disabled people.[47]

Although UPIAS had only applied its *Fundamental Principles* to people with physical impairments, the distinction between disability and impairment could readily be applied to the difficulties faced by other groups of disabled people.

Oliver was only too aware that the success of the social model was double-edged, and that many of its new converts had a commitment to it that was superficial at best:

> [T]he social model has been incorporated into the agendas and practices of governments, welfare agencies, 'quangos' (quasi-non-government organisations), charities and a variety of other organisations worldwide...without any...substantial change to their practices; we still have international charities who incarcerate disabled people all over the world claiming to work to the principles of the social model and governments who endorse it yet continue providing individualising responses to the problems of unemployment and discrimination.[48]

As the leaders of the disability movement in the UK increasingly placed their hopes in a future New Labour government, the social model began to be identified with a "rights" model centred on achieving legislative change and at the same time to be challenged outright for its perceived inadequacies.

Critics

The first challenges to the social model came from within the disability movement, shortly after the publication of Oliver's *The Politics of Disablement*. In 1992, Liz Crow argued that the social model needed to be "renewed" and later critics argued that it had to be "rectified." Vic Finkelstein noted:

> By the year 2000 the 'rectifiers' were secure enough to state: 'We need to produce an updated social model of disability that; includes a positive statement about us; recognises our diversity and difference; recognises institutionalised discrimination; talks about choice; recognises that not all the things that exclude us are about society's barriers'[49]... This statement is generalised enough to cover all human social behaviour and is quite useless as a 'disability' model—a real

'shopping basket' approach which enables people to pick and choose any interpretation which happens to suit their personal ambitions; and it perfectly matches the privatisation programme of New Labour for a free market in health and social services.[50]

The most sustained and serious challenge to the social model came from a former supporter, disability studies academic and activist Tom Shakespeare. He argued in 2002 that the social model had become "outdated" and a "new orthodoxy". Four years later in his book *Disability Rights and Wrongs* he compared the disability movement in the UK to a "fundamentalist religion" because, in his view, the model had not been "developed or revised or rethought" for 30 years.[51]

For Shakespeare the social model defined impairment in individual and biological terms, in practice ignoring impairment altogether to focus on disability as a form of oppression which by definition had been socially created. While accepting many parallels between disability and other forms of oppression, Shakespeare argued that impairment had an "inextricable interconnection" to disability:

> [T]he oppression which disabled people face is different from, and in many ways more complex than sexism, racism and homophobia… even in the absence of social barriers or oppression, it would still be problematic to have an impairment, because many impairments are limiting or difficult…in most cases, disabled people are experiencing both the intrinsic limitation of impairment, and the externally imposed social discrimination.[52]

On one level, this argument is clearly correct. Disability does differ from other "equality strands", as they are now called, just as these differ from each other. However, Shakespeare's argument is that the nature of impairment dictates that disabled people will always face disadvantage. For him, it is not so easy to distinguish between impairment and disability: "the strong social model [this is, Oliver's version] overstates the social creation of disability, and fails to give an adequate account of the complexities of disabled people's lives".[53]

This charge drew the following response from Michael Oliver and Colin Barnes:

The distinction between impairment and disability is a pragmatic one that does not deny that some impairments limit people's ability to function independently. Nor does it deny that disabled people have illnesses at various points in their lives and that appropriate medical interventions are sometimes necessary. But independence is a relative concept. Human beings are social, and no one, regardless of impairment, can function completely independently.[54]

Oliver also pointed out that the social model is "a campaigning aid concentrating on the collective experience of disablement, not the individual experience of impairment". Drawing on the precedents of the struggles for black, gay and women's liberation and rejecting biological explanations of social inequality, he insisted that "there is no causal relationship between impairment and disability".[55]

The question of impairment

Paul Abberley had already argued (in 1987) that the social model viewed impairment in individual and biological terms and that its supporters rarely examined or questioned it as a concept: "impairment...always and only occurs in a particular social and historical context which determines its nature...where a given impairment may be prevented, eradicated or its effects significantly ameliorated it can no longer be regarded as a simple natural phenomenon".[56] By their very nature, human beings are "unnatural":

> We do not yet walk 'naturally' on our hind legs, for example: such ills as fallen arches, lower back pain and hernias testify that the body has not adapted itself completely to the upright posture. Yet this unnatural posture, forced on the unwilling body by the project of tool-using, is precisely what has made possible certain aspects of our 'nature': the hand and the brain, and the complex system of skills, language, and social arrangements which were both effects and causes of hand and brain. Man-made and physiological structures have thus come to interpenetrate so thoroughly that to call a human project contrary to human biology is naive: we are what we have made ourselves, and we must continue to make ourselves as long as we exist at all.[57]

Abberley argued that disability differs from other forms of oppression in one respect in particular:

> While in the cases of sexual and racial oppression, biological difference serves only as a qualificatory condition of a wholly ideological oppression, for disabled people the biological difference...a consequence of social practices, is itself a part of the oppression. It is crucial that a theory of disability as oppression comes to grips with this 'real' inferiority, since it forms a bedrock upon which justificatory oppressive theories are based and, psychologically, an immense impediment to the development of political consciousness amongst disabled people. Such a development is systematically blocked through the naturalisation of impairment... the 'really normal' ideology...finds its expression in everyday life in the exceptionalism of 'but I don't think of you as disabled', denying a key aspect of a disabled person's identity in what is intended as a compliment. Compare this phrase to 'played like a white man' and 'she thinks like a man'.[58]

For disability discrimination to be seen as analogous to racial and sexual oppression it must be demonstrated that disadvantage for disabled people is ultimately a social and not a biological product. Oliver himself conceded that "an adequate social theory of disability must contain a theory of impairment".[59] Abberley's starting point was that "[a]s far as the majority of the world's disabled people are concerned, impairment is very clearly primarily the consequence of social and political factors, not an unavoidable 'fact of nature'." He provides a range of examples to illustrate this:

> At the World Mental Health Congress in Brighton in July 1985, Dr David Hill, Senior Psychologist...argued that 25 million patients throughout the world had suffered irreversible brain damage as the result of the administration of powerful tranquillisers such as Largactil...polio is by no means a 'disease of civilisation'; recurrent outbreaks are still endemic in much of the world, where vaccination has been seen as unnecessary or where methods of administration have been ineffective...such a view does not deny the significance

of germs, genes and trauma, but rather points out that their effects are only ever apparent in a real social and historical context, whose nature is determined by a complex interaction of material and non-material factors. For example, while the link between tobacco consumption and lung cancer, bronchitis and ischaemic heart disease is demonstrably a material one, the occurrence and incidence of tobacco consumption is to be understood primarily in terms of social factors, as is the level and kind of ameliorative provision available.[60]

Advances in science and technology mean that the point at which impairment becomes classified as disability changes. To take the example of visual impairments, the recent advent of laser treatment in particular means that many of its less serious forms (for example, short or long-sightedness and astigmatism) can be rectified provided that there is access to treatment. Most people who wear glasses neither think of themselves as disabled nor are regarded as such by others. This is in turn linked to social expectations. Until recently, for example, it was commonly seen as embarrassing for women to wear spectacles as it undermined sexual attractiveness ("boys seldom make passes at girls who wear glasses")[61] or indicated high and supposedly unfeminine intelligence. In this case, therefore, impairment became linked to sexism, another form of oppression.

Most impairments are acquired over the course of an individual's lifetime and a large proportion occur at work. The website of Britain's Health and Safety Executive (HSE), for example, shows an estimated 1.2 million people in 2013-2014 as suffering from an illness they believe was caused or made worse by work. Musculoskeletal disorders, stress, depression and anxiety accounted for 80 percent of new work-related conditions in 2013-2014.[62] HSE research suggests about half of the reduction in non-fatal injuries up to 2012 was linked to changing employment patterns and occupations.[63]

The medical model

While Mike Oliver prefers to contrast "individual" or "tragedy" models of disability with the social model, many of the latter's supporters perceive its opposite to be what they call the "medical model" of disability. Well-known US disability activist and writer Paul Longmore describes this model as follows:

> The medical model defines disability as the physical and psychological experience of biological defect deriving from any one of a series of illnesses or injuries located within the bodies of 'afflicted' individuals. Medical practitioners have seen cure, or at least correction of functioning, as the only possible way to bring about the social integration of people with disabilities.[64]

Medical practice and research is focused on cures and treatment for illnesses and impairments. Disabled individuals have many times been made the objects of expert intervention, identified by and often reduced to their particular impairment. Medical practitioners have for over a century determined who qualifies as disabled and therefore their eligibility for benefits, rights and services. The medical model sees the medical profession as a whole to be the source of disabled people's oppression. This approach is both highly understandable and highly problematic.

It is true that disabled people have on many occasions been subject to appalling treatment at the hands of the medical (and "caring") professions, as later chapters in this book will show. Nevertheless, the medical model is a one-sided and unhelpful formulation. Firstly, it assumes the greatest difficulties faced by disabled people relate to medical conditions or are caused by medical staff, rather than wider social and economic factors. Medical practitioners do not, however, make and are rarely key in enforcing government policies, which they may in fact oppose. In addition, the medical profession is not homogeneous. Rather, it is historically shaped, internally differentiated and influenced by wider society. UK doctors' organisation the British Medical Association (BMA), for example, resisted the foundation of the NHS but now presents itself as its strongest advocate. A vote at the BMA's 2013 annual congress also contributed to the removal of Atos from its position administering the notorious work benefit tests. Last but not least, those often most responsible for poor medical practice are not practitioners at all, but those who restrict or remove medical services from people who need them.

The attitude of disabled people towards doctors has much to do with their status as "gatekeepers" who deny or confirm the legitimacy of someone's suffering—and therefore access to pensions or benefits, as well as to relief, drugs or even a cure. In *The Rejected Body: Feminist Philosophical Reflections on Disability* Susan Wendell describes one patient with chronic and serious symptoms who expressed her sheer joy and relief, on finally being diagnosed: "We had a name to something. We could deal with it. I was not a neurotic lady. It was OK to slow down, to quit work. It was OK to say no to things." Another patient also described a "feeling of euphoria... Something was wrong and this is what it is. I remember feeling kind of special and important. I could just have hugged that doctor for taking me seriously and deciding to get to the bottom of this".[65]

The subjective nature and the diversity of impairment mean that some people may be desperate to give a label or a name to their pain or limitations, whereas others may be very hostile to this. The subject of medical cures or therapy often leads to lively debates among disabled people. The point here is that they are not "incompatible with social change and civil rights".[66] On the contrary, they have demonstrably helped to extend and improve human lives in general. Their applicability in terms of individuals is usually a personal choice, albeit one influenced by a range of social factors.

A series of alternative or additional models of disability—such as the charity, moral, economic and affirmative models—have been mooted by other writers. None has had anywhere near the impact of the social model itself. One in particular, however, has become increasingly popular among policy-makers in the advanced economies. The biopsychological model[67] (a term borrowed from psychiatry which places the emphasis on an individual's behaviour as a primary factor in disability) represents a huge attack on disabled people by those responsible for reducing the number classified as such, cutting benefits and services in the name of "reform" and "modernisation."

Evaluating the social model today

As Oliver and Barnes wrote in their 2012 book *The New Politics of Disablement*, which revisited Oliver's original work 22 years later, the "social model is a simplified representation of a complex social reality. Although it has been linked to various theories of disablement, it is not a social theory".[68] Oliver originally drew up the individual and social models of disability as a "binary distinction" to help the social work students he was then teaching to understand disability as a form of discrimination.

The individual or tragedy model can easily be interpreted as a criticism of individuals. Coming to terms with disability can indeed feel like a tragedy. For many people to be disabled means to be unattractive, unwanted and a burden to others, a perception sometimes shared by parents or relatives of disabled children and by the majority of disabled people who acquire impairment later in life, often due to accident or sudden trauma.

The social model's sheer simplicity and flexibility made it immensely useful as a campaigning tool. These same virtues, however, have facilitated its embrace by national and international bodies. Witness the following excerpt from *Fulfilling Potential*, one of a series of reports produced by the UK Coalition government of 2010-15:

> For much of recent history a medical model of disability combined with a spirit of benevolence…often led to a focus solely on impairment…over deterministic, too prone to think in terms of blame, cure and rehabilitation and to treat disabled people as objects of pity and charity… The social model of disability, which is at the heart of the UN Convention, now commands much (but not full) support amongst disability professionals and campaigners. It offers insights into the importance of attitudes, social support, and accessible information and environments in influencing the quality of life of disabled people.[69]

The social model, in other words, often seems to mean all things to all people. Its acceptance by successive UK governments has not prevented savage cuts in disability-related benefits and services. These are necessary, we are told in those familiar weasel words, in order to "target benefits at those most in need":

> Cuts in our benefits are now being justified on the grounds that the intention is to give more to those who are severely impaired and less to those who are not. Our differences are being used to slash our services as our needs are now being assessed as being moderate, substantial or critical and many local authorities are now only providing services to those whose needs are critical...it has taken us back more than 30 years to the time before the social model came into existence. Those who have talked down the social model while failing to replace it with something more meaningful or useful must bear a heavy burden of responsibility for this state of affairs. Disabled people urgently need a reinvigorated social model—or something new to replace it.[70]

As we shall see, some contemporary writers wish to extend the concept of the social model into mental health, a complex venture which is nevertheless further evidence of the model's continuing relevance. Its survival serves as a constant (if often unwelcome) reminder to Disability Studies scholars of the origins of their discipline. This is part of the reason it continues to provoke such intense academic debate today. In the final instance, its value as a political tool has given it the durability it deserves.

4.
It wasn't always so

The first obstacle to providing a historical account of disability is the widespread assumption that such discrimination is a permanent feature of human society. This includes even some historians of the subject. In his study of disability in ancient Greece and Rome, Robert Garland states baldly: "a perennial problem confronting those afflicted with severe deformity…is how to escape the myths and stereotypes which divest them of a full, complex and rounded humanity".[71] In her bestselling book *Scapegoat*, Katherine Quarmby writes in a similar vein about "the stereotypes that have surrounded disabled people since recorded history began".[72] Such approaches are deeply ahistorical.

An increasing body of research strongly suggests that such discrimination did not exist, certainly not prior to the rise of class society, and very likely before the rise of capitalist society. Such evidence needs to be treated with care, not least because of the tendency to examine early societies through the distorting lens of modern prejudices: the concept of disability itself, for example, is very new in terms of human history. Second, early humans, lacking access to insulation, health care or mobility aids, were both more dependent on and more vulnerable to the whims of nature and so far less likely to survive into adulthood if injured or impaired. Third, any hunter-gatherer or other "non-class" communities still in existence today have inevitably been reshaped or at least influenced by modern capitalist society in a multitude of different ways.

Despite these obstacles, anthropologists, archaeologists and others have identified evidence indicating that what we today know as impairment was likely to have been understood and dealt with very differently in earlier human societies. This chapter comprises a summary of this evidence.

Pre-class society

Impairment is a fundamental feature of the human condition, present in every stage of history. There have always been accidents, chronic illness and congenital "defects" and the longer people live the more likely they are to experience some degree of impairment.

We know from skeletal remains that all sorts of diseases and conditions like arthritis as well as congenital impairments affected the earliest humans. Several examples indicate that long-term support was provided for people who would have been unable to look after themselves. Remains found in Kenya of a female Homo ergaster, the first human-like species, were dated to around 1.5 million years ago. Examination suggested that she had hypervitaminosis A, an extremely debilitating disease greatly hindering capacity for independent survival. Living as she did in the African savannah, she must have been fed by others who also protected her from carnivores.[73]

Other examples providing evidence of long-term care among archaic humans include remains from Dmanisi in Georgia (around 1.77 million years old), those of a young child (about 530,000 years old) in Sima de los Huesos in Spain, a diseased jaw found at Bau de l'Aubesier in France (around 180,000 years old), and a Middle Palaeolithic woman from Salé, Morocco.

> A review of more than twenty records of lesions and non trivial pathologies in Lower and Middle Palaeolithic early humans by Hong Shang and Erik Trinkaus produced evidence for at least some degree of survival from severe injuries in all cases...the remains of many Neanderthal individuals also show evidence for long term care, dating back as early as 190-160 thousand years ago... It seems that neither age nor the type of affliction, whether it be injury or genetic defect, recoverable or life-long, detracted from the care given by these archaic humans. This is perhaps all the more remarkable since life was hard in

such times, the risk of serious injury was high and records from teeth show that periods of food shortages were common.[74]

Archaeologist Lorna Tilley knows of 30 individuals whose impairments were so severe that they must have had care in order to survive, including the remains of several Neanderthals from a site in Iraq dating to 45,000 years ago. "Shanidar 1" had a badly withered right arm amputated below the elbow, loss of vision in one eye and other injuries sustained at a young age, yet died much later, at around 40 years old.[75] "Shanidar 3" was buried in the same grave, aged 40-50 at death, making him one of the oldest known Neanderthals. He had a "severe degenerative disorder in his right foot", meaning it would have been very difficult for him to walk around or to find his own food. "The fact his condition developed indicates he had been living with significant injury for some time, sufficient for the degenerative disease to emerge".[76] Seriously hampered in their ability to survive independently, both lived to such a late age because their communities must have cared for them.

"Windover boy", whose 7,500-year-old remains were found in Florida, had a severe congenital spinal malformation, yet lived to around 15 years old. A 10,000-year-old skeleton found in Italy in the 1980s belonged to a teenage boy named Romito 2. His severe dwarfism gave him very short arms, so the nomadic band of hunter-gatherers to which he belonged "would have had to accept that he couldn't run at the same pace or participate in hunting in the same way others did".[77]

Another example concerns the remains (up to 4,000 years old) of a young man found in northern Vietnam. Man Bac Burial 9 (M9) lived for 10 years after becoming paralysed from the waist down as a young adolescent and had "at best very limited upper body mobility." The challenges to maintaining his health and quality of life would have been enormous, yet M9 lived until he was over 30. "M9's survival reflects high quality, continuous and time-consuming care within a technologically unsophisticated prehistoric community".[78]

Kim Neilsen has written about impairment in the earliest North American communities. Impaired individuals could still contribute in some way to the community. If a young man with a cognitive impairment, for example, was reliable in carrying and transporting water, he was valued accordingly. "He lived in reciprocity and lived in balance. His limitations shaped his contributions, but that was true of everyone else in the community as well".[79]

> Prior to European conquest, the worldviews of indigenous peoples understood body, mind and spirit to be one. These beliefs allowed for fluid definitions of bodily and mental norms, and fundamentally assumed that all had gifts to share with the community—and that for communities to exist in healthy balance, each individual needed to do so. A young man who no longer controlled the movements of his arm after falling from a tree or cliff while scouting neighbouring peoples would learn other means by which to hunt, fish, drum, and please his sexual partners. His gift might be that of sharing and teaching the community's past.[80]

The earliest human societies—which comprise some 90 per cent of our history as a species—were nomadic hunter-gatherers, living for the most part in small bands of 30 to 40 people. These communities depended wholly on "nature's bounty"—foraging for nuts and berries and trapping, fishing or hunting small game. All group members had a role.[81] Such societies practised egalitarian sharing and participation: their immediate dependency on nature left them no option. As we have seen, people with impairments were not marginalised or excluded.

The first class societies

Among the Dalegura, a group of Australian Aborigines, and the Kenyan Masai, life is extremely harsh. However in both societies infanticide is prohibited, age is considered a sign of authority and respect, and impaired individuals are not rejected or excluded. Among the Masai "the fact that an individual is impaired in one way or another is just an aspect of his/her person":

> Certainly Masai notice 'disabilities' and look upon them as bad or unfortunate things... They both name the difference and mark it, but...

this indicates acceptance and lack of fear of the different or abnormal. To give birth to a disabled child is not culturally defined as a crisis requiring specific actions and precautions. It is part of life's experience.[82]

The Punah Bah of central Borneo ban anyone with mental impairments from marriage on the grounds that they are only "half a person". Otherwise, there is no prejudice directed at them and all impaired people play a full and productive social role.[83]

Other earlier class societies explained impairment in religious terms, seeing it as a mark of either good or evil. Artefacts left by the Olmecs of ancient Mexico (approximately 1500BCE (Before the Christian Era)—300CE (Christian Era) indicate that they revered impaired people as godlike. The Spanish conquistadors later noted this as a feature of the Aztec royal court. As Michael Oliver has written;

> [W]hat is construed as an impairment and what is regarded as an appropriate social response are far from universal features: 'The disfiguring scar in Dallas becomes an honorific scar in Dahomey.' Moreover, the assumed 'defects' that mark individuals out as unacceptably different may include features that other cultures regard as benign, such as freckles, small or flabby buttocks, and protruding navels.[84]

A society's treatment of its older members, who have lost the ability to hunt, fish or cultivate the soil, amounted to a form of enlightened self-interest. Jared Diamond calls the elderly the "library" of pre-literate societies as their accumulated experience could be vital to a community's survival. Rennell Island lies in the "cyclone belt" of the south-west Pacific. After a hugely destructive *hungi kengi* (cyclone) in around 1910, the islanders were able to survive by eating certain plant species they normally avoided. When Diamond visited in 1976, only one woman in her eighties remained who had detailed and direct experience of what plants were safe and edible after the *hungi kengi*. She attributed her own survival to the elders of the time who carried the same valuable knowledge.[85]

Classical antiquity

Some authors in the field of disability studies, such as Colin Barnes, would accept the above evidence. Like others such as Tom Shakespeare, however, he believes that "the roots of disabled people's oppression lie in the ancient world of Greece and Rome".[86] The main evidence Barnes cites for this is that in ancient Greece: "Infanticide in the form of exposure to the elements for sickly or weak infants was widespread and in some states mandatory".[87] Such beliefs are widespread, but the actual evidence of such practices is rather more complex, varied and often ambiguous.

The first substantial records concerning social attitudes towards people with impairments in antiquity relate to ancient Egypt, a civilisation which began over 5,000 years ago and ended shortly after the Roman occupation in 30BCE. The only unambiguous evidence—in writings and from natural and artificial mummification—concerns the role of dwarfs. Their many human remains include several high-ranking figures and at least two dwarf gods, Ptah and Bes. Achondroplastic dwarfs[88] appear to have been associated with divinity and other dwarfs in ancient Egypt are portrayed in a positive way in a wide range of occupations.[89] Blind people, meanwhile, are "most commonly depicted in specific roles, such as harpists or singers".[90]

The records from ancient Greece, an empire which began with the first Greek city states in the 6th century BCE and ended with the death of Alexander the Great in 323BCE, provides considerably more material about its impaired citizens, as does the Roman empire which succeeded it. The Roman republic was established in the 6th century BCE, leading to an empire of 600 years' duration in the west and lasting in the east until the fall of Constantinople in 1453.

Martha Rose begins her study of ancient Greece by stressing that, although there were terms for specific impairments (such as blindness or deafness), there was no Greek equivalent for the modern overarching term "disability". Physically disabled people were not segregated, excluded or marginalised. Rose rejects the idea that children with impairments were routinely left to die, shows that there is scant information about "exposure" of any baby—disabled or not—in ancient Greece, and argues that "sweeping conclusions" are unwarranted in the light of this "scant evidence".[91]

Many people with severe impairments would not have survived in the ancient world. Survival from a spinal-cord injury, for example, has largely only been possible since the 1960s. On the other hand, impairments rarely seen in today's Europe—such as "clubfoot, broken bones that have not healed properly, and the effects of epidemic diseases such as tuberculosis"[92]—would at that time have been relatively common, as were gout and infectious arthritis.

It is therefore likely that impairment was common in ancient Greece and Rome. According to one study, 10 percent of all known ancient Greek skeletons have at least one bone fracture. Four out of every five of these are male, with warfare the likely cause of many injuries. Two examples, however, are of particular note:

> unusually well-preserved skeletal remains in the fourth century AD [Roman] cemetery at Cirencester in Gloucester. From a sample of 299 adults, it is estimated that about 80 per cent of the population suffered from...osteoarthritis...a progressive disease which in its advanced stages involves debilitating pain, gross deformity and, ultimately, paralysis... Of 233 skeletons in a Greek cemetery at Pantanello near Metapontum in southern Italy, 131 (ie 56 per cent) exhibited bone pathologies due to fractures, metabolic disorders and systemic infections. In light of what appears to have been a general decline in average lifespan in the ancient world from the fifth century until the early centuries of the Christian era it is quite possible that incapacitating and disfiguring diseases actually increased over time and became more rife in the Roman period, since life expectancy is an important indicator of the health of any population.[93]

The ancient Greeks sometimes made fun of impairment "in ways that would make us shudder".[94] Terms for physical impairment, however, were very general, describing only appearances or symptoms, in contrast to today's "technical, medical generalisations of specific physical conditions".[95] The fact that unusual or undesirable physical traits were pointed out, however, does not necessarily indicate that people were routinely discriminated against.[96]

Rose points out that the original sources for claims of exposure or killing of disabled children in ancient Greece amount to five short passages. Plato's *Republic* and Aristotle's *Politics* are frequently cited as evidence. *Politics* certainly recommends infanticide.[97] However, both Plato and Aristotle were writing about what they saw as ideal societies, not the practice of their contemporary Greeks. How much any given baby was wanted was determined by factors such as the economic situation of the parents, the type and degree of impairment and the gender of the infant (baby girls were sometimes rejected due to inadequate aesthetic appeal). Rose notes that there are plenty of references in the records to babies "with congenital anomalies" who survived. Further:

> In the ancient world, one would not have been shocked to deliver a baby with some anomaly or other…what we would call a deformed baby today would not necessarily have been an unacceptable baby in ancient Greece… Modern assumptions about the economic worth and aesthetic appeal of deformed people, cloaked in the standards of modern health, do not provide an appropriate framework of interpretation for the evidence about the lot of anomalous infants in ancient Greece.[98]

In many cases, babies were left in known locations where others would take them away. Roman babies were exposed not just due to a perceived deformity or other physical inadequacy, but also for other reasons such as the shame of illegitimacy on the part of mothers or the presence of ill omens prior to the birth. "Another orator says that slave mothers sometimes expose their infant children because they are unwilling to bring them up in slavery."[99]

Childbirth in general was a huge risk. This meant that, as Mary Beard puts it in relation to Roman women, "the boundary between contraception and infanticide was a blurred one, and disposing of children after birth was safer than getting rid of them before".[100]

Intriguingly, ancient Greek culture provides scattered accounts of people with different impairments involved in a wide range of economic activities, with no indication that this was seen as unusual. The "crook-foot god" Hephaestus "is often depicted in paintings with his smithing tools; even in a whimsical red-figure painting from the fifth-century BCE, portraying a drunken Hephaestus being led home by a satyr, he carries his identifying emblems, a pincers and hammer".[101] The ultimate measure of a Greek man's stature and worth was his participation in the military. We know of soldiers and even generals who were "lame" yet took part in war, with the contemporary comment that "the army has need of those who stand and fight, not those who run away".[102]

Exposure was certainly more widely practiced in the "high" Roman Empire, though possibly not in earlier republican Rome.[103] This did not always necessarily lead to the child's death:

> The best known of all Roman evidence is Pliny's exchange of letters with Trajan. He consults the emperor about the threptoi, in other words 'those who having been born free, were exposed, then picked up by someone and brought up in slavery', a great issue, he says, concerning his entire province).[104]

The epileptic Julius Caesar became dictator of all Rome, and Claudius, who had severe physical impairments possibly including cerebral palsy, became a Roman Emperor. Blindness was not a bar to fame or respectability for either the Greek poet Homer or the Roman seer Capys. Among the victims of the 79CE volcanic eruption of Vesuvius was a rich and heavily pregnant young woman. Her remains indicate she was from a wealthy Pompeii family—and that she had spina bifida. She had nonetheless retained her position in society, with her age at death estimated at 17. In this individual example at least, a woman with an obviously visible impairment appears to have enjoyed the status and material rewards common to her contemporary class and gender.[105]

Some authors note a sharp contrast in Roman ruling class attitudes towards people considered deformed or ugly between the period of the Republic and that of the later Principate. In the Republic, some of those regarded as "monstra" (androgynous and severely impaired people, such as Siamese twins) were put to death and aristocrats with certain impairments were excluded from political mandates. In the Principate several accounts describe emperors and aristocrats buying and keeping physically or mentally impaired people such as dwarfs, "androgyns" and slaves with highly visible deformities as household pets, for entertainment.[106]

Classical antiquity featured mythological creatures such as the Minotaur or Cyclops, which were referred to as monsters. But "monstrum" and its synonyms were also used to describe ugly people or strange animals:

> With the Emperor Claudius it comes close to denoting a disabled person, as is also the case in reference to the birth of deformed babies. The morally ugly, too, are sometimes called monstra. The most famous…is Cleopatra, whom Horace calls fatale monstrum. Suetonius called Caligula monstrum because of his horrible deeds; the activity of bone breakers (ossifragi), who turn people into beggars by mutilating them, is also called monstrous.[107]

Monstrum is defined as "a divine omen indicating misfortune, an evil omen, portent; a monster, monstrosity". The word also has etymological roots in the verb monstrare, meaning to show. Another term more frequently used in the later Roman Empire is *mirabilium*—something "to be wondered at, wonderful, marvellous, extraordinary, admirable, strange, singular".[108] So the myth and culture of classical antiquity portrays impaired individuals as cursed but also blessed, feared but also revered, not quite human (monstrous) but also more than human (associated with divinity).

While people with particular impairments were often subjected to ridicule or worse, there is no reliable evidence that the ruling classes of ancient Greece and Rome discriminated against disabled people as such. In respect of Greece Rose may have a better case for concluding that "disability was defined and negotiated between individuals on a case-by-case basis within the community, rather than as a medical one, in which what was conceived of as a 'problem' was inherent in the individual".[109] In Greece at least, outward physical perfection was believed to reflect inner moral virtue.[110] Attitudes in both societies towards their weaker (and particularly their poorer) citizens are likely to have much to do with the fact that both were highly militarised empires prizing individual physical ability. The parading of dwarves or others considered as "monstra" may be best explained as a means for

Roman rulers to display their superiority by making sport out of those below them.

The central characteristic of these societies was slavery. It was slaves who built the cities, temples and amphitheatres—and most citizens were expected to own at least one. The speech writer Lysias records the trial of an unknown Athenian citizen with an undefined impairment in the 4th century BCE, who was accused of the Ancient Greek equivalent of benefit fraud. In his defence, he says that he is so poor that he could not afford to employ a slave.[111]

It would be foolish to deny the cruelty and humiliation Roman and Greek rulers inflicted on individuals perceived as "monstrous" or in some way physically inferior. However, such cruelty and humiliation was widely practised and the identity of the victims was often arbitrary. Most important, however, is that these societies had no concept of disability and we must therefore look later in human history to clearly establish the roots of disability discrimination.

Feudal society

Few surviving records provide an idea of what life for disabled people was like in early feudal society. Natural disasters such as severe storms or prolonged drought could mean social disaster, with settled agricultural communities lacking the mobility of hunter-gatherer bands. Various Latin terms for illness or impairment were interchangeable. The relevant medieval terminology was often extremely vague:

> 'Disease' was a general term in Middle English usage for trouble, misfortune or misery, encompassing both a notion of bodily discomfort, suffering or pain, as well as a notion of corporal infirmity or impairment. 'Sickness' was also a blanket term for an abnormal or special state of health, and could sometimes signify a specific mental or physical disorder.[112]

The Middle Ages have received little historical attention by writers on disability. The first and most important reason for this is a lack of primary sources. Stereotypes undoubtedly play their part too. One writer on contemporary disability issues dismisses the period thus: "in the Middle Ages, disabled people were subject to a host of superstitious ideas, which led to their persecution. Impairment was believed to be the result of divine judgement and therefore a punishment for sin. Abuse of disabled people was sanctioned by the church... During the Middle Ages disability was associated with evil and witchcraft".[113]

Opposition to such "dungeons and Dark Ages" notions, and the belief that all older societies invariably linked sin and illness or impairment, sometimes appears in surprising places. The website for government-sponsored body English Heritage provides a potted summary of life for disabled people in the Middle Ages:

> In medieval England, the 'lepre', the 'blynde', the 'dumbe', the 'deaff', the 'natural fool', the 'creple', the 'lame' and the 'lunatick' were a highly visible presence in everyday life. Some thought such people were being punished for sins, while others believed that they were closer to God, suffering purgatory on earth rather than after death and would get to heaven sooner.
>
> With no state provision, impaired people lived and worked in their communities, supported by family and friends. If they couldn't work, their town or village might support them, or they resorted to begging. The Church's teachings led monks and nuns to feed, clothe and house the poor, visiting them when in prison or sick, offering drink to the thirsty, and burial for the dead.[114]

Archaeological evidence shows that labour "such as spinning, weaving, leather working, carpentry and carving carried with them a high risk of RSI [repetitive strain injury] as well as ongoing trauma. Burns, scalds, hernias and respiratory disorders occasioned by the inhalation of dust, smoke and pollutants must have been equally common".[115]

Most contemporary sources discussing impairment during the feudal period belonged to the religious intellectual elite based in monasteries, cathedral schools and universities who preserved, translated and reinterpreted earlier classical and biblical texts.[116] How far their ideas actually represented or influenced the attitudes of the majority of the population is questionable. Contrary to myth, accidents at work were usually seen as natural (or man-made) and not divinely caused punishments and so were subject to human alleviation. Miracle stories were written by monks as advertisements for a particular shrine, saint, and cathedral, so each of the latter has its own archive. Of the 500 examined by medieval historian Irina Metzler, "only about 4 or 5" mentioned sin in connection with disability. One example from the 12th century concerns the builder of the cathedral in Canterbury, William of Sens. The scaffolding on the building gave way and the fall left him paralysed. "Nobody, in any of the sources that tell this story, accused him of doing anything sinful. It was just, 'Oh, poor chap'".[117]

Sin and disability is linked in the teachings of Christianity, as it is in other religions. But how far did people really believe this and apply it to their friends and neighbours? If a baby was born with impairments, the church blamed its parents for deviant sexual practices:

> Sexual activity while a woman is pregnant, during menstruation, on Sundays, on a saint's feast day, during daylight…anything that's improper could result in a defective child. People in the Middle Ages were much more pragmatic, almost turned a blind eye…to the church's teaching about what may or may not be sinful, and…got on with their lives.[118]

A study was made in the 1930s of 456 skeletons buried in mass graves from the battle of Wisby, fought on the Swedish island of Gotland in 1361, and of 37 skeletons at Towton in England from another battle during the Wars of the Roses. In both cases, the remains included soldiers with healed fractures, who must have fought and died alongside their comrades.[119]

On the other hand, religious hospices of the period in Western Europe excluded the lame, one-armed and blind on the grounds that such impairments "did not constitute sickness." As Henri-Jacques Stiker observes of the Middle Ages, "the categorization of various impairments and disabilities is far from clear. [D]isability…is neither inventoried, nor excluded, nor organized, nor viewed in any special way: it is simply there, part of the great lot of human misery".[120]

Over this period a nationwide network of hospitals based in (or near) religious establishments began to emerge. Specialised hospitals for leprosy, blindness and physical disability were created. England's first mental institution, later known as 'Bedlam', was originally the Bethlehem hospital in the City of London. At the same time, almshouses were founded to provide a supportive place for the disabled and elderly infirm to live.[121]

Metzler has found little evidence of any change in the varying and ambiguous attitudes or beliefs concerning sin and illness or impairment over the period 1100 to 1400. On the contrary, they were encoded in canon law through an article passed in 1215 at the Fourth Lateran Council: "Theologically, all human ills were caused by sin, due to the primeval Fall from grace, so that all illnesses, without any hierarchical qualifications, were in a very wide sense caused by sin".[122]

Records also suggest that early Islamic society treated people we now describe as having learning difficulties with respect:

Europe was still in the Dark Ages of science and medicine but in the Islamic world Avicenna (980-1037) wrote a textbook the Canon of medicine in which he mentioned hydrocephalus, meningitis and other mental disorders. He recognised and defined various levels of intellectual functioning and knew that brain injury could affect memory and speech. There were mental hospitals in Cairo and Baghdad in the 11th and 12th centuries. Ibn Al-Baitar also wrote about learning disabilities during the first half of the thirteenth century.[123]

In 1270, asylums were founded for people with mental impairments in Damascus and Aleppo. In the Judaic Tradition, although Leviticus "described how people with any disability were forbidden to become priests or enter the sanctuary...parts of the Talmud advocated disability as a holy state and a means of getting to heaven and similar sentiments were expressed towards those who helped disabled people".[124]

Self-mutilation by amputating fingers or toes as an expression of mourning or to appease spirits and causing deformities for begging purposes have been known in various parts of the world. Medieval punishments for crime included "mutilation of the ears, lips and tongue, amputation of hands and feet, gouging out of the eyes".[125] Some examples of mutilation, such as footbinding—the deliberate deformation of upper class women's feet practised in China between the 10th and the early 20th centuries—were clearly attributable to women's oppression.[126]

Stiker describes the likely attitude of medieval society towards impairment:

> Normality was a hodge-podge…it was only natural that there should be malformations. This was more than tolerance; it was real life, with which one compromised as best as one could, without wishing to change it by various techniques and various treatments, and without wishing to exclude it either. There was an acceptance, at times awkward, at times brutal, at times compassionate, a kind of indifferent, fatalistic integration, without ideology but also without confrontation…[T]he disabled and powerless…were, first and for a long time, poor persons to be helped and not representatives of a strangeness to be exorcised.[127]

Elsewhere, the 3rd century Buddhist emperor Asoka is said to have organised care institutions for people with impairments, a practice revived in the 4th century by Ceylonese ruler Buddhadasa. "Chinese pilgrim Fa-Hien, c 400CE, reported a city house of treatment for disease and disability, in Buddhist north India", which reappeared around 645CE.[128] Future research across the Global South will undoubtedly reveal further evidence of this "vast and complicated history":

> At least 3,500 years of substantial South Asian experience and evidence exists, in which varied responses to disability and people with disabilities appear… Some…is well known, involving for example characters such as blind King Dhritarashtra and his blindfolded wife Gandhari, Ashtavakra the brainy supercrip and Hanuman the divine but crack-jawed monkey, cunning and vengeful Manthara, even Shiva the (occasional) Simpleton; while vastly more characters and

episodes, such as Khujjutara the humpbacked female thief turned religious teacher, are known mainly to scholars.[129]

The crisis of the late Middle Ages led to intensified and religiously inspired discrimination and persecution. The evidence prior to then does not indicate the presence of any "culture of oppression" against disabled people. Congenital and other kinds of impairment, including those acquired later in life, such as "river blindness" or broken or damaged limbs were attributed to divine displeasure at an evil action or human disobedience to a command. These social interpretations and explanations for impairment reflect human powerlessness in the face of nature that determined, for example, whether the harvest would be immensely successful or utterly disastrous. Despite increased productivity compared to ancient slave society, feudalism remained highly dependent on nature.

The ambiguity towards impairment identified in early class societies, therefore, can be explained by a need to appease the capriciousness of nature due to a far greater degree of dependence on its favours than appears to be the case under capitalism.[130] The lives of people with impairments were determined by the general conditions of exploitation and oppression that obtained in these (often brutal) societies. But there is no evidence of any *specific*, systematic discrimination levelled at them.

5.
Late feudalism and the origins of disability

The rich man in his castle,
The poor man at his gate,
The lord made them high and lowly,
And ordered their estate.
—Cecil Frances Alexander, All Things Bright and Beautiful

The evidence now available to us suggests that the origins of disability as a form of discrimination lie in the social and economic changes of the late feudal period, as the new forms of merchant and agricultural capital grew in influence.

In feudal society the lives of those working the land were largely dictated by the seasons, with long periods of leisure interspersed with shorter periods of intense labour. Families often lived and worked as large extended groups, enabling greater networks of support for child-rearing and caring for the elderly. For most people there was no concept of literacy or intellectual ability. Every family member would have taken part in the daily grind of fetching water and firewood, ploughing the fields, or feeding the animals. It was often officially recognised that not everyone could do any kind of work, such as the hard manual labour required during the harvest season:

> Once the main harvesting had been done with scythes and sickles, this left a reasonable amount behind. Gleaning, or collecting the remaining ears of corn, was the job of everyone else not fit enough to do the harvesting. The reeves of royal manors defined who was able-bodied or not, as in this example from 1282: 'Let it be established that the young, the old, and those who are decrepit and unable to work shall glean in the autumn after the sheaves have been taken away,

but that those who are able if they wish to work for wages will not be allowed to glean.' Anyone hired as a labourer was by definition forbidden from gleaning.[131]

This way of life, typical for much of the world's population for thousands of years, was to virtually disappear over the course of just 300 years. The social and economic crisis of the 14th century set in train a series of changes that ultimately led to revolution and the rise of industrial capitalism. This chapter examines these changes and how they affected the lives of people with impairments.

Late feudalism and work

The way feudal society was organised around production did not readily facilitate new methods of work, even when these were self-evidently superior to older ones. The heavy-wheeled plough, for example, could cope with heavy but fertile soil. Although invented in the 6th century, it took 300 years for its use to spread throughout Europe. This slow pace of development was also true of other innovations such as the water mill, new methods of harnessing horses and the use of beans and other legumes to replenish the soil. The cumulative effect, however, was that grain yields had doubled by the 12th century. This enhanced food surplus promoted the development of merchant trading networks and in turn the growth of towns which tied together previously isolated villages. The traders and artisans who established these towns increasingly found that their interests diverged from those of the feudal lords.

Europe's monarchies came to see towns as a valuable counterweight to the power of the feudal lords and so helped promote their growth.

> The traders needed to keep accounts and written records of contracts in a way which the feudal lords of the earlier period had not. They also wanted formal, written laws rather than the ad hoc judgements handed down in the villages by the lords... Literacy was no longer confined to the monasteries and Latin ceased to be the only written language.[132]

This enhanced ability to keep records led to the translation of information on productive techniques and innovations from older societies, such as ancient Greece, Rome, China and the later great Islamic civilisations. It also made it easier to spread knowledge and understanding of new inventions. The Catholic Church, feudalism's biggest landowner, feared that the new faith in reason would undermine superstition and threaten the hold of the church on the minds of its members.

The great crisis of the 14th century saw famine and plagues spread across Europe, killing up to half the population and leading to a catastrophic fall in economic production:

> This is the era of great epidemics, widespread dislocation and wandering, criminality. An era, in particular because of the plague, of substantial demographic and hierarchical upheaval. Great families disappeared entirely. Roving gangs sprang up. Authorities responded with repressive measures. Poverty, illness, disability, are often linked with theft, profiteering, petty criminality. Society begins to make the marginalized the object of 'treatment'.[133]

This was also an era of huge urban and peasant revolts. At its end, market networks continued to grow, and urban traders reshaped life in the countryside by encouraging craft industry particularly through the "putting-out" system where rural workers turned raw materials into finished products in their own homes. These changes undermined the power of the feudal lords and moved production methods a step closer to capitalism.

> [S]ome of the later medieval urban production processes (eg, wage earners working for an artisan/craft master, 'clocking on/off' of the workforce) are already premonitions of the later production methods of early industrial and mercantile systems... Perhaps, with regard to the position of medieval disabled persons as labourers, as active participants in the various crafts, trades and occupations, one should place greater emphasis on the difference between urban and rural patterns and systems of work, a difference that became greater with the growth of markets and towns from the high Middle Ages onwards.[134]

In the earlier feudal period "people tended to work slowly and inefficiently, and to stop whenever possible. It is said that their activities were not measured or timed accurately, and they worked until the job was completed...to use modern phraseology, they were 'task-oriented' rather than 'time-oriented'." [135] With few instruments to measure time, there were no general standards to regulate work. Life was governed by "natural rhythms like day and night, the seasons, the sequence of harvests, or the revolutions of the moon as indicators of the process of time, and local groups of settlers in villages were accustomed to control their own time rather than being controlled by it". [136] But this began to change with "the development of precise time measurement in monastic as well as urban spheres", leading by the early 14th century to standardised measurement units. "Pioneered in the Italian cities, public clocks came to be installed, followed in the mid-fourteenth century by town halls in north-western Europe, and with the clocks came the expectation to "keep time". [137]

The growth of merchant trade also gave money greater importance, with goods or services acquiring their own "exchange value". This implied a challenge to the feudal ideology that everyone's place in society was fixed by God:

> Market relations rest on the assumption that, however unequal people's social standing, they have an equal right to accept or reject a particular transaction. The buyer is free to offer any price and the seller free to reject the offer. Mandarin and merchant, baron and burgher, landlord and tenant have equal rights in this respect. In so far as the market spreads, old prejudices come under siege from calculations in terms of cash. [138]

The mass of peasants and workers in handicraft industries, the latter often based at home instead of the towns, still retained a large degree of control over their working patterns. The rural production process and the extended nature of the feudal family would have permitted many people with impairments to participate in daily economic life. A population census in 1570s Norwich found a "lame" and one-handed 80-year-old woman who worked by spinning and winding yarn and a blind man who worked as a baker.[139]

Idiots, fools and the crisis of late feudalism

Modern psychological concepts of intelligence and disability have their origins in the period from the Reformation to the Enlightenment when a specific category of mental impairment began to evolve. Ancient Greek philosophers Plato and Aristotle were *idiotai*—meaning private citizens detached from power and the public arena. In his book *The Laws*, Plato:

> classifies ultimate ignorance under the genus 'unreason' (anoia), a broad category of cosmic disorder. By contrast with ignorance as simple lack of knowledge (agnoia), which though 'ugly' is merely an absence, unreason as it occurs in the human realm is positively evil. In The Laws, it covers a wide range of conditions: being mad, immature, senile, female, drunk or a poet... The modern emphasis on speed of thought was foreign to Plato, Aristotle and Socrates, all wealthy landowning philosophers who embraced a life of leisure, although it was more valued in Athenian public life.[140]

When Alexander [the Great] distinguished between philosophers and idiotae, the latter meant those naturally lacking ideas or abilities—and all ordinary people. This attitude remained for centuries; "ideas above your station...were ideas as such".[141] An eminent Oxford scholar wrote in the late 1240s: "physical activity is more suited to insignificant and common people, the peace of meditation and study to the noble elite; in this way, everyone has an occupation fitting his station in life".[142]

Modern ideas about intelligence began to develop in the 12th century, along with the growth of merchant trade and urbanisation. The belief that nature was god's creation and so could not make a living being without his guidance was still widespread—but as such discussions moved from the monasteries to the academies, attempts were made to explain what was observed. Universities began as training schools for the church and state authorities so the concept of intelligence remained primarily a religious one, although this was soon to change.

Foolishness in medieval and early modern medicine covered everything from infancy and old age through to eccentricity, melancholy, drunkenness and the simulations of the court jester, and was a disposition rather than a personal possession. So a medieval doctor could empathise with foolishness as a state of mind that was not seen as abnormal, whereas a modern one could not. Thirdly, absence of thought, in addition to slowness, came to characterize the idiot. The records of Bedlam Hospital in the early seventeenth century show that its governors took increasing care to weed out 'idiots' because they were deemed to be incurable.[143]

Fools were a feature of European royal courts from the 13th to the end of the 17th centuries. What should we make of this medieval fool, ubiquitous in literature from Chaucer to Shakespeare?

Medieval fools were called fools because of their behaviour and not because of their lack of cognitive and other mental skills. The medieval and early modern period therefore distinguished between 'natural' fools (those coming closest to the modern notion of the mentally disabled) and 'artificial' fools (who were professionals acting out a role they had voluntarily taken on). Both natural and artificial fools could function as courtly or public entertainers.[144]

A few individuals, who might be described today as learning disabled, enjoyed a privileged life at court, with a 'keeper' who looked after them. These 'natural fools' were seen as a source of wisdom and humour. Will Somer, Henry VIII's 'natural fool' and 'Jane the Fool' can be seen in paintings of the Royal Family from this period. The learning disabled were held to have 'access to a divine wisdom', and to keep a fool absolved one's sins.[145]

For medieval and Renaissance writers, intellect was still associated with the soul. Only later was it seen as a separate entity of the mind. James I's physician Helkiah Crooke wrote in 1615 of those:

who are 'esteemed foolish idiots...even by the common people', that is, by those who simply by virtue of being common would usually be termed idiots themselves. Crooke was also keeper of Bedlam, which would have placed him at the centre of legal controversy over the sequestration of incompetents' estates, and the hospital's records show that its governors were taking increasing care to weed out 'idiots' because they were not deemed to be curable. It took another two centuries for the medico-legal brew to be fully digested, however.[146]

This last point is important, as the decline of the fool can be linked to the new Enlightenment values of reason and science. The first change was the replacement of the coarse and raucous "natural" fool by the Elizabethan court's more refined "artificial" fool, representing Renaissance ideals of free speech. By the end of the 16th century the fool was primarily associated with the clown/fool figures of Elizabethan drama.

At the beginning of the 18th century, permanent mental difference (as natural folly) and temporary mental difference (as a psychiatric condition) became amalgamated. The fool became an object of medical research, and later of special education and rehabilitation. This was linked to the emergence of the "norm" in statistics (see chapter 7) with degrees of "deviance" in cognitive ability measured on a continuum of normalcy and anomaly.[147]

In the 1650s, during the tumult of the English Revolution, there were a series of debates in the Church of England about who should be excluded from participation in the ritual of communion. Thomas Aquinas had already singled out people born with a lack of reason as associated with those "possessed by unclean spirits"—a group likely to include heretics, atheists and those exhibiting disruptive behaviour. Agreement in the church hierarchy on this issue:

> sprang from the need for a united front against an encroaching tide of doctrinal relativities exacerbated by civil war. The underlying need for all sides to maintain church unity preceded and actually created...a common and absolute exclusion... This shift coincided politically with the loss of power of kings and ecclesiastical authority to dictate

a uniform political and religious doctrine. Since the supposedly universal 'common ideas' had in fact been the property of an elite with the authority to proscribe them, typically human psychological operations such as abstraction or logical reasoning occurred only in such people. But the civic disorder of the mid-seventeenth century, especially in England, was an omen: the lower orders were 'getting ideas', of their own and on their own.[148]

The gradual intrusion of the term "idiot" (in the sense of someone permanently lacking reason) into theology had much to do with the previous machinations of the Court of Wards, a loose grouping of intellectual thugs and royal hangers-on abolished by the Revolution's new parliament:

> Late Tudor and early Stuart monarchs…had set up this Court to distinguish between the limited rights of the lunatic to his estate…and the permanent lack of rights of the born, incurable idiot, the profits from whose estates could be used to finance the state—though it must be repeated that the characteristics exhibited by these idiots scarcely corresponded with those attributed to modern 'intellectual' disability.[149]

As Oliver Cromwell re-established a centralised, quasi-monarchical authority by becoming Lord Protector, the dispute in the church died down: the threat to its unity had passed. The concept of "intellectual" disability therefore emerged for practical reasons of self-interest on the part of the monarchy on the one hand and on the part of the church on the other.[150]

The rise of the institution

Between 1500 and 1650 England's population doubled and the proportion of the population living in towns increased to one in 12.[151] Growing numbers of poor people "were left to roam the country without a livelihood as the barons dismissed their old armies of retainers and landowners, 'enclosed' old common lands and deprived smallholding peasants of their plots".[152] At the end of the 16th century a series of Poor Law Acts authorised the whipping and branding of "sturdy vagabonds", now seen by successive monarchs as "voluntary criminals". This, however, excluded those seen as lunatics, blind, lame or unable to work: "all these...are to be provided for by the overseers of necessary relief and are to have allowances...according to...their maladies and needs".[153]

St Bartholomew's and St Thomas' Hospitals in England had catered for the sick and the poor since the mid-12th century. Usually run by the church, such institutions fed and sometimes raised those deemed to be in need. But by the 14th and 15th centuries, a new specialisation was apparent:

> with the result that prostitutes, pilgrims, and the disabled are no longer mixed together. In Paris, for example, pilgrims and transients are sheltered in the Hôpital Saint-Jacques du Haut-Pas, while the foundation of Quinze-Vingts admitted only the blind. This last establishment did not intern its clients, who continued to go out and beg in the streets. The disabled and sick were directed towards the Hotel-Dieu. What would become the hospital in the modern sense of the term accepted only these two categories.[154]

General hospitals—secular institutions whose sole function was the practice of medicine—were first founded in France in 1656, followed later by more specialist institutions. In Paris, these included the Hospital for the Incurable and the Hotel des Invalides for disabled veterans, the latter founded in 1674 by Louis XIV. "The Hotel des Invalides was intended as a model, and based on the charitable houses established by Vincent de Paul in the first half of the century; with good hygiene, heating, surgery—and a productive workforce which produced shoes, clothing and tapestries".[155]

The priory of St Mary of Bethlehem was founded as a religious refuge in London in 1247. By the 14th century it was specialising in the treatment of mental illness. In 1547 control over what was still England's only institution for mentally ill people passed to the Corporation of London and its first medically qualified superintendent was employed. Mental illness was increasingly being seen as a matter for medical treatment.[156]

Madness began to feature more prominently in culture. It is a central theme in Shakespeare's *King Lear*, *Macbeth* and *Hamlet*, in which the eponymous hero's vacillations and inability to act make his insanity ambiguous. Alexander Pope and Jonathan Swift made lunatics the focus of their satires, and Bethlem/Bedlam itself was the scene for Hogarth's series of panels *A Rake's Progress*.[157]

Reform and reaction

Guilds emerged with the development of urban craft industries. These were associations of artisans or merchants formed to control trade in a particular town. They collected funds and distributed benefits to their impaired members. The carpenters' guild in London had a passage in their 1389 statutes: "each brother and sister of his fraternity shall pay to the helping and sustaining of sick men which have fallen in disease, as by falling down of an house, or hurting of an axe, or by diverse sicknesse, twelve pennies per year".[158]

> For Paris at the end of the thirteenth century it has been estimated that around 20 of the 101 registered craft guilds made explicit statements in their statutes to provide charitable aid, both to guild members who had fallen on hard times as well as to the needy in the wider community; that the other guilds did not specify such aims in their statutes is not evidence for lack of collective support but simply evidence for a perceived superfluity to record such statements of intent in writing.[159]

The statutes of the guild of the Blessed Virgin Mary in Yorkshire, founded in 1357, provided that guild members who became "infirm, bowed, blind, dumb, maimed, or sick, whether with some lasting or only temporary sickness" received a pension of "sevenpence every week...so long as he lives".[160]

Beliefs in the Devil and natural magic actually intensified in the last centuries of feudal Europe as successive crises led to new inroads for capitalist development, cumulatively undermining the power of feudal rulers. The notorious *Malleus Maleficarum* (written in 1486) was followed over a century later by a treatise on witchcraft written by King James VI of Scotland (soon to be James I of England). Martin Luther argued that impaired children were the result of sexual intercourse with the devil, although the evidence that he advocated infanticide is less definitive than often supposed.[161] It is sometimes claimed that this period provides proof of the systematic persecution of disabled people but the evidence instead suggests that women and the elderly, as well as "the heretical and the physically awkward, are much more incriminated in the medieval fever of the witch hunt... The mentally ill were involved in the witch trials not primarily as defendants but as evidence of the witchcraft practised by others".[162]

The Catholic Church responded to heresy in its own ranks with the Counter-Reformation, beginning in the 1560s. Copernicus had not faced persecution for arguing in 1543 that the Earth moved round the Sun, but 90 years later Galileo was forced by the Pope's Inquisitors to recant his own support for the Copernican system. The repression unleashed by the Inquisition, especially in the Catholic states of France and Spain, lasted until the second half of the 18th century.[163]

The focus for scientific advance now shifted to the new Dutch republic and post-revolutionary England. Enlightenment anatomists undertook dissections on the bodies of executed criminals, revising mistakes uncorrected since Galen's time. Their new models of the nervous system fitted with the mechanistic models of Newtonian science. Philosophers like John Locke saw the mind at birth as a blank slate, emphasising the educability of man. The rational mind was contrasted with the material body, with madness seen as rooted in the latter. Scottish psychiatrist W A F Browne argued that "derangement" was a disease, not of understanding, but "of the centre of the nervous system... In all cases where disorder of the mind is detectable...it must and can only be traced directly or indirectly to the brain".[164]

The ideas of the Enlightenment represented the ideas of a new rising class—the bourgeoisie. A series of revolutions, especially those in England and then in France, cleared the way for its rule across the globe, which led to the most profound transformation of human society since its turn to settled agriculture 10,000 years previously.[165]

6.
The rise of disability

[M]ore than any other mode of production, [capitalism] squanders human lives, or living labour, and not only blood and flesh, but also nerve and brain. Indeed, it is only by dint of the most extravagant waste of individual development that the development of the human race is at all safeguarded and maintained in the epoch of history immediately preceding the conscious reorganisation of society.
—KARL MARX [166]

The Industrial Revolution was the most fundamental transformation of human society in recorded history. It made Britain a global power of unprecedented dominance and determined the subsequent development of the entire world economy.[167] It also crystallised the rise of an entirely new type of labour, which in turn led to the rise of disability as a specific form of discrimination.

From the mid-19th century onwards, new advances in chemistry and electricity gave science and technology a growing role. This in turn led to mass education systems rapidly becoming crucial to industrial development. Britain's success forced its competitors to push through their own industrialisation programmes. By 1895, Germany and the US each produced more steel than Britain. Much of it helped build vast new railway networks stretching across Russian steppes, American prairies and Alpine mountain ranges. In 1840, 45,000 miles of railway were open across the world. By 1880, the worldwide total was 2,284,000 miles,[168] concentrated mainly in North America and Europe. Railways and steamships hugely boosted trade, exports and foreign investment: between 1850 and 1870, world trade increased by 260 percent.[169]

The late 19th century saw the US overtake Britain as the world's leading industrial power—and the one with the most industrial accidents. In 1890, it was estimated that 42 percent of Colorado railroad workers were injured on the job every year. "In 1910, American Federation of Labour leader Samuel Gompers said of compensation for the victims of railroad injuries that no other issue 'was of half the importance'."[170] "By 1900 industrial accidents killed thirty-five thousand workers [in the US] each year and maimed five hundred thousand others".[171]

This fast pace of industrialisation also led to a rapid and continuing growth in the world's population, increasingly concentrated in urban centres instead of sparsely distributed across the countryside. As Marx and Engels explained in *The Communist Manifesto*, capitalism is by far the most dynamic system the world has ever seen:

> The bourgeoisie...has accomplished wonders far surpassing Egyptian pyramids, Roman aqueducts and Gothic cathedrals... It must nestle everywhere, settle everywhere, establish connections everywhere... The bourgeoisie, during its rule of scarce 100 years, has created more massive and more colossal productive forces than have all preceding generations together. Subjection of nature's forces to man, machinery, application of chemistry to industry and agriculture, steam navigation, railways, electric telegraphs, clearing of whole continents for cultivation, canalisation of rivers, whole populations conjured out of the ground—what earlier century had even a presentiment that such productive forces slumbered in the lap of social labour?[172]

The industrial revolution

In arguing that the roots of disability lie in this historical period Vic Finkelstein and Mike Oliver highlight two factors in particular: the growth of factory production and the segregation of people with impairments in institutions. The development of the asylum system over the same period has been the subject of much separate debate and is also discussed here.

Following Marx, Finkelstein first showed how the rise of capitalism forced people off the land. In Britain production for the market began on a scale sufficiently small to be carried out in the home and therefore impaired people could still play a role. But this gradually became harder:

> [T]he rural population was being increasingly pressed by the new capitalist market forces, and when families could no longer cope the crippled members would have been most vulnerable and liable to turn to begging and church protection in special poor houses. Market forces soon favoured machinery which was more efficient and able to produce cheaper, more plentiful woven material. Those working larger looms would more likely survive and cripples would have had greater difficulty working such equipment...
>
> Spinning machines...had to be usable by any worker freely employed on the labour market. Such a worker could not have any impairment which would prevent him or her from operating the machine. It was, therefore, the economic necessity of producing efficient machines for large scale production that established able-bodiedness as the norm for productive (ie socially integrated) living... production for profit undermined the position of physically impaired people within the family and the community.[173]

Industrialisation in Britain began with cotton mills, which produced for export on a scale rapidly outstripping the old craft and cottage industries. Exports from cotton production, primarily based in Lancashire, increased tenfold in the 20 years up to 1770. This promoted the growth of slavery on the plantations of the West Indies and then the southern US states, the profits from which in turn contributed to more intensified and diverse industrial development.

By the middle of the 19th century, Britain produced "perhaps two thirds of the world's coal, perhaps half its iron, five sevenths of its small supply of steel, about half of such cotton cloth as was produced on a commercial scale, and forty per cent (in value) of its hardware".[174] The population of England and Wales grew "from perhaps six and a half millions in 1750 to over nine millions in 1801, and to sixteen millions by 1841".[175] The expansion of the factory towns sucked in new workers from the countryside. Whereas "in 1750 there were only two cities with more than 50,000 inhabitants—London and Edinburgh— by 1851 there were 29 and the majority of people lived in towns".[176]

The new factory towns destroyed the old extended family structures. The end of craft workshops and peasant holdings meant that the new working class, removed from any control over the means of production, had no source of income other than a cash wage. People were now reduced to the status of machine "operatives" or "hands".

As pottery boss Josiah Wedgewood put it, the object of industry was "to make such machines of the men as cannot err".[177] Ability to work was determined by the requirements of the new machinery. Deprived of community or family support, those with all sorts of impairments now found themselves "unfit" for factory work. Those in work meanwhile were often permanently injured due to appalling conditions. High casualty rates among a largely female and child workforce led to increasing pressure for reform. The report leading to the 1833 Factory Act included these statistics from a school in Bolton:

> 165 boys were factory workers, 46 had been injured by machinery, 3 had lost fingers, 3 were deformed at the knees, 17 had coughs, 6 had loss of appetite, 9 were consumptive. Of 171 girls, 27 had been injured by machinery, 5 were deformed at the knees, 19 complained of coughs, 31 had loss of appetite, 9 were consumptive.[178]

In 1842, another damning report by Edwin Chadwick, secretary to the Poor Law Commission, on working class living conditions appeared. Three years later, Friedrich Engels drew on these findings for his famous *The Condition of the Working Class in England*. Unlike Chadwick, however, Engels did not blame the working poor for their conditions. He showed that factories and mills produced the smoke choking poor neighbourhoods and the pollution turning rivers into putrid streams. He also showed that in industrial cities like Manchester and Liverpool mortality from diseases such as scarlet fever, whooping cough and measles was four times as high as in the surrounding countryside. Conditions even posed a threat to the rich:

> [T]he repeated visitations of cholera, typhus, small-pox, and other epidemics have shown the British bourgeois the urgent necessity of sanitation in his towns and cities, if he wishes to save himself and family from falling victims to such diseases.[179]

Liberal reformers such as novelist Charles Dickens campaigned against such conditions, believing them to be against the long-term interests of capitalist society. Huge class struggles in the 1830s and 1840s exerted further pressure for change. Workers' resistance to long working hours led to legal limits being imposed on night-time and Saturday working. The 1848 Public Health Act created national and local public health boards, providing for improvements in infrastructure and sanitation.

Accidents at work had acquired what Borsay calls a "public political presence" by the early 19th century:

> Children crippled through employment in mines and factories became a potent issue...in the 1830s and 1840s; revelations in the mid-1840s of the shocking conditions in which railway navvies sustained countless injuries and fatalities became a matter of public concern; and cognizance of accidents in coal mines led to the creation of a miners' inspectorate...in 1850. But factory reform, rather than the causes of the breaking of innocent bodies, was the object of the focus on children; the concern with railway labourers focussed on their living conditions rather than their accidents; and the legendary injuries and fatalities of miners mostly provided social statisticians with a resource for moral exhortation.[180]

Marx quotes from one public health report in 1863, concerning workers in the Staffordshire pottery industry, who are described as "stunted in growth, ill-shaped, and frequently ill-formed in the chest; they become prematurely old, and are certainly short-lived". A particularly common form of chest disease was "peculiar to them, and is known as potter's asthma, or potter's consumption".[181] Other writers detailed "the green hair and teeth of brass and copper workers, the blue gums of pottery and earthenware workers, the "trembles" of those who worked with mercury, and the skin boils of confectionery workers".[182]

In 1917, military surgeons in Wales calculated the number of civilians who had lost limbs in peacetime at home. The answer was "1 in 810 in a population of nearly two million of whom we received a record. Applied to England and Wales, this 'datum line' produced a figure of 46,722 civilian limbless cripples".[183]

Industrial capitalism required able-bodied workers to operate the new machines, but this work itself led to injury and illness on a massive scale.

The development of the institutions

The 18th and 19th centuries saw the development of new institutions such as workhouses and special schools. A combination of old and new categories identified those of the poor who were unfit for work; "the sick, the insane, defectives, and the aged and infirm".[184] These were increasingly separated from the rest of the population. As Colin Barnes put it:

> the widespread incarceration of disabled people is directly attributable to the transition from agriculture and cottage-based industries to the large-scale factory-type system. Segregating the poor into institutions...had several advantages over domestic relief: it was efficient, it acted as a major deterrent to the able-boded malingerer, and it could instil good work habits into the inmates.[185]

Although the workhouse never housed more than a small minority of society, the threat it represented was a valuable means of social control. The first workhouses were built towards the end of the 17th century. By 1750 there were 600, essentially local state institutions that "sought to increase the nation's manufacturing output, to reduce the poor rate by deterring requests for assistance and to turn jobless paupers into morally virtuous labourers through regulated employment." Although there were many examples of sadistic and barbaric practice, "in practice, conditions in the 4800 institutions that had developed by 1834 were diverse".[186]

Popular protests against the more repressive provisions of the Poor Law Amendment Act included demands for better or specialised treatment for the "aged and infirm". In the mid-1860s, leading medical journal *The Lancet* sponsored a survey of the sick poor in metropolitan workhouses, and found that: "a harsh and repulsive regime intended for the repression of idleness and imposture had been and was still applied to persons suffering from acute diseases, permanent disability, or old age".[187]

It was not just the development of large-scale machinery or institutions, however, or even the industrial revolution itself, which led to the marginalisation of people with impairments. It was something more fundamental to the capitalist mode of production.

Wage labour

In feudal society, serfs exercised some degree of control over production, including (at least to some degree) the land, and could access a portion of the crops or livestock they raised to feed themselves. Many owned their own plough and animals and all production took place in or near the home. Under capitalism, production shifted away from the home and the mass of labourers lost control over production as well as over the products of their labour. In order to survive, they must sell their labour power (capacity to work) to the capitalist and can only access the products of their labour by buying them on the market.

The value created by labour is considerably more than the value or cost of labour power; workers produce more value in goods during a day's work than they get in wages. The difference between these is what Marx called surplus value, and its rate can be increased in two ways. The first method is to increase "absolute surplus value"—to lengthen working hours. Marx describes in *Capital* how "in the early phases of the industrial revolution, capitalists sought to extend the working day as long as possible, forcing even nine year-old boys to work three 12-hour shifts in the hellish conditions of the iron foundries".[188]

The second method, raising the rate of "relative surplus value", involves increasing productivity, for example by increasing the intensity of work, through technical innovation or by a more efficient division of labour. Capitalism involves a constant re-division of the labour process into ever smaller parts, combining with automation to enforce rigid repetition and undermining individual talents or skills. Marx described the application of this method to factory work:

Factory work exhausts the nervous system to the uttermost, it does away with the many-sided play of the muscles, and confiscates every atom of freedom, both in bodily and intellectual activity... The special skill of each individual insignificant factory operative vanishes as an infinitesimal quantity before the science, the gigantic physical forces, and mass of labour that are embodied in the factory mechanism and, together, with that mechanism, constitute the power of the master.[189]

Marx also distinguished between "concrete labour", the specific character of work performed by a car worker, checkout assistant, telemarketing worker or a teacher, and "abstract labour", which abstracts from the particular character of acts of labour and which is measured by what all work has in common. This is known as "socially necessary labour time"—how long it takes on average for a worker to complete a particular task. Through exchange, the labour of each individual is continually compared with that throughout the system as a whole: "All the different kinds of private labour, which are carried out independently of each other...are continually being reduced to the quantitative proportions in which society requires them".[190]

Under feudalism, the process of exploitation was transparent: landlords extracted profit from peasants in the form of unpaid labour, surplus crops, rent and taxes. This was restricted by the limited markets existing at the time, due to the limits imposed by the personal consumption of the lords. In capitalist society, almost all production is for the market, very little is for immediate consumption. Production is also driven by competition between capitalists, entailing constant changes in production. Since workers are paid by the day or the week, the relationship between the wealth they create and what they receive is therefore not obvious. Capitalists look only at the rate of return they get on their total investment, including labour, machines and raw materials, and therefore have little interest in the fate of workers damaged by the labour process or of those excluded from it. The actual value of labour power is determined by what is deemed socially necessary to keep workers alive and fit to work.[191] This has little to do with the *specific* needs of the individual worker.

Some disabled people cannot reproduce their labour power effectively, given the same value advanced, due to additional costs incurred *outside* the process of production (such as medical assistance, personal support, equipment or travel). However, if a disabled person lives in poverty and can stay fit enough to keep working (with a lower standard of living than other workers) capitalists are indifferent to this. In this sense, *neglect* is more important than active discrimination.

Other ways in which disabled people are disadvantaged are that first, their impairment may make them less productive using typical technology or forms of cooperation. Second, they may require adjustments to the workplace and the labour process in order to work as quickly or efficiently as others. These additional costs cut into profits. Capitalists therefore regard disabled workers as potentially "wasted" investment as they may require extra training or need to be replaced prematurely. Capitalists therefore often refuse to employ disabled people because it is contrary to their interests and purpose: the accumulation of wealth.

The market forces individual capitalists to maximise exploitation, in the process making the labour of workers increasingly interdependent. Production takes places on an ever-larger scale, within a complex division of labour where most workers no longer produce a complete single output. The production of cars or computers, for example, can involve several different countries, in a process running from raw material extraction through to the manufacture of the finished product. In place of individual workers tied loosely to other producers, capitalism creates what Marx called the "collective worker".[192]

Within the labour process, labour is treated as relatively interchangeable and homogeneous (given appropriate education, training and experience). So the working class is collectively exploited, despite being internally differentiated. The diversity of impairment, however, means that individual disabled people are less likely to be able to fulfil all the tasks expected of the "collective worker", just as they may not be able to play certain sports or engage in specific leisure activities. The development of capitalist society, therefore, leads to the exclusion of impaired people from work.

Alienation

Alienated labour, Marx's more philosophical interpretation of what he later mainly referred to as wage labour, is central to his analysis of capitalism and essential to a full understanding of disability.

The theory of alienation describes how human beings are deprived of control over their lives and how this leads to a sense of powerlessness. The central paradox Marx pointed to was that the same revolutionary form of production that made it possible for the first time in history to provide for everyone also comprehensively undermined the control which human beings exercised over that production. As Marx explains:

> Labour is external to the worker i.e. does not belong to his essential being; that he therefore does not confirm himself in his work, but denies himself, feels miserable and not happy, does not develop free mental and physical energy, but mortifies his flesh and ruins his mind. Hence the worker feels himself only when he is not working; when he is working he does not feel himself. He is at home when he is not working, and not at home when he is working. His labour is therefore not voluntary but forced, it is forced labour. It is therefore not the satisfaction of a need but a mere means to satisfy needs outside itself. Its alien character is clearly demonstrated by the fact that as soon as no other physical or other compulsion exists it is shunned like the plague.[193]

This description brilliantly conveys the daily experience of work for the vast majority, characterised in today's world by increasing regimentation, surveillance and performance or productivity targets. More and more professions formerly seen as autonomous or relatively privileged—such as teaching, medicine, social work and mental health services—are subject to these pressures.

The first two elements in the theory of alienation are that workers under capitalism have no control over what they produce and that they have no control over the process of work (see above). The third aspect of alienation is estrangement from our human nature or "species being," the essence of which is our ability to create and recreate the world we live in. Our intentional and social productive activity is the means through which we express and develop the powers which differentiate us from other animals.

> In tearing away from man the object of his production...estranged labour tears from him his species life, his real species objectivity, and transforms his advantage over animals into the disadvantage that his inorganic body, nature, is taken from him. In the same way as estranged labour reduces spontaneous activity and free activity to a means, it makes man's species life a means to his physical existence.[194]

Production is not only the most fundamental human activity; it is above all a social one. How production is organised in any society is therefore of fundamental importance, as for Marx this is what shapes human nature. The "life activity" of workers, through which they affirm their humanity (or species being), becomes merely a means to survive.

The final dimension to Marx's theory is how we are alienated from our fellow human beings. The competition between workers compelled to sell their labour power on the market gives rise to competition in every area of life, from housing and education to fashion and cosmetics. We see other people through the lens of profit and loss—as competitors, inferiors or superiors. Mass commodity production continually creates new needs, creating yet more forms of competition from which more profits can be generated:

> Each attempts to establish over the other an alien power, in the hope of thereby achieving satisfaction of his own selfish needs...becomes the inventive and ever calculating slave of inhuman, refined, unnatural and imaginary appetites. He places himself at the disposal of his neighbour's most depraved fancies, panders to his needs, excites unhealthy appetites in him, and pounces on every weakness, so that he can then demand the money for his labour of love.[195]

Marx distinguishes between use values and exchange values. Labour power is a use value because it can transform the world in ways that may benefit or hinder humanity. The removal of workers from control over the means of production means that their labour power is only useful to them insofar as it can be sold or exchanged in the market. Labour power's role as a use value is therefore subordinated to its role as an exchange value.

The products of labour power also have both use and exchange values. The use value of food is in feeding people, realised when the food is consumed. However, the production of food under capitalism is not about feeding people but making a profit. The latter is realised only when the food is exchanged for money—sold on the market. If it is not sold, it will rot, even though people go hungry. So exchange values dominate use values: the needs of the market determine what happens to the products of human labour—not the needs of humanity.

Production within capitalism is subordinated to the needs of the market—itself nothing more than a mechanism for the exchange of what is produced. Commodities are "fetishised"—attributed with a magical power over human beings—even though they are nothing more than products of our own imagination and labour.

For Marx, "commodity fetishism" describes how a "definite social relation between men" takes on "the fantastic form of a relationship between things." This is particularly true of money, a special "universal" commodity that can be exchanged for all others, which therefore in a real sense *does* have power:

> Money's properties are my, the possessor's, essential properties and essential powers. Thus what I *am and am capable of* is by no means determined by my individuality. I am ugly, but I can buy for myself the *most beautiful* of women. Therefore I am not ugly, for the effect of ugliness, its deterrent power, is nullified by money. I, according to my individual characteristics, am lame, but money furnishes me with 24 feet. Therefore I am not lame. I am bad, unscrupulous, dishonest, stupid; but money is honoured, and therefore its possessor. Money is the supreme good, therefore its possessor is good. Money, besides, saves me the trouble of being dishonest: I am therefore presumed honest. I am *brainless*, but money is the *real brain* of all things and how then should its possessor be brainless? Besides, he can buy clever people for himself, and is he who has a power over the clever not more clever than the clever? Do not I, who thanks to money am capable of all that the human heart longs for, possess all

human capacities? Does not my money, therefore, transform all my incapacities into their contrary?[196]

While the vast majority of people have no real power in society, a tiny minority exercise huge and unaccountable power over the lives of everyone else. But this capitalist class are not free either; competition with their rivals constantly compels them to find more effective means of exploitation and more sources of profit, even if this means war or environmental destruction. The capitalists are also alienated, but as Marx put it, they are "happy in their alienation."

In a society where everyone's value is measured in money, it is small wonder that those who struggle most with work or are excluded from it feel most alienated by it.

This account of alienation does not amount to a permanent or mystical mental trap within which humanity is hopelessly imprisoned.[197] Instead, Marx explicitly associates alienation with a particular historical form of society; in other words, as a material and social process which can be overcome through a far-reaching reorganisation of society. Capitalism's need to continually find new ways to exploit workers more efficiently also forces them to organise to defend themselves and in the process to counteract alienation with collective values of community, solidarity and co-operation.

Class, gender and madness

What of the casualties of this new capitalist juggernaut, which so completely transformed the lives of its subjects? How would the new industrial society deal with those seen as "melancholic" or mad? They were increasingly separated from society, living isolated at home with their families or warehoused in the new asylums under the care of a layer of new professionals who studied, categorised and invented a growing diversity of mental health "conditions" or "disorders."

Medical professionals treated mentally distressed human beings as malfunctioning machines. The therapy used to treat the madness of King George III was a prominent example of how this theory was put into practice. For "much of the eighteenth century, the treatment of mental illness relied on the socializing potential of fear and terror, and so the King—like his subjects—was restrained, beaten, starved and verbally abused to restore his reason".[198]

> the second half of the 18th and the early 19th centuries saw
> experiments with strange technologies to produce such severe frights:
> whirling chairs...'baths of surprise', where seemingly solid floors were
> designed to collapse and suddenly deposit unsuspecting lunatics
> in vats of cold water; elaborate contraptions that held patients
> under water and persuaded them they were about to drown; and
> the American Benjamin Rush's famous 'Tranquillizer', a chair that
> encased the madman's head in a padded box that excluded light and
> sound, and kept his arms and legs pinioned in place, while warm and
> cold water was applied to head and feet.[199]

The notorious "madhouses" of Georgian England were an unregulated open marketplace, but even by the end of the 18th century, they housed no more than 3,000 people.[200] The 19th century began with a new optimism among medical practitioners in Western Europe and in the US about the therapeutic possibilities of a reformed asylum system.

At the height of the French Revolution in 1790, the clinician Philippe Pinel wrote: "Scarcely one year has gone by, and everything has taken on a new countenance... 'I feel better since the revolution' has been said by many people honoured by that sentiment".[201] In March 1790, a new law abolished *lettres de cachet*, which allowed the arbitrary internment of anyone by order of the king on petition. This change, "combined with transfers of power to the justice system, the administration, and the medical profession, meant that yesterday's lunatic, locked up without any kind of due process, became a citizen in need of evaluation, a patient to be cured".[202]

Pinel was appointed as the head of the Bicêtre asylum in Paris at the height of the Revolutionary Terror in 1793. Credited with removing the chains of inmates, he ended brutal methods such as bleeding, purging, and blistering.[203] His new "moral therapy" involved close contact with and careful observation of patients, often several times a day, engaging them in lengthy conversations. This was used to build a detailed case history of each patient's illness. After gaining an inmate's trust however, Pinel's next method was intimidation: "One of the major principles of the psychological management of the insane is to break their will in a suitably timed manner, [to tame them] without causing wounds or imposing hard labor. Rather, a formidable show of terror should convince them that they are not free to pursue their impetuous willfulness and that their only choice is to submit".[204]

Meticulous, monotonous tasks were supposed to cure insanity through the effort and hard work they entailed, draining the body to the point of exhaustion. Pinel provided a user's guide for these miraculous therapies, laying down the law for the model asylums of the nineteenth century, whose ascendance was paralleled by the rise of factories. "The patients who are suitable for work are divided at daybreak into various separate groups, each headed by a guide who assigns tasks to them, and who directs and supervises them. The day is spent in continuous activity which is only interrupted by rest breaks, for tiredness at night brings sleep and calm".[205]

This model of servitude and mental exhaustion mirrored the rise of factory production and the rise of alienated labour. While Pinel's "moral therapy" was adopted only by a handful of asylums, such as the York Retreat which opened in 1796,[206] his other innovations anticipated a wider transformation in the asylum system across Europe—especially in Victorian Britain.

The Victorian age saw the transformation of the madhouse into the asylum into the mental hospital; of the mad-doctor into the alienist into the psychiatrist; and the madman (and the madwoman) into the mental patient... Madness was increasingly seen as something which could be authoritatively diagnosed, certified, and treated only by a group of legally recognized experts.[207]

The small private madhouses in Britain had until now mainly catered for the wealthy. They were often hugely profitable, with their methods attracting widespread mockery and cynicism. The first publicly funded "asylums" were established under the 1808 County Asylums Act, partly to address the problem of "pauper lunatics". In practice, most of the latter continued to be jailed as prisoners and criminals.

The increasing outrage at abuses in the madhouses led to demands for greater regulation. The 1845 Lunacy Acts made it compulsory for local authorities to open more public asylums, with a new Lunacy Commission to inspect conditions and monitor the treatment of inmates, who now began to be described as patients. New treatment regimes, combining "moral" as well as medical remedies, were discussed in English, French, and German journals. Professional associations of asylum doctors were formed, debating whether to adopt the new French name "aliéniste" or its German equivalent, "Psychiater". The new "mad doctors" advocated confinement of the insane in order to facilitate therapeutic isolation, with the restorative power of reason preferred (at least in theory) to coercion and restraint.

It was agreed that madness was a greater risk to the rich than to the poor. "With civilization" warned the Scottish alienist W A F Browne "come sudden and agitating changes and vicissitudes of fortune; vicious effeminacy of manners; complicated transactions; misdirected views of the objects of life; ambition, and hopes, and fears, which man in his primitive state does not and cannot know".[208] Limited to simple toil, the backward and illiterate working class was seen as mostly immune to mental disorder.

A series of "lunacy panics" in the press publicised cases of wealthy individuals fraudulently committed by spouses or relatives in order to seize their property. One magistrate, having freed several such patients, went so far as to write: "For the poor, all are interested in the recovery. For the rich, all may be interested in their retention".[209] In the US, Elizabeth Packard, a clergyman's wife whose husband had her confined as mad, launched a one-woman crusade across several states. Another former patient, Louisa Lowe, labelled private asylums "English Bastilles" and spent years agitating against their very existence.[210] These and other celebrated cases fed middle class fears. Working class people rarely became the focus of concern over wrongful confinement.[211]

The arguments of the reformers against the existing asylum conditions led in practice to a rapidly expanding asylum population. Tertiary syphilis, diagnosed at the time as general paralysis of the insane, accounted for 10-15 percent of admissions, with a similar proportion accounted for by alcoholic poisoning and "delirium tremens". In addition, difficulties with co-ordination or communication were often defined as "mental deficiencies" when the cause was cerebral palsy or problems with sight or vision.[212]

Contrary to myth, committals were not always for life: around one third of each year's asylum intake was discharged within 12 months, although a high annual mortality rate of 10-15 percent also reduced numbers. In England overall, county asylums now housed more than 90 percent of the institutionalised mentally ill.[213] In Britain and internationally, the trend was clear:

> Asylums that housed a hundred or two inmates at mid-century had grown to a thousand and more by century's end. Mental hospitals (as they were relabelled late in the 19th century) grew into miniature towns... London magistrates...built a series of establishments for a total of up to 12,000 patients on a single site at Epsom. At Milledgeville in Georgia, the Central Lunatic Asylum eventually confined almost 14,000 patients, and a whole series of asylums on New York's Long Island...together provided for more than 30,000 inmates. Asylums with patient censuses in the thousands likewise became common in France, Germany, and elsewhere in Europe... In Germany, the ratio of lunatics confined in asylums grew from 1 in 5,300 in 1852 to 1 in 500 in 1911. In England, over a 50-year period, 1859 to 1909, the rate of confinement more than doubled, from 1.6 to 3.7 per thousand of the general population. The promise of the reformed asylum had vanished.[214]

Every year, a substantial fraction of patients remained committed, so the median length of stay in the asylum grew longer and the number of chronic, "incurable" patients increased. This "horde of the hopeless"[215] increasingly came to dominate popular perceptions of the asylum. One British physician lamented that "after the best application of the most sagacious and ingenious measures, the results are so barren and incommensurate, that in defiance of sympathy and solicitude, misery and violence, and vindictiveness should predominate".[216]

In 1826, the first year statistics were available, fewer than 5,000 people were confined in asylums throughout England. By 1900, 77 institutions housed over 74,000 patients. Although public asylums now admitted private patients too, the vast majority of asylum inmates were by then paupers,[217] a large proportion of them women identified as suffering from "hysteria".

Nervous disorders had long been associated in the Hippocratic tradition with the womb, the Greek name for which was *hystera*. The ancient Roman physician Galen believed sexual deprivation could cause disorders of the female body. Disorders of the reproductive system imposed immense strain on women's smaller brains and nerves, prompting hysteria or even outright insanity. The term was applied to a whole series of bizarre and perplexing behaviours: episodes of paralysis and trances, fits, spasms and contortions, roaring cries, grimaces and mood swings.

The English Malady, published in 1733 by physician George Cheyne, argued that only the refined and delicate were susceptible to hysteria: those "whose Genius is most keen and penetrating, [with] the most delicate Sensation and Taste". The lower classes, "Fools, weak or stupid Persons...are seldom troubled with Vapours or Lowness of Spirits". For Cheyne the condition was "as much a bodily Distemper as the Smallpox or a Fever". Males with such traits were weak, lacking appropriately masculine qualities. This diagnosis, flattering as it was to their sensibilities, proved hugely popular among the English upper class.[218]

From the 1840s, anaesthesia (and later anti-sepsis) made routine invasive surgery possible for the first time. From 1858, London gynaecologist Isaac Baker-Brown, believing hysteria to be caused by female masturbation, began removing the clitoris of numerous women as a remedy. It was not, however, the operation's brutality that led later to Baker-Brown's downfall, but his relentless self-publicity, which the emerging medical profession saw as a threat to their moral standing.[219]

Another surgical cure for hysteria was popular in America, and to a lesser extent Britain, from the 1880s to the mid-1890s. Possibly tens of thousands of ovariectomies (removal of the ovaries) were carried out. Although some Victorian women may have seen the operation as a solution to repeated pregnancies, improved medical knowledge and cumulative evidence of failure led to its downfall.[220]

Some 150 years after Cheyne had identified hysteria as a mark of uniquely English refinement, another popular book contended that in the new US, the pace of social change and striving for success meant that hysteria "like American invention or agriculture, is at once peculiar and pre-eminent." In *American Nervousness* (1881), New York neurologist George Beard coined the term "neurasthenia" to describe weakness of the nerves due to overwork and stress. Like Cheyne, Beard emphasised that neurasthenia affected only those in society most exposed to the pressures of modernity, "the civilized, refined and educated, not the barbarous and low-born and untrained".[221]

The 19th century neurologist Silas Weir Mitchell's "rest cure" involved prolonged isolation and confinement in bed, force feeding, and sensory and intellectual deprivation. It was rapidly adopted as the standard approach to the hysterical and neurasthenic on both sides of the Atlantic.[222] The problem remained however, that hysterical patients, although lucrative, seldom seemed to get better. Weir Mitchell himself often referred to hysteria as "mysteria".

Jean-Martin Charcot mapped out lesions and disorders of the nervous system through his study of deceased patients' brains at the Salpêtrière hospital in Paris. His identification of conditions such as multiple sclerosis, aphasia and Tourette's syndrome (an assistant's name) led to his being hailed as "the Napoleon of the neuroses." In the 1880s, he staged increasingly elaborate, sexually suggestive displays of his hysterical female patients before huge audiences: "His exhibits were brought onto the stage to be examined, poked and prodded, hypnotized, all-but-anatomized...their foibles and physical contortions made the centre of the week's entertainment and instruction".[223]

Despite these "hysteria circuses", Charcot held progressive views on women's rights, with women trainees among his staff. He believed hysteria to be a disorder of the nerves not the womb, which also affected men, and opened the first-ever ward for hysterical males at the Salpêtrière in 1882. He also sharply contradicted his contemporaries, arguing that "neuropathic heredity is scarcely the exclusive privilege of the wealthy in life. It extends its reach to the working class as to everywhere else".[224] His unrivalled position meant that French medical circles abandoned a belief in hysteria's organic roots only some years after his death in 1893, with the term likewise disappearing from use.

Feminist historian Elaine Showalter has speculated that female hysteria was a form of protest against the roles in which Victorian women were imprisoned.[225] The 19th century saw the rise of the nuclear family, supported by a range of new laws and ideas entrenching the oppression of women. Even in the asylums, "matrons, female nurses, and attendants were paid on a much lower scale than male workers, were regarded as less reliable, and were subject to more rules and restrictions... Not until 1927 were state mental hospitals in England legally allowed to employ women doctors".[226]

The belief among the rich that only they were prone to madness was increasingly replaced by fear of a new and increasingly combative working class, including refugees from the Irish famine of 1840. Contempt for Indigenous populations across the British Empire was also directed towards:

> the 'sunken race' of poor Irish peasants, outcast slum dwellers of the urban slum districts and degenerate women who debilitated the military forces by infection. [Visits] by physicians and philanthropists were often dramatized as explorations into darkest England, a comparison often made with medical expeditions in remote and exotic regions of the world.[227]

The optimistic vision of the previous century's mad doctors was turned on its head. Now the poor, not the rich, were predisposed to madness. Edwardian psychiatrist Charles Mercier concluded that: "Insanity does not occur in people who are of sound mental constitution" but "occurs chiefly in those whose mental constitution is originally defective".[228] Politicians, physicians and intellectuals alike discussed decadence, degeneration and national decline. In the US and Western Europe, the new psychiatrists insisted that madness was not only rooted in the body, but was hereditary and therefore incurable. Worse, the biologically defective working class were breeding at a rate that threatened society's very future:

Such people were...vermin, 'moral refuse', parasites whose pedigrees, in the memorable phrase of another British alienist, 'would condemn puppies to [drowning in] the horse-pond'. These were sentiments that simultaneously reinforced and drew sustenance from the Social Darwinist ideas that circulated widely in late 19th-century culture.[229]

Michel Foucault's hugely influential *Madness and Civilisation* provided important insights into the development of the asylum and the segregation and control of its population and prompted much greater study of what he called "the great age of confinement". However, his work is also seriously one-sided. Contrary to his account, the development of the asylum system was not a linear or unproblematic process. Instead, it was marked by constant tensions between central regulation and local autonomy as well as others described above.[230] As Finkelstein recognised, not all these changes, "whereby cripples were transformed into disabled people", were negative:

It is clear that to be given charity rather than being punished for not working has its advantages... Having a captive population of disabled people made it possible to study some of the underlying physical conditions more carefully and systematically and this went hand in hand with the general advance made by the medical profession at the turn of the century.[231]

Mental impairment, for example, was seen as a single category until Langdon Down's reports at the Royal London Hospital in 1866, which identified (among other conditions) what became known as Down's syndrome.[232] With human labour now a commodity whose components were separately identified and valued, so mental health conditions were increasingly categorised—and stigmatised.

Freak shows

Freak shows spread throughout Europe from the 17th century onwards,[233] and were most popular in Britain and the US during the 19th century, part of the popular entertainment on sale at fairs, in market places and in music halls. "Monsters" were those presented as deformed and disabled; "the long train of pinheads, dwarfs, fat ladies, armless and legless 'wonders', and others...whose presence formed the heart of the freak show over many decades".[234] The Irish, described in the British press as "apelike", frequently featured in freak shows portraying African "savages" or "primitives".[235]

The "Aztecs", a man and woman named Maximo and Bartela, were exhibited as "degenerate members of an almost extinct race." Forbidden by law, their souvenir pamphlet claimed, "from intermarrying with any persons but those of their own caste", Aztec society had shrunk, "in the course of many centuries, to a few insignificant individuals, diminutive in stature, and imbecile in intellect".[236] In London, Queen Victoria attended, as did, according to the show's publicity, 400,000 others. Medical journal *The Lancet* "regularly published case reports on freak exhibitions, accompanying the description of the fantastic body on display with a medical diagnosis".[237]

Animals and humans were initially exhibited jointly as "living curiosities".[238] After the publication of Darwin's *Origin of Species* in 1859, human oddities such as the Bear Lady, the Tiger Lady and the Elephant Man were presented as the missing evolutionary link between the animal and human worlds.[239] Krao, a small Indochinese woman whose body was covered in soft, brown hair, was billed as "Living Proof of Darwin's Theory of the Descent of Man".[240] Krao's promotional pamphlet told of her capture among "wild tribes" and she appeared in the dress and elegant black boots of a middle class girl, showing Victorian society's "ability to turn even the most primitive peoples into good British subjects".[241]

Krao continued to market herself as "the original missing link" on the international freak show circuit in France, Germany and the US, increasingly monopolised by the new "Big Top" circus tours.[242] P T Barnum popularised the freak show in the US, particularly with the American Museum in New York City (1841-1865).[243] One of the most popular attractions in Dreamland, a huge amusement park on Coney Island, was "Lilliputia", an entire village scaled to the size of the 300 dwarfs that lived there.[244]

Physician Frederick Treves wrote an account of the story of Joseph Merrick (later the basis for the award-winning film by David Lynch), better known as The Elephant Man. Treves claimed that he had rescued Merrick from a life "little better than a dismal slavery" in 1886. He claims of Merrick that: "when he writes, he does so with the naiveté of a child; and when he reads, it is with the untutored wonder of a primitive savage." Before being taken in by Treves, however, Merrick had written "an autobiographical pamphlet [for his show] that poignantly detailed his sufferings".[245]

Tom Norman, previously one of Merrick's business managers, wrote his own book contradicting Treves, arguing that Merrick had contacted showmen on his own initiative, had been treated with dignity and had made a tidy profit from his freak show career. By this account, Merrick "was compromised not at the moment he was compelled to exhibit his deformity for profit, but rather once he had become a permanent resident of the London Hospital and relinquished all control over the manner in which his body could be viewed".[246] Treves described Merrick as a "childlike creature", frequently photographing him in the nude and exhibiting him to other medical practitioners.[247] Recaptured by Treves after fleeing the hospital, Merrick died shortly afterwards. Both Treves and Norman believed it was a suicide. The former attributed the cause to Merrick's frustrated desire to be "normal", whereas for Norman it was Merrick's "last expression of bodily control…an explicit refusal to be further objectified and pathologised by medical science".[248]

Freak shows went into decline in Britain towards the end of the 19th century, with fairs replaced by permanent entertainment venues such as zoos, music halls and theatres. Increasing exploration and knowledge of the world gradually undermined the crudest notions about strange "races" of people and their equally alien customs. The huge casualty toll of the First World War, which led to many soldiers being permanently disfigured, also changed popular attitudes. People who were "physically deformed could no longer be comfortably "othered", for they were undeniably sons, fathers, husbands, brothers, fellow citizens and even national heroes".[249] The rise of cinema, with its own monsters and mysteries, helped to further marginalise exhibitions of human oddities. Although it continued for some decades elsewhere, the freak show—at least in its original form—ceased to exist in Britain.

The 19th century freak shows helped to promote a new duality of the "normal" and the "other," with their popularity greatest in the three countries where, as we shall see, the new pseudo-science of eugenics would intensify discrimination against a range of socially oppressed minorities.

Conclusion

In many ways, capitalism represented a huge advance from previous societies. For the first time in history, humanity exercised the productive capacity to feed, clothe and house the entire global population. Scientific and medical advances offered the prospect of understanding and curing diseases. The astonishing achievements of industry shrank the world, created new technologies and opened up new sources of wealth. As Marx brilliantly put it in *The Communist Manifesto*:

> The bourgeoisie cannot exist without constantly revolutionising the instruments of production, and therefore the relations of production, and with them the whole relations of society. Conservation of the old modes of production was…the first condition of existence for all earlier industrial classes. Constant revolutionising of production, uninterrupted disturbance of all social conditions, everlasting uncertainty and agitation distinguish the bourgeois epoch from all earlier ones.

The new working class creating this wealth, however, was excluded from any control or say over what was produced and how, leading to huge numbers of deaths and injuries. Others marginalised or excluded from production, on the grounds that their existing impairments made their labour less profitable, were marginalised or excluded from wider society. New professions and industries classified, regulated and graded individual human capacities according to their relationship with production. The new world, from the fields of work to science and entertainment, justified and promoted discrimination against social groups identified as different or as a threat to new social norms. In this way, capitalism created disability as a particular form of social oppression.

7.
From eugenics to Nazi genocide

While delivering the Margaret Thatcher Lecture in the City of London in November 2013, the then Mayor of London Boris Johnson said:

> Whatever you may think of the value of IQ tests it is surely relevant to a conversation about equality that as many as 16 percent of our species have an IQ below 85 while about 2 percent have an IQ above 130... the harder you shake the pack the easier it will be for some cornflakes to get to the top. And for one reason or another—boardroom greed or, as I am assured, the natural and God-given talent of boardroom inhabitants—the income gap between the top cornflakes and the bottom cornflakes is getting wider than ever.[250]

Just under 40 years previously, darling of the Tory right and leadership hopeful Sir Keith Joseph gave a rather less subtle speech on the same subject. Unmarried mothers of "low intelligence" were threatening Britain's "human stock". These women, he warned, were "producing problem children, the future unmarried mothers, delinquents, denizens of our borstals, sub-normal educational establishments, prisons, hostels for drifters".[251]

The political storm over Joseph's speech torpedoed his chances of becoming Tory party leader. Johnson's lecture, however, its eugenicist message disguised by concern over widening inequality, neither received much publicity nor did any obvious damage to his own Tory leadership prospects.

Less than a century ago, such views were accepted and promoted far more widely in British society. The politics of eugenics began in Britain, and were subsequently exported to the US and in particular to Germany, where they were fully put into practice in the gas chambers. When the genocidal scale of the Nazis' crimes against Europe's Jews became fully known, it dealt a huge blow to the respectability of eugenics. But just as Hitler's crimes against disabled people—equally inspired by eugenicist convictions—received far less attention and remain far less well known, so too did the role of US and British eugenicists in providing the theories which inspired the fascists.

British origins

Charles Darwin's groundbreaking *Origin of Species*, published in 1859, expounded his theory of evolution by natural selection. Darwin showed that organisms with variations best adapted to their particular environment were the ones most likely to survive, thus shaping the development of species. Darwin also showed that this selection could be artificially manipulated: animal breeders could, for example, produce animals with specific characteristics. Scientists and political theorists quickly began to apply Darwin's theory to human beings.

Using the concept of "the survival of the fittest" (a distorted version of Darwin's ideas), social Darwinists questioned the provision of medical treatment and social services for disabled people as this enabled those who were "not meant to survive" to live and potentially have children. They believed that this would undermine the natural struggle for existence and lead to the degeneration of the human race. They claimed that people were poor, criminal or unhealthy because of hereditary factors rather than as a result of their upbringing or environment.

Francis Galton, who coined the term eugenics (derived from the Greek word meaning "of noble birth") in 1883, was a cousin of Darwin. He was obsessed with *Origin of Species*, especially its chapter on the breeding of domestic animals. Galton believed human mental and physical abilities, like plant and animal traits, were inherited and worried that the rich were marrying late and having too few children. He argued that early marriage between healthy, mentally strong families should be encouraged by financial incentives, while reproduction by the "feeble-minded" should be curtailed.

The development of wage labour and the drive to accumulate wealth required the measurement, comparison and ranking of units of capital according to their value, including the labour power of workers. This stimulated the use of statistics as "political arithmetic" to promote state policy. The leading members of the first British statistical societies were industrialists or had close ties to industry. They were also, in the main, eugenicists.[252]

As the population of European cities mushroomed during the course of the 19th century, the intelligentsia became increasingly concerned about issues of criminality and madness. Notions of mental and physical inferiority (*dégénérescence*) were associated in particular with the French physician B A Morel in the 1850s, and later with the Italian criminologist Cesar Lombroso.[253] It was during this period that a new concept appeared:

> The word 'normal' as 'constituting, conforming to, not deviating or differing from, the common type or standard, regular, usual' only enters the English language around 1840. (Previously, the word had meant 'perpendicular'; the carpenter's square, called a 'norm', produced the root meaning.) Likewise, the word 'norm', in the modern sense, has only been in use since around 1855, and 'normality' and 'normalcy' appeared in 1849 and 1857 respectively. If the lexicographical information is relevant, it is possible to date the coming into consciousness in English of an idea of 'the norm' over the period 1840-1860.[254]

The creation of the norm divided the population between standard and nonstandard, or "deviations" from the norm. Galton changed the name of the statistical bell curve from "the law of frequency of error" to "the normal distribution" curve. In the "error curve", the curve's extremes are the least accurate. For human traits, extremes of tallness, intelligence, ambition, strength or fertility were therefore "errors" or deviations. To avoid such traits being defined by the average, Galton divided his curve into ranked quartiles so that, for example, the first quartile equated to low intelligence and the fourth quartile to high intelligence. His work led directly to "intelligence quotient" (IQ) and scholastic achievement tests.[255] In a section of his book *Essays on Eugenics* entitled "Profit and Loss", he anticipated a time when the value of a prospective child could "be estimated by an actuary, and consequently the sum that it is appropriate to spend in favouring an X parentage".[256] Galton's views rapidly became popular in establishment circles, and gained support on both sides of the Atlantic. His many honours included a knighthood granted just before his death.

The views of eugenicist Henry Maudsley evolved from an optimistic to a more apocalyptic form of social Darwinism in the last decades of the 19th century, based on increasing fear of social revolt:[257]

> There will be a grim experience and a troubled future for the nation that has not known, before that hour comes, how to guide these forces in the right way, and to absorb and embody them in fitting forms of social and political organization. The French Revolution was momentous enough as an event, but it is perhaps more so as an awful example teaching how silently the great social forces mature, how they explode at last in volcanic fury, if too much or too long repressed.[258]

The eugenics movement called for government policies to improve the biological quality of the human race through selective breeding. It linked physical and learning disability to social problems including crime, vagrancy, alcoholism, prostitution and unemployment. These ideas gained ground when the Boer War (1899-1903) revealed that many young men from slum backgrounds were unfit for military service.[259]

A Royal Commission on the Blind, Deaf and Dumb concluded in 1889 that intermarriage between these groups was to be strongly discouraged. Its report was based on advice from Alexander Graham Bell, the inventor of the telephone. In 1896, the National Association for the Care and Control of the Feeble Minded was established to campaign for the segregation of disabled people.

Sir James Crichton-Brown, giving evidence before a 1908 Royal Commission, recommended the compulsory sterilisation of those with learning disabilities and mental illness, describing them as "our social rubbish" which should be "swept up and garnered and utilised as far as possible... We pay much attention to the breeding of our horses, our cattle, our dogs and poultry, even our flowers and vegetables; surely it's not too much to ask that a little care be bestowed upon the breeding and rearing of our race".[260]

A popular textbook published in 1911 advised that "the segregation of physically defective children is necessary only among the poorer classes...whose parents, if the child remained at home, have neither the leisure to teach him themselves nor the means to provide a governess or a master for that purpose. The same group of children, among the well-to-do, [should] remain at home and be taught privately".[261]

In 1912, London hosted the first International Eugenics Conference. It was addressed by Arthur Balfour, former Tory Prime Minister, and attended by numerous dignitaries and several European ambassadors.[262] On passing into law the Mental Deficiency Act 1913, then Home Secretary and eugenics enthusiast Winston Churchill said:

> The unnatural and increasingly rapid growth of the feebleminded classes, coupled with a steady restriction among all the thrifty, energetic and superior stocks constitutes a race danger. I feel that the source from which the stream of madness is fed should be cut off and sealed up before another year has passed.[263]

The Mental Deficiency Act was the high point of eugenicists' success in Britain, but it is worth noting that it was a diluted version of the original Bill. Sterilisation and compulsory segregation of the "mentally deficient" were both dropped. New powers authorised taking illegitimate children of "paupers" into care and the removal of "feeble-minded" schoolchildren, once identified by IQ tests, to special schools. By 1939, 17,000 children attended such schools.[264] As author G K Chesterton, one of the Act's most public opponents, argued, the Act's real target was the poor.[265]

Support for eugenics was not confined to the political right. Harold Laski, Bertrand Russell and the founders of the Fabian Society, Sidney and Beatrice Webb, were avid supporters. As one contemporary put it: "The Webbs supported eugenic planning just as fervently as town planning". In July 1931, the *New Statesman* claimed that the aims of eugenics "are not inherently incompatible with the outlook of the collectivist movement." Playwright George Bernard Shaw wrote: "The only fundamental and possible socialism is the socialisation of the selective breeding of man." Other supporters of eugenics included author H G Wells, John Maynard Keynes, the *Manchester Guardian* and William Beveridge, architect of the post-1945 welfare state. [266]

Labour MP Will Crooks described disabled people as "human vermin" who "crawl about doing absolutely nothing, except polluting and corrupting everything they touch". In 1931 another Labour MP, Archibald Church, proposed a bill for the compulsory sterilisation of certain "mental patients" on the grounds that they were "a burden to their parents, a misery to themselves and in my opinion a menace to the social life of the community".[267]

> With shell shock in WW1, 'the very scale of the phenomenon produced a managerial and conceptual crisis. Army statistics revealed that officers were more than twice as likely to suffer from breakdown on the battle field as men of the ranks; the much vaunted fortifying ethos of the public schools seemed to be futile. Earlier hereditarian ideas about degeneration collided with the quintessential 'nobility' attributed to the war volunteers... Shellshock, Martin Stone concludes in a recent essay [1985], 'brought the neuroses into the mainstream of mental medicine and economic life and set psychiatry's field of practice squarely within the social fabric of industrial society.' The problem of mental illness could no longer be conceived as that of a restricted realm of degenerates with weak hereditary constitutions.'[268]

Another blow to the eugenicists, of course, was the fact that the labour of many of those previously considered "unemployable" was suddenly found vital to the war effort. A range of disparate forces, from the trade unions and the Labour Party to the Catholic Church and the British Medical Association, opposed further eugenic sterilisation proposals, as did geneticists like Lionel Penrose.[269] The writer G K Chesterton published a polemic in 1922 in which he wrote that eugenics was "no more to be bargained about than poisoning".[270]

As the threat of fascism grew in the 1930s, eugenics became increasingly associated with the far right. Another prominent opponent, the zoologist and statistician Lancelot Hogben, put it nicely: "I dislike football, economists, eugenicists, Fascists, Stalinists, and Scottish conservatives. I think that sex is necessary and bankers are not".[271]

The United States

The recent revelation that 148 female prisoners in California were sterilised between 2006 and 2010 is a stark reminder of the legacy of eugenics in the US,[272] where the dominant concerns of the period were race and immigration.

After the devastation of the Civil War (1861-1865), a newly unified US capitalism expanded and industrialised rapidly. Supporters of eugenics in the US saw it as a means to purify society of those deemed undesirable—a category that included newly emancipated Blacks, Jews and other "races", as well as the poor, the infirm and the disabled. More than 26 million immigrants arrived in the US between 1870 and 1924. Many soon discovered that they were not welcome.

In July 1867, following the end of the Civil War and in the ferment of the Californian Gold Rush, "a poor, half demented" former Union soldier was arrested in San Francisco under a new city law. This legislation prohibited anyone "diseased, maimed, mutilated or in any way deformed" from begging or even appearing in streets or public spaces. Those convicted but unable to pay the fine were committed to a new purpose-built alms house. The city also passed new mass quarantine measures and public health orders, supposedly to halt infectious epidemics among (mainly Chinese) immigrants.[273]

Several US cities passed a version of these "Ugly Laws", including Chicago in June 1881:

Any person who is diseased, maimed, mutilated, or in any way deformed, so as to be an unsightly or disgusting object, or an improper person to be allowed in or on the streets, highways, thoroughfares or public places in this city, shall not therein or thereon expose himself to public view, under the penalty of $1 for each offence.[274]

The peak period of these laws coincided with anti-immigrant legislation (in 1891) specifically excluding those who were "insane" or had a "loathsome or dangerous contagious disease".[275] The "unsightly beggar ordinances" (the most common title for the laws) proved largely unenforceable, however, partly due to their vagueness and ambiguity and because most police forces in practice ignored them.[276]

The 1882 Immigration Act, the first in a series of increasingly restrictive and racist laws, prohibited entry to any "lunatic, idiot, or any person unable to take care of himself or herself without becoming a public charge." The US Congress extended the list of exclusions in 1903 to include epileptics, "imbeciles" and "feeble-minded persons". The category of "poor physique" was added in 1905 "to reject individuals suspected of sexual perversion (homosexuality), having bodies with ambiguous sexual organs, or simply being undiscernibly distinctly male or female".[277] From 1917, immigration officials were instructed to refuse those deemed to have "any mental abnormality whatsoever...which justifies the statement that the alien is mentally defective".[278]

In 1899 Dr Henry Sharp of the Indiana Reformatory instituted a sterilisation programme in order to prevent the spread of hereditary defects. He warned ten years later: "There is no longer any questioning of the fact that the degenerate class is increasing out of all proportion to the increase of the general population." According to Sharp, this included "most of the insane, the epileptic, the imbecile, the idiotic, the sexual perverts; many of the confirmed inebriates, prostitutes, tramps and criminals, as well as the habitual pauper found in our county poor asylums; also many of the children in our orphan homes".[279]

Institutions for those considered insane or feeble-minded became less concerned with education and assimilation and more concerned with simple custody. These "colonies" reflected the imperialist outlook of the US authorities. Dr William Spratling, who ran the

Craig Colony for Epileptics in New York, described the ideal colony as a beehive:

> The innumerable hives picturesquely scattered through sweet smelling fields...stand, in colony life, for contented and happy homes: the ceaseless hum of the wings of the busy little toilers stands for the activity of head and heart and hand of the common inhabitants of the colony, each striving for the common good; while the inevitable drones of the hives find their prototype in the lame, the unteachable and the mentally blind among the colonists, who are driven to seek refuge in such a home.[280]

The term "colony" was an appropriate descriptor for these new institutions. Each comprised several such "happy homes", housing up to 50 inmates each, segregated from wider society and presided over by a separate and central administrative centre.

The first US sterilisation law, passed in Indiana in 1907, authorised compulsory sterilisation for "criminals, idiots, rapists and imbeciles".[281] Other laws, also enforcing segregation or marriage restrictions, followed in 26 more states. A total of more than 63,000 sterilisations were performed. One third of these were carried out in California, mostly on women, a disproportionately large number of whom were of Mexican descent. The diagnoses included being "oversexed" or "sexually wayward" or having what was deemed an abnormally large clitoris or labia.[282]

Carrie Buck was a young, poor white woman who bore a child outside marriage. In 1924, her child was taken from her and she was institutionalised. Three years later, the US Supreme Court endorsed her compulsory sterilisation. Justice Oliver Wendell Holmes wrote:

> Carrie Buck is the probable potential parent of socially inadequate offspring...she may be sexually sterilized without detriment to her general health and that her welfare and that of society will be promoted by her sterilization...It is better for all the world, if instead of waiting to execute degenerate offspring for crime, or to let them starve for their imbecility, society can prevent those who are

manifestly unfit from continuing their kind...Three generations of imbeciles are enough.[283]

This infamous decision opened the floodgates for thousands of people to be coercively sterilised or otherwise persecuted as subhuman. The annual average number of compulsory sterilisations across the US increased from 230 in the 1910s to 2,273 in the 1930s.[284] At the Nuremberg trials just over 20 years later, the Nazis quoted Holmes's words in their own defence.

By 1914, 44 American colleges and universities already offered courses in eugenics.[285] Big business, specifically the Carnegie Institution, the Rockefeller Foundation and the Harriman railroad fortune, sponsored eugenicist academics and research at prestigious universities such as Stanford, Yale, Harvard and Princeton. By 1926, Rockefeller had also donated some US$410,000 (the equivalent of around US$5.5 million today) to eugenics research in Germany.[286]

Hitler praised US eugenics in *Mein Kampf*, published in 1924, and in particular that year's US National Origins Act. "There is today one state in which at least weak beginnings toward a better conception [of immigration] are noticeable. Of course, it is not our model German Republic, but [the US]... By refusing immigration on principle to elements in poor health, by simply excluding certain races from naturalisation, it professes in slow beginnings a view that is peculiar to the People's State." Hitler even wrote to US eugenics leader Madison Grant, calling his race-based eugenics book *The Passing of the Great Race* his "bible".[287]

During the Reich's early years, many US eugenicists welcomed Hitler's plans as the logical fulfilment of their own efforts. Some republished Nazi propaganda for US consumption. Nazi scientific exhibits were displayed in August 1934 at the L A County Museum for the annual meeting of the American Public Health Association.[288]

The US *Encyclopaedia of the Social Sciences* (1935) discussed German work on degeneration:

> The literature of Aryanism and Nordicism and of eugenics have stressed the probability of a present degeneration of racial quality among Western nations. The former writers base their views largely

on belief in the gradual inundation of supposedly pure Nordic types by the Westward push of Slavic elements and the assumed deleterious effects of race mixture... It is not impossible that a rich and humane civilisation may permit the undue multiplication of defective and parasitic types.[289]

Nazi Germany

Germany's imperial ambitions had been dealt a humiliating blow by defeat in the First World War. For the nationalist right, defeat was due to a combination of treacherous generals and the 1918-1923 German Revolution. Support for eugenics gathered pace during the traumatic economic slump of the early 1930s. By 1932, more than 40 courses at German universities offered the study of "race hygiene".[290] German citizens "had to produce family genealogies that indicated the presence of Jewish ancestors or relatives with hereditary diseases. Furthermore, Nazi eugenicists frequently included Communist Party membership in family trees as an undesirable trait".[291]

The Nazi regime did not treat all disabled people in the same way. In fact, they were separated into three distinct groups. Firstly, disabled war veterans were portrayed as "neglected and betrayed heroes" and given a series of privileges in accordance with their status as "wounded warriors" of the Fatherland.[292] Secondly, members of official Nazi organisations for blind, deaf, and physically impaired civilians were seen as having potential as productive citizens. Although decisions did not always follow these categories, it was overwhelmingly a third group, the "feeble-minded" and those with hereditary impairments, that was targeted by increasingly horrific policies.[293]

The Law for the Prevention of Genetically Impaired Progeny was implemented on 14 July 1933. From then until 1 September 1939, around 350,000 people were sterilised on the grounds they had heritable conditions such as "congenital feeble-mindedness", schizophrenia or heritable epilepsy. The categories could be arbitrary: non-hereditary conditions such as "severe alcoholism" were included, whereas congenital conditions such as haemophilia were excluded. Candidates could sit a test, answer all the questions correctly, yet still be sterilised because the examiner found behaviour or appearance suggestive of feeble-mindedness.[294]

Blatant hypocrisy was another hallmark of Nazi policy. In 1938, SS Reichsführer Heinrich Himmler banned German "freak shows" in opposition to, as one Nazi journal put it, those who "speculate on the desire of fairgoers for sensations and try to make money out of human misery, from pitiful, deformed human beings".[295] In practice, commercial freak shows had already been replaced with an officially sanctioned version, albeit with a very specific purpose:

> An educational pamphlet issued 5 years earlier (What Must the National Socialist Know About Heredity?) outlined two important tasks for institutions for inferior people. First, they must sterilise inmates. Second, they must educate the healthy, especially Nazi cadres, through regular tours and lectures for the public: "Every young person, and especially every Volk comrade of either sex who desires to get married, must be led once through the wretchedness and unspeakable misery of an insane asylum, a cripples' home or a similar institution." In 1935, over 2,000 people toured one asylum in the Rhineland alone. From 1933-39 over 21,000 people toured the Elfing-Haar asylum near Munich, almost 6,000 of them members of the SS.[296]

Adult euthanasia was introduced in September 1939 after a personal order from Hitler extended the powers of specific doctors so that "after the most careful assessment of their condition, those suffering from illnesses deemed to be incurable may be granted a mercy death." It was never codified in German law, very likely because it would have met public opposition.

Nazi propaganda did nevertheless aim to win over large sections of the public and was not restricted to crude documentaries. The film *Ich klage an* (*I Accuse*), which won a major award at the Venice Biennale in 1941, had by the end of the war been seen by 15.3 million people in Germany alone. The plot features two doctors, one a rational young man of science and the other a kindly and older liberal. At its conclusion, the latter—as well as the viewer—is manipulated into seeing euthanasia as "a welcome deliverance from disability and illness".[297]

The killing operation, based at T-4 Tiergartenstrasse, was referred to as the T-4 programme. The secret government department responsible for implementing T-4, the innocuously titled Foundation for the Care of Institutions in the Public Interest, systematically disguised the programme's true nature. The Foundation collected money for the care of patients from their families, and continued to levy charges even after the disabled person's murder. Another new organisation, the Reich Association of Sanitoriums and Nursing Homes, was responsible for administration. Finally, the Charitable Patient Transport Company (known as Gekrat) moved people by van and bus from their institutions to the killing centres.[298]

Patients were selected for conditions such as schizophrenia, depression, mental retardation, dwarfism, paralysis, epilepsy, sometimes delinquency, perversion, alcoholism and anti-social behaviour. In order to avoid weakening army morale, veterans of the First World War were exempted, but only if they had received medals, or been wounded, or fought with special valour.[299]

Mass killing in gas chambers was first developed under the T-4 programme, and only later used in the concentration camps. "An elaborate charade was used to disguise the fate of these patients. Families were first notified that they had been transferred to another institution, which in turn told them that visits were prohibited. Families were then later informed that the patient had suddenly died, but that the remains had been cremated due to the danger of epidemics".[300]

Doctors carried out the killing. Although half of Germany's 15,000 doctors joined the Nazi Party, some actively resisted:

After attending the initial T-4 briefing, Professor Gottfried Ewald, himself a disabled veteran of the First World War, wrote letters of protest to the authorities: he was ignored, but not punished. Professors Pohlisch and Panse called a secret meeting of physicians in Bonn to work out a sabotage strategy. For example, the questionnaires could be faked to show that the individual was working and important to the war effort. Professor Walter Creutz managed to save 3000 out of 4000 people designated for euthanasia. Other doctors said no to the instructions, took patients off the Gekrat buses or refused to co-operate.[301]

Public opposition and unrest, not least among relatives of murdered patients and those living near the killing centres (due to the smell and smoke from the cremations, and the ominous grey buses which always arrived full and left empty) led to their closure at Grafeneck and Brandenburg. It also led to the Bishop of Munster going public with his opposition, resulting in the formal end of the T-4 programme in August 1941.[302]

The killing continued, however, particularly in the concentration camps. A study for the Nuremberg trials of leading Nazis after the war estimated that 275,000 disabled people had been killed—a figure which excludes those who died in the concentration camps as well as those who died after the formal phase of T-4 ended.[303] No compensation was ever paid, either to those sterilised, or to the heirs of murdered disabled people. Many doctors known to have participated in the euthanasia programme continued practising afterwards. It was not until 1989 in a speech at the German Federal Chamber of Physicians that there was any formal acknowledgement of the medical profession's role in T-4.[304]

Eugenics after the Nazis

As the horrors of the Holocaust became more widely known after the Second World War, eugenics fell from favour. Enforced sterilisation, however, continued for several decades in some countries including Canada, Denmark, Sweden and Switzerland.[305] In India several million people were forcibly sterilised under family planning policies that only ended after huge protests and the assassination of Sanjay Gandhi in 1980. Similar policies have been implemented more recently in China and Uzbekistan.[306] The governors of five US states, including California, publicly apologised for abuses linked to the eugenics movement. In 2009 the Czech Prime Minister followed suit after an official report admitted to the compulsory sterilisation of many thousands of Roma women in the post-war period.[307]

In 2012 *Guardian* editor Jonathan Freedland wrote a column arguing that eugenics is "one of the grisliest skeletons in the cupboard of the British intellectual elite, a skeleton that rattles especially loudly inside the closet of the left".[308] As we have seen, many figures on the left did support eugenics; some held racist or imperialist views too. There were two things, however, which were common to all supporters of eugenics. The first was an uncritical faith in science as a force for progress (however "progress" might be defined), and the second was a deep fear of the "lower classes" whose place it was to be the objects of change, never its subjects.

In Britain and elsewhere, liberal reformers combined eugenic views with support for a welfare state that would provide capitalism with a healthier and fitter workforce. William Beveridge, architect of the post-war welfare state and later director of the London School of Economics, was a keen eugenicist who believed university teachers were self-evidently "fit" and should therefore be encouraged to have children. Steven and Hilary Rose recall that, as junior academics in the 1960s, "we received £50 per year added to our salaries for each of our children".[309]

> [For] Alva and Gunnar Myrdal, the theorists of the social democratic Swedish welfare state…eugenics was integral to the always nationalist project of the welfare state—without state intervention and compulsory sterilisation, the new welfare services would be overwhelmed by the increase of the feeble-minded and degenerates.[310]

The contempt for and fear of working people which inspired the eugenics movement finds a contemporary echo in discussions about "chavs" and "the underclass"—condemned in similar terms for their "lifestyle choices", their "culture of dependency" and for having too many children. Much of today's ruling class believe their own wealth and status to be attributable to breeding and intelligence. In reality, Boris Johnson's elite 2 percent owe their place to an accident of birth or a combination of greed, luck and ruthlessness—and the labour of others.

Ethical debates about the rapidly evolving field of genetics are likely to grow both more complex and controversial. A major current project by the UK Department of Health aims to sequence 100,000 genomes from National Health Service (NHS) patients in the space of three years.[311] Meanwhile, selecting against human embryos with gene "defects" which cause cystic fibrosis or breast cancer is likely to become increasingly common. It will soon be scientifically possible to "edit" the genome of a human fertilised egg (the current UK ban on such actions may be lifted in future).

In an era of global warming and nuclear stockpiles, widespread suspicion of the claims of science to be a force for progress extends well beyond issues of eugenics and genetic engineering. As John Parrington has put it: "while we can now sequence a human baby's genome in twenty hours or image its brain patterns as it learns to speak, at the same time other children are dying for lack of clean water or being blown up by smart missiles in some distant war".[312]

8.
War and disabled veterans

Far from disability and impairment being an unfortunate by-product of an otherwise civilised society, this society frequently prepares, plans and deliberately inflicts death and injury on a large scale. The war veterans who survive this killing and maiming are allocated a place at the top of the impairment hierarchy and are made the recipients of public sympathy and private charity. The rulers and media of nation states enthusiastically exploit the patriotic appeal of disabled veterans in particular, while at the same time minimising state responsibility for their welfare. This balancing act, however, has often proved to be unstable.

Revulsion at the horror and devastation of war has sometimes led to major social change. This was particularly true of the aftermath of the two hugely traumatic world wars of the 20th century whose millions of newly disabled veterans took seriously slogans promising a post-war world "fit for heroes". Although often believing that they are more "deserving" of support than disabled civilians, the activism of disabled ex-soldiers has been an important—if largely ignored— factor in winning wider welfare provision as well as welfare policies for all disabled people.

During the French Revolution, the 4,000 residents at the Hôtel des Invalides in Paris, the famous home for disabled veterans, elected their own management committee. As politics later swung to the right, their republican activism was seen as a threat. "[F]or a few months in 1798, dissident veterans became the main police problem in the capital for both the civil authorities and military police".[313] Napoleon's rise to power put an end to self-government at the Hôtel and the authoritarian hierarchy was restored. Although veterans' benefits remained relatively high, many of the wider social gains of the revolution were reversed.

The American Civil War represented a step change in the scale of warfare.[314] At least 2 million men fought for the Union and 750,000 for the Confederacy. Around three quarters of the estimated 60,000 operations performed during the war were limb amputations.[315] After the war, the Grand Army of the Republic (GAR) was set up to lobby for the interests of Union army veterans. Its influence, in the wake of the social convulsions of revolutionary war, was extensive:

> [W]ith more than 400,000 members by 1890, the GAR was a voting machine for the Republican Party. Politicians of both parties vied for the veterans' favor... By 1891, military pensions accounted for one dollar of every three spent by the federal government, and at the peak in 1902, 999,446 persons (including widows and dependents) were on the pension rolls... The most important aspect of Union veteran culture, however, was its intensely conservative nationalism, visible in the GAR's crusades against anarchy, flag desecration, and 'impure' school textbooks in the 1890s. Veterans of the Union army were the first to assert a privileged relation to the national state.[316]

Later veterans' movements would repeat this pattern of revolution and reaction on a larger canvas.

The Great War (i): shell shock in the UK

The global conflict of 1914-1918 was the first modern war between imperialist states of similar economic strength and size. Scientific and technological advances facilitated destruction on a previously unimaginable scale. By the war's end, 20 million soldiers and civilians were dead. Richard Holmes describes graphically the nightmare reality of war at the Front:

> Men might be killed instantly, but without apparent damage, by concussion; blown to tatters by direct hits; cut up as if by some malicious butcher; crippled by flying fragments of their comrades' bodies or shocked into babbling incoherence by a capricious hit

which left them unscathed among the remnants of their friends. Evidence of death was all too abundant; splintered trees turned to gibbets, heavy with dismembered limbs and glistening ropes of entrails. One French Officer (at the Battle of Verdun) wrote of 'a place where one can't possibly distinguish if the mud were flesh or the flesh were mud'.[317]

More than half of the 3 million British troops who fought lost limbs, were blinded, became deaf or suffered severe mental trauma or brain damage. It was "shell shock", however, affecting much smaller numbers of troops, which became the signature injury of the war.

By December 1914, up to 10 percent of British officers and 4 percent of enlisted men were identified as suffering from "nervous and mental shock". Charles Myers of the British Psychological Society made the first diagnosis of shell shock in 1915. By October 1917 this new condition was "responsible for one-seventh of all discharges from the British Army, and one-third if wounds were excluded".[318] By the end of the war the army had dealt with more than 80,000 cases.

From the outset, Myers faced opponents who argued that shell shock was simply cowardice or malingering, the answer to which was greater military discipline.[319] A diagnosis of shell shock could mean medical treatment instead of a court martial. Officers showing the symptoms were diagnosed as suffering from neurasthenia (or nervous collapse). For soldiers the same symptoms were usually interpreted as a lack of moral fibre or "hysteria", which the 1910 edition of *Encyclopaedia Britannica* defined as a psychological condition primarily associated with women, Jews and Slavs.[320]

Shell-shocked officers were allocated their own rooms in idyllic country retreats. Private care homes were careful to specify their intended clientele: St Andrew's Hospital for Mental Diseases in Northampton advertised itself as "For the Upper and Middle Classes Only". Other ranks were sent to traditional field hospitals where they were likely to die of disease or infection due to filthy conditions. A small number of men were sent to asylums.[321]

Shell shock was initially believed to be brain damage caused by exposure to exploding shells. But many showing the symptoms had not been exposed to artillery fire and they were soon treated differently. The British Army in France was told that if a soldier's breakdown did not follow a shell explosion, "he was labelled "S" (for sickness) and was not entitled to a wound stripe or pension".[322]

For the top brass, firing squads were necessary to stiffen the resolve of the rank and file and to prevent the "weak-willed" infecting the strong. Over 3,000 death sentences were pronounced on British soldiers found guilty of cowardice or desertion, 10 percent of which were carried out. The accused had no right to legal representation, although some were allowed a "prisoner's friend". Condemned men weren't told of their right to petition the King for clemency—so none did. From January 1915 onwards, General Routine Order 585 reversed the assumption of innocence so those accused were guilty until proved otherwise. In general, the court-martialled were young working class soldiers and those who tried them upper class officers from public schools, mirroring the class divide in magistrates' courts at home. Records show officers referring to soldiers as "worthless" or "shirkers". One officer's statement on a soldier's character said: "I consider him an insubordinate man of low class".[323]

In February 1916, Private James Crozier was found guilty of deserting his post and was shot. Two weeks earlier, 2nd Lieutenant Annandale had been found guilty of the same offence but escaped a death sentence due to "technicalities". That summer, an army directive stated that all cases of cowardice were punishable by death and that medical excuses would not be tolerated—apart from officers suffering from neurasthenia. Of the 306 who were executed, only three, all from modest backgrounds and lacking "connections", were officers.[324]

The Army banned any further diagnoses of shell shock in 1917, but admitted it into its judicial procedures in March 1918—partly due to "external factors". Disturbances in the army followed larger-scale mutinies in the French army that summer, coinciding with the Russian Revolution. Armed Forces Commander Haig worried aloud in November 1917 that: "advanced socialistic and even anarchical views" were being expressed in the army.[325]

Two British veterans' organisations were founded in 1917. Their activities included a demonstration at the Albert Hall in March 1918 followed by a mass rally later that month. Luton council's exclusion of ex-servicemen from victory celebrations led to the town's peace riot of 1919. Veterans lined the path of the parade and hung a banner reading: "Don't pity us, give us work".[326] In the same year, London veterans organised a march on Parliament Square, which was baton charged by police.[327] Ex-servicemen disrupted Armistice Day events several times during the 1920s.[328]

These struggles did lead to reform. By 1920, the Parliamentary Labour Party had publicly linked shell shock and executions at the front. A Royal Commission was set up to reassure the public and silence criticism of the army. Its chair, Lord Southborough, said: "The subject...cannot be referred to with any pleasure. All would desire to forget it." Predictably, the Commission's report was a whitewash.[329]

For eugenicists, shell shock was proof of the physically and mentally degenerate state of the Empire's workers.[330] But in Britain popular anti-war feeling was largely directed at the rich. Shell shock seemed to symbolise a senseless and traumatic war whose original justification few could remember. By the beginning of the Second World War, the term shell shock had been dropped in favour of the more neutral "combat stress reaction".[331]

The Great War (ii): revolution and counter-revolution in Germany

The Russian Revolution of October 1917 initially led to military gains for Germany. But the wave of radicalisation led to widespread mutinies and ultimately to the disintegration of the German armed forces. An uprising in November 1918 ended the Kaiser's rule and signalled the onset of five years of revolutionary upheaval.

More than 700,000 German civilians died of starvation and malnutrition during the allied wartime food blockade. This was extended in response to the revolution (to discourage "Bolshevism"), leading to around 250,000 more deaths. Almost 1.5 million newly disabled soldiers returned to a hugely polarised society where their own sympathies also divided rapidly.

The biggest organisation of disabled veterans, the Reichsbund, was formed in May 1917 by members of the Social Democratic Party (Europe's foremost left-wing party, whose support for the war came as a huge shock to the international socialist movement). The Bund (as it became known) demanded wealth redistribution and a new pension system to care for disabled veterans and widows, to be paid for by war profiteers. It grew to 25,000 members by spring 1918 and to 640,000 by 1921.[332]

In July 1918, a crowd of about 1,000 marched on the town hall in the Bavarian town of Hof, demanding improved rations and working conditions. One official reported that disabled veterans were the "chief troublemakers". One letter to the War Ministry complained: "even the simple presence of wounded soldiers makes police action very difficult. I need only think of the serious consequences which would result if a wounded soldier were trampled by police horses".[333] The consequences of the revolution were more far-reaching:

> The changed political situation seemed, however, to have a remarkable effect on many patients still in hospital. When rumours of the revolution swept into the neurosis station at Mergentheim, an hysterical soldier about to be examined by [a psychiatrist]…at once 'ran to the town's market square and delivered a fiery political speech to an excited crowd.' Many of Max Nonne's neurotic patients suddenly shed their symptoms and became revolutionary leaders: 'In my ward, one refractory shaker, who had complained of being treated too roughly, took on the function of the soldiers' council, and was in high spirits, responsible for his "subordinates" from morning to evening'.[334]

One psychiatrist, Dr Kurt Singer of Berlin, made the diagnosis that the revolution, "by inverting the social system, had removed the social function of neurosis".[335] Some recognised that the end of the war—and along with it the removal of the threat of being sent back to the front—would in itself lead to a rapid improvement in the condition of many veterans.

Veterans marched to demand state assistance and recognition. One frequently seen banner read: "Is this the thanks of the Fatherland?" Demonstrations included amputees in wheelchairs or on open carts and blind men led by family members or guide dogs.[336] The Reichsbund held a huge rally of 10,000 war victims at the War Ministry on 22 December 1918. Another protest ended in the drowning of the Saxon War Minister in the River Elbe.[337]

At the turn of the year, the KPD (German Communist Party) was launched as a new explicitly revolutionary workers' party. Their founding conference voted to leave the official trade unions and set up "red" unions. In line with this policy, a new disabled veterans organisation—the Internationaler Bund—was formed as a rival to the Reichsbund. The suppression of the KPD-led uprising in Berlin only days later, involving the murder of Rosa Luxemburg and Karl Liebknecht, led to further polarisation.[338]

During the mass layoffs after the war, fighting had broken out at the Spandau factories in Berlin between disabled and non-disabled workers over who should be laid off first. At least one disabled veteran received gunshot wounds. The Reichsbund responded by arguing that women "must take second place behind the disabled veterans"[339] in competing for jobs. New right-wing veterans' organisations attracted those disillusioned by the left. By 1921, the Labour Ministry calculated that the seven different organisations of disabled veterans had a total membership of almost 1.4 million.[340]

The trade unions and the left (except the new breakaway Independent Social Democratic Party) demanded a quota system to ensure injured veterans were employed in mainstream workplaces at the proper rate for the job. In 1920, in face of opposition from the employers, the Reich government finally passed the Law of the Severely Disabled. This legislation remains in many respects the most progressive law for disabled people anywhere then or since. Workplaces with 25 or more workers had to employ at least one disabled person, with a quota of 2 percent for larger workplaces. This covered all those classified with impairment in physical function of 30 percent or more. The new legislation made it harder to sack disabled workers and protected their right to strike alongside their workmates. The left successfully demanded the law should be extended to the around one million workers injured in industrial accidents. Those seen as unemployable, however, such as people considered insane or epileptic, were excluded.

The National Pension Law (RVG) of the same year covered all 1.5 million disabled war veterans, as well as war widows, orphans and dependants. Doctors now classed individual impairments as percentage units of ten starting at a 20 percent threshold: 40 percent was "lightly disabled" and 50 percent was "severely disabled".

Although the level of pensions was very low, the entire system collapsed under the impact of the wider political and economic crisis. An abortive right-wing rising, the Kapp Putsch of 1920, was followed by a French invasion of the Ruhr, prompting hyperinflation. The defeat of the October 1923 revolution was a decisive blow. It led directly to another right-wing rising (the Munich "Beer Hall" Putsch, this time led by Hitler).[341] Although this was defeated, German workers were soon to pay a terrible price for the revolution's failure.

For almost ten years, unemployment among working-age disabled people remained virtually zero. But the recession of the 1930s hit Germany harder than any other major state. Industrial production fell by almost half and unemployment jumped from just over 6 percent in 1928 to nearly 30 percent by 1932. Thousands of workers suddenly lost employment protection. Emergency decrees slashed the value of pensions, leading to protests in every major city. The Reichsbund estimated that 500,000 veterans joined demonstrations in May 1932.[342]

The Nazi Party capitalised on the alienation of many disabled veterans, setting up a special section in its directorate for war victims in September 1930 under the slogan: "Even a poor fatherland can be grateful". They promised sweeping reform of the pension machinery and to honour war victims. Hitler himself, fascist pamphlets pointed out, was a wounded veteran.[343] In April 1933, five of the seven disabled veterans groups merged in a new organisation aligned with the Nazis.

As the Nazis became more powerful, uniting the forces of the right behind them, the left continued to fight each other. The Internationaler Bund followed the new KPD line of "social fascism", according to which the Reichsbund, the SPD (German Social Democratic Party) and the Nazis were equally reactionary.[344] The SPD and the KPD remained opposed to each other until their offices were raided and their organisations outlawed.[345]

On coming to power, the Nazis reversed the worst cuts in disability pensions and reinstated the original disability threshold for employment quotas. While Nazi supporters injured in street fighting were covered by these measures, in February 1934 new laws excluded all Communists.

The Nazis' policies were deeply contradictory. On the one hand, disabled war "heroes" were used to promote militarism and the value of self-sacrifice, becoming "first citizens of the state". They received a special medal, concessions for public transport and priority employment under the quota law. In the Reichstag elections of November 1933, uniformed disabled veterans joined rallies. Nazi propagandists published photographs of Hitler thanking them for their sacrifices, while ensuring that those with the most severe impairments were hidden from view. On the other hand, disabled people with hereditary or congenital impairments were increasingly demonised, leading to their mass murder under the T-4 programme (see chapter 7).

The USSR: heroes and traitors

The main inspiration for the German revolution had been its successful counterpart of October 1917 in Russia. The negotiations and punitive peace treaty with Germany that followed the Russian Revolution triggered a trade blockade of Russia by its former military allies, further damaging an already devastated economy. The new state abolished all charities and passed laws providing for social welfare, but could offer no financial support to nearly 3 million disabled veterans from the First World War and the Russian Civil War (1918-1921) until the late 1920s.[346] By then, the failure of the revolution to spread had led to its degeneration and to the rise of Stalinism.

Russia suffered by far the biggest casualties of any country during the Second World War, with 20 million dead and a further 18 million soldiers reported physically impaired, 3.8 million of whom had been discharged as disabled.[347] The state media declared: "caring for disabled veterans of the Great Patriotic War is the sacred duty of the whole soviet people".[348] Throughout the new Eastern Bloc the new communist dictatorships promoted idealised images of:

> heroic labourers, medal-winning sportspeople or victorious soldiers, [with] an official championing and near fetishisation of bodily strength, functioning and ability...disability and other possible impediments to work were increasingly equated with deviation.[349]

"War invalids" were excluded from official accounts of the war.[350] Few veterans received jobs, and pensions remained woefully inadequate. Dishevelled war veterans begging or selling their possessions became a common sight on the streets[351]—and were increasingly targeted as "anti-Soviet elements":

> During the late 1940s and 1950s disabled veterans were dispersed from Moscow and other large cities for forced resettlement in remote areas... [K]olkhoz supervisors in rural areas, in order to shed inefficient disabled workers, sometimes turned them in as 'parasites'; such workers were then deported, presumably to labor camps. Penal camps were established in the Soviet Union for disabled prisoners and disabled veterans... The most infamous of these is the Spasskaia labor colony near Karaganda, Kazakhstan, to which 15,000 disabled prisoners were sent in the late 1940s and early 1950s.[352]

Stalin's death, combined with unrest resulting from workers' uprisings in East Germany and Hungary, led to a series of reforms allocating disabled war veterans and their dependents substantially higher pensions than other disabled people. Each veteran also received a free car which was replaced every seven years, free driving lessons and public transport, priority for health resorts and housing lists, and reductions in electricity and gas bills.[353]

State policy involved a hierarchical ranking of impairment, as described by Lev Indolev, journalist and key figure in the Russian disability rights movement. His satirical comment on post-Soviet Russia applies equally well to the Stalinist period:

All invalids are not created equal... At the head of the line stand the all-important invalids of the Second World War. Behind them we find...participants in squelching anti-communist protests in Hungary and Czechoslovakia, and ending with those wounded in Afghanistan and Chechnya. Further back [in the line] are invalids of military service, the ministry of internal affairs, the KGB and other 'forces'. Then invalids of the workplace and those injured 'at the hands of others' get their turn. Those accident victims, who are themselves at fault, come in last, along with the congenitally disabled, who have no one at all to blame.[354]

These categories reflected official views as to which groups were most deserving of help, although many of those entitled to "extras" never actually received them.[355]

The US: in the shadow of Vietnam

US war veterans' organisation The American Legion was founded immediately after the First World War with the declared aim of resisting "Bolshevism" and other radicalism. Its members helped break strikes and attacked activities by "reds".[356] However, the dominant pattern of veterans' activism in the US was later to take a very different character.

The Legion's rival organisation, Veterans of Foreign Wars, took up the demand for the payment of a bonus under a law passed in 1924.[357] At the height of the Great Depression in summer 1932, 40,000 war veterans and their families gathered in Washington, DC. This "Bonus Army" set up camp in the nation's capital to demand immediate payment of the bonus. Around a fifth of the protesters were disabled. On 28 July 1932, President Herbert Hoover ordered the army to clear the campsite. Troops and tanks burned it to the ground, shooting two veterans dead and wounding dozens more. The subsequent scandal helped ensure the election of Franklin D Roosevelt's Democrat Administrations. The new President, however, opposed paying the bonus, even after more than 400 more Bonus Army veterans were killed when a hurricane hit a ramshackle government camp built on the Florida Keys shoreline.[358] The bonuses were finally paid in 1936 against a backdrop of labour unrest, alongside the wider reforms of Roosevelt's second term New Deal.

> The rise of a general social welfare system under the New Deal decreased the need for military pensions and made aid to ex-soldiers seem less like "special benefits." Thus, when the 12 million veterans of World War II returned home, debate was minimal over the largest package of veterans' benefits in American history. The GI Bill (1944)...provided World War II veterans with free college education and medical care, unemployment insurance for one year, and guaranteed loans up to $4,000 to buy homes or businesses... By the 1970s, VA [Department of Veterans Affairs] spending was greater than all but three cabinet departments. By 1980, benefits distributed under the G.I. Bill totaled $120 billion, an enormous investment in 'social capital' and social mobility.[359]

The two rival empires dominating the post-war world mirrored each other in many respects, not least in their policies towards war veterans. The armed forces of the US were by far the largest and best equipped in the world, reflecting and enhancing its position as the dominant industrial power. The new war in Vietnam therefore attracted widespread optimism and support throughout US society— but the enthusiasm was to prove short-lived.

In 1970, it was reported that US psychiatric casualties had fallen from 101 per 1,000 troops in the Second World War to 12 per 1,000 in Vietnam.[360] In that same year, however, a psychiatrist arriving for duty in Da Nang found that the hospital's entire mental health team had been disbanded for agitating against the war. In 1971, the American Psychiatric Association passed a motion voicing concerns about the war's "grave effects on morale and on the rate of alienation, dehumanization and divisiveness among the American people".[361] In *Born on the Fourth of July*, Ron Kovic describes his experiences on returning from the war. Languishing in an understaffed and under-funded veterans' hospital, he started asking questions:

The wards are filthy. The men in my room throw their breadcrumbs under the radiator to keep the rats from chewing on our numb legs during the nights... The sheets are never changed enough and many of the men stink from not being properly bathed. It never makes any sense to us how the government can keep asking money for weapons and leave us lying in our own filth... I still tell people, whoever asks me, that I believe in the war. But more and more what I tell them and what I am feeling are becoming two different things. The hospital is like the whole war all over again.[362]

Kovic went on to help form Vietnam Veterans Against the War, and to play a key role in the famous anti-war protest at the 1972 Miami Republican National Convention.[363] The belief that ordinary people had nothing to gain from the war spread rapidly across US society. Ethnic minorities and the poor were doing most of the fighting, killing and dying, while the sons of the rich avoided the draft. One New York analyst was reputed to have written 75 letters a week at US$250 a time, declaring men "emotionally unfit for military duties".[364] Psychiatrists sent soldiers back to the front on drugs that in civilian life would have banned them from working on machinery. Marijuana was widespread and heroin use was so endemic that in 1971 more soldiers were evacuated for drug use than for wounds.[365]

Vietnam veterans successfully campaigned to have Post Traumatic Stress Disorder (PTSD) recognised in the *Diagnostic and Statistical Manual*. A report to US Congress found that 479,000 of the 3.14 million Americans serving in Vietnam still suffered from PTSD 15 years after the war's end and that 960,000 men and 1,900 women at one time or another had the full-blown disorder.[366]

Current US veterans have been described as "the most medically and mentally troubled generation of former troops in history." Some 45 percent of the 1.6 million veterans of the wars in Iraq and Afghanistan have sought compensation for service-related injuries.[367]

Tomas Young died on 10 November 2014 at the age of 34. The most prominent US veteran to speak out against the invasion and occupation of Iraq, he was the subject in 2007 of the TV documentary *Body of War*. Young's story in many respects parallels that of Kovic: the memories of war, the trauma of paralysis and rehabilitation, mental torment, bitterness and alienation. Both regained self-respect through becoming involved in the anti-war movement. The contrasts are also significant. Kovic went to Vietnam a gung-ho patriot and volunteered for a second tour of duty. When he turned against the war after being shot and paralysed in 1968 much of the public still supported it. When Young went to Iraq in 2004 he was, like millions of others, already sceptical and he joined an anti-war movement which more clearly reflected wider public opinion.[368] This has left its mark on today's US armed forces:

> [G]oing back to at least 2008 and in other years since, more American soldiers have committed suicide than have been killed in combat… while the number of suicides had roughly doubled among Iraq and Afghanistan veterans, the numbers had trebled among military personnel who had never been deployed… [Veterans are] struggling not only with PTSD but a host of other problems, not least alcohol and substance abuse, domestic violence, personal financial problems and inability to find jobs at home.[369]

Prosthetics and rehabilitation

Modern warfare prompted the development of a prosthetics industry. The large-scale loss of labour power led nation states and capitalists to invest in devices that would allow disabled veterans to return to the work force.

The American Civil War led to the first mass artificial limb-making industry, a response to an estimated total of 60,000 amputations.[370] But prosthetic limbs were bulky, noisy and uncomfortable. Many veterans were unable to wear artificial legs because surgeons left too much bone at the end of their stumps.

The carnage of the First World War similarly allowed plenty of opportunity for medical innovation. The UK Ministry of Pensions estimated that there were "300,000 newly amputated ex-servicemen worldwide", of whom "around 41,000 were British".[371] New weaponry led to more hugely disfiguring injuries. US sculptors made masks for casualties across the world, using pre-injury photographs of faces to reproduce missing parts with materials like metal and soft rubber and painting the masks to match skin colours. In the UK, 21 different manufacturers set up facilities at Queen Mary Hospital in Roehampton, collaborating with surgeons, other specialists and patients. The new research centre won a worldwide reputation for excellence in treating amputees.

The war economy also (quite literally) shaped the development of artificial arms. The pre-war "Sunday arm", named for its cosmetic use on holidays, was immobile and carved from lightweight wood. The scale of the slaughter at the front led to labour shortages in the warring states, leading industrial firms such as Siemens in Germany to design a variety of "workers arms". These sacrificed aesthetic appeal for practical function, accommodating a range of workplace tools. One example, the "work claw", consisted of a metal hook or clamp attached to the end of a leather casing which then slipped over the stump enabling the wearer to hold objects. The Hamburg naval hospital's prosthetics factory, meanwhile, trained men with such prostheses in locksmithing, blacksmithing, plumbing, cabinet making, lathe turning and other wood-working trades and as tailors, shoemakers and harness makers.[372] These industry-specific designs, however, meant that a veteran with a specially crafted "arm" or set of working hands could not easily change jobs.

German ocularists had dominated the glass eye-making market since the Franco-Prussian war of 1870-1871, primarily because of their superior raw materials:

The soda glass from German factories was well suited to eye making. Sand from the Black Forest had a low iron oxide content, which meant the glass made with it resisted corrosion from human tears... [unlike] the lead glass commonly available in France, England and the United States... During the mobilization of German industry for [World War Two], the Nazis forbade exportation of many products and raw materials, including glass. The first acrylic eyes were developed in the US a few years later.[373]

Modern rehabilitation also has its roots in war. The US National Defense Act of 1916 provided vocational training to disabled soldiers in an attempt to return them to the workforce:

> Even at this early date...the concept of *cost-effectiveness of social intervention* was introduced and argued by legislators. *Costs* were defined only in terms of economic costs to the state and/or employer, and *effectiveness* was defined in terms of successful re-employment and removal from the unemployment welfare rolls.[374]

Further legislation, including the Soldier Rehabilitation Act of 1918 expanded this provision. Modern physiotherapy is reputed to have begun with the recruitment by the US Surgeon General's Office of graduates from the first school of physical therapy, established at Walter Reed Army Hospital in Washington, DC.[375] This group of almost 800 women, trained in physical education, massage and corrective exercise, were assigned to the US Army in 1918.[376] Occupational therapy is credited with similar origins, with 118 women assigned to work as technical assistants to army physicians, teaching crafts to rehabilitate the wounded.[377] The Second World War led to more standardised prosthetic devices and the introduction of treatment protocols.

In the advanced economies today, leg amputations are mainly caused by vascular problems associated with ageing. In civil war zones from Afghanistan to Bosnia and Sierra Leone, landmines are the main cause. In these countries, most amputees have to make do with crude crutches or sticks. Their experiences differ starkly from those of John Kremer of the US Navy, who lost both his legs below the knee after stepping on a mine in Afghanistan in 2010:

> with the encouragement of therapists at the Naval Medical Center, Mr Kremer was walking in two months, running in five and skydiving after nine. He did his first 10-kilometer race, about six miles, one year after stepping on the mine. Today he runs, swims or bikes almost daily and competes for the Navy's wounded warrior team in swimming, shooting, seated volleyball and wheelchair basketball.[378]

The treatment and rehabilitation of disabled war veterans places a premium on developing athletic prowess and body strength. The London *Evening Standard* recently explained why they should be seen as a worthy addition to the workplace:

> Prince Charles is right to say that business should take the trouble to recruit ex-service people... There are excellent reasons of self-interest as well as public spirit for them to do so. In the armed services, recruits are given extensive training. They are disciplined and by definition can work as a team. They have a strong sense of corporate identity and often have excellent vocational skills... What makes a good soldier or officer also makes an exemplary employee.[379]

Disabled war veterans may receive three or four prostheses: one each for walking and running, another for biking and other sports.[380] In the UK, "injured servicemen could leave Headley Court [military rehabilitation centre] with £50,000 worth of equipment. Difficulties come later when they leave the military, and the NHS does not have the budget to replace the equipment".[381]

The success of the 2012 London Games, and the raised expectations and aspirations this briefly gave some disabled people, led to worry in some quarters that the next generation of prosthetics would be even more expensive than those currently available on the NHS:

> The "Paralympic effect" may mean that not only elite athletes will want to have the benefit of ever advancing technology... Compensators should brace themselves for a rise in the costs of amputation claims. However, as improvements in the functionality of prosthetic limbs allow amputees to live fuller and more independent lives, this may be offset by a substantial reduction in the amount of care and help that claimants require in the future. Loss of earnings claims should be similarly reduced. Whether such savings will offset the increased cost of the prosthetic limbs entirely remains to be seen.[382]

Modern trauma

Medical records show that the ways in which mental injuries are experienced varies widely. British soldiers in the Boer War complained of joint pain and muscle weakness, which doctors called "debility syndrome". In the American Civil War battle-traumatised soldiers experienced an aching in the left side of the chest and the feeling of a weak heartbeat, labelled "Da Costa's Syndrome." Another variant was withdrawal and lethargy thought to be caused by homesickness. As one writer has commented: "although the potential psychic damage of war is indisputable, the process by which that damage becomes an outward symptom is a reflection of the cultural beliefs in a particular time and place".[383] We now know that "shell shock" is likely to have been applied to a range of different conditions or responses to war trauma.

Today, nearly half of all current US veterans file for disability benefits. One Harvard economist estimated the health care and disability costs of recent wars at up to US$900 billion.[384] As mentioned above, record numbers of US soldiers have committed suicide in recent years.[385] The list of causes, however, remains constant: trauma, alcohol and substance abuse, domestic violence, personal financial problems and inability to find jobs at home.

The prominent coverage given to appeals for military charities illustrate how little has changed. Just as many victims of shell shock never reached the Front in the First World War 100 years ago, many of those expected to fight the wars of today become traumatised by brutal and dehumanising military training. A common factor between the uprisings which ended the slaughter of the First World War and the struggles of today's generation is an international movement against imperialist war, which has already led some of today's soldiers to confront the true nature of their role, if not yet to actually turn their weapons against their masters.

The social position of disabled veterans remains contradictory: lionised as heroes to glorify war, yet hidden away as a reminder of its reality; lauded by politicians as "most deserving", yet provided with minimal state support. Most importantly, they are "wounded warriors" for capital whose experiences can sometimes turn them against the society in whose name they fought. As such, they are likely to play an even more important role in future battles for "hearts and minds".

9.
Politics and movements

In February 1988, the All-Union Society of Disabled People
(AUSDP) was officially launched in Moscow—an event treated by
the Soviet state and media as of historic significance. Three years
into President Mikhail Gorbachev's "perestroika" reforms and
after decades of official hostility or indifference, Russia's disabled
population now ran and controlled their own national organisation,
similar to those previously established in the west.

None of these, however, were the world's first such organisations.
That distinction belonged to the All-Russian Cooperative of Disabled
People (VIKO), launched in December 1921. It was formed four years
after the October Revolution, following a vote by the Council of
People's Commissioners. This was followed by the formation of the
All-Union Society of the Blind in 1925 and the All-Union Society of
the Deaf the following year.

VIKO's structure was similar to that of the AUSDP today. All
decisions were made democratically and only disabled people could
vote. But as an institution founded by a still-revolutionary state
VIKO exercised far greater power and influence. It provided work
opportunities for disabled people with special production lines and
established kindergartens, resorts and health retreats, vocational
schools and sport centres.[386]

Another significant fact that VIKO and the AUSDP had in
common is that both existed for only a few years. VIKO disappeared
with the rise of the Stalinist state and the AUSDP did not survive the
fall of the Berlin Wall and the disintegration of the Stalinist empire
in 1990. Many other organisations for and of disabled people have
risen to prominence only to disappear after a comparatively short

period. This chapter examines disability organisations and politics in different countries to illustrate how wider factors have shaped the role of disabled people.

Origins of the disability movement

The origins of what is commonly seen as the first disability movement lie in the social changes set in train during the Second World War and the long economic boom which followed. Before then, the word disability was virtually unknown and welfare states did not yet exist. Many disabled people were primarily housebound, financially dependent on families or charities. Others lived in isolated and squalid institutions unchanged in decades and whose continued existence reflected and reinforced widespread ignorance or even fear of disabled people.

Many of the warring states had given large numbers of disabled people—previously considered unfit or unsuitable for factory work—a substantial role in wartime production.[387] Although many of these jobs disappeared after the war, there was particular pressure on governments to rehabilitate disabled veterans. Economic expansion, technological and scientific advances and the foundation of welfare states allowed more disabled people to live longer and carry out activities of which they had until then been considered incapable:

> Of particular importance was the availability of domestic appliances which could be operated with the minimum of physical energy and skill. Teaching a physically impaired person how to go to a well, fetch a pail of water, collect firewood and light a fire to make a pot of tea may have been impossible last century, but teaching a similarly impaired person to fill an electric kettle with water, switch on a button, etc. to make a pot of tea today is well within the accepted aims of modern rehabilitation practice.[388]

These changes did not, however, immediately transform the lives of disabled people. Although services (at least in the UK) were now in theory allocated according to need, disabled people were in practice rarely consulted. Instead, they remained passive recipients of services prescribed or imposed by medical or other professionals. The number of patients in mental asylums in the UK and the US continued to rise and many physically disabled people remained institutionalised until the 1970s or even later.

Long-term changes, meantime, were pulling in the opposite direction. In the 1960s, full employment led to large numbers of disabled people joining the workforce—for the first time in a period of peace. The development of more specialist professions in health and social services led to the first public questioning of institutionalisation and the patronage of charities and also of the labels imposed on disabled people as deviants, dependents or patients.[389]

The United States

Disability activism has a particularly rich history in the US, not least in the years of the Great Depression. In 1935, three years after the famous struggle of the Bonus Army,[390] the League for the Physically Handicapped was formed in New York. Over a lifetime of barely three years, its members (in total somewhere between 40 and 200) won jobs for up to 1,500 of the city's disabled population—despite federal New Deal legislation categorising disabled people as "unemployable".[391] In the same period, 17 blind workers employed by a New York Jewish welfare organisation joined a nationwide wave of sit-down strikes to demand a minimum wage, supported in turn by a sympathy sit-down of 83 workers at another New York workshop for the blind.[392]

The modern disability rights movement began with the admission of Ed Roberts to a new residence programme at Berkeley's University of California in 1962. Paralysed from the neck down due to childhood polio, Roberts overcame opposition to gain a university place and was housed initially in the campus hospital. Seeing other students challenge discrimination gave him confidence: "When women talked about being objects, I understood...underneath I got more and more angry at the way people perceived me as a vegetable with no future. We were all talking about the same issues".[393]

A headline in a local newspaper proclaimed, "Helpless Cripple Attends UC Classes." Within a short period of time, several other men and women with disabilities joined him on campus. Dubbing themselves the "rolling quads," they banded together to fight for better services and for permission to live independently, rather than at the hospital. With a grant from the U.S. Office of Education, they created the Physically Disabled Students' Program [PDSP], the first of its kind on a college campus. It was, in effect, the beginning of the independent living movement.[394]

The new activists, whose main inspiration was the black civil rights struggle, organised self-advocacy and taught those skills to others. They demanded an end to the control and patronage of medical professionals and institutions, stressing what were seen as key American values of self-reliance and economic consumer rights. The PDSP provided services to students including assistance referrals and wheelchair repairs, but it was soon taking calls from other disabled people with similar concerns. The first centre for independent living opened in Berkeley in 1971, providing peer support, referral services, advocacy training and general information.[395] Versions of these centres soon spread across both the US and the world.

The example of the independent living movement inspired wider activism. Another quadriplegic, Judy Heumann, obtained the necessary grades, but was refused her teaching certificate after failing a medical exam. She went to the press. "You Can Be President, Not Teacher, With Polio" ran the headline in the *New York Daily News*. After securing her certificate, Heumann set up a new overtly political disability rights group, Disabled in Action, in 1970.[396] One of its first initiatives was joining disabled Vietnam veterans to demand a debate with Republican nominee Richard Nixon during the 1972 US presidential election.

Disabled people lobbied Congress to demand the inclusion of their civil rights in new legislation. Despite two previous vetoes, the Republican administration passed a much-revised and diluted Rehabilitation Act in 1973. They had, however, overlooked Section 504, a one-sentence paragraph prohibiting disability discrimination in any government-funded service or activity. "In one of American history's ironies, Richard Nixon had signed into law a major civil rights statute" the implementation of which became the focus of the new disability movement's most famous protest.[397]

> [T]here was an expectation that the incoming Carter Administration would fulfill its promise to issue the [Section 504] regulations. When it became obvious that the Democrats' policy makers were stalling... disability rights activists mobilized in nine cities across the United States. In Washington, three hundred demonstrators occupied the offices of the Health, Education and Welfare (HEW) Secretary for some twenty-eight hours despite the termination of the office's telephone lines by authorities and the refusal to permit food through to the protestors.[398]

None of the other demonstrations lasted as long as that in Washington—except in San Francisco, where up to 120 activists maintained an occupation of the HEW federal building for an astonishing 25 days. In contrast to the protests elsewhere, they had built alliances in advance, winning wider political support as well as practical assistance:

> A network of volunteers from such groups as the Black Panthers and the Delancey Street Foundation would risk arrest to bring the protestors food donated not just by churches and unions, but even by Safeway and McDonald's. HEW officials in Washington quickly saw that if they tried to starve out the demonstrators, they might provoke a larger protest involving many other groups.[399]

The occupation attracted huge and largely supportive media coverage.[400] Many participants "literally risked their lives, as they were without their personal care attendants or assistive devices".[401] It became clear to the Carter administration that its only alternatives to capitulation—forcibly evicting or starving out the demonstrators—risked provoking a major backlash. The regulations were issued unamended. It was a spectacular and memorable victory.

In 1983 American Disabled for Accessible Public Transit (ADAPT) was formed in several cities to campaign for accessible public transport. Its direct action tactics often led to mass arrests.[402] As Atlanta activist Mark Johnson put it: "Black people fought for the right to ride in the front of the bus. We're fighting for the right to get on the bus." In March 1990, three dozen ADAPT activists crawled up the 83 marble steps of the Capitol building to highlight society's lack of accessibility for disabled people.[403]

On signing the Americans with Disabilities Act (ADA) into law in 1990, President Bush Senior famously declared: "Let the walls of exclusion come tumbling down." The ADA describes disabled people in the US as "faced with restrictions and limitations, subjected to a history of purposeful unequal treatment, and relegated to a position of political powerlessness in our society".[404] The legislation led to significant improvements in access to buildings, goods and services and inspired the passing of similar laws across the world in subsequent years.

The reality, however, fell far short of the rhetoric. Those drafting the legislation, all appointees of the previous president, Ronald Reagan, ensured that business had nothing to fear from the ADA:

> employment discrimination provisions are lax, there is no mandated affirmative action, and there are loopholes to delay and stall access. In short, compliance is largely voluntary... Any business can claim that it will be 'a significant difficulty or expense' to conform with the law... [Bush] vetoed the 1990 Civil Rights Act, which would have allowed disabled people to join women and other minorities in suing companies for damages for discrimination.[405]

Even before the ADA became law, the liberal *New York Times* had declared, under the headline "No one wishes to stint on helping the disabled", that access "costs too much".[406] As historian Edward Berkovitz put it: "Admitting [black student] James Meredith to the University of Mississippi cost nothing in an economic sense. All of the costs were political. Meredith required courage to attend classes, not ramps and wide toilet stalls with grab bars".[407] In contrast to anti-discrimination measures for other minorities, those for disabled people often cost money.

On Election Day 2000, ten years after the ADA's passage, the General Accounting Office found that eight out of every ten polling places visited had at least some access problem.[408] Economist Thomas DeLeire argued that the ADA wasn't working because it tried to regulate business, making disabled people "less employable." Added costs and threats of prosecution, he argued, "led firms to avoid hiring some disabled workers in the first place".[409] There seems to be a grain of truth in DeLeire's argument in that studies consistently show fewer disabled people in work since the passage of the ADA.[410] In more than 94 percent of job discrimination cases however courts had found in favour of the employer.[411]

Germany

Having been a prominent issue in both the Weimar and Nazi periods, disability became almost a taboo subject in Germany's "hungry years" after the war (along with other issues that evoked memories of the Nazi era). However, the many disabled war veterans begging on the streets were a visible and ever-present reminder of defeat. Allied occupiers refused to pay their military pensions, claiming that favourable treatment for war veterans had helped to promote militarism in the Weimar period.[412]

Obliged to seek alliances due to an allied ban on organisations for war victims, war veterans were the first disabled group to organise themselves. On 26 March 1950 several thousand marched in Munich demanding jobs and higher pensions. In 1959, the War Disabled, War Survivors and Social Pensioners (VdK) mobilised against threatened benefits cuts, organising demonstrations of 25,000 in Dusseldorf and another 20,000 in Stuttgart with a banner reading "Justice Not Pity". In 1955, a disabled war veteran (one of many who joined the peace movement) addressed 150,000 people at a Hamburg anti-nuclear rally, demanding that his generation be "the last war victims of all times".[413]

With the onset of the Cold War and the partition of Germany, *realpolitik* governed post-war attitudes to the Nazi regime and its supporters. War criminals had initially received heavy sentences at the Nuremberg trials,[414] but after the founding of the Federal Republic, judges who had been Nazi Party members were reinstated, as were medical personnel who had carried out euthanasia programmes.

Their disabled victims, in contrast, received no compensation until decades later.

> Historians estimate that about twenty thousand patients died in state hospitals and nursing homes during the four years of the occupation period up to the founding of the two German states in 1949. While almost all these deaths were from starvation, in at least one institution, in the state hospital in Kaufbeuren, patients were still murdered after the war ended.[415]

Compensation for those sterilised or for relatives of the murdered was refused on the grounds that eugenic policies had not been unique to Nazi Germany. Surviving victims "felt understandable fear and shame about speaking out, and...hardly had any strong advocates to speak on their behalf".[416]

The problems in the supposedly egalitarian East Germany and the supposedly free West Germany were remarkably similar: the retention or return of former Nazi officials to their posts, segregated institutions and schools, discrimination and bureaucratic opposition to change. Skilled jobs were easier to access in East Germany, where it was compulsory "to make suitable apprenticeships and jobs available...in contrast to West Germany (and reunified Germany), where employers could (and still can) avoid employing their small quota of disabled people by paying a small fine".[417] The difference in the West was that disability activists could organise and challenge discrimination openly.[418]

Disabled East German citizens who remember the days before the fall of the Berlin Wall "sometimes sum up their situation today by saying that their living conditions have improved but their work status has worsened. As has always been the case in West Germany, most disabled East Germans are now unemployed, underemployed, or only working part time".[419]

The modern German disability rights movement began after Gusti Steiner and non-disabled journalist Ernst Klee founded a course at Frankfurt's Adult Education Centre in 1973. After their requests to make specific buildings and services accessible were ignored, course participants blocked roads during the rush hour.

Further protests led to a ramp being installed outside Frankfurt's main post office, inspiring similar actions elsewhere. One initiative, the "Golden Crutch", highlighted discriminatory practices. Its first annual award in 1978 was for an advert for car seat belts with the slogan: "To be crippled for the rest of your life is a fate worse than death". This, campaigners pointed out, echoed the Nazi concept of "life unworthy of life".[420]

On 25 February 1980 Frankfurt's district court endorsed the compensation claim of a West German woman against a travel agency on the grounds that her Greek holiday was ruined by the presence of a group of learning disabled people staying in the same hotel. Part of the court's decision read:

> it is a matter of deformed, mentally disturbed people who are not in command of language, who sometimes emit inarticulate screams in an irregular rhythm... There is suffering in the world, and this cannot be changed. However, the plaintiff is justified in not wanting to see it during her vacation.

The verdict led to Europe's biggest yet protest for disability rights. Gusti Steiner told a crowd of 5,000: "We won't let ourselves be equated with defective toilet seats or be made into a vacation problem".[421]

A series of actions targeted events marking the UN International Year of Disabled People in 1981. January's official launch ended in farce after protesters occupied the stage, with Federal President Karl Carstens forced to deliver his keynote address from a locked room. The occupiers declared:

> We...reject the congratulatory speeches of politicians and experts... Today and tomorrow we are allowed to use the special transportation that has been brought here with so much fanfare. The day after tomorrow we will be sitting at home again. The policy of special institutions, special equipment, special treatment, etc., has led to nothing but ghettoization, isolation, dependence and mistreatment".[422]

At a second event five months later, in full view of the media, one protester hit Carstens with a crutch, shouting that the President was again endorsing an event where "people were talking about us but not with us." An article in *Die Welt* on 14 December 1981 said the protests had transformed the "Year of the Disabled" into the "Year of the Disablers".[423] A few years later, the first of many Centres for Independent Living in Germany opened, following a visit to Berkeley in California by several West German activists.[424]

Disability began to feature more prominently in the West German media. After reunification in 1990, disability and bioethical issues became a major subject of debate, initially prompted by a controversy involving the writer and academic Peter Singer.[425] A major exhibition on the history of disabled people, held in Dresden in 2000, attracted 170,000 people.[426] In 2005, disability activists lobbied the ruling SPD-Green Party coalition government to adopt an anti-discrimination law:

> As in the United States, the main opponents of the proposed law in Germany came from the CDU and the Free Democratic Party (FDP), which represented various sectors of the business community...[which threatened] a huge flood of lawsuits if the legislation were passed.[427]

Despite CDU and FDP opposition, the General Law on Equal Treatment was passed in June 2006. However, its record in key areas is not impressive.

Recent campaigns by German disability activists have highlighted the failures of a chronically under-funded education system. Compared to the US and the rest of Europe, a far higher proportion of children attend separate "special" schools. Inclusion declines at each stage of education: 62 percent of disabled children attend mainstream pre-schools and kindergartens, with this figure falling to 34 percent for primary schools and only 15 percent for high schools.[428]

Proportionately fewer disabled students enter higher education in Germany than in the US.[429] Twice as many disabled pupils leave German schools without any formal qualifications compared to their non-disabled peers. For pupils of special schools, the figure is 77 percent. Studies show that inclusion can only work with more and appropriately qualified teaching staff and smaller classes. However, the concept "has been used as a means for making cuts, with special schools shut down without savings being used to support more accessible education. This has led to many parents believing that their children are better off in special schools".[430]

Only around half of disabled people aged between 16 and 55 are employed, with a limit of only €2,600 in savings before they are ineligible for benefits.[431] Although almost one third of German employers are legally obliged to hire severely disabled people, in most cases the law is ignored, with this group comprising less than 1 percent of their employees.[432] New minimum wage legislation introduced in January 2015 excludes around 250,000 disabled people employed in sheltered workshops on the grounds that they are not legally classed as employees.

The role of the UN

China's first moves to develop state policy on disability were prompted by a UN disability advocacy programme, rather than by initiatives from below such as those in Germany and the US.[433] UN Secretary General Kurt Waldheim's speech for the 1981 International Year of Disabled People campaign included an estimate of the disabled population as 10 percent of the global total. His speechwriter later admitted this figure was "largely invented... People don't tend to think an issue is big unless you have big numbers." After a national survey in 1987 estimated China's disabled population to be a far smaller proportion of the whole, the government launched the Chinese Disabled Persons Federation (CDPF).[434] The new state body quickly co-opted leading disability activists, as one of them explained:

> Two or three men among us...got real government positions within the Federation. Most everyone else, though, was offered posts that were largely symbolic... Some were angry that [this] work...involved spending lots of precious state money on public events rather than on disability assistance.

Many Chinese saw the CDPF as corrupt: "cronyism was a big factor in staff hiring policies; Federation employees usually had neither experience with nor interest in disability assistance".[435]

Although passed in the same year as the new US legislation, China's Law on the Protection of Disabled Persons guaranteed no "entitlements or personal rights but [only] a loose declaration of ethics".[436] The government later admitted that it had proven more difficult to implement the law "because deep-rooted prejudice against the disabled still exists".[437] However, the 2008 amendments to the law, which "prohibited" discrimination but imposed no penalties and left enforcement up to local authorities, showed little had changed on the government's part. The law defines disability in medical terms as "abnormalities" which involve losing "wholly or in part the ability to perform an activity in the way considered normal".[438]

The CDPF, which has around 120,000 full-time employees, declares its key functions as to: "represent the common interests and safeguard the rights of persons with disabilities; provide comprehensive services...[and] supervise the administration of disability-related affairs".[439] The Federation therefore performs an advocacy role for disabled people—insofar as this is acceptable to the authorities—while simultaneously acting as an official government department.

The Indian parliament's passing of the Persons with Disabilities Act in 1995 likewise owed "more to international pressure than to lobbying and protests by disability rights groups". To mark the launch of another UN disability initiative in 1993, the Indian government organised a seminar in New Delhi. This led to the formation of the Disabled Rights Group which then lobbied for and helped to draft the new law. A census in 2001, however, showed India's disabled population as amounting to only 2.1 percent of the population (21 million people).[440]

In 2014 the Indian Supreme Court condemned the national government's failure to implement the quota system in the 1995 Act. This requires public sector bodies to reserve 3 percent of posts for disabled (or "differently abled") employees.[441]

In Japan the employment rate of disabled people (58 percent) is relatively higher than in the US and OECD countries, although many work in sheltered workshops.[442] However, the employment quota system introduced by the Japanese government in 1976 has been largely ignored: "[n]ot once in the last 30 years have the quotas been achieved".[443] The record is similar in Germany and France, with employers preferring to pay a penalty than to meet the required quota.

The record suggests that attempts to introduce disability reforms from above—whether prompted by international bodies such as the UN or by national governments—have fared no better and in some cases clearly worse than those campaigned for from below.

Russia and the former Soviet Union

Residential care in the Soviet Union, like Western Europe until the 1970s, was seen as the most appropriate form of support for disabled children, who were mostly brought up and educated in special hospitals and boarding schools.[444] Few found work or continued in education after leaving.

The Soviet Union gained notoriety for locking up dissidents in psychiatric institutions on the grounds that they were mentally ill; its less publicised harassment of disability activists was more effective. Informal networks of disabled people nevertheless developed across the Soviet Union throughout the 1970s and 1980s. In October 1987, during the period of reforms initiated by Mikhail Gorbachev, 200 disabled people taking part in the TV show *Perestoika Projected* successfully demanded the government consent to setting up a national organisation.[445] Although the growth of the new organisation was cut short by the collapse of the Soviet Union, its Russian successor, the All-Russian Society of Disabled People (ARSD), had by 2000 reached a membership of over 2.5 million.[446]

The ARSD helped draft the Social Protection of Disabled People, which became law in 1995. The new legislation defined social protection in extremely broad terms, mentioning equality of opportunity but not discrimination. Although individuals can file private complaints under the law, as yet there is no enforcement commission.[447] Periodic state initiatives, charities and other non-governmental organisations (NGOs) alike are regarded by disabled activists as bureaucratic, leading them to form numerous local clubs and societies to provide legal and advocacy services to members.

Nearly 30 percent of disabled children still live in state orphanages notorious for violence and neglect. Children interviewed in 2014 said that staff beat them, injected them with sedatives, and sent them to psychiatric hospitals for days or weeks at a time to control or punish them.[448]

State paternalism has in many cases been replaced by the paternalism of charities. International non-governmental organisations (INGOs) tend to blame cultural influences in non-Western countries when a project fails or when initiatives do not work "presenting themselves as rescuers and sole defenders of children's rights…national professionals were often excluded if they did not speak English and did not conform to a particular agenda".[449] One INGO worker in Bulgaria observed:

> British, French and German NGOs donated really enormous amounts of money to residential institutions…and now after several years they see that everything is stolen or hidden and none of the toys or equipment they provided is used…I tell them you should pay salaries, you should train people and never buy clothes, shoes, but that is the donor mentality, they continue to do that.[450]

According to research for the UN published in 2009, the number of disabled people employed in Russia under the quota system introduced by the 1995 legislation fell from 57,146 in 2000 to 10,906 in 2007.[451] In the Putin era, reduced state support and services for disabled people has paralleled a widening gap between rich and poor. Placing responsibility on local government for service provision has led to huge disparities in the level of disabled pensions across the regions.[452]

Disability in the Majority World

If the understanding of "disability as a concept and an identity" is uneven and contradictory in the developed countries, this is even more the case in the Global South,[453] where living standards are in general lower and health and welfare systems poorer. Fewer people survive being born with impairments and those (predominantly the elderly) who acquire them later die younger than others. Nine in ten disabled children in some poor countries die before the age of 20 and a similar percentage with cognitive impairments do not live beyond 50.[454] As Barnes and Mercer have written:

> Specific diseases once common but now rarely recorded in industrialised countries remain widespread and in some cases are increasing...in India, the prevalence of polio and blindness is at least four times higher among people who are below the poverty line compared with those who are above it...around three-quarters of India's 60 million disabled people live in areas where public amenities like clean water, electricity, sanitation, and medical services are in very short supply.[455]

One in nine of the world's population has no access to clean water. Twice as many—2.5 billion people—have no access to a toilet.[456]

Poverty and a lack of health and social care are not the only factors producing impairment. Other causes include industrial accidents and pollution. One of the world's worst industrial disasters took place at Union Carbide's pesticide plant in Bhopal in India in December 1984. This led to the release of 40 tons of deadly gas, killing at least 10,000 people and leaving over half a million others with medical problems.[457] The WHO estimates indoor air pollution was linked to 4.3 million deaths in 2012, mainly among the almost 3 billion people living in homes using wood, coal or dung as their primary cooking fuel. Air pollution is also known to be a primary cause of cardiovascular and respiratory diseases and cancers.[458]

More generally, practices outlawed in the more advanced economies are often still permitted elsewhere. The role of asbestos in causing cancers (especially lung cancer) and mesothelioma, for example, is now well established. The incidence of mesothelioma across the European Union, where asbestos use peaked in the mid-1970s and was finally banned in 1999, is expected to peak around 2020. From 1994 to 2008, there were 174,000 mesothelioma cases reported in 56 countries. Today "Asia and parts of Eastern Europe use [approximately] 70 percent of the world's production of this mineral".[459] In India, asbestos is still used widely in construction: "Fibro, a mixture of asbestos and cement is sold cheaply...to roof makeshift slum houses... Much of the asbestos is imported from Canada, where it is illegal to build using the fibre".[460]

In one of their two books on attitudes to disability in poorer countries, Ingstad and Whyte comment: "If there is a danger that disabled people are presented as Others, not like us, then there is a double danger in the study of people with impairments in other cultures [of presenting them as] both foreign and disabled".[461] Although focused on rural communities, where religious beliefs are stronger than in the towns and cities, these studies nevertheless challenge conventional thinking. In the case of East Africa, Whyte points out that:

> cultural conceptions of epilepsy are not in fact simple structures with clear lines and clear functions built by an anonymous contractor called culture. Rather, they are homemade jerry-built affairs made of available materials and subject to remodeling by worried parents, curious neighbors, and healers, both traditional and untraditional. In fact, they are not finished structures at all, but ongoing processes. Sometimes they are messy—people disagree, or they are unsure or vague, or worst of all, they don't know... Our analyses must be built on the assumption that people are actors within social contexts, not prisoners of a fixed cultural construction.[462]

During Ingstad's fieldwork in rural Botswana in the mid-1980s, she frequently heard stories about disabled people "being hidden, abused and neglected by their families". She was told of one village where a mentally disturbed man was kept locked up by his parents in a mud hut next to the family home. On visiting the family, however, they told her that caring for their son became increasingly difficult as he grew older and were persuaded to send him to a local mental hospital. During their regular visits, they noticed his condition worsen and repeatedly requested his discharge. When this was finally granted, the condition of release was that he must be kept locked up to avoid danger to others—with the family personally responsible if anything happened. They often did let him out under supervision, but this became more difficult when his father died. Rarer outings sometimes led to him becoming violent and scaring the neighbours. Fearing the authorities would detain him again, the remaining family members now left him almost permanently locked in the hut. "The practical arrangements that outsiders interpreted as 'hiding' and 'abuse' were partly a result of this struggle, and partly necessary precautions that might have been relaxed had there been a better-developed (and better-functioning system) of support locally."[463]

Helander compares perceptions in a Somali village where two boys had similar degrees of mental impairment. One belonged to a prestigious family. His "problem" was explained by the fact that his mother was of insufficiently high status, but he was not regarded as mad and was well treated. The other boy, a homeless orphan, was said to be possessed by a spirit. He was teased and despised and children threw stones at him.[464]

In his examination of leprosy in India, Staples criticises the "worldview that continues to dominate the public agenda on disability" according to which ultimate responsibility for ill-health, disability and even poverty, lies with disabled people and their families, deflecting "culpability for disabling conditions away from social institutions":

> Responses to disability, from this perspective, require no change to the status quo, just a shift in the behaviour of those careless enough to get themselves into such a position... conceptualising the disabled and the sick as a feckless other, captivated by superstition and outmoded practices, allows them [the able-bodied] to distinguish themselves as modern and stake claims of social superiority...the poor, contra stereotype, were also less resistant to biomedical solutions than their affluent peers, and were usually keen to access medical support when socio-economic circumstances permitted. Against such a background, calls for more public health education will continue to fail [and] to miss their intended targets.[465]

This finding that better-off disabled people are more likely to hold conservative and traditional views is a valuable corrective to conventional narratives of illiterate and ignorant populations in the Global South. Impairment is often perceived differently in rural societies:

> Where the family is the basic unit of production, it seems easier for people with disabilities to make a contribution. Working conditions

are flexible, tasks are varied, [with] support from other family members and neighbors. Impairment does not usually disqualify people for work in subsistence production, domestic tasks, or even home-based handicraft production for the market. When labor is a commodity sold on a competitive market in fixed time and skill units, the participation of people with disabilities is more problematic.[466]

A large majority of the wars occurring since the Second World War have been in the Global South. Many were "proxy" wars between the Soviet Union and the US during the Cold War, or direct interventions by the superpowers, most notoriously in Vietnam and Afghanistan. In Afghanistan, almost one million people have been disabled in conflict-related incidents. The 2001 film *Kandahar* conveys some sense of the consequent social impact. It features Hayat, a young man with an amputated arm (presumably due to a landmine), who is shown trying to sell prosthetic legs to a passer-by. The latter responds: "I have my own, thank you". Hayat retorts, again very matter-of-factly: "These fields are full of mines; it's good to have replacements".[467]

In Cambodia and Rwanda, an estimated 100,000 people lost limbs as a direct result of the combatants' use of landmines.[468] These wars led to efforts to establish rehabilitation services for disabled veterans and injured civilians similar to those seen in Western countries after the two world wars, albeit often with fewer resources available.

In the case of Nicaragua, government programs for disabled veterans were instituted as other organizations of disabled people were becoming active... In Zimbabwe, which also suffered a devastating civil war, the first major effort toward rehabilitation was the construction of a large institution for disabled veterans. Later, this institution was reorganized as a resource center for several disability groups, and the government has implemented a policy of decentralized community-based rehabilitation for not only war veterans but all disabled people.[469]

A 2009 report identified Uganda's disability movement as "one of the most vibrant throughout Africa" that "has played a key role in the promotion of disability rights throughout the continent".[470]

The country's civil war caused many thousands of casualties, not least due to landmines. In 1987, 17 urban-based disability organisations united to form the National Union of Disabled People in Uganda (NUDIPU). Legislation in 1996 reserved seats for women and for disabled people in the national parliament and thousands of local government councillors are also disabled.[471] However, critics argue that quotas have led to little more general progress.[472] In 2004, 72 percent of disabled people in Northern Uganda were living in "chronic poverty".[473] New national disability legislation was passed in 2006, but to date no regulations have been passed for its implementation. Much existing provision in Uganda is due to the intervention of Western NGOs:

> Danish International Development Assistance funded the Uganda National Institute of Special Education, which trains teachers and rehabilitation workers... Schools for the deaf and the blind anchor and reproduce specific forms of communication and consciousness. The Norwegian Association of the Disabled supported a community-based rehabilitation (CBR) program... Geoffrey Wandera, who now so articulately speaks for rights not charity, did his apprentice and journeyman years in a CBR project funded from Norway.[474]

When the African National Congress was elected to govern post-apartheid South Africa in 1994, it introduced a Bill of Rights prohibiting discrimination including against disabled people. The Office on the Status of Disabled Persons is staffed entirely by disabled people and an Integrated National Disability Strategy was produced in 1997. Despite all this, only 1 percent of disabled people are employed in the formal sector of the economy. As in Uganda, "a whole raft of disability-related legislation has been introduced with the avowed aim of mainstreaming disability issues and access", but "[m]eaningful change has been seriously hampered by a chronic lack of funding".[475]

The growth of NGOs and charities has led to a greater emphasis on changing individual attitudes, which often becomes:

an exercise in victim-blaming...an excuse to justify paternalism and the righteousness of programs that are often created with little or no contact with the people they concern. In many—perhaps most—cases, however, the difficult circumstances of the disabled person are the result of the difficult life of the whole household or care unit. The problem may be poverty due to scarcity of resources, unemployment, or natural disasters such as drought—anything that makes the care unit extra vulnerable when one of its members become disabled. It may also be lack of support from outside.[476]

In reality, ideas of disability are constantly changing, with people adapting their ideas to fit the circumstances within which they find themselves. For example, one study of a group of Turkish immigrant women concludes: "Living in Sweden while maintaining close links to their village in Turkey, they confront radically different situations and must adjust their understandings of normality, responsibility, and the validity of 'deviant' children".[477]

Britain[478]

The coalition central to Britain's disability movement emerged from "single issue" campaigns in the 1960s and 1970s, principally the Disability Income Group (DIG) and the later Union of Physically Impaired Against Segregation (UPIAS). DIG campaigned for a national income for all disabled people who were unable to work and increasingly focused on parliamentary lobbying. UPIAS, which never grew beyond a couple of hundred members,[479] is remembered chiefly for pioneering in 1975 the distinction between impairment and disability. Their *Fundamental Principles* (see chapter 3) declared that disability, far from being biologically determined, was a social creation—a distinct form of oppression that could be challenged and eliminated.[480] This simple but illuminating insight, was often hugely empowering:

> To tell disabled people that it wasn't their impairments that were disabling as much as it was the barriers in society was just magical. You could see people actually growing from submissive, grateful people into assertive, powerful people.[481]

Establishing a new coalition for and of disabled people was a difficult and often frustrating process. Who should it represent, and what should be its principal aims? Should it focus on "helping individuals practically or on struggling collectively to achieve broader social changes?"[482] For some, disability was first and foremost a human rights issue. Others saw "able-bodied society" as the problem, with disabled people perceived as having different interests. This in turn led to more divisive notions such as who was "really disabled". Black people, LGBT supporters and women pointed to discrimination against them by fellow disabled activists.[483]

Having successfully negotiated (if never fully resolving) most potential divisions, the British Council of Organisations of Disabled People (BCODP) was launched as a "formal organisational focus for a range of issues" in 1981. The same year also saw the foundation of Disabled People's International, a new grouping which urged disabled people to unite in multi-impairment coalitions.[484] The BCODP grew slowly until its first national protest in July 1988 at the Department of Health and Social Security in London. Barbara Lisicki was one of around 2,000 people who attended and remembered it vividly:

> bloody Nicholas Scott (Minister for Disabled People) was holed up in there...Nobody would come out and meet the march, even though they had advance notice of it... People just said 'How dare you treat us with such contempt.' Everybody just sat down and blocked the Elephant and Castle roundabout. It stopped and blocked the traffic. I thought it was enormously powerful.[485]

One of the BCODP's principal aims was to expose and discredit the main "establishment" disability organisations—wealthy disability charities such as RADAR, Mind and Cheshire Homes—and promote instead organisations run and controlled by disabled people, a principle of organisation required of all its affiliates. By the early 1990s, the BCODP claimed to represent 400,000 disabled people.[486] Two protests in 1990 and in 1992 targeted ITV's annual *Telethon* event—a marathon TV fund-raiser criticised for reinforcing patronising stereotypes of disabled people.[487] The second demonstration attracted up to 2,000 protesters[488] and led ultimately to the show's cancellation (although its rival, the BBC's *Children in Need*, continued to thrive).

Smaller scale direct actions followed, in this case by the Direct Action Network (DAN) and the Campaign for Accessible Transport (CAT). Protests began with disabled people queuing at bus stops, and escalated quickly to sit-down blockades of main streets, with activists chaining themselves and their wheelchairs to buses. Some DAN activists embraced "separatism", seeing all non-disabled people as their enemies:

> Disabled people, for our sins, encounter a whole range of people throughout our lives: parents, carers, brothers, sisters, professionals like doctors, nurses, OTs [occupational therapists], social workers—even celebrities who sometimes adopt us...some will be surprised to find out that, not only are they not our allies, but, in fact, are the beast itself.[489]

Despite this background of hostility, the BCODP formed an alliance with the disability charities in 1990. The Disability Benefits Consortium campaigned for new state benefits to compensate for the extra costs of disability. The lobbying clout of the major disability charities proved decisive. A significant new state benefit, Disability Living Allowance, was introduced in April 1992 (immediately prior to a General Election the government feared it might lose) the very success of which made it a target for "reform" 20 years later.

A second alliance—Rights Now!—demanded anti-discrimination legislation similar to the ADA in the US. On this issue at least there was near-universal consensus. Laws against race and sex discrimination had been in place for two decades, but the Conservative administration blocked successive attempts to introduce similar legislation on disability. In May 1994, Minister for Disabled People, Nicholas Scott, talked out another bill as a group of Labour MPs left the Commons chamber for their ex-leader John Smith's funeral.[490] Scott's daughter Vicky, then working for the disability charity RADAR, publicly denounced him and (successfully) demanded his resignation. The government's subsequent U-turn led to the Disability Discrimination Act (DDA) becoming law in 1995. It was the 19th attempt to introduce the legislation.[491]

Narrow in scope and lacking any enforcement agency, the DDA was widely criticised by disability activists (DDA = "Doesn't Do Anything"). The breakthrough nevertheless led figures such as Bert Massie to argue for a focus on amending and enforcing the legislation. Labour leader Tony Blair's pledge to do both effectively neutered the movement. The alliance with charities and New Labour seemed to many the only way to achieve broader social change. Single impairment charities had long been a vital source of welfare support or social networks, while Labour, in opposition for longer than many cared to or could remember, at last looked certain to form a majority government. The disability movement fragmented, and political divisions—previously more or less successfully managed—came to the fore. As Mike Oliver and Colin Barnes later put it:

> [W]e no longer have a strong and powerful disabled people's movement... since the late 1990s the combination of Government and the big charities have successfully adopted the big ideas of the disabled people's movement, usurped its language, and undertaken further initiatives which promise much yet deliver little.[492]

Few figures at the time had an alternative strategy or saw any limitations in civil rights legislation. In 1996 Vic Finkelstein sounded an isolated warning:

> The adoption of Anti-Discrimination Legislation (ADL) is about to drive a wedge through the heart of the disabled community as the artificial alliance promoting ADL predictably falls apart. The disability movement with its adoption of pressure group politics campaigning for this legislation not only followed all the mistakes of yesterday's DIG but is threatening to end up the same way, having started full of enthusiasm and ending up as..."a disappointing affair".[493]

In 2011, an influential critique by Jenny Morris explained how aspirations for more independence and control over disabled people's lives, for example in personal care, have been corrupted and co-opted by successive governments:

we did—when making the case for direct payments—use language which fitted well with the individualist political framework which was becoming more and more dominant. Thus we emphasised disabled people's rights to autonomy and self-determination, which resonated with the Conservative Government's agenda; and drew attention to the way a lack of choice and control could undermine human rights, which then fitted well with New Labour's agenda... The problem is that we seem to have more or less lost the battle for "collective responsibility for welfare" with the rise of an "individualist framework", which—while it started in 1979—gained an increasing hold under New Labour and is rapidly triumphing under the current government.[494]

This problem, of course, is more than one of terminology. In the same year Morris wrote her report, another by Liz Sayce (now chief executive at Disability Rights UK) endorsed—in the name of disability rights—the closure of Remploy factories across Britain, with the loss of over 1,800 jobs.[495] It is this "corporate approach to diversity"[496] which lies behind the enthusiasm of successive governments for direct payments and personalised services, alongside a rhetorical commitment to independent living.

The generalised nature of austerity cuts (in Britain at least) has led to a revival of disability activism. Rights and benefits successfully campaigned for in the 1980s and 1990s are now under systematic attack. This dramatically changed context has prompted recognition of a need for wider alliances. In contrast to its predecessors, who were often indifferent or even hostile to support from the labour movement, Disabled People Against Cuts (DPAC) sought and won affiliation from major national trade unions such as the Public and Commercial Services (PCS) civil service union, the National Union of Teachers and the University and Colleges Union.

DPAC was launched at an anti-cuts demonstration directed at the Conservative Party Conference in Birmingham in October 2010. Along with another new network—Black Triangle (whose title was taken from the symbol identifying disabled prisoners in the Nazi concentration camps)—it has initiated a wide range of local and national actions directed against disability benefit cuts in general and against Atos and Work Capability Assessments in particular.[497] When 80,000 spectators booed Chancellor George Osborne at the Paralympic Games, the campaign against Atos won international attention. The protests finally led to Atos announcing, in March 2014, withdrawal from its contract.[498]

DPAC organised support for Remploy workers taking strike action against factory closures in 2012. Its policy statement begins: "DPAC is about disabled people and their allies" and goes on to say:

> DPAC is for everyone who believes that disabled people should have full human rights and equality. It is for everyone that refuses to accept that any country can destroy the lives of people just because they are or become disabled or sick. It is for everyone against government austerity measures which target the poor while leaving the wealthy unscathed.[499]

The emergence of alliances such as DPAC with its outward-looking perspective is timely and hugely encouraging. Its forces, however, are tiny, particularly when compared to the challenges it faces. The prospects for disabled people in Britain and elsewhere remain grim, with governments determined to pass on the costs of austerity and economic failure to their respective populations for many more years. In Britain, this has already led to reports showing a general rise in scapegoating and discrimination.[500]

The disability movement's slogans, such as "nothing about me without me" or "rights not charity", and principles such as empowerment or independent living for individuals, partly reflect the isolation and limited power of disabled people to effect change on their own. As a small minority in society, hindered by a range of additional obstacles to their participation in political activity, it is clear that disabled people cannot defeat these attacks or win fundamental social change without being part of a more powerful force.

Disability arts

Virtuous or heroic characteristics have long been associated in culture with beauty and athleticism, while evil or villainous traits have likewise been linked to physically deformed and disabled people. This context has informed debate around the increased involvement of disabled people in different areas of arts or culture in recent years. For some, this is a political issue: if someone's work is "informed directly or indirectly by their experiences as a disabled person, then it makes clear sense for them to identify as a disabled artist".[501] Many others, however, "abhor the thought of making Disability Art" and want their work to be seen on its own merits rather than treated differently.[502]

The marketing campaign and title of *The Undateables*, a popular UK Channel 4 TV series about the dating fortunes of people with a diverse range of impairments, deliberately utilised disability stereotypes, even if the content of the programmes themselves were often less offensive.[503] Another area of controversy is "cripping up"—a term used to describe non-disabled performers portraying disabled characters. Disabled actors on the other hand, are unlikely to be allocated more than a narrow range of roles, almost always as disabled characters.

Comedy has been a particularly fruitful area for disabled artists in the UK, with particularly successful acts such as Francesca Martinez, Laurence Clark, Lee Ridley and the Abnormally Funny People group. In her own work Seaneen Molloy draws on her experiences of mental distress, which for her, far from being abnormal, "just exaggerates experiences that everybody goes through". Clare Allan, in a similar vein, sees comedy "as a means of exploring and coping with difficult subjects":

> Comedy is...a means of connecting. If you make a joke and I laugh at it, this is an act of recognition: we have something in common. For many people, the thought of having anything at all in common with someone with mental health problems is deeply concerning. Humour can be a means of staying afloat, of transcending adversity, even. Spike

Milligan, who suffered from bipolar disorder, (and others) put it: "Blessed are the cracked for they let in the light".[504]

These debates reflect the contradictory way in which disability's profile in culture and the arts has developed. They express both a degree of change and also the fact that disability is still a "special interest" issue that is chronically under-represented in the media and in culture in general. The Edinburgh Festival Fringe is one of the world's most diverse and inclusive events for the arts. Its summer 2015 programme featured over 3,300 shows including record numbers of disabled artists and performers. However, it was far less inclusive for audiences: only half of the listed festival venues were wheelchair accessible, one in ten shows had hearing loops installed, and only 47 performances were signed.[505]

Sometimes it seems very much a case of one step forward and two steps back. The climate of austerity has impacted negatively on the arts as it has on many other areas. Arts Council England (ACE) announced a fall in the number of disabled-led organisations it supports from April 2015, leaving the latter with less than 0.5 percent of ACE funding as a whole.[506]

Disability has also been used by non-disabled artists in different and often controversial ways. Otto Dix, for example, painted the damaged bodies of German soldiers as grotesque to attack what he saw as a capitalist war machine. In several of his plays, Samuel Beckett deprives his characters of movement to varying degrees:

> In *Happy Days*, Winnie spends the first half of the play buried up to her waist in sand and the second half up to her neck (similar to spinal injury). Her happy days are social or interpersonal events. In *Murphy*, the hero seeks solace in a rocking chair 'to free his mind.' In the third novel of his trilogy, *The Unnameable*, the narrator spends all his time, devoid of movement or bodily feeling, in a container. Life is endured without question or complaint.[507]

In a more positive vein, Tom Shakespeare has observed how the experience of impairment can sometimes open up new possibilities. David Hockney said his deafness enabled him to more effectively concentrate on the visual. The famous cut-out shapes Henri Matisse produced in his later years were necessitated by his failing health, as was true of the final works of Francisco Goya and Paul Klee. The latter said of himself, he "has found his style when he cannot do otherwise." As Shakespeare concludes: "the challenges of old age and impairment can spark new creativity and resourcefulness".[508]

Conclusion

The slogan "rights not charity", first seen on a national British march of the blind in 1920, expresses memorably and clearly the desire for disabled people to exercise control over their lives instead of being the objects of "able-bodied" charities which are in practice unaccountable to the impairment groups on whose behalf they claim to act.

As we have seen, however, the distinctions between organisations for and of disabled people are often blurred and disability charities have sometimes supported specific campaigns to secure or to defend benefits and services. Disabled people have in recent decades joined their staff, even becoming their chief executives.[509] In the case of the Spinal Injuries Association, its users have run the organisation since its formation in 1973.[510] One of Britain's biggest ever protests of disabled people and their supporters was organised by the disability charities (mainly the same as those which joined the earlier alliances of the 1990s). Among the 5,000 people who attended the Hardest Hit March in May 2011 were significant delegations from the PCS, Unison and GMB trade unions. Many grassroots organisations of disabled people, in contrast, largely avoid a political stance, adopting a role as service providers and in many cases actually are registered as charities. Indeed, a chronic lack of resources forced the BCODP itself to apply for charitable status in order to survive.[511]

Disability charities promote stereotypes of disabled people as needy and tragic victims in order to generate income. Although pressure from disability activists has led to improvements in their image and operations, they remain businesses that compete for private or state contracts to provide their services. The reliance of charities on increasingly scarce government funding for much of their income encourages a commitment to negotiating or endorsing the status quo rather than confronting it. A long-running publicity campaign by Scope, titled *End the Awkward*, focuses on inappropriate individual behaviour towards disabled people—arguably a relatively minor problem in the context of government attacks on disability-related benefits and services.[512] The popular UK charity Comic Relief, meanwhile, was recently exposed for its large investments in shares in arms and tobacco firms.[513]

It is possible to make some generalisations from the international experience. In many countries, the distinct needs of particular impairment groups led to their separation from wider society. Residential schools and institutions run by charities or state agencies, particularly for blind or deaf people, brought them together to be educated or trained to join the workforce. This also provided groups with a sense of identity. Social clubs set up by school attendees evolved from networks of friends and mutual support groups into organisations taking up economic and policy issues, creating the basis for the disability movement. This history of simultaneous bringing together and separation is common to many countries and partly explains why disability movements often comprise a relatively small and narrow section of the disabled population.

Wheelchair users, many of whom had experienced life in institutions during the post-war decades, comprised the single largest impairment group in each of the disability movements discussed above. In the case of UPIAS, Vic Finkelstein saw "good historical reasons" as to why this was the case:

> They tended to be less isolated and so had greater awareness of significant social changes that were already taking place in the health and welfare services as well as political struggles and the general state of the economy. Many had been able-bodied and were familiar with social movements.[514]

The tensions between struggle for legal reform and for wider social transformation have sooner or later asserted themselves in every social movement. The anti-racist and women's movements were stymied and split by the compromises involved in the parliamentary reforms they helped achieve, as was the disability movement which followed in their footsteps. The leaders of these struggles rarely saw their fortunes as linked to workers' movements, reinforcing the sense of a social group with distinct and separate interests. Disability activists for the most part saw their struggle as about civil or human rights and were hostile to any wider class identity. Inevitably, other identities based on gender, race and sexuality—often treated as mutually exclusive—came to the fore.[515] This move towards individual rights also coincided with—and helped to disguise—a simultaneous move on the part of governments away from genuine social reform towards cuts in benefits and service provision.

The above observations aside, this highly selective summary demonstrates that where disabled people have been able to organise for themselves, they have exerted an influence on national and even international policy as well as on wider perceptions of disability. As in the case of China, national governments have initiated their own programmes and laws to address the costs as well as economic potential of their own disabled populations. In all cases, the severe limitations of disability rights legislation points to a need for more fundamental social and economic change. The experience of VIKO in Russia almost a century ago provides a glimpse of what might be possible when revolutionary movements address their potential to root out all forms of oppression.

Treatment for mental distress: crude devices used in the eighteenth and nineteenth centuries did not offer any real relief. Depressed patients were spun at high speeds in the circulating swing (top left). The Tranquilizing Chair (top right) was invented in 1769 as treatment for mania, by US doctor Benjamin Rush, considered the father of modern psychiatry. The crib (bottom) was widely used to restrain violent patients. (Image from http://bipolarworld.net/Bipolar20%Disorder/History/hist12.htm)

Shell-shocked British soldier in the trenches of the First World War.

Blind people marching, UK, 1920. Note the banner slogan: "Justice not Charity."

Eugenics was mainstream in US culture: cartoon from *New York Tribune*, 10 November 1921.

Nazi eugenics propaganda poster. Text reads: "This person suffering from hereditary defects costs the community 60,000 Reichsmarks during his lifetime. Fellow German that is your money too."

Hitler greets disabled veterans, Berlin, March 1939.

Deaf students at the Capitol building during their occupation at Gallaudet University, Washington DC, March 1988.

Greek demonstration against cuts hitting disabled people, October 2013; banner reads: "We demand a life with dignity—we are not begging." Photo: Stelios Michailidis/Workers Solidarity

This satirical cartoon about our education system is often accompanied by a quote attributed to Albert Einstein: "Everyone is a genius. But if you judge a fish by its ability to climb a tree, it will spend the rest of its life thinking that it is stupid."

Advertisement for a self-propelled wheelchair from 1910. Wheelchairs were very expensive to buy, and poorer parents often made their own DIY versions in order to help their children become mobile.

10.
Mental distress— not all in the mind

All the people like us are We, and everyone else is They
—RUDYARD KIPLING, We and They[516]

In every cry of every Man,
In every Infants cry of fear,
In every voice: in every ban,
The mind-forg'd manacles I hear
—WILLIAM BLAKE, London

For most of the time, the lives of the vast majority of people under capitalism are characterised by a lack of power and control, a situation which Marx saw as rooted in alienated labour. The despair, frustration and isolation this breeds, especially when combined with poverty and inequality, are the key factors giving rise to mental distress.[517] If much mental distress is caused by our lack of control over what happens in society, then—as the evidence suggests—the prospect of and the struggle for social change can also put an end to a lot of that distress.

Marx described commodity fetishism as the process whereby the products of human labour confront workers as alien entities, imbued with a status constantly denied to most humans. Nightly news bulletins report on the relative health of the stock markets, which have, we are told, had a good or a bad day. On the rare occasions mental distress is discussed, diagnostic labels and medications are given primary importance while the actual experiences of those directly affected are disregarded as subjective or of little value.

Impairments impacting on mental function are perhaps the most feared and stigmatised of all.[518] In areas such as housing, education and employment, mentally distressed people are one of the most deprived social groups. Almost 90 percent are unemployed—the lowest rate of employment across all disability categories.[519]

Much discussion of what is usually referred to as "mental illness" focuses on its economic rather than its human cost. The *Financial Times* reported that 15.2 million days of sickness absence in the UK in 2013 were due to stress, anxiety or depression—significantly higher than the 11.8 million days lost in 2010. The OECD estimated the cost to the British economy at £70 billion a year in productivity losses, higher benefit payments and increased NHS spending.[520]

Some 60 percent of employers say they would not hire someone with a "mental health condition".[521] A similar proportion in a 2010 survey said any such person should be kept in a psychiatric hospital. Further research a year later found that 77 percent of people believed that "mental illness is an illness like any other".[522] These contrasting findings reflect a widespread ambivalence towards those affected by mental distress.

A common theme that is at least implicit in government and social policy as well as in media coverage is that those with "mental health problems" must be controlled by means of either compulsory detention or powerful mind-controlling drugs. With their impairments largely invisible, mentally distressed people are treated as "least deserving" of support, identified on the one hand as benefit "cheats" or "scroungers"[523] and on the other as psychopaths posing a danger to others.[524] The power of these stereotypes, despite plentiful evidence to refute them, serves to divert attention from cuts in mental health services and to reinforce the isolation of those directly affected. For those in this disparate, isolated and woefully misunderstood social minority, scapegoating and prejudice often present a greater obstacle than the original problems.

Debates on the issue are often highly polarised, provoking strong emotions. Psychiatric and psychological treatments alike have many supporters as well as enemies. This is partly due to people's hugely varied experiences of drugs or therapies. The diversity in outcomes has led to a wide range of views about the value and role of drugs and the drug companies, and of mental health services.

Who is affected by mental distress?

Record numbers of people across the world are experiencing mental distress. A key UK report said in 2014: "Among people under 65... nearly as much ill health is mental illness as all physical illnesses put together".[525] The number of prescriptions for antidepressants has increased sharply across the economically advanced countries. For example in Spain and Portugal (two of the countries hardest hit by the financial crisis of 2008) their use rose by over 20 percent in the five years to 2013.[526]

In 1987, one in every 184 Americans was receiving social security disability insurance payments for "mental illness". By 2007, this figure had risen to one in 76.[527] According to the WHO, the US has the highest prevalence of mental distress of any country with 26.4 percent of the population thought to have a diagnosable disorder. China, its nearest rival, is expected to claim the title soon, along with the more welcome one of the world's largest economy.[528]

This increase is most commonly attributed to greater accuracy in diagnosis and to the success of safer and more effective drugs in treating the chemical brain imbalances seen to be responsible for poor mental health. Critics argue that the growth in mental "disorders" is due to an alliance of psychiatry and the drug companies and driven by profit and a desire to control. They maintain that many behaviours classified as "mental illness" really express unhappiness and alienation. The answer may well involve a combination of these factors as well as a rise in distress due to worsening social and economic conditions.

What counts as mental distress? Scull, who prefers the more controversial term "madness", provides a useful (if somewhat uncritical) summary of the range:

> Those who lose control of their emotions, whether melancholic or manic; those who do not share the commonsense reality most of us perceive, who hallucinate or make claims about their existence people

around them conclude are delusions; those who act in ways that are profoundly at variance with the conventions and expectations of their culture, and are heedless of the ordinary corrective measures their community mobilises to get them to desist; those who manifest extremes of extravagance and incoherence, or who exhibit the denuded mental life of the demented.[529]

Not everyone is equally at risk. People with long-term health conditions are two to three times more likely to experience mental distress. There is a high level of "co-morbidity" between depression, anxiety and dementia, for example, and common physical illnesses such as cardiovascular diseases, diabetes, chronic obstructive pulmonary disease and musculoskeletal disorders.[530] About a third of people diagnosed as physically ill would also be diagnosed with "mental illness".[531]

Mental distress costs lives. Figures show that seriously mentally distressed people die 15 to 25 years earlier than others.[532] In a recent UK survey, nearly a third of mentally distressed people said that stigma had made them want to give up on life, while 80 percent said they had experienced discrimination.[533] Part of this stigma is due to the way in which people are reduced to their diagnostic labels, with complex problems crudely reduced to single causes. Anorexia, for example, is commonly attributed to an irrational desire among girls and young women to look thin:

Eating disorders are the only mental illness that people still assume is caused by something identifiable and external. No sensible person would ask anyone why they became schizophrenic, why they suffer from clinical depression. But eating disorders are different, and this is partly because of the behaviour of those who suffer from them. In the grip of the disorder, your world shrinks to the size of a pinhole: your brain fixates entirely on weight, calories; and, if you're underweight, being so cold it feels like you have icicles for bones... So why did I stop eating? Because I was unhappy. Because I didn't know how to express it vocally. Because I didn't understand I was allowed to respond to my own needs. Because I was scared of growing up. The specific causes of eating disorders are varied, but those factors are pretty common.[534]

People aged 15-44 are the age group most likely to suffer mental distress.[535] A UK government census in 2005 found that "black men and mixed race men are three or four times more likely than the general population to be admitted to a psychiatric unit. Women from the same groups are two or more times more likely to be admitted." Black men are also more likely to be sectioned under the Mental Health Act and for longer than their white counterparts.[536] UK immigrants, many of whom also face chronic poverty and discrimination as well as social isolation, are more likely to experience psychosis and schizophrenia but less likely to be able to access services.[537]

> US teenager Leelah Alcorn killed herself on 28 December 2014 after being subjected to "transgender conversion therapy". She ended her suicide note pleading: "My death needs to be counted in the number of transgender people who commit suicide this year. I want someone to look at that number and say 'that's fucked up' and fix it. Fix society. Please." In the United States, 40 percent of transgender people attempt suicide, compared to 4.6 percent of the general population, and up to 20 percent for lesbian, gay and bisexual adults.[538]

As with physical ill health, mental distress is linked to social class. In 2014 a report for the WHO found that of 115 studies "on common mental disorders and poverty in low-and middle-income countries… over 70 percent reported positive associations between a variety of poverty measures and common mental disorders." Analysis of eight former Soviet Union countries identified "higher levels of psychological distress among women than men, and associations with social and economic factors including poverty, unemployment, low education, disability, lack of trust in people, and lack of personal support".[539]

Inequality in the UK and elsewhere has widened enormously in recent decades and evidence has linked this directly to health: the more extreme the level of inequality in any given country, the worse the general health of the population.[540] As one writer was able to conclude as early as 1996:

> A very simple statement will serve to summarise all the research findings on this matter: for nearly every kind of disease, illness or

disability, "physical" and "mental", poorer people are afflicted more than richer people; more often, more seriously and for longer—unless of course they die from the condition, which they do at an earlier age.[541]

Stressing the importance of social and economic factors is not, of course, to deny that biological factors may play a role in certain psychotic conditions, as they clearly do in organic conditions such as epilepsy or Alzheimer's disease.[542]

Defining mental distress

The belief that mental distress is a disease of the brain can be traced back to the ancient Greek and Roman physicians Galen and Hippocrates. They saw the body's health as determined by the balance of four interrelated "humours" (blood, phlegm, yellow bile and black bile) which were in turn influenced by factors such as diet, exercise or emotional trauma. The key to good health was keeping the humours in equilibrium, so "when the patient fell ill, the physician's task was to deduce what had become unbalanced and to use the therapies at his disposal to readjust the patient's internal state".[543]

This view of human health explicitly rejected any idea that the causes of illness were divine or supernatural. It also made sense of symptoms without any sharp distinction between physical and mental health and sickness. This biomedical understanding of the body and the brain became the dominant ideology of medical science, remaining virtually unamended until the end of the 18th century and, in its essentials, remains mainstream medical opinion today.

Ancient Roman methods, such as "bleeding" patients or ducking them in cold water, were widely used until the mid-19th century.[544] Other invasive or "shock" physical treatments remained the dominant practice until the 1950s. The prefrontal leucotomy, involving the removal of part of the brain, was introduced in the 1930s, as was insulin coma therapy, but both methods were rapidly discredited and abandoned. Electroconvulsive therapy (ECT), when first used in the 1940s, caused spinal fractures and broken bones. The use of anaesthetics and muscle relaxants overcame these problems and ECT remains today both hugely controversial and in regular use.[545]

The first psychiatric drugs were developed due to scientific breakthroughs in physical medicine. Improved anaesthetics, sedatives, antihistamines and anticonvulsants affected the central nervous system in different ways. Side effects were identified in some of these drugs as being beneficial for psychiatric conditions, leading to their development in the early 1950s as the first antipsychotics. Politicians and scientists celebrated this unintended outcome as the first step in a new "mental health revolution" centred on drugs in place of physical treatments. Surely these successes in general medicine could be repeated in the field of psychiatry? Could drugs conquer "mental illness" in the same way as they had defeated so much physical illness?

The *Diagnostic and Statistical Manual* (*DSM*) and the *International Statistical Classification of Diseases and Related Health Problems* (produced by the WHO) provide the mental health and related industries with definitions of mental disorders. The first *DSM* appeared in 1952 in response to demands for a guide to diagnose US military servicemen.[546] Robert H Felix, Director of the new US National Institute for Mental Health (NIMH), explained the reasons for the manual's emphasis on social factors:

> mental and emotional disorders are associated with difficulties in meeting life's problems... Because of special circumstances, however, the problems may be especially difficult and not capable of satisfactory solution. In any case, the mental disturbances represent an attempt at adjustment that is inadequate and that generally produces more problems than it solves.[547]

Other social factors were soon to exert a more direct influence on what appeared in the manual. From the late 1960s, gay rights activists campaigned to remove homosexuality as a mental disorder in the *DSM* under the category of sexual deviance. The issue was settled in April 1973 by a referendum of American Psychiatric Association (APA) members.[548] Vietnam War veterans, in contrast, organised to demand that Post-Traumatic Stress Disorder (PTSD) be added to the manual. Their successful protests—galvanised by huge public opposition to the war—were further politicised by the US authorities' refusal to recognise the atrocities soldiers had witnessed (or perpetrated). Veterans used research on Holocaust survivors and a team working with burns victims that identified similarities in many symptoms, including flashbacks and survivor guilt.[549]

As the struggles and movements of the 1960s and 1970s receded, the biomedical approach to mental distress returned with a vengeance. The *DSM* developed as an anti-intellectual checklist of psychiatric diagnosis, using symptoms agreed by committee and linked to treatment with a particular class of drugs. "Indeed, soon enough the polarity would be reversed, and the creation of a new class of drugs would lead to the creation of a new psychiatric 'disease' to match".[550] Constant criticism and revision, not to say scandal, has led to cumulatively larger and more complex manuals. Definitions became increasingly technical, with greater emphasis on the individual. As the latest edition, *DSM-5*, published in 2013, puts it:

> A mental disorder is a syndrome characterized by clinically significant disturbance in an individual's cognition, emotion regulation, or behavior that reflects a dysfunction in the psychological, biological, or developmental processes underlying mental functioning. Mental disorders are usually associated with significant distress in social, occupational, or other important activities. An expectable or culturally approved response to a common stressor or loss, such as the death of a loved one, is not a mental disorder. Socially deviant behavior (eg, political, religious, or sexual) and conflicts that are primarily between the individual and society are not mental disorders unless the deviance or conflict results from a dysfunction in the individual, as described above.[551]

The "psychiatric bible" continues to further entrench the power and profits of the pharmaceutical companies.[552] With its classifications treated as a global standard, psychologists and psychiatrists in the US and other countries are obliged to give *DSM* diagnoses in order to obtain payment from their patients' medical insurance schemes. Researchers in search of industry funding must use *DSM* categories and definitions.[553] These diagnostic categories and definitions arise in turn, not from scientific discovery but from agreement by committee, itself the product of social pressures.

A review in business magazine *The Economist* described *DSM-5* as "a vehicle for misdiagnosis, overdiagnosis, the medicalisation of normal behaviour and the prescription of a large number of unnecessary drugs".[554] Another reviewer saw the *DSM*'s approach as based on the belief that "recognised varieties of mental illness should neatly sort themselves into tidy blocks, in the way that plants and animals do".[555] NIMH, the world's biggest funder of mental health research, announced in 2013 that it would no longer[556] use the *DSM* when deciding what to fund. As its director Thomas Insel explained: "*DSM* diagnoses are based on a consensus about clusters of clinical symptoms, not any objective laboratory measure."

The challenge of anti-psychiatry

Soon after the end of the Second World War, a series of exposés condemned inhumane conditions in US mental hospitals. Albert Deutsch, who had visited Nazi concentration camps, famously compared them with asylum wards in his 1948 book, *Shame of the States*:

> As I passed through some of Byberry's wards, I was reminded of the Nazi concentration camps at Belsen and Buchenwald. I entered buildings swarming with naked humans herded like cattle and treated with less concern, pervaded by a fetid odor so heavy, so nauseating, that the stench seemed to have almost a physical existence of its own. I saw hundreds of patients living under leaking roofs, surrounded by moldy, decaying walls, and sprawling on rotting floors for want of seats or benches.[557]

Erving Goffman's book *Asylums* (1961) echoed this comparison, arguing that the crucial factor creating mental patients was the institution, not the illness. He denounced institutions as ineffective, anti-therapeutic "brain-washing machines" where staff completely controlled and infantilised patients.

Three more influential books published between 1960 and 1961 also questioned the legitimacy of psychiatric theory and practice, albeit from very different perspectives: Michel Foucault's *Madness and Civilisation*,[558] R D Laing's *The Divided Self* and Thomas Szasz's *The Myth of Mental Illness*. This politically diverse current of opinion formed the basis for what became known as the anti-psychiatry movement. Associated in particular with dissident psychiatrists Szasz and Laing, anti-psychiatry remained highly popular until the end of the 1970s. This remarkable development—medical practitioners challenging the scientific basis of their discipline—is unique to the psychiatric profession.

Szasz shared Goffmann's view that "mental illness" did not exist, but his rejection of psychiatry was based on libertarian conservatism, more akin to a moral crusade. He later allied himself with L Ron Hubbard's Church of Scientology, forming the Citizens Commission on Human Rights to expose psychiatry's crimes and abuses.[559] Hubbard himself argued that every "institutional psychiatrist" should be "arraigned and convicted of extortion, mayhem and murder".[560]

Among this group, British writer R D Laing was most celebrated at the time, in both the US and his own country. In *The Divided Self* Laing rejected the idea that schizophrenia was a disease, describing it instead not only as the product of a disturbed family life, but also as an existential fight for personal freedom. The seemingly nonsensical monologues of psychoses, he argued, expressed in distorted form a struggle to cope with and make sense of an unbearable environment.

Laing appealed to a generation of young workers and students influenced by the new social movements of the 1960s and opposition to the war in Vietnam. As Laing's fame increased, his ideas became increasingly chaotic and inconsistent. By the mid-1960s, he had adopted the view that psychosis could be both a rational reaction to an irrational world and a positive, transcendental journey. He helped found the Philadelphia Association, which set up over 20 therapeutic communities throughout England, most famously at Kingsley Hall community centre in East London. Here, staff and patients assumed equal status, the use of medication was voluntary and that of psychedelic drugs frequent.[561] What is still known as "schizophrenia"—memorably described by Peter Sedgwick as "a rudimentary dustbin category for a variety of psychic ills which may have little logically or biologically in common"[562]—was the sole focus of Laing's work. His solidarity with those so labelled was only one factor in his mutual if brief flirtation with the political left.

The ideas of anti-psychiatry achieved wider popularity in 1973 after a famous experiment by US psychologist David Rosenhan. Eight volunteers agreed to present at 12 different mental hospitals and report hearing voices. All were admitted, with seven subsequently diagnosed with schizophrenia and one with manic depression—even though after admission all had been told to behave normally. Although none of the staff spotted the imposters, patients sometimes did. As one said; "You're not crazy. You're a journalist, or a professor...checking up on the hospital".[563] All researchers were eventually released, after detentions lasting up to 52 days, with a label of "schizophrenic in remission". Following the public sensation caused by his results, Rosenhan accepted the challenge from a leading research and teaching hospital which had been most critical of his work to repeat the experiment. Over a three-month period, staff identified 41 fakes among 193 new patients—but this time no volunteers had been sent.[564]

Hollywood echoed the anti-psychiatric mood. The film *One Flew Over the Cuckoo's Nest*, based on Ken Kesey's bestselling 1962 novel, appeared in 1975 and won all five major Academy Awards:

> Here was a damning portrait of the mental hospital and those who ran it. The patients are victims of the mental health machine, not of their psychopathologies. The hospital is an inhuman environment that damages and destroys. Psychiatric treatment is at best punishment, whether in the form of the dehumanizing group therapy sessions sadistically employed to destroy patients' sense of self, or in the convulsions produced by the electroshock machine that are used to punish misbehaviour. At worst, as with the lobotomy visited upon the otherwise indomitable character of Randle P McMurphy, played by Jack Nicholson, it is a device to tame, to eliminate the individual, by reducing him to a human vegetable. Psychiatry...the ultimate means of enforcing conformity.[565]

In 1978, following campaigns by the *Psychiatria Democratica* movement, the Italian government outlawed all further admissions to its large psychiatric hospitals. Over the next 12 years, a network of smaller community mental health clinics replaced the old system. Franco Basaglia, the dissident psychiatrist who founded *Psychiatria Democratica*, had first made his name by transforming the Gorizia asylum in northeast Italy. This allowed patients free movement, banning all restraints and coercive treatment and setting up a programme of discharges. Basaglia's view was that mental distress was rooted in social adversity, the "political dialectical inability" of patients to face up to the contradictions of reality.[566]

From 1971 to 1980, sales of psychiatric drugs in the US fell from 233 million drugstore prescriptions to 153 million[567] and the proportion of medical school graduates studying psychiatry dropped from 11 to less than 4 percent.[568] Anti-psychiatry's success reflected the huge social struggles of the period, which led millions of people to see the main priority as changing the world rather than the individual. The demise of these wider struggles also led to the decline of anti-psychiatry. Its influence, however, led to a revision of committal practices and encouraged a more flexible and nuanced approach to disease labels, with many of its criticisms absorbed and incorporated into mainstream psychiatric practice.

Big Pharma

By 1955, an estimated two million patients in the US alone were taking the first "anti-psychotic" drug, Thorazine. Its success prompted each of the pharmaceutical companies to develop marginally different versions of the drug that they could patent as their own—establishing a pattern that has been repeated many times since.

Academics and scientists involved in drugs research are routinely obliged to sign gagging clauses that prevent publication, analysis or even discussion of trials data without permission.[569] Those who protest risk having research funding withdrawn and their careers wrecked. New drugs are often tested against a dummy placebo or poor competitor—or against a strong competitor at an excessively low or high dose.[570] Only half of all drug trials are published: those with negative results are twice as likely to go missing as those with positive ones. This means that the evidence on which medical decisions are based systematically overstates the benefit of drug treatments.[571] In 2012 GlaxoSmithKline (GSK) was fined US$3 billion (the biggest fine imposed on any drug firm in US history) to settle charges of illegal drug promotion, failure to report safety data and false price reporting.[572] GSK had withheld research findings about its drug Paroxetine showing an increased risk of suicide among children who received it.[573]

The drugs industry also uses front organisations to drown out dissenting voices. In 2009, the US National Alliance on Mental Illness was forced to disclose that it had received 56 percent of its funding from pharmaceutical companies.[574] This kind of sponsorship would not have been a financial burden:

> The global pharmaceuticals market is worth US$300 billion a year, a figure expected to rise to US$400 billion within three years. The 10 largest drugs companies control over one-third of this market, several with sales of more than US$10 billion a year and profit margins of about 30 percent. Six are based in the United States and four in Europe. It is predicted that North and South America, Europe and Japan will continue to account for a full 85 percent of the global pharmaceuticals market well into the 21st century. Companies currently spend one-third of all sales revenue on marketing their products—roughly twice what they spend on research and development.[575]

These are stupendous sums. Even in the UK, where the medical profession receives more independent, publicly funded information than in many other countries, promotional spending by pharmaceutical companies is 50 times greater than that for public information on health. As the APA president lamented in 2005: "As a profession, we have allowed the biopsychosocial model [of mental illness] to become the bio-bio-bio model... Drug company representatives bearing gifts are frequent visitors to psychiatrists' offices and consulting rooms... We should have the wisdom and distance to call these gifts what they are—kickbacks and bribes".[576]

Do the drugs work?

It is a remarkable fact that the huge increases in the sales of drugs for mental distress bear little relation to their success in treating the conditions for which they are prescribed. Even where drugs are successful, this is often based on guesswork:

> A patient may end up taking a drug indicated for a different diagnosis, or a cocktail of pills—one to quell his hallucinations, one to temper his agitation, one to relieve his depression, and one to help him sleep—and the combination may change monthly or even weekly, or it may work for a while and then stop. No one will be able to explain why that happened, any more than they will be able to explain how the drugs worked in the first place.[577]

Sales of Thorazine and the new antidepressants, as they became known, made pharmaceutical firms "the darlings of Wall Street".[578] Soon after Valium's arrival in 1963, "mother's little helper" became a huge bestseller across the Western world.[579] Outpatient sales of antidepressants and antipsychotics increased almost 50-fold in the US between 1985 and 1998.[580]

Research from as early as 1958, compiled from 68 US and European studies, showed no overall improvement in outcomes over the previous half-century—including the first years of the new "wonder drugs". The same study also found that "patients recovered less well during periods of economic recession than during periods of economic boom".[581] Later evidence showed that prescription drugs provided minor symptom relief in the short term, but risked tolerance, dependency and withdrawal (often mistaken for relapse) in long-term users. Patients became less able to do without and withdrawal was shown to be often difficult or dangerous—especially if done abruptly instead of gradually. A major 1997 study found that half of those who stopped their antidepressant medication relapsed within 14 months, a rate which increased according to how long someone had been on the drug. As one speaker at the 2008 American Psychiatric Association AGM put it in relation to antidepressants: "Can fifty thousand psychiatrists be wrong? I think that the answer is yes, probably".[582]

In 2001, NIMH showed that antipsychotics, antidepressants and other psychotropic drugs, when taken over a period of time, disrupted the workings of the brain. Medication can actually turn an acute episodic condition into a lifelong chronic condition:

> Prior to treatment, patients diagnosed with schizophrenia, depression, and other psychiatric disorders do not suffer from any "chemical imbalance." However, once a person is put on a psychiatric medication, which, in one manner or another, throws a wrench into the usual mechanics of a neuronal pathway, his or her brain starts to function...abnormally.[583]

Further NIMH research in 2007 found that medicated patients had one-eighth the recovery rate of unmedicated patients and were three times more likely to do badly in the long term.[584]

Two international studies carried out over 25 years for the WHO provided even more startling results. People diagnosed with schizophrenia living in Colombia, India and Nigeria—where drugs are rarely available—had significantly longer periods of remission and higher levels of social functioning than those living in Denmark, Taiwan or the US.[585] Other evidence showed that Eastern Europe, parts of North Africa and the Middle East have higher rates of depression than North America and Western Europe.[586] So on the one hand, the incidence of mental distress is probably higher in the Global South than in the more economically advanced countries, but on the other recovery rates in the former are better. These differences expose as a myth the notion that life is simpler and less stressful in poorer parts of the world.[587]

There are other reasons as to why genetic factors are less likely to be responsible for mental distress than previously supposed. A gene responsible for producing specific proteins may be more or less active (and so produce more or less of that protein) depending on environmental influences.[588] Similarly, inherited characteristics may make some people more likely to experience psychosis, but it is the experience of hardship, abuse or trauma which would trigger any such incidence. As Tom Insel, Director of NIMH since 2002, recently commented: "Whatever we've been doing for five decades, it ain't working...the numbers of suicides, numbers of disabilities, mortality data—it's abysmal, and it's not getting any better".[589]

Manufacturing illness?

The symptoms of depression have been described with remarkable consistency since the time of Galen and Hippocrates, when they were known as "melancholia." But it is only in recent decades that it has become widely seen or treated as an illness. When a new antidepressant was developed in the mid-1950s by a Swiss psychiatrist, the pharmaceutical company Geigy at first refused to back the drug's development in the belief that the market for it was too small.[590]

Japan provides a good example of how the drug companies created a mass market for antidepressants. When the *DSM* category of depression was first introduced there in 1982, it was widely rejected as a meaningful mental illness. Japanese psychiatrists had focused principally on *utsobyô*—chronic and severe mental illness—at the time considered to be very rare. A capacity to experience great sadness was seen as a national characteristic and a mark of strength and distinction.

This began to change in 1991, following the highly publicised suicide of a young city worker employed by Dentsu, Japan's biggest advertising agency. The company's lawyers argued that his suicide was due to a pre-existing mental weakness, but legal evidence revealed frequent bullying and overtime averaging 47 hours a week. The Supreme Court ruled that workplace stress had led to his depression, with Dentsu liable for the death. Western researchers responded to the verdict by pointing to high suicide rates in the 1990s as proof of an epidemic of depression.[591]

Concern about mood disorders and high suicide rates mounted through the recession of the 1990s. The Kobe earthquake in 1995 boosted the notion that Japan was behind the times on mental health. A coalition of US drug companies co-operated to break open the market, attacking Japanese testing and other practices as "junk science". Their new adverts called depression *kokoro no kaze*, a "cold of the soul". This effective metaphor suggested a commonplace illness, non-stigmatising and less severe than until then believed.

The drug companies promoted bestselling books and articles in academic journals, creating and funding advocacy groups ostensibly set up by patients. A leading business magazine ran a 26-page cover story advising people to seek help with depression. Reflecting the themes of almost a century previously, the article suggested that the most talented and hard-working employees were most susceptible to depression.[592] All this led to a dramatic shift in public opinion. In the first year of its Japanese launch, sales of leading antidepressant Paxil were over US$100 million. By 2008, these had increased to US$1 billion per year.[593]

Watters shows how the type and character of mental distress is shaped by specific social contexts:

> [D]elusional guilt is most often associated with Judeo-Christian cultures, as are religious hallucinations such as hearing the voice of god. Such hallucinations are rarer in Islamic, Hindu, and Buddhist populations. Schizophrenic patients from Pakistan are more likely to have visual hallucinations of ghosts and spirits than are British schizophrenics, who are more prone to hearing persecuting voices. In traditional Southeast Asian villages, where it is often frowned upon to strive wilfully for personal status, delusions of grandeur are rare. In the United States, where celebrity, wealth, and power are popular fetishes, people with schizophrenia commonly believe they are famous or all-powerful... Those living in urban settings in the US and Europe appear to suffer more from the disease than those living in the country or the suburbs.[594]

There is also significant variation in how people express mental distress across different cultures:

> A Nigerian man might experience a culturally distinct form of depression by describing a peppery feeling in his head. A rural Chinese farmer might speak only of shoulder or stomach-aches. A man in India might talk of semen loss or a sinking heart or feeling hot. A Korean might talk of tightness in the chest, and an American Indian might describe the experience of depression as something akin to loneliness.[595]

Other examples Watters provides, such as the rise of anorexia in Hong Kong and attempts by Western aid agencies to impose the concept of Post-Traumatic Stress Disorder on post-tsunami Sri Lanka[596] also demonstrate how perceptions, diagnosis and treatment of mental distress are influenced by social norms.

There are contrary trends too. Even in Western countries many people never contact mental health services because their experiences—which others may find strange—are not distressing to them. Up to 10 percent of the general population hear voices at some point in their life. While for many people such experiences are very distressing, for others their voices say relatively neutral, pleasant or even helpful things. In Islam, such voices are not seen as abnormal and are commonly attributed to *djinn* (or *jinn*), largely invisible human-like creatures whose messages may be threatening or comforting.[597] As Sally Edwards put it:

> I see the voices I hear as parts of myself that hold the strong emotions it didn't feel safe enough to feel. They are parts of me without which I would not have survived. To see them as a symptom of a mental illness is insulting, and failing to acknowledge their pivotal role in my survival as a human being. I want to thank them, not get rid of them![598]

From asylums to community care

The closure of psychiatric institutions was not the breakthrough previously hoped for. As one mental health advocate noted in 1980:

> Tens of thousands of mental patients have been released in the United States through court suits in the last ten years... It has been a disaster. Institutions have been shut but there has been nowhere for the patients to go. They have ended up in prison, or exploited by private landlords, readmitted to other mental hospitals or just dying... Courts are unable to plan, budget or build alternative facilities.[599]

For anti-psychiatry campaigners and others, it only later became clear that the closure of mental institutions had little to do with their arguments. In California, conservative Governor Ronald Reagan was enthusiastic about closing down "superfluous" institutions. In 1961, Minister for Health Enoch Powell became the first major UK politician to champion closures. Powell had resigned from the previous Conservative administration only three years earlier due to its refusal to make huge public spending cuts.[600] Despite evidence of significant financial savings for the state, it was a full decade before another UK Conservative government announced its intention to close all mental institutions within 15 years. A final indictment of the asylums came in 1975, when research showed that 40 percent of asylum inmates had been incarcerated for over 20 years.[601]

Political support for the philosophy of community care quickly became the new political consensus, but adequate and appropriate funding has been another matter entirely. In practice, newly liberated patients have often been simply handed back to their families. With support from health and social services inadequate or non-existent, this has placed an often intolerable burden on unpaid (usually female) carers. Community care is, as one official survey of British practice put it, "a poor relation: everybody's distant relative, but nobody's baby".[602]

> For thousands of the old, already suffering in varying degrees from mental confusion and deterioration, deinstitutionalization has meant premature death. For others, it has meant that they have been left to rot and decay, physically and otherwise, in broken-down welfare hotels or in what are termed, with Orwellian euphemism, "personal care" nursing homes. For thousands of younger psychotics discharged into the streets, it has meant a nightmare existence...[603]

Boarding houses and prisons are often now the biggest local providers of mental health "care", a situation not unlike that 200 years ago before the large-scale building of asylums. The substance of health or social insurance schemes developed since then—ensuring welfare support to individuals—has in recent years been greatly diminished.[604] As one UK service user explained: "general hospitals have emergency psychiatric wards, with a limited number of beds and as fast a turnover of patients as anti-psychotic drugs can sustain. Then, you're on your own with the pills, and the underfunded, understaffed, sometimes mythical care in the community".[605]

The growing trend towards the closure of institutions did, however, provide more space and opportunity for mentally distressed people to begin to find collective voices of their own. Service users are often highly critical of community care. However, the problem is not the model itself (few people would advocate a return to institutionalisation), but rather the chronic lack of funding. The same difficulty applies to new individualised services such as direct payments or personalisation: the money is simply not there to put into practice policies that can seem impressive on paper.

A social model of mental health?

The costs of mental distress have in recent years been the subject of unprecedented public comment and policy initiatives by business and politicians alike. It is, however, much harder to find such concern about its social and economic causes. The *DSM* categories are "neutral with respect to theories of aetiology"; in other words, silent on causes.[606]

For most psychiatrists, trained in medicine and specialising in what they believe are diseases of the brain, drugs are the preferred method of treatment. Psychologists, on the other hand, usually believe mental distress is caused by intolerable stress and advocate mainly therapeutic treatments. The British Psychological Society (BPS) suggests that the causes of psychosis are often social:

> A review found that between half and three-quarters of psychiatric inpatients had been either physically or sexually abused as children. Experiencing multiple childhood traumas appears to give approximately the same risk of developing psychosis as smoking does for developing lung cancer...psychosis is often no more and no less than a natural reaction to traumatic events...one recent paper [concluded] 'There is abuse and there are the effects of abuse. There is no additional "psychosis" that needs explaining'.[607]

A lack of safety and equality, the BPS report argues, is key to the incidence of psychosis and so meeting our basic needs is the most important element in making us feel safe and secure. Noting that more equal societies are associated with greater trust and less paranoia, it concludes that: "rather than primarily targeting our efforts at individuals, the most effective way to reduce rates of 'psychosis' might be to reduce inequality in society".[608]

Rates of reported mental distress are five times higher in the most unequal countries compared to the "least unequal". In the US around one in four people are affected every year, compared to less than one in ten in Germany, Italy and Japan. Studies show that this is linked to conspicuous disparities in wealth, with the majority bitter and dissatisfied with their relative poverty.[609]

Common causes of mental distress include unemployment, domestic violence, housing problems and homelessness and the effects of discrimination. More contemporary examples include stress and anxiety associated with apparently arbitrary decisions concerning benefits or immigration status. Work is also a significant causal factor, with the most frequent triggers identified as bullying, excessive workloads and performance targets. A survey in 2013 found that UK workers felt less secure and more pressured at work than at any time in the past 20 years. Forty percent said they worked at very high speeds for 75 percent or more of their working time, against 23 percent in 1997 and 38 percent in 2001.[610] Extreme distress may be partly due to past traumatic events such as childhood sexual, physical or emotional abuse, accidents, illness, bereavements or violence.

As the incidence of mental distress often fluctuates, those affected experience periods of greater or lesser lucidity and wellbeing. As one service user put it: "the key lies in how I think of myself when I am well".[611] In response to "medical model" approaches to mental distress, which see changing brain chemistry or the behaviour of individuals as the key, writer and activist Peter Beresford advocates the creation of a social model of mental health. This stresses the parallels between physical and mental impairment:

> The social model of disability does not seek to deny the individual experience of impairment and nor does a social model of madness and distress ignore the distress that people experience. Rather the aim is to challenge the oppression and discrimination that both groups

face as a result and to develop more appropriate responses to their circumstances and experiences.[612]

Beresford sees this new "social model of madness and distress" as prioritising the experiences and voices of mental health service users and survivors and putting these in a wider context. He and other disability activists are establishing common ground between mental health service users and people with sensory or physical impairments more commonly seen as disabled. His 2010 research, however, revealed considerable obstacles to developing such an account. Its very association with disability has led some service users to reject a parallel social model of mental health, believing that identifying as disabled could only add to the stigma they already experience. Some dislike the terminology of "distress" and others reject the term madness. Many in the survey did feel disabled as service users, but did not see this discrimination as underpinned by any actual impairment.[613] A further difficulty is that many people in mental distress avoid or have no access to mental health services at all and are neither service "users" nor "survivors."

The social and economic context of mental distress, therefore, presents a major obstacle to those wishing to campaign for change. Individuals have nevertheless increasingly organised themselves precisely for this purpose.

Taking over the asylum?

In December 2013, the UK National Union of Students (NUS) announced its support for a "Coming out as Disabled Day" in a conscious attempt to emulate the efforts of gay and lesbian activists in the 1990s.[614] The fact that many mental health problems are concealed or controlled through the use of medication would seem to add weight to the parallel. Nicola Field's comment from that period, however, seems apposite:

> Obviously in a society where normalised heterosexuality and the family are pushed as the only valid expression of sexuality, individual "coming out" is more or less the only way to reject dominant values

and live as an out gay person. However, the vast majority of working-class people who experience lesbian or gay feelings cannot go through this individualised process because they do not have the necessary levels of independence, support and confidence to do so.[615]

The NUS initiative compares unfavourably to earlier more radical and collective campaigns. In the 1970s, overtly political service user organisations were formed by and for patients, or "survivors", to represent their views and defend their rights against what they saw as a politically oppressive psychiatric system. These groups also pioneered innovations such as advocacy programmes, "crisis cards" (which users kept on their person, providing emergency information and contact details) and crisis houses.

In March 1973, BBC radio broadcast an interview with Andrew Roberts about his part in forming the new UK Mental Patients Union (MPU). Roberts recalled that it "took them three hours to decide if it was safe to let a mental patient into Broadcasting House." Over 100 people attended the union's subsequent inaugural meeting in west London.[616] The MPU, formed after a similar Scottish initiative, saw psychiatry as the "high priest" of capitalist society, exorcising the "devils" of social distress through electroconvulsive therapy, lobotomy and medication. In the same way that workers formed trade unions, the MPU believed that mental patients also needed a union to fight for their rights against political oppression and social control.[617] Other UK organisations included: Protection of the Rights of Mental Patients in Therapy, formed in 1976 (which ten years later became the Campaign Against Psychiatric Oppression); Survivors Speak Out, a national networking group formed in 1986; and the radical action group Mad Pride, founded in the 1990s.[618]

The San Francisco-based Network Against Psychiatric Assault, founded in the early 1970s, was influenced by the libertarian individualism of Szasz and railed against "The Therapeutic State". In contrast, the Mental Patients' Liberation Project (MPLP) was formed after patients in New York joined with their psychiatrists to charter a subway train on which they rode to lobby City Hall in opposition to cuts in mental health services.[619] The MPLP, while also campaigning against psychiatric malpractice, demanded better welfare services, including support for "crisis centres" based on non-medical alternative models of care.[620]

The popularity of anti-psychiatry in the 1960s and 1970s was part of a period of general social upheaval that involved opposition and analysis of all kinds of oppression and exploitation. "It was tempting", as O'Grady has commented, "to ascribe all suffering to social causes and even to interpret psychotic experiences like delusions and hallucinations as transformative experiences towards personal growth as Laing did." However, by the end of the 1970s, radicalism was on the wane and social solutions were abandoned in favour of individual ones. In the mental health field, biological reductionism "elevated the status of doctors and chemists as authorities and experts and undermined the standing of sociologists, psychologists, journalists and others with a more social and less individual approach".[621]

While generally less radical than those of the 1970s, today's service user and survivor movements have absorbed some of their insights. Mutual support networks help people see benefits as well as challenges in "psychotic" experiences (for example, links between "madness" and creativity) and how users are often dehumanised by aspects of mental health services. The UK National Survivor User Network is a service user-led charity providing a single voice for mentally distressed people on policies and services.[622] The Hearing Voices Network (HVN) unites over 180 UK self-help groups for "people who hear voices, see visions or have unusual perceptions", explicitly recognising the diversity of views held about the nature and causes of such experiences. Regular meetings allow members to talk freely and to support one another. HVN is also active internationally.[623] Similarly, self-harm organisations have helped "reframe self-harm as a valid coping mechanism, pioneering approaches such as self-harm minimization that are now well respected".[624]

Fewer of today's users and survivors groups oppose psychiatry as a whole or reject outright the use of medication. David W Oaks, "psychiatric survivor" and founder of US campaign MindFreedom International, describes his organisation's more nuanced and practical approach: "We're prochoice about prescribed psychiatric medication, and some of our members choose to take such drugs.

What we're concerned about is people being pressured to take drugs and the unavailability of nondrug alternatives. That's a human rights violation".[625]

Some organisations have begun to establish common cause with dissident voices in the medical profession. Founded in 2013, the All Trials campaign is backed by 130 patient groups representing over 100 million patients. Founding member, author and doctor Ben Goldacre recently claimed "more progress on transparency in drugs trials in the past 12 months than in the past 25 years".[626] For the most part, however, today's mental health campaigns comprise alliances of users and providers struggling to defend precious local facilities facing relocation, cuts or closure.[627] Coalitions of service providers—such as the UK's Social Work Action Network, Psychologists Against Austerity and Psychotherapists and Counsellors for Social Responsibility—work with service users and others to help such groups build more effective resistance.[628]

Mental health treatment and services

Just as people are not equally affected by mental distress, so access to support is grossly unequal. A privileged few pay thousands of pounds a week to stay at exclusive residential clinics such as The Priory Hospital in Britain, which promises treatment for "behavioural addictions" such as compulsive text messaging and spread betting.[629] For those with the means to pay, private therapy is available immediately. For everyone else, drugs are often the only alternative to long waiting lists.

The dominant trend to prescribe drugs for mental distress is not universal. Dutch family doctors, for example, decided to do so mainly in cases of more severe depression, leading to levels of antidepressant usage remaining static in the Netherlands between 2008 and 2013. In Germany, the UK and Spain, by contrast, prescriptions have doubled over the past decade.[630]

Many of those in need in the UK find that the relevant services provide only crisis management and intervention. Repeated government pledges to "direct help at those who most need it" has meant in practice removing help from most seen as not at immediate risk. Recession, unemployment and benefit cuts have led to rising demand and shrinking resources. Sue Bailey, outgoing president of the Royal College of Psychiatrists, described mental health services in England in June 2014 as "a car crash".[631] A study for the London School of Economics found that three quarters of people with depression or anxiety got no treatment.[632] The chronic lack of cash and resources impacts on service providers too: "the average NHS member of staff still takes one day off sick for every 25 days...one in five staff members has experienced bullying or harassment from a colleague in the past three months, and two in five have had work-related stress within the past year".[633]

Decades of research on psychosis and schizophrenia have failed to identify any biological cause. The idea that these are biological illnesses, however, is still widely accepted, particularly among mental health practitioners:

> As a result workers have often not tried to understand the experiences in the context of the person's life, or prioritised talking to the person about their experiences. The 'brain disease' idea has also contributed to a climate in which the main, or only, treatment tends to be medication. This in turn has meant that other approaches to helping, such as talking treatments, have often been unavailable. It has also diverted resources away from the circumstances of people's lives, not only in the way that we try to help people in distress, but also in research and in efforts at prevention.[634]

Most people in the UK experiencing mental distress don't see psychiatrists or clinical psychologists unless they are deemed to have extreme, severe and urgent problems. Instead, they see a psychotherapist or counsellor (most often an "Improving Access to Psychological Therapies" therapist), either within the NHS or via agencies such as council social work services, employee assistance providers, voluntary organisations or private practitioners. Counsellors tend to be low paid and female, seeing people whose distress is due to a wide range of social problems. Many of their clients have attempted or are contemplating suicide and may be affected by excessive alcohol or drug consumption, used to cope with intolerable circumstances. Given the nature of their caseload, most counsellors therefore have little time or respect for the "brain disease" approach.

There are many varieties of counselling and psychotherapy, including psychodynamic and cognitive behavioural therapy (CBT).[635] Economist Richard Layard was "happiness tsar" in Tony Blair's New Labour government. In his 2014 book *Thrive* he favours CBT, which he calls "evidence-based", in contrast to most person-centred talk therapy, which tends to be longer, more expensive and much harder to measure.[636] CBT is standardised so that therapists can be trained very quickly, with patients treated by phone, online or with self-help books. The NHS also favours CBT because it has shown positive results in relatively few sessions, limiting the scope of therapy, but returning those affected back to work as soon as possible.

The relative merits of CBT are, however, disputed. Research to date consistently shows that the type of therapy has little bearing on outcomes.[637] General factors such as the degree of trust between patient and therapist are regarded as more important. Although many people find psychological "talking therapies" helpful, high demand and chronically low funding means that they are often unavailable. Nine out of ten people who could benefit currently have no access to CBT.[638]

For the support that is available, BPS guidance emphasises that service providers should tailor help to the needs of individuals rather than providing standardised packages of care:

> the causes of a particular individual's difficulties are always complex. Our knowledge of what might have contributed, and what might help, is always tentative. Professionals need to respect and work with people's own ideas about what has contributed to their problems. Some people find it helpful to think of their problems as an illness but others do not. Professionals should not promote any one view, or suggest that any one form of help such as medication or psychological therapy is useful for everyone. Instead we need to support people in whatever way they personally find most helpful, and to acknowledge

that some people will receive support partly or wholly from outside the mental health system.[639]

Studies in Finland recently inspired some UK mental health professionals to initiate trials of "open dialogue" which "fully involves the patient and their social network, from the very beginning; with a flattened hierarchy, a shared agenda and the aim of 'being with', rather than 'doing to.'" Under this system, over 70 percent of those presenting with acute psychosis were discharged from services within two years, with far less hospitalisation or high-dose medication than in the UK.[640]

Conclusion

The drugs industry—and much of the mental health profession—sees mentally distressed people as malfunctioning machines. It medicalises problems that are social in nature and pathologises behaviour once considered normal. This does not mean that all drug treatment can be dismissed as useless or worse. Many people's lives have been stabilised, transformed or even saved by effective medication and see their treatment as unequivocally beneficial. Others have found talking therapies the best way to manage their distress.

The positions of these different camps can be polarised and one-sided. Some of those highlighting abuses in mental health services tend to uphold a core practice which, if conducted according to certain prescribed norms, is seen as ethically and politically unproblematic. Supporters of anti-psychiatry, on the other hand, tend to indict "institutional psychiatry" wholesale as a system of state-sponsored oppression and violence. As Peter Sedgwick commented over 30 years ago: "Those who reject both the short-sighted denunciation of mere 'abuses' and the wholesale indictment of psychiatry as an enterprise of state-sponsored violence have no easy task in developing an alternative to these simplicities".[641] Meeting welfare needs and defending individual freedoms, however, need not be mutually opposed goals. In more recent years, they have often been seen as equally important in alliances between service providers and users.

Many of the most important advances in the control of physical disease or impairment were, of course, not medical at all. The creation of clean water and efficient sewage systems, the reduction of the working day, and the provision of warm and secure housing were all social measures which did more to prevent infections and illness than the impressive discoveries of medical science. Ending mental distress will similarly require extensive social change. In the case of anorexia, for example, it is necessary to tackle the roots of women's oppression:

> If experts really want to help those with eating disorders, they should look at why so many people are so unhappy; they should teach schoolkids how to talk about their feelings without resorting to masochism; they should look at why so many girls and women feel they ought to put themselves last; and, most of all, they should look at the causes of self-loathing as opposed to the manifestations of it.[642]

The "maddening world" we live in seems to encourage irrationality and contrary ways of thinking. As one mental health service user points out:

> While people always say that what they want most in the world is peace, what characterises it constantly are war and conflict. While in recent years mental health service users/survivors have come under growing attack for being threatening and dangerous—for their association with homicides—ours is a world that in other contexts celebrates the military, has exhibitions of its killing machines and at particular times expects men to carry out orders to kill in war, unless they can offer convincing 'conscientious objection' to doing so...
> The manufacture of weapons is one of the greatest polluters of the environment, yet we focus instead for a greener future on campaigns against the use of plastic shopping bags.[643]

These examples reflect the fundamental contradiction of a world with more than sufficient means to meet the needs of everyone which is structured instead around maximising the profits of a tiny minority. Given this "sickness" underpinning all aspects of our world, it is perhaps surprising that only a relatively small proportion of society experiences mental distress at any one time.

The transient and often hidden nature of mental distress, combined with its diverse manifestations and interpretations, make it difficult to sustain organisation. At any one time, the numbers of people directly affected are relatively small. The first consequence of these facts is that the oppression experienced by this highly isolated and marginalised section of society "is much less systematic, and, from the point of view of the ruling class, much less significant as a tool to 'divide and rule'." [644] Second, alliances have proved necessary to win or to defend even piecemeal reforms in services. People in mental distress must therefore look to wider forces to effect fundamental change in how the issue is perceived and how it is addressed.

There are many campaigns to defend existing services and others to demand better and more of them. Besides the possibility of winning their objectives, these struggles also help counter notions of "us and them". These notions help maintain divisions between a wholly fictional "normal" majority and others seen as different or dangerous because they are "mentally ill". But even the most successful of such campaigns can at best only help us cope with an increasingly stressful and unhealthy environment, wreaking ever more havoc on our bodies as well as our minds.

There is an old saying that when your house is flooded there is little point mopping the floor if the tap is still running. Much of mental distress is in reality a fully sane response to living in a dysfunctional society rooted in alienation,[645] poverty and inequality. The cure is not medication or therapy: these are at best a means to help people manage or minimise the effects of their distress. Many individuals resolve their difficulties for good through improved social circumstances. To remove the basis for this distress, therefore, and to provide proper support for those still affected, it is necessary to fundamentally alter these social circumstances and to create a society that promotes genuine social inclusion and the fully rounded development of the individual.

11.
Deafness and sign language

What matters deafness of the ear, when the mind hears? The one true deafness...is of the mind.
—Victor Hugo

By whom, then, are signs proscribed? By a few educators of the deaf whose boast is that they do not understand sign and do not want to; by a few philanthropists who are otherwise ignorant of the language; by parents who do not understand the requisites to the happiness of their deaf children and are inspired by false fears... What heinous crime have the deaf been guilty of that their language should be proscribed?
—Robert McGregor, first president, National Association of the Deaf, 1896

As the disability rights movement developed, so disputes began over who was or was not disabled. Many members of one "impairment group" in particular consciously rejected a disabled identity, arguing that profoundly Deaf[646] people have a separate culture and history and constitute an oppressed linguistic minority. Why?

First, although the concept may at first seem obvious, the reality of deafness is poorly understood. Any concept of loss or impairment (of hearing) has no meaning for those who were born or became deaf at an early age. Second, there is a qualitative difference between any degree of hearing impairment and profound deafness. Deaf people often cannot understand speech and rely on sign language and lip-reading.[647] Language is a defining feature of humanity—the means through which we communicate, acquire and share information. The history of sign, the language of Deaf people, has been a central factor in their lives. Finally, Deaf people have been segregated from wider society for much of recent history. Whereas for other disabled people, marrying within their impairment group is seen as neither a priority or even desirable, around 90 percent of Deaf people who marry choose a Deaf partner.[648]

For over 130 years, the vast majority of Deaf children have been educated in separate (often residential) schools using "oralist" methods that attempt to enforce the use of speech. In 1979, a shocking report by Oxford University researchers—largely ignored by the media—found that Deaf children left school with a reading age averaging less than nine. In most cases, their speech was intelligible only to their teachers and families and their ability to lip-read no better than that of hearing people. It is estimated that over 80 percent of the world's Deaf children receive no education at all.[649] It is difficult to imagine the cumulative damage caused to their self-esteem and mental health.

This began to change in the 1960s as campaigns to officially recognise sign language and to reinstate its use in schools also helped to stimulate wider interest. At Further Education level in the UK today, British Sign Language (BSL) is the second most popular language course, while American Sign Language (ASL) is estimated to be the third most widely used language in the US (after English and Spanish).[650] Estimates of the Deaf population vary from one or two per 1,000, with between 50,000-70,000 Deaf people in the UK,[651] around 250,000 in the US, and an estimated 4-5 million sign language users across the globe.[652]

The history of sign language

Until recently, sign languages were believed to be based on the spoken word or confused with sign "systems", gestures used by hearing people in place of spoken language, such as those used by American Plains Indians and in hunting by Australian Aborigines.

> These substitutions are word-for-word translations of spoken language. A sign language, by comparison, is generally the first language of the person who uses it...[and] differs in grammar, syntax,

expression, and idiomatic usage from the spoken language used by hearing members of the same community... Only 10 per cent of those born deaf have deaf parents...most hearing parents have no prior knowledge of deafness.

Wherever there are enough deaf people over time to systematise and pass along a language from one generation to the next, a mature, comprehensive sign language may develop. The use of signs by groups of deaf individuals has been described from Rennell Island, Providence Island, Grand Cayman Island, a group of Indian villagers in Surinam, the Adamorable in Ghana, and the Engha of New Guinea. People affected by iodine deficiency [which sometimes causes deafness] in the Andes and Himalayas use sign language. Undoubtedly many more instances exist.[653]

The first written record of deaf people is from the 5th century BC. Classical Greek and Roman societies conceived of them as a distinct group. Aristotle wrote that "hearing is the sense of sound, and sound the vehicle of thought: hence the blind are more intelligent than deaf-mutes." Justinian law in the sixth century AD limited the rights of people born deaf, whereas those deafened later in life who were literate could exercise these rights in writing.

Christianity conceived of deafness as synonymous with demonic possession, although a 12th century papal decree allowed deaf people to marry so long as it was clear from their signing that they understood the concepts involved. Leonardo da Vinci recommended a deaf teacher of painting to a colleague: "Do not laugh at me because I propose a teacher without speech to you...he will teach you better through facts than will all the other masters through words." Many deaf people worked in the Turkish Ottoman court between the 15th and 20th centuries. Their signing system was used regularly by several Sultans and held high status, regarded as capable of expressing ideas of whatever complexity. Noblemen of the court also had deaf attendants. Sir George Downing (after whom Downing Street is named) knew sign language, having been brought up in the Weald in Kent where sign is known to have been practised.[654]

Systems of sign language have been traced to silent monastic orders in either 529 AD or 910 AD and this is where the teaching of sign language most likely began. Recent research found evidence of one system of sign, the origins of which "date back to the 11th-century Benedictines from Cluny, but the Cistercians took it over and developed further".[655] Benedictine monk Pedro Ponce de Leon taught deaf children to speak in the monastery of San Salvador in Burgos, in northern Spain until his death in 1584. There are other records of sign usage in England and Holland in the 17th century, but it is in France that modern Deaf history really begins.[656]

The first schools for the deaf were established in Leipzig, Edinburgh and Paris. The latter was opened by the Abbé de l'Epée in 1760, with support (but little money) from King Louis XVI. The Abbé conducted regular public "exercises" of pupils, both to demonstrate that the deaf were educable and to secure sponsorship. He developed a system of "methodical" signs combining "the mimicry of the impoverished deaf"[657] with signed French grammar. Epée died in 1789, having trained many deaf teachers and founding 21 deaf schools across France and Europe. His successor, Abbé Sicard, described sign as opening "the doors of intelligence".[658]

The French Revolution inaugurated the first publicly funded deaf school following an appeal to its National Assembly by Sicard. This opened in 1791 in a seminary taken over following the abolition of all church property.[659] Deaf people fought and died in the revolutionary army, and deaf artist Claude Deseine was commissioned to sculpt busts of several French revolutionary leaders. Pierre Desloges had composed the first "deaf" text, in 1779, in defence of the use of sign language: "when the isolated deaf man arrives [in Paris], he learns to polish and order his signing...[and] the art of portraying all his thoughts, even the most abstract... We express ourselves on all subjects with as much order, precision, and rapidity as if we enjoyed the faculty of speech and hearing." As an ardent supporter of the revolution, Desloges wrote a series of widely read political pamphlets—including *Letter Addressed to the Voters of Paris*, printed the day after the fall of the Bastille—until his disappearance with the fall of the Jacobins in 1794.[660] The French system of sign language was instituted across Europe in the wake of Napoleon's armies.

Deaf residential schools and the rise of oralism

In the pre-Civil War Union of America, another former preacher, Thomas Gallaudet, agreed to educate the deaf daughter of Mason Cogswell, a wealthy friend of his family. Cogswell won his support to establish an American school for the deaf, and Gallaudet left for Europe to get help and advice. Laurent Clerc, a pupil at the Paris Institute, met Gallaudet while he was in London with Abbé Sicard in 1815. Following unsuccessful efforts to get help from Thomas Braidwood and his school in Edinburgh, Gallaudet left for Paris.[661] It took less than three months of study to convince Gallaudet of the superiority of education in sign language and he then persuaded Clerc to emigrate with him to set up the new school.[662]

The Connecticut Asylum for the Education and Instruction of Deaf and Dumb opened in Hartford on 15 April 1817. Rehoused and renamed as the American Asylum in 1821, it supplied founders and teachers for other deaf residential schools across the US.[663] It was estimated that by 1869, there were 550 teachers of the deaf worldwide and that 41 per cent of those in the new US were themselves deaf.[664] Gallaudet's son Edward founded Gallaudet College (later University) in 1864 as the world's first higher education institution for the deaf.

From the outset, there had been heated debates over whether instruction in sign ("manualism") or speech ("oralism") was the best method of educating deaf people. The first US "oralist" school for the Deaf was founded in Massachusetts in 1867. Supporters included social reformer Samuel Gridley Howe and Boston millionaire Gardiner Greene Hubbard, but by far the most influential was scientist and teacher of "visible speech" Alexander Graham Bell, who married Hubbard's daughter Mabel. Like Bell's mother, Mabel had lost her hearing when young. Her attitude to other Deaf people was uncompromising: "I have helped other things and people…anything, everything but the deaf. I would have no friends among them".[665]

In his infamous *Memoir Upon the Formation of a Deaf Variety of the Human Race* (1884), Bell opposed deaf teachers, deaf marriage, deaf residential schools, and advocated the dispersal of deaf children and the abolition of sign language. He admitted: "If we have the mental condition of the child alone in view, without reference to language, no language will reach the mind like the language of signs." He went on, however: "The main object of the education of the deaf is to fit them to live in the world of hearing-speaking people".[666] Deafness was a condition for which children needed to be cured: "We should teach them to forget that they are deaf".[667] Bell's work was used to justify the sterilisation of deaf people, often against their knowledge or will, although his theories about the nature of hereditary deafness were subsequently proved to be wrong.[668]

For the oralists, sign language represented irrationality and backwardness, while education in speech represented reason and progress. Many manualists, however, partly agreed, seeing sign language as rudimentary and primitive "mimicry"—at best a bridge to acquiring languages which (whether in spoken or written form) they also believed were more cultured and civilised. The French system of methodological signs was designed to replace "natural" sign language,[669] whereas in Britain the latter was accepted as deaf people's preferred means of communication, but signed versions of the English alphabet were developed for learning.[670]

Presented thus as in keeping with the scientific mood of the times, oralist methods grew in influence. The first schools for deaf children in the US had educated rich and poor alike, but the new industrialists wanted their children to integrate with their hearing peers and to learn speech, with money no object. The turning point came in Italy at the infamous Milan Congress of 1880.

Most major Italian cities were practising oralism by this time, along with Austria, Belgium, Norway and Switzerland. Balestra, its principal advocate at the Congress, organised in advance to ensure victory. A close ally arranged the agenda, editing advance submissions and sending a report hostile to sign language to all delegates.[671] Of the 164 who attended, those from Italy and France made up seven-eighths of the total. The five US delegates (one of which was the only deaf delegate at the conference), represented more schools and pupils than all the other delegates put together, but were outvoted ten to one by those from Milan alone. Only six of the eight British delegates had any experience of teaching deaf students, and only one voted with the American delegation[672] against a resolution "exalting the dominant oral language and disbarring sign language whatever the nation".[673]

Repression and reaction

Oral and manual methods alike were often justified in religious or moral terms. As the Milan Congress president put it: "Speech alone, divine itself, is the right way to speak of divine matters." The oralist method removed the "indocile and wild spirit peculiar to those who express themselves by the fantastic and passionate method of gestures, and also renders them more obedient, respectful, affectionate, sincere, and good." The London *Times* hailed the outcome of the Congress with an editorial stating: "Deafness is Abolished", adding that it showed a "virtual unanimity of preference for oral teaching" in deaf education.[674] The falseness of this claim was shown by the strident protests and campaigns provoked by the decision. These, however, rarely succeeded and the formal teaching of sign language all but disappeared over subsequent decades.

Various methods were used to try and "cure" deafness. Even at the height of the Paris school's fame, the school's physician carried out a series of increasingly brutal experiments.

> After applying electricity to the children's ears, Itard then tried leeching and piercing of eardrums (one child died of the latter). His next move was even more drastic still—he inserted a probe into the eustachian tube and attempted to flush out the suspected (and hypothetical) 'lymphatic excrement.' This was applied to 120 of the school's pupils, almost all—'save for some two dozen who would not be subdued.'[675]

Less brutal and more commonly used methods involved the use of metal rods to control tongue movements, or manipulating the shape of the mouth in laborious and usually unsuccessful attempts to enforce speech.

In keeping with the eugenicist world view of the period, the poor were equated with and seen as closer to nature—especially the deaf—whereas oralist methods were more appropriate to the needs of the "leisured class". Thomas Arnold, Britain's leading champion of oralism, was hugely celebrated by the wealthy elite for his education of Abraham Farrar, who lost his hearing at the age of three. After exhaustive tuition, Farrar went on to graduate from London University in 1881. As one critic commented, however:

> Mr Farrar had every advantage that the average victim of Pure Oralism has not. He had intelligence, means, individual instruction for a practically unlimited period, and a prince of teachers; yet he admits that he cannot take in an average sermon or lecture by lip-reading, and that his speech is adequate only to the ordinary transactions of life... Mr Farrar is the brilliant exception that proves the rule that the Pure Oral method is quite unsuitable for general application.[676]

In 1901, a French government report found that pupils "after seven or eight years at the institution, were incapable, not only of speaking, but of writing the teacher's name, or even their own." This indictment of oralist methods reflected how far the education of deaf pupils comprised for the most part a continual speech lesson. As one speaker at the oralists' 1909 convention wondered out loud:

> It has always seemed to me that there is something terribly wrong with oralism when it cannot turn out deaf graduates who appreciate the value of the methods by which they were instructed...how thrilling it would be to have a deaf man...stand up here and defend the Oral method orally...we have met together to talk about the education of the deaf, and the deaf themselves reject what we are having to say.[677]

Given this systemic failure, the only remaining option was to stress the subnormality of deaf people, now seen as childlike or savage, requiring institutionalisation, like the blind, insane or ill, with special forms of rehabilitation and education.[678] Such attitudes certainly reflected the wider concerns of the main nation states which supported the ban on sign language.

At the time of Milan, the new Italian state was less than ten years old. Its creation involved the imposition of a national language in place of local dialects. Italy went on to join in the late 19th century's "scramble for Africa" in which the main European powers—especially France and Britain—colonised 90 percent of the African continent in the space of just over 20 years. Some English and French linguists developed an "evolutionary" theory of language according to which European languages were superior to all others. One British report of 1925, written in relation to West Africa, could have easily been discussing sign language:

> It is clear that there is comparatively little, if any advantage, in the continuation of a crude dialect with practically no powers of expression. It is also evident that the need for a common language is not essential to a large group of people…living under conditions that do not require much intercommunication.[679]

African languages were labelled as primitive and European languages as modern. This was the context for the historic defeat of sign language at Milan: the rise of imperialism and eugenic ideas. Both were enthusiastically embraced by supporters of oralism.[680] In 1920 Bell himself warned that: "children of foreign-born parents are increasing at a much greater rate…the interests of the race demand that the best should marry and have large families and that any restrictions on reproduction should apply to the worst rather than the best".[681]

By 1899, the views of one educationalist were also typical across the USA: "the English language must be made the vernacular of the deaf if they are not to become a class unto themselves—foreigners among their own countrymen." Sign language made the deaf person an outsider; "not an Englishman, a German, a Frenchman, or a member of any other nationality, but, intellectually, a man without a country".[682]

Officially sanctioned racism led to every US deaf school in the southern states separating its black and white pupils until desegregation began in 1955. The South Carolina School for the Deaf and the Blind had four separate departments: two for black and white deaf children and two for black and white blind children, with separate classrooms and sleeping and eating quarters. White students lived in a new building, but black deaf children lived in older, decrepit quarters without electricity.[683] In 1890, the school added two further subdivisions, oral and manual. By the end of the century, nearly 40 percent of deaf students were educated primarily or exclusively in the oral method, increasing to 80 percent by 1920.[684] Louisiana School for the Colored Deaf and Blind was the last segregated school to close— in 1978.[685] Gallaudet, at the time the world's only university for the deaf, registered its first black student in 1951, while the National Association of the Deaf (NAD) did not allow black members until the 1960s.[686]

Resistance and the return of sign

In the same year as the oralist victory at Milan, the NAD was founded, contributing in large part to sign's preservation in the US. Its president George Veditz argued that "sign language was the greatest gift God gave to deaf people",[687] reinforcing views of sign as based on emotion rather than reason.[688] Conferences and campaigns to defend sign language were organised in other countries.

The ban on sign was enforced unevenly. In some schools it applied only to the classroom; in others it extended to residential dormitories, with pupils encouraged to inform on each other. Deaf students often defeated the best efforts of teachers to stamp out its use, while some of the latter chose to defy the ban.[689] In a few places, resistance to oralist methods lasted many decades. Sign language survived in many British schools until after the Second World War,[690] and Catholic schools in the Irish republic taught in sign until the 1960s. There were similar exceptions across Europe and the US:[691] In Australia, rebellions against oralism in 1929 and 1931 were serious enough to result in police intervention.[692]

The lives of deaf and many other disabled people were transformed with economic changes during and after the Second World War when large numbers of them joined the workforce. Large deaf clubs, vibrant social centres which sprang up during the war, survived until the 1960s or later. Akron Club for the Deaf, at the huge Goodyear industrial complex in Ohio, opened round the clock seven days a week and New York City had at least 12 different deaf clubs. The US Government

Printing Office employed nearly 9,000 workers, 150 of them deaf. Almost all were members of the powerful International Typographical Union (ITU), which strictly controlled access to the shop floor.[693]

Other deaf clubs were founded as early as the 19th century. In the UK, church control meant that it was 1967 before the first deaf club (in Coventry) secured a licence to serve alcohol. Although there were still around 250 local clubs across the UK in 2003, the pattern of long-term decline followed that of the US.[694] Many deaf people, having moved into new jobs that brought them into daily contact with hearing people, increasingly saw clubs as an anachronism. The availability of hearing aids with the founding of the NHS led to many hard-of-hearing people no longer seeing themselves as deaf.[695]

The shift towards deinstitutionalisation in the 1960s and 1970s also led to the closure of many deaf residential schools. While these had often helped to nourish and preserve sign language, they had also isolated generations of deaf people from wider society and made them more vulnerable to abuse. Something else led to a wider interest in sign language developing among hearing people:

> by the 1960s, campaigners in support of sign language began to shift to a new rhetoric, one that embraced rather than countered the scientific-rational theme, and argued that there were studies showing that sign language education had a positive effect on the development of intelligence, academic performance and psychological well-being. Their argument was a revision of an earlier rhetorical tradition that sign language was natural, not in the sense that it descended from ancient times, but in the sense that it was easy to use, and that it promoted normal development in addition to supporting communication within families.[696]

A new academic field, sign language linguistics, helped to promote an understanding of sign as a language in its own right, with its own structure, syntax and grammar. The key breakthrough was by William Stokoe. His findings in 1960, made five years after being appointed as a professor of English at Gallaudet, were at the time treated as absurd or heretical. As he put it: "the entire Gallaudet College faculty rudely attacked me, linguistics, and the study of signing as a language".[697] Many deaf people saw sign language as so natural and familiar as to need no theoretical explanation. However, the academic interest in sign did contribute to a widespread change in attitudes—as did other factors, not least the development of linguistics as a discipline. The starting point for linguistics, that all languages are seen as equal, became widely accepted in the 1960s, although the implications of this took time to make themselves felt.

On 6 March 1988, Gallaudet University's Board of Trustees announced that the sole hearing person from three candidates had been appointed as president. The news shocked staff and students alike: the campaign in support of a deaf president had included a 3,000-strong rally at the university only five days previously. Crowds of students immediately blockaded the campus. The board's appointee, Elisabeth A Zinser, threatened to "take action to bring [the protest] under control". The chair of the board justified their decision with the infamous statement: "Deaf people are not able to function in a hearing world." The national media seized on this hugely inflammatory soundbite, prompting more coverage for the campaign and stimulating wider support.

Deaf schools shut across the country in solidarity. The president of the American Postal Workers Union personally delivered a US$5,000 cheque. On his arrival at the occupation, author Oliver Sacks noted one placard in particular; "LAURENT CLERC WANTS DEAF PREZ. HE IS NOT HERE BUT HIS SPIRIT IS HERE. SUPPORT US".[698] After four days, Zinser resigned with an unexpectedly moving statement, recognising the campaign as an "extraordinary social movement of deaf people...a civil rights moment in history." On the following day, 2500 students and their supporters, from as far away as South America and New Zealand, marched on Congress. On 13 March, the university agreed to all the campaign's demands, and Dr I King Jordan was named the first deaf president of the university. Having originally supported Zinser's appointment, Jordan now hailed a "historic moment for deaf people around the world... The world has watched the deaf community come of age." "The highest praise", he added, "goes to the students at Gallaudet." It was a victory that galvanised the campaign for Deaf rights everywhere.[699]

The "Deaf Prez Now" campaign traced its origins back to Epée and Clerc, but it is unlikely to have occurred without Stokoe's research over 30 years earlier. The increasing prestige of sign language was leading to changes well beyond the field of education.

Deaf culture

The birth of a new deaf arts scene can be traced to 1967, with the founding of the US National Theater of the Deaf. The company performed its first play in sign language (as opposed to signed English) in 1973 and the use of sign then spread to areas such as poetry and dance. Deaf people and issues began to appear more regularly in literature, documentaries and drama, symbolised for example by the success of the play, book and film *Children of a Lesser God* in the 1980s.

A second, more restrictive concept of "Deaf culture" denotes a separate community of the deaf who communicate only in indigenous sign languages, characterised by a capitalised "D." Its advocates see the distinct history of Deaf residential schools and Deaf clubs as similar to that of oppressed national minorities ("linguistic colonialism").[700] Hearing society is seen as indifferent or even uniformly hostile, and its members passively or actively complicit in Deaf people's oppression. The new notion of the Deaf as a linguistic minority led to a rejection of any disability identity, with the Deaf no longer understood as having an impairment but instead defined by their difference. This approach even led to advanced US plans for a separate town for the Deaf in Laurent, South Dakota,[701] an echo of earlier demands for a "deaf nation" raised at the "silent banquets of the deaf elite of Paris in the 1830s (and also by John Flournoy in the US), in response to the growing influence of oralist methods.[702] This separate existence was imposed from above in some former Eastern Bloc countries where deaf people worked and lived in "their own" factories and "Deaftowns".[703]

This alternative "separatist" concept of Deaf culture developed through the 1980s and 1990s, but has begun to decline more recently. This may be partly due to its sometimes rose-tinted view of a shared past in institutions and clubs which were themselves an expression of neglect and discrimination. With more Deaf people attending schools and growing up alongside their hearing peers in recent years, stereotypes have begun to break down and interest has grown in the lives, language and culture of people who happen to have been born or become deaf. New technology such as telephone teletype services and closed captions for TV in the 1970s and 1980s, through to more recent innovations such as video relay services, smartphones and computer software, have all helped to break down barriers to Deaf people's involvement in society.

It was thanks to campaigning by Deaf activists that some of these technological innovations were made more widely available. The rise of another invention for Deaf people, however, has proved hugely controversial. Cochlear implants (CIs) were initially denounced by many Deaf people as another "miracle cure"; *British Deaf News* in 1985 described it as "Oralism's Final Solution".[704] The CI is a surgically implanted electronic device providing a sense of sound to those with severe or profound hearing loss. As a prosthetic substitute, it cannot cure deafness or hearing impairment and its sound quality is (as yet) inferior to normal hearing. CIs do not work for everyone who is deaf, but are often hugely beneficial for individual users. With early technical problems largely overcome, CIs are now widely available in some countries. Although currently free on the UK's NHS, they cost around $60,000 in the US, with their price and availability elsewhere varying enormously. Many parents choose CIs for their children. By December 2012, around 324,000 people worldwide had CIs, almost 100,000 of them in the UK.[705] Initial concerns that they would lead to the end of sign language have partly receded, although the issue remains controversial.[706]

Conflicting trends

The *New York Times* recently reported: "In 1867, all twenty-six schools for the deaf used ASL. By 1907, all 139 such schools had forbidden its use in an effort to make the deaf more like hearing people. Instead, they were taught to read lips or [sic] to speak. New York's embrace of American Sign Language reflects a pendulum swing back".[707] This, however, is far from the whole story.

On the one hand, a growing academic interest in sign has led to more hearing students taking up courses. ASL has become the fourth most popular language (after Spanish, French and German) studied in the US.[708] Sign language "laboratories" have been established at universities in a number of countries. In Japan and Scandinavia sign is taught in government-funded interpreter training programmes run by community organisations. In the UK sign language is taught both as a further education subject and as a degree course at some universities.[709]

Although sign has been reinstated in many schools, it is usually not indigenous sign language, but a system of "Signed English" similar to the Abbé de l'Epée's "methodical sign" of over 250 years ago. Deaf pupils are forced to learn signs "not for the actions they want to express, but for phonetic English sounds they cannot hear".[710] The UN Convention on the Rights of Persons with Disabilities (2006) includes the right to receive education in sign language at all levels of a country's respective services. Education in mainstream schools, however, often means a child being placed there as the sole Deaf pupil with teachers who may not know sign language. This also creates a higher risk of abuse and isolation, the opposite of officially stated intentions to integrate Deaf children,[711] who are more likely to experience mental distress than their peers.[712]

In January 2015, figures on examination results from the UK Department for Education showed that only 36.3 percent of Deaf children in England hit national GCSE benchmarks, compared to 65.3 percent of their hearing classmates.[713] A UK report in 1995 showed that Deaf children were leaving school at 16 with a reading age of less than 10[714]—findings which were almost identical to those of an Oxford University report 16 years previously. Recent cuts to inclusive education and classroom support[715] and the threat of deeper cuts in the future are in part why many parents still prefer Deaf schools for their children.

Other UK research shows that Deaf adults are twice as likely to experience mental distress such as depression and anxiety, but it is also harder for them to access support. The most favoured treatment, "talking therapies" are virtually impossible to obtain as few practitioners are literate in BSL.[716] The picture is no better for physical health: of 900 videos on the NHS Choices website, just ten are available in BSL. A recent study found that 70 percent of Deaf people surveyed who hadn't been to their GP recently had wanted to go but didn't, mainly because there was no interpreter.[717]

In such circumstances, it is unsurprising that Deaf people have such fond memories of deaf-only institutions. On meeting for the first time, the first question among deaf people is still usually about what school or Deaf club they attend/ed, a constant reminder of the possibility of a real and practical sense of community.

Conclusion

There are many sign languages and many different dialects of sign, which are linguistically just as complex and expressive as any spoken language, and there are good reasons to promote wider use of the former. Research shows that children who learn sign alongside their spoken language tend not only to speak sooner, but also to have a larger vocabulary[718] and that knowing a signed language can enhance visuospatial cognition.[719]

Contrary to myth, most defenders of "manualism" did not take an either/or attitude to methods of educating deaf people. More than 150 years ago, Edward Gallaudet, after touring deaf schools in 14 European countries, concluded that the best approach was to prioritise individual need, which often meant a combination of teaching in both sign language and speech.[720] Although no radical, Gallaudet believed that he spoke for "those who are merely teachers and not capitalists".[721] His message, in a time of cuts and austerity, is surely an essential part of contemporary approaches to Deaf education.

The UK's Federation of Deaf People (FDP) was set up in 1997 due to anger at the lack of action by existing organisations such as the British Deaf Association and the Royal National Institute of the Deaf (the latter was christened "Really Not Interested in the Deaf") to win recognition of BSL.[722] The FDP staged four national marches in the space of five years in London. Some 9,000 Deaf people and their supporters attended the biggest of these in July 2000. The UK government finally agreed to recognise BSL in March 2003,[723] but the legislation's value is little more than symbolic and does not provide any right to BSL interpreters. The Scottish Parliament is currently consulting on a new law promoting the use of BSL. The Bill, first introduced in October 2014, "does not go as far as imposing an explicit statutory requirement on authorities to provide BSL interpreters or translation services", instead seeking that "BSL should be on a similar footing to Gaelic in Scotland [as a minority language]".[724] Several other countries have recognised sign as an official language, but only Finland, Norway and Slovenia provide a right to be educated in or to have services provided using sign language.[725]

Campaigns demanding official recognition for the sign language of the majority are hugely important, but often also involve marginalising and suppressing other minority sign languages—mirroring the earlier development of national spoken languages. Indonesia in particular includes many geographically dispersed communities. In similar vein, the Australian government's recognition of Auslan as the national sign language excludes any consideration of Aboriginal languages, as well as those of immigrant populations without a UK or Irish background.[726] These struggles need not prompt further division; they offer opportunities to draw parallels and to make links between forms of oppression.

There are many good reasons for Deaf people to find common cause with wider struggles. Recent research, for example, shows that 96 percent of deaf children are born to hearing parents.[727] As one US disability activist commented of contemporary advocates of a separatist Deaf culture: "they are perpetuating the notion that disability is bad. And they're not really helping themselves since the disabled majority is still going to think of [Deaf people] as disabled".[728] As we have seen in respect of the disability movement more generally, Deaf separatism expresses the political approach of a new layer of middle class deaf professionals who have rejected wider social change in favour of a Deaf "lifestyle" based on a supposedly distinct set of interests for all Deaf people.

There is a common history to the issues affecting Deaf and other disabled people in the post-war years—the closure of institutions; the economic changes which helped many to join the workforce for the first time; the contradictory role of charities; the realities of official integration versus genuine resources to promote diversity; the gains and shortcomings of anti-discrimination legislation. The rights and services won for and by Deaf people in recent decades are as fragile as those of other disabled people. Winning genuine equality and inclusion demands unity against those who seek to dismantle them.

12.
Some controversies

This chapter looks in a little more detail at specific issues only touched on or not yet discussed, which are nevertheless an essential part of this book's analysis.

Whether or not a particular impairment is real or involves disability, as discussed earlier in relation to deafness or mental distress, is often hotly disputed. Other impairments, the existence of which may also be contested, are relevant only in particular social contexts. This is especially true of both general and specific learning difficulties, the subject of the first two sections. These are discussed principally in relation to the educational context in which they most often appear.

Independent living is a central demand of the disability movement, but as a goal it is no less difficult to realise than that of civil rights and raises a series of complex questions. The third section examines the history and politics of independent living, especially the changing environment within which activists have campaigned to make it a reality.

The chapter concludes by examining perhaps the most controversial issues concerning disabled people. The first concerns the rise of disability hate crime, asking how prevalent this is in Britain and how it compares with hate crimes motivated by racism or homophobia. The final issue discussed here concerns the difficult and slippery concept of "quality of life". Many debates about disability rights touch on this question: none more so than that of assisted dying or suicide. The last section therefore looks at the history of this question and the context within which it is raised, before settling on a clear position that is consistent with a disability rights as well as a socialist perspective.

Education and 'special needs'

The liberal notion that education under capitalism must be a force for progress ignores the way in which it mirrors and reinforces social inequality and competition. Education is shaped by and reproduces class divisions; its primary purpose to meet the requirements of the economy.

There is nevertheless a recurring tension between those working in education who see it as a means of expanding the horizons of pupils and students and those whose overriding priority is to meet the demands of society's rulers. This tension is if anything greater when it comes to educating children deemed to have learning difficulties.

One in five English schoolchildren are diagnosed as having "special educational needs" (SEN)[729]—a hugely elastic term which refers to anything from a minor hearing impairment to profound learning difficulties. SEN children are far more likely to be excluded than their peers, comprising more than seven in ten of those permanently excluded.[730] Academies, meanwhile, which are beyond the control of local authorities and have no legal obligation to accept SEN children in the first place,[731] are nevertheless twice as likely to exclude SEN pupils as other schools.[732]

The Conservative Party promised in its 2010 election manifesto to end "the bias towards the inclusion of children with special needs in mainstream schools".[733] It described the benefits of inclusion as "far outweighed by the grievous damage that this policy has caused, not just to children with SEN but to their peers in mainstream education, their teachers, and their parents".[734]

Research in 2014 by the Centre for Studies on Inclusive Education (CSIE) showed the practical consequences, with the first rise since 1983 in the proportion of children with a statement of SEN being sent to special (segregated) schools. The report also found huge unevenness in provision. From 2007 to 2013, Newham in east London (one of the country's poorest boroughs) sent just two in every 1,000 children to a special segregated school. The figure for Torbay council in contrast was 14 in every 1,000 (the average across England is eight in every 1,000, or 0.8 percent).[735]

Whether special or mainstream schooling is best for teaching children with widely varying impairments is an issue that remains hugely contested by parents and educationalists alike. Many parents have to fight for the right to send their child to a mainstream school, while for others inclusion means their child is placed in such a school with no appropriate resources or support. As Alan Dyson, professor of education at Manchester University, put it: "Special needs is just an administrative category. The only thing these kids have in common is that they've been labelled special needs".[736]

A study in the late 1970s "found that headteachers, teachers, psychologists, medical officers, welfare officers, psychiatrists and others who dealt with slow-learning or disruptive pupils referred as potentially ESN-M [educationally subnormal-mild] used ten different accounts to define such a child." As a consequence, the experience of education for many thousands of children was even more neglectful and alienating than that of their peers:

'We couldn't possibly cope with him here—he should be at the special school.' These words from the head of the local infant school sentenced me to seven years at the local education authority's 'physical handicap' day school. It was six miles from where I lived and operated in a time warp all of its own. People arrived late and went home early. Lessons—in English and Maths—only took second place to physiotherapy, riding and swimming. There was to be no pressure and so there were no apparent goals.[737]

This same lack of consensus still characterises the assessment of those with mild learning difficulties.[738] One parent's dilemma is representative of many others:

At the moment, the focus is where Alex will go to secondary. The local choices are limited. There is the giant comprehensive in which he would have to shunt distressingly from class to class throughout the day, and where there is no great expertise on site. There is an academy with a massively oversubscribed autism unit. There is a special school that attempts to meet 'a rainbow' of wildly divergent needs, where a large minority of students have complex behavioural and emotional difficulties, and GCSE results are very low. It is a pretty typical local picture, which may explain why the number of SEN pupils in private schools almost trebled over the past decade.[739]

Cuts of more than 40 percent in local authority funding between 2010 and 2015 have led to reductions in SEN services and redundancies among support staff. In one national survey, 83 percent of respondents reported severe or significant cuts in local authority provision of educational psychologists, 50 percent reported cuts in child and adolescent mental health services, 70 percent in speech and language therapy and 71 percent in behavioural support outreach.[740]

The answer to the frequently asked question "why do children fail?" has more to do with the nature of society than anything intrinsic to individual ability. Until recently, children with literacy or numeracy difficulties could expect to work in manual labour. With the decline in this type of work and the relative permanence of mass unemployment, the labour of children from the poorest or ethnic minority families is increasingly seen as either marginal or no longer needed. Special needs education reproduces their social position for the next generation, legitimating differential treatment while in itself being seen as a legitimate and humane provision.[741]

State-funded education developed much later in Britain than in many of its competitor countries. Economic success convinced Britain's rulers there was no need for the educational advances in which its rivals invested. State secondary schools were first introduced in England in 1902, around a century after France, Germany and the US.

The eugenics movement had a strong influence on the development of education. In 1908, the UK's Royal Commission for the Care and Control of the Feeble-Minded reported that women working in factories were "neglecting their homes and their families... They often go out to work so that their husbands can loaf and drink...unless there is some reform in this matter of female labour the number of defectives in the next generation will be greatly increased".[742] The Wood Report on Mental Deficiency suggested in 1929 that if only "all the families containing mental defectives" could be segregated, the "overwhelming majority of the families thus collected would belong to that section of the community we propose to call the social problem class".[743]

The ability of the rich to provide privately for their own children has helped entrench a commonly held assumption that only children from poorer families are likely to have learning difficulties.

The first school for the blind, opened in Liverpool in 1791, discharged all those seen as "incapable of any labour".[744] This concern—how the maximum number of children can be made productive and self-sufficient at the minimum possible cost—has remained central to government policy. The *Times Educational Supplement* noted of a 1980 government White paper on SEN: "the three words that appear most often...are not...special educational needs, they are Present Economic Circumstances".[745]

Across Europe as a whole in 2006, there were over 2 million children with SEN, of whom 57 percent attended segregated special schools.[746] A UN report records the most rapid and radical changes as taking place in some of the world's poorest countries, such as Egypt, Morocco, Palestine, Vietnam and Yemen. "In Uganda and Arab countries, the integration of children with special needs coincides with the integration of girls into mainstream schools".[747] As anti-racist campaigners will testify, however, integration often means having to adapt to an overburdened, under-resourced and consequently rigid system that in practice enforces conformity instead of promoting diversity.

In 1988, Sally Tomlinson concluded an influential article with an observation as relevant now as it was then:

> Demands for a return to traditional methods, national control of the curriculum, recording pupil achievements, and monitoring and assessing teacher performance are now commonplace. As teachers understandably feel pressured to raise standards, and credential more pupils via more examinations, they are forced to exclude the Johnnys with reading problems from their own time and often from access to large and important areas of the curriculum.[748]

Research in 2015 demonstrated that pupil progress in general is not linear. At some points, children can make leaps in cognitive understanding, while at others they cannot fully understand concepts. Children seen as "low-attainers" in their first school years often perform well by the end of their secondary education. The use of test-based learning, however, restricts the curriculum, robs it of creativity and divides children into successes and failures from an early age. The study concludes: "the assumptions of many pupil tracking systems and Ofsted inspectors are probably incorrect".[749]

Discrimination is also a problem for teachers. Nearly half of disabled teachers commented in a National Union of Teachers survey that they were not confident in disclosing their disability or health condition on applying for a new job and reported high levels of harassment and negative stereotyping in the workplace. One in three disabled teachers who had left teaching said they had done so because the job was too tiring, stressful and difficult with their impairment or health condition.[750]

Schools are not socially disinterested or culturally neutral places, but operate largely as knowledge factories, where children learn to rule or to be ruled. They are also sites of conflict where different visions of education are contested. Teaching unions argue, rightly, that flexible teaching and assessment methods are needed for pupils to develop their potential. It is here that the ideas of Lev Semyonovich Vygotsky have huge relevance for today.

Vygotsky and an alternative approach

Vygotsky was a psychologist and educationalist in post-revolutionary Russia in the 1920s and 1930s who worked and wrote extensively on "defectology", particularly in education. He worked mainly with children who had physical or sensory impairments and others with what are now called learning difficulties. He believed the "special" schools attended by Russian disabled children should promote meaningful productive labour so that pupils could benefit fully from a social education and no longer see themselves as inferior.[751]

The economic crisis and civil war which followed the October 1917 Revolution left huge numbers of Russian children malnourished, orphaned and homeless, with many also mentally or physically damaged. Vygotsky's approach was first to understand the individual "defect" (impairment) and then, crucially, its social, emotional and developmental impact on the child. As he put it, the: "social effect of the defect (the inferiority complex) is one side of the social conditioning. The other side is the social pressure on the child to adapt to those circumstances created and compounded for the normal human type".[752] For him, disabled children were primarily "normal" people who may have exceptional talents.

Vygotsky referred to special schools in Russia as "schools for fools". He believed that if a child's needs meant she had to be educated in a special setting, this should be for as short a period as possible. The "fundamental idea is to overcome the very notion of handicap",[753] with individual "compensatory" programmes the best means of promoting development.

> the traditional education of children with mental defects...has been weakened by a tendency toward pity and philanthropy; it has been poisoned by morbidness and sickliness. Our education is insipid; it nips the pupil in the bud; there is no salt to this education. We need tempered and courageous ideas. Our ideal is not to cover over a sore place with cotton wadding and protect it with various methods from further bruises but to clear a wide path for overcoming the defect, for overcompensation.[754]

While recognising that some impairments may be physiologically caused (for example, due to problems at childbirth or genetic disorders), Vygotsky saw most "retardation" as due to difficult conditions at home or school. Changing social attitudes and circumstances could help many "uneducable" or "unmanageable" children to thrive. For him, disabled children developed differently because they are seen and treated as such. This led to "disontogenesis"—the distortion of a child's development by the prevailing environment.

Vygotsky believed that children "compensated" for impairment by developing their other senses. When the famous deaf and blind American revolutionary, Helen Keller, visited Russia, Vygotsky wrote:

"her defect did not become a brake but was transformed into a drive which ensured her development".[755]

In addition to providing a tailor-made curriculum, Vygotsky argued that teachers should treat the disabled child as they would any other, being positive about his or her potential, using strategies to overcome stigma, and adopting collaborative, interactive learning (including games) to promote the rounded development of all pupils.

Vygotsky was particularly influential in Soviet psychology between 1929-1931, but the consolidation of Stalin's rule led to his demotion and the banning of his books. Two years after his death of tuberculosis in 1934, all discussion of his work was prohibited. His approach was hugely ahead of his time and of significant benefit to those working with SEN children today.

There are many teachers in education who do attempt to develop alternatives. As one puts it: "my purpose with all these strategies, then, is ultimately to blur the divide between disabled and non-disabled, to multistream rather than mainstream, to complicate that binary rather than eradicate differences in some kind of elusive or illusory search for universals".[756]

As Michael Rosen has commented of education under capitalism more generally:

> Education has broken knowledge up into 'subjects' that neither correspond to parts of the brain nor to the real world... This false subject division also involves a hierarchy...some knowledges or intelligences are regarded as better than others. At present education proceeds by ranking pupils and students according to their success in a very narrow range of abilities—mostly logical and mathematical ones. The rest, unless they have private education, are shunted around in what the pupils themselves perceive as less important courses for people like them who are 'not intelligent'. In one stroke, we teach the majority of people (mostly working class) that they are incapable human beings.[757]

The struggle to defend education as a right for all requires a vision of a social good that anyone can enjoy at any point in their lives. Any education system worth the name must promote creativity and critical thinking for staff and students alike, with everyone's contribution equally nourished and valued. Capitalist society, however, is incapable of meeting this aspiration.

What is neurodiversity?

Neurodiversity is the modern umbrella term for a group of support needs including specific learning difficulties (SpLDs) such as dyslexia, attention deficit hyperactive disorder (ADHD) and autism. The core principles of neurodiversity are that these "conditions...are 'real' and neurological in nature",[758] that neurodiverse people should be seen as a social minority distinct from the neurotypical majority, and their differences should be recognised as natural human variation instead of being pathologised.

Dyslexia and ADHD (and also autism) were identified in a 30-year period from the 1880s onwards as employers increasingly demanded a more literate and specialised workforce and as psychology and psychiatry became more established as specialist disciplines.[759] Interest in SpLDs increased with the expansion of higher education and white-collar work in the decades after the Second World War. Dyspraxia[760] and ADHD were categorised as mental disorders and placed in the Diagnostic Service Manual. Opponents of this "medicalisation" argued that there is no such thing as, for example, dyslexia—a position still taken by some critics today.[761]

This section examines some of the myths associated with these "disorders," and asks what their rise tells us about disability, impairment and society.

Specific learning difficulties

The term dyslexia describes problems with aspects of reading and/ or spelling. Both dyslexia and dyspraxia are best seen as a spectrum, with clusters of difficulties varying in severity and affecting individuals in different ways. The more obvious symptoms of dyspraxia, such as clumsiness and co-ordination problems, usually become less noticeable in adulthood, but difficulties with aspects of memory, organisation of thoughts and elements of perception remain harder to identify.[762]

People diagnosed with dyslexia or dyspraxia later in life frequently recall being labelled by teachers as slow, stupid, lazy or careless and being isolated or bullied by other children. Working class children in general, and black and Asian children in particular, are less likely to be diagnosed due to lower expectations while at school.[763] Isobel remembers her good intentions always being thwarted: "I'd spend a lot of time on homework and it would come back covered in red pen. And I'd think, what's the point?"[764] Diagnostic techniques are highly standardised and include the use of controversial IQ tests. Assessments of older adults are also more complex, due to compensation techniques they develop for their difficulties.[765]

Studies from England, Sweden and the US suggest that between 30 and 52 percent of the prison population in all three countries may be dyslexic.[766] These figures are a shocking contrast to the estimated prevalence of dyslexia in the general population, ranging from 4 to 10 percent in Britain and 10 to 20 percent in the US (where definitions of dyslexia are much broader).[767]

Some people counter the myth that people with dyslexia are less intelligent by arguing instead that they are more creative,[768] preferring careers in subjects like art, science or technology which require less reading and writing.[769] On being asked whether being dyslexic had influenced his photography, David Bailey replied: "I feel dyslexia gave me a privilege. It pushed me into being totally visual." Psychologist and writer David Grant observed of Bailey's response:

> I'm not so sure that dyslexics are born to be creative, visual thinkers. I suspect it is the experience of *being* dyslexic that leads to many dyslexics becoming creative, and *being* dyslexic that influences their choice of which profession to enter.[770]

When the famous English painter J M W Turner was asked for advice, he relied: "The only secret I have is damned hard work." Most dyslexic and dyspraxic students do have to work more intensely than their peers, and greater social isolation may also help promote habits more beneficial for creative work.[771]

It was believed until recently in Western countries that dyslexia did not exist in Japan or China, due to the difference in writing scripts. Research in Japan, Taiwan and the US, however, found that the proportion of children with SpLDs in each country (around 6 percent) was almost identical.[772] There is also a genetic component, with a one in two chance that a dyslexic parent will have a child who is also dyslexic.[773] Finally, although it is untrue that males are more likely to have SpLDs, differences in behaviour, confidence levels and in the expectations commonly imposed on the sexes may help to explain why girls are less likely to be diagnosed at school.

The first medical paper on what became classified as ADHD—the most researched of all neurodiverse differences—appeared in 1798. ADHD is known to have a neurological basis and some individuals with higher degrees of hyperactivity may respond to medication (although some forms of behaviour, particularly among children, are often mistaken for ADHD "symptoms" and duly medicated as such).[774] Attention deficit also exists on a spectrum, with groups of features of varying frequency and severity. Despite the title,[775] hyperactivity is not always present in people diagnosed with ADHD. The latter is frequently found alongside other SpLDs, and is often overlooked because these may be more prominent. On the other hand, clumsiness in some people with SpLDs can be due to inattention and impulsivity associated with ADHD rather than poor motor co-ordination and poor reading skills may be due to concentration problems.

In the US, nearly one in six boys under the age of ten has been diagnosed with ADHD, with most of them placed on medication. In most developed countries, the incidence is estimated at around one child in 20. Business magazine *The Economist* recently noted that the Israeli government allows ADHD medication to be obtained on prescription to help boost performance at work. The use of similar stimulants on US college campuses "prompted the Food and Drug Administration (FDA) to crack down on their supply, though the prohibition was short-lived because it also made it harder for parents to get hold of medication for their children".[776]

Autism

For most of the 20th century autism was believed to affect only three or four children in 10,000. An enormous increase in prevalence rates from the 1990s onwards led to much talk of an epidemic, with the US Centre for Disease Control estimating that one in 68 children was affected.[777] Against all the available evidence, many people still believe it is caused by a vaccine, the wrong diet, or exclusively by genetic factors. The explanation for the rise, however, is more complex.

The term "autism" was wrongly associated with schizophrenia, before being adopted by psychologist Eugen Bleuler in 1911 to describe a form of uncommunicative and asocial behaviour. In the US and (particularly) the Soviet Union of the 1940s and 1950s, autism was seen as a psychological condition affecting only the upper classes—echoing earlier views of neurosis or hysteria. This was partly due to the work of Leo Kanner, who classified autism as a very rare form of infantile psychosis caused by cold and unaffectionate parents. Kanner's work led to the twin psychoanalytic notions of "refrigerator" and "smother" mothers, attributing autism (and ADHD) to poor parenting. Popularised in the media and women's magazines, these highly misogynistic "theories" led to a number of suicides by guilt-stricken mothers.[778]

British psychologists Lorna Wing and Judith Gould, who rejected these theories as "bloody stupid", conducted a study in the 1970s which found that Kanner's criteria for autism were severely flawed.[779] This led them to the work of German paediatrician and psychiatrist Hans Asperger, whose theories preceded and contrasted sharply with those of Kanner. Asperger identified autism as a lifelong impairment with many causes, but also as a diverse continuum whose traits, although always common among humans, had never been fully identified. He worked with his autistic pupils to develop creative forms of education which best suited their needs.[780] The fact that Asperger's work took place under Nazi rule in the 1930s and 1940s was a strong contributory factor in its being neglected for over 30 years.[781] Its rediscovery led to his name becoming popularly associated with a specific sub-type of autism without learning difficulties or speech delay: Asperger's Syndrome.[782]

Research in 1977 proved that autism had a genetic component, leading to its designation as a "disorder" in the *Diagnostic and Statistical Manual* (*DSM-III*, 1980). This drew on new evidence of a "triad of impairments" (difficulties in the areas of social behaviour, language and communication, and flexibility of thought). Further research in the 1990s pointed to autism as a developmental disability, with a distinction between "low-functioning" and "high-functioning":

> Recruiters have noticed that the mental qualities that make a good computer programmer resemble those that might get you diagnosed with Asperger's syndrome: an obsessive interest in narrow subjects; a passion for numbers, patterns and machines; an addiction to repetitive tasks; and a lack of sensitivity to social cues. Some joke that the internet was invented by and for people who are "on the spectrum", as they put it in the Valley. Online, you can communicate without the ordeal of meeting people.[783]

The identification of broader criteria and better testing methods (and the popularity of the film *Rain Man* in 1988) led to a huge increase in diagnosis.

The medicalised view of autism is still dominant. An appeal in 2005 by the US charity *Cure Autism Now* ended: "It's time to triple our efforts, to make finding the cause or causes of autism a national priority just as we did for polio in the 1950s and the AIDS virus in the 1980s".[784] A renewal of the US Combating Autism Act in 2011 led to huge investment in research, despite much of it being discredited— most notoriously, Andrew Wakefield's study linking the measles/mumps/rubella (MMR) vaccine with autism and gastrointestinal disorders. Wakefield "still has many supporters despite retraction of his 1998 study by *The Lancet* over significant concerns about research ethics, conflict of interest, and falsification of data".[785]

Adults with autism began to form their own organisations in the 1990s,[786] increasingly challenging assumptions that the key issue is changing, curing or controlling the "abnormal" child—rather than changing the environment or adapting teaching or care methods. The campaign for greater recognition and improved services led in the UK to The Autism Act of 2009.

A large-scale UK study in 2013 found that girls were about 75 percent less likely to be diagnosed with an autistic spectrum "disorder" than boys. The prevalence rate for autism in the UK, about four in every 1,000 children, is also substantially lower than the equivalent US figure of about 11 in every 1,000.[787] Allen Frances, the US psychiatrist who chaired the task force that produced *DSM-IV*, now argues that overdiagnosis has led to a "false epidemic'" and children "who would have been called eccentric, different, were suddenly labeled autistic".[788]

This led to the makers of *DSM-5* dropping Asperger's Syndrome as a diagnosis. One of them, David Kupfer, told the *New York Times*: "It involves a use of treatment resources. It becomes a cost issue".[789] People "on the spectrum" are now grouped under the single title of Autism Spectrum Disorder. Some "Aspies" worry that their exclusion from *DSM-5* will lead to greater discrimination. As one put it: "When you hear the word autism, you think of institutionalization, speech delay, diapers. It's a scary word. It's going to make me want to be even more concealed".[790]

Whatever one thinks of this view, autism remains a vague term covering a large spectrum of behaviours and debates over its nature and how it is best addressed are likely to continue. Actor and comedian David Mitchell describes some of the "interventions" available to those who can afford them:

> Some [autism therapists] work for local care-providers, some are freelance; some are occupational therapy specialists, some focus on speech and language, some advocate Floortime (a play-based treatment), some "applied behaviour analysis" (rewards and measurements); some are evangelical about one approach, some take a more pragmatic "whatever works, works" approach... Some [costs are] refundable, if the official criteria for the tutor are satisfied, but for the most part you're on your own. Therapy during school holidays is not repayable, because the authorities believe autism ceases to exist outside term time.[791]

Diagnoses of autism are still more likely for children of white, middle class professional families[792] and class also influences the content of a diagnosis. As one parent succinctly put it: "The difference between high-functioning and low-functioning is that high-functioning means your deficits are ignored, and low-functioning means your assets are ignored".[793]

Conclusion

Many people with SpLDs or autism prefer the term neurodiversity, partly due to individual variation and diffuse boundaries within diagnostic categories, as well as a desire to resist stereotyping and discrimination. For similar reasons, there is an increasing preference for the term "specific learning difference" instead of "specific learning difficulty," also reflecting recognition that there are many ways to learn. The widespread use of reading and writing is, after all, relatively new in human history.[794]

People who are blind or unable to walk are sometimes seen as a burden, but neurodiverse people whose behaviour may be due to differences in brain function are more likely to be held responsible, in effect blamed, for their impairments. These differences are often exaggerated or pathologised, reinforcing the sense of "the Other". One writer countered this idea particularly well, saying that the autistic response is one "many of us have used in certain situations. Block out the intruder. Strangers are dangerous. Touch is bad. Change is scary. Barriers are important. Mysterious forces control us, and only our routines and our rituals keep us safe".[795] Neurodiverse people may experience a more intense version of fears shared by many others—for example, when starting at university:

It is the morning that I am due to go to the university...for the first time. As a 19 year old who has never lived away from home, I am fearful of what lies ahead. I pace up and down my parents' lounge without direction, contemplating what lies in wait. My head is full of uncontrollable thoughts and questions. Who will I live with? Will they like me? Will I be able to make friends... Will I be able to cope with the course? Is this really what I want to do with the rest of my life?[796]

Teachers and practitioners working with neurodiverse people have found new ways to learn, think and visualise that could be of much wider social benefit, but the necessary resources are rarely available.

Carl Jung is sometimes credited with the claim that collecting a sample of 1000 pebbles would make it possible to calculate the average weight of a pebble on a given beach. The chances of finding an actual pebble of this exact weight are, however, virtually non-existent. This analogy is perhaps even more appropriate in relation to the ubiquitous and often pernicious concept of normality. Capitalist society categorises human behaviour not to promote individuality but to promote the interests of profit. A rhetorical commitment to diversity is, therefore, accompanied by a practice that promotes stigma and enforces conformity.

Independent Living

Independent living is often described as a key goal of the disability movement, second only to civil rights. The term does not express a desire by disabled people to do everything alone or to live in isolation, but instead refers to a demand for:

> the same choices and control in our every-day lives that our non-disabled brothers and sisters, neighbors and friends take for granted. We want to grow up in our families, go to the neighborhood school, use the same bus as our neighbors, work in jobs that are in line with our education and interests, and raise families of our own. We are profoundly ordinary people sharing the same need to feel included, recognized and loved.[797]

Such demands may seem unremarkable, but making them a reality is increasingly possible only for disabled people who can afford the time, effort and expense involved. Costs and resources are the principal (though not the only) reasons as to why independent living has from the outset been a complex and contested issue.

Ed Roberts and his allies were the founders of independent living centres (ILCs) in the US.[798] They saw the first ILCs, established in Berkeley and Boston in 1972, as "organising centres for disabled people advocating for and empowering themselves." In reality, this meant predominantly "young, white and middle class physically disabled college graduates". By the 1990s, Congress was funding 400 ILCs, reflecting and reinforcing the wider trend of deinstitutionalisation. By then ILCs also included (some) adults with mental health and learning difficulties and from minority ethnic backgrounds.[799] With US federal law requiring that a minimum of 50 percent of their managers and staff be disabled people, ILCs now "provide core services such as personal attendant services, benefits, housing and transportation information, along with a diverse range of others, with different programs, staffing organization and funding sources".[800]

This shift towards community living has faced opposition, both in the earliest days of ILCs and at present. Factors such as lack of funding, carers worried about isolation and a lack of community services and media-fed scares about the danger posed by former asylum inmates have been cited as obstacles to independent living initiatives in several European countries.[801]

As part of their campaign for greater personal autonomy, disability activists in Britain demanded "direct payments". First legislated for in the early 1990s, this allows disabled people to employ their own helpers. However, the implementation of the scheme (as well as that of its successor, personalisation) has been immensely problematic. The first difficulty is that some disabled people prefer to obtain support from a friend or family member or from a local authority or voluntary organisation. Many do not want the stress or responsibility of being an employer. Others may be too socially or geographically isolated to exercise any meaningful choice or control over their support.

The take-up of direct payments or personalisation has been lower among those with learning or mental health difficulties and the elderly, who may need advocacy, advice and emotional support. Many individuals express no preference between nursing, residential or family care and independent living—assuming there is no abuse, and that their needs are met. Where lifelong dependency is inevitable, "the priority may be to provide stimulation and enjoyment".[802]

Personal assistants (PAs) are less likely to be unionised, and are vulnerable to low pay, unsocial hours and inappropriate demands such as lifting and carrying.[803] A large majority are women, comprising 87 percent of PAs in the UK and 85 percent in Norway. Many PAs are also likely to be migrants, with a lack of employment rights making them vulnerable to abuse.[804] Even when PAs have decent pay, terms and conditions, there are other complex and more personal difficulties. Some disabled people employing PAs may prefer unskilled workers because they are more likely to do as they are told; others may treat their PAs as more akin to a paid friend and confidante. In both cases, this compromises "the separation of practical and emotional roles on which independent living is based."[805]

Support services are notoriously uneven, with inadequate resources and training. Many desperately poor disabled people choose direct payments because it presents the best chance to have even the minimum degree of choice in their lives, such as what to eat or what time to get up or go to bed. The only alternatives are often either residential homes or care agencies which provide an inferior service (as well as inferior pay and conditions for their staff). Decades after the adoption of the social model by public sector services, the treatment of disabled people in social care often continues to undermine dignity and autonomy. This is unlikely to improve under the impact of further funding cuts and lack of recognition for care work.

Decades of cost-cutting, performance management and marketization aimed at turning service users into customers have left deep scars on many public sector workers. Disabled people often relate instances of brutal or unfeeling treatment, leading them to regard medical and social services professionals as uniformly hostile to or opposed to disabled people's interests. The approach that "the professionals know best" indeed has deep historical roots and remains a feature of modern social services. It is also vital, however, to recognise that there are allies to be found there too:

Those who have made disability their life's work may have an insight into the problems and priorities... A disabled person may generalise from their own limited experience, while a professional may have a much broader knowledge of the impairment group... many [of them] have played important roles in developing self-help and advocacy groups for and with disabled people and their families...radical professionalism...promotes interdependence, focuses on capacity and takes a back seat.[806]

In 2008, the Labour government in Britain published the Independent Living Strategy, supported by all the parliamentary parties, and based on the findings in the key government report, *Improving the Life Chances of Disabled People*. This stated the key goals of independent living to be "providing disabled people with choice, empowerment and freedom" assisted by the provision of "individualised budgets", which "should be used to get whatever type of support the individual needs—whether it is equipment, personal assistance, housing adaptations, help with transport to work or something else entirely".[807] Anticipating the similar approach taken by its successor, the report added: "government is moving increasingly towards a menu-driven approach. People should be able to access support from a range of choices, focusing their own package of support on their own personal needs".[808]

In 2013, a report found there had been no progress in one of the strategy's two most important aims, namely greater choice and control in the lives of disabled people. Overall, the years since 2008 had seen "serious reversals for independent living after decades of sometimes slow but positive improvement".[809] Another report in the same year found that worst affected were those "with low socio-economic status".[810]

In a society dominated by huge inequalities, everyone cannot have the same degree of autonomy and choice. Wealthier individuals exercise qualitatively greater control over their personal affairs, including the use of private sector services where resources are not restricted in myriad different ways. Successive governments, as we have seen,[811] have used the rhetoric of choice and independence for disabled people to justify privatisation and cuts in public services. A far bigger factor undermining meaningful community living is the relentless cuts to public services, which particularly affect disabled people. Personalisation continues to be promoted as the key to independence, but there is little point in disabled individuals being "empowered" with their own budgets when many of the services they rely on have been cut back or closed down.

The notion of individual autonomy is a carefully nurtured illusion. At various points in their lives, people are more or less autonomous or dependent and may provide personal support for others, particularly elderly relatives. Some of those receiving personal support may also provide it to someone else. Every human being depends on a complex network of services over which individuals have little or no control. The planning and organisation of these services, from health and personal support to transport and electricity, is increasingly driven by commercial and not public interest. The key to securing the most appropriate support for individuals is to campaign for more collective and democratic control over these services—a process that ultimately demands fundamental social and economic change.

Disability and hate crime

In January 2015, the UK's *Daily Express* newspaper ran a shocking headline story claiming that hate crimes against disabled people had increased by 213 percent.[812] Less spectacular increases were subsequently reported in the Scottish media, echoing other earlier newspaper stories. After the 2012 London Paralympics, *The Guardian* claimed "disability hate crime is at its highest level since records began".[813]

The concept of hate crime first became widely known in the UK[814] after the racist murder of Stephen Lawrence in 1993. An influential report in 2008, *Getting Away With Murder*, was the first major attempt to apply the concept to cases where disabled people were the victims. The report highlighted several horrific examples, including the murder of Raymond Atherton, a 40-year-old man with learning difficulties who had also been diagnosed with schizophrenia. In May 2006, after being badly beaten and having bleach poured over him, he was thrown in the River Mersey. He had considered his attackers, teenagers who had regularly robbed and beaten him over the previous nine months, to be his friends.[815]

The report explained that, in contrast to racist and homophobic hate crime, perpetrators of such offences against disabled people are frequently well known to their victims as friends or carers.[816] Police or judges often described such crimes as "senseless" and "motiveless" and referred to disabled victims (such as Raymond Atherton) as "vulnerable". Offences consequently attracted lesser sentences than for comparable offences deemed racist or homophobic.[817]

The Crown Prosecution Service (CPS) urges caution about the use of the term disability hate crime. "Some crimes are committed because the offender regards the disabled person as being vulnerable and not because the offender dislikes or hates disabled people".[818] The government defines a vulnerable disabled adult as someone who "is or may be in need of community care services…is or may be unable to take care of him or herself, or unable to protect him or herself against significant harm or exploitation".[819]

A Scope report agreed that many cases appeared to be motivated by a combination of vulnerability and hostility, but countered that disabled people "are not innately vulnerable, though they may be if they do not receive the services they need" and may (like everyone else) become so "in situations where someone wishes them harm".[820]

Hate crimes deemed to be racist "are often, or taken to be, attacks on a whole community [for example, Muslims or Roma people] whereas disabled people may be picked on because they are particularly isolated".[821] Research by the Equality and Human Rights Commission (EHRC) found that some people thought only crime motivated by clear hatred or hostility should count, while others felt that offences based on seeing certain groups of disabled people as vulnerable or as "easy pickings" should also be judged as hate crime.[822] Erin Pritchard may be closer to the truth in arguing that disabled people may be targeted because they are seen as less likely to be able to fight back or defend themselves. Crimes may not be due to hate, but rather "perceived vulnerability".[823]

Some disabled people rely on personal support workers or carers who may be unpaid but who also have a(nother) job, may live in the same household and/or support a family. In this respect, there are similarities to domestic violence (usually against women), where the victim may have strong family or emotional attachments to, and/or is dependent on, the abuser. Like women in such situations, disabled people may not see their experiences as abuse, but may instead blame themselves or see the abuse as an inevitable part of the relationship.[824]

How prevalent is disability hate crime?

Disability hate crimes were first recognised in UK law in 2003, but only in respect of sentencing guidelines, and began being separately recorded in statistics four years later. Police recording practices about such offences vary widely, as does the likelihood of disabled people reporting them. The most recent Home Office report shows a rise of 8 percent in the year 2012/13 to 2013/14.[825]

This report goes on to say, however, that it "is less clear whether increases in disability, sexual orientation and transgender hate crime reflect a real rise in these offences or whether they reflect improved identification and recording practices by the police." Stephen Brookes, co-ordinator of the Disability Hate Crime Network, argued that statistics showing large increases in such crimes are highly misleading, leading to "fear among certain groups of disabled people that they will be a victim". Even if there is both more reporting by and greater awareness among disabled people, however, an estimated 97 percent of incidents are either not reported to police or not recorded by them.[826] According to the EHRC, overall levels of disability hate crime have remained stable year on year since 2007 (at an estimated 72,000 per year for England, Scotland and Wales combined).

A number of factors make it hard to estimate actual levels of disability hate crime. An EHRC report in 2013 asked disabled people why they did not report such incidents. The most common reasons were: "the police could not have done anything (36 percent); the police would not have been interested (31 percent); or the incident was too trivial to report (17 percent)".[827] These responses, similar to those for other types of hate crime,[828] suggest a widespread distrust of the police.

The police often perceive people with learning difficulties or in mental distress as more likely to be perpetrators rather than victims of crime and so as "unreliable witnesses".[829] However, these groups are the most likely to be victims of disability hate crime, having been shown to be more susceptible to befriending people who abuse them as well as more likely to be socially isolated.[830] They are also far more likely to report such crimes to health and other professionals such as social workers rather than to the police. An investigation by the charity Mencap in 2010 showed that people with learning difficulties found police officers "rude" and "patronising" and that they were ignored by officers who talked only to support workers even when they were present.[831]

A more general difficulty is the nature of hate crime against disabled people. The relevant legislation, Section 146 of the Criminal Justice Act, simply requires evidence of hostility. Crimes against disabled people "more generally get mislabelled as 'abuse' or 'bullying' so that the police do not perceive the incidents to be [their] business".[832] The causes of under-reporting include "fear of not being believed, learned helplessness, disabling barriers in the criminal justice system" and a fear among disabled victims that they will not be believed in court. They may, "like victims of sex crimes, feel that the court system can be a form of 'repeat victimization'—feeling like they are on trial, rather than the offender".[833] The Scope report of 2008 also made this connection:

> Women are still told not to walk around alone at night, or not to wear revealing clothes in case they invite unwanted attention. Disabled people are told to avoid certain areas, not to carry a white stick or to move house to escape harassment from neighbours.[834]

Causes and solutions

The rise of disability hate crime as a concept is itself rooted in an increasingly hostile portrayal of disabled people as an undeserving or fraudulent drain on hard-pressed public finances. Restrictions in disability benefits began with the replacement of Invalidity Benefit in 1995. Cuts and further restrictions to disability-related benefits have intensified year on year since, with increasingly drastic benefit sanctions accompanied by a constant stream of media headlines about benefit scroungers and cheats.[835]

In the autumn of 2010, Chancellor George Osborne announced £4 billion in benefit cuts. A "welfare cheat", he said, was no different to a mugger who robs you on the street, claiming that the figure "lost in this way" was £5 billion. This frequently cited figure adds the amount in fraudulent benefit claims (£1.6 billion, or 1 percent of total claims) to the (far larger) estimated total lost due to error. Deceptions such as these have led to wildly inaccurate public perceptions as to the scale and nature of benefit fraud, as well as to who actually receives benefits (mostly an ageing population).[836]

Media campaigns in papers like as *The Sun* "declaring war on feckless benefits claimants" and its "shop a cheat" initiative,[837] TV programmes such as Channel 4's *Benefits Street* and the government's widely promoted National Benefit Fraud Hotline have all helped to create the impression that this is a central problem. With tax avoidance by the wealthy amounting to the far larger sum of around £25 billion, disabled people are easy scapegoats in a climate of economic uncertainty and austerity. In this context, by far the worst offenders in perpetrating hate crime against disabled people are not alienated and brutalised youngsters, but the government and the media.

The phenomenon of disability hate crime may also be seen as an indictment of the process of deinstitutionalisation, with people left to fend for themselves against a background of fear and distrust of "the other", with concepts such as independent living often more of a comforting slogan than a practical reality. As criminologist Nils Christie commented of the situation in Norway in 1989:

> Through deinstitutionalisation some of the people in need of help are back to ordinary society, but in a special way. They are, but they are not. It is as if an invisible wall of glass exists between them and us. They are in our streets, our buses, our schools, our houses and our places of work. Close but distant, among us but lonely.[838]

Just as wealthy black or gay and lesbian individuals are at less risk of hate or other crime than their poorer counterparts, so are wealthy disabled people. As one respondent to an EHRC study in 2010 said: "Money protects. For example, taxis, nicer environments, more choice about where you live. Living alone on a council estate might make you more vulnerable to abuse, for example, being 'befriended' by an abuser".[839]

The record since the Macpherson report on the investigation into the murder of Stephen Lawrence suggests that campaigns aimed at changing police attitudes to hate crime are unlikely to succeed.[840] Proposals to introduce longer sentences for offenders have not been shown to have any impact on crime levels in any other area. Any effort to reduce the incidence of hate crime must instead address its underlying causes, particularly in "deprived (often urban) areas in which poverty, homelessness, unsettled, poor-quality housing and tensions from segregation of communities may worsen crime levels."[841]

Assisted suicide

Until 1970, campaigners sought the legalisation of both assisted suicide and euthanasia (the term means "good death", and involves active killing by someone else). They dropped suicide because this is seen, particularly since 9-11, as pejorative and morally tainted. Dignity in Dying (formerly the Voluntary Euthanasia Society) says "assisted suicide refers to providing assistance to someone who is not dying." But who defines who is dying and how? Under what time limits would someone with a terminal illness qualify? Are "the dying" a separate moral category?[842]

The unexpected election of a Conservative government in the UK in May 2015 prompted a fresh campaign to introduce assisted suicide legislation, only months after the previous one had been abandoned. Sarah Wootton of UK campaign group Dignity in Dying argued that the question is "the pressing social issue of our time", with "more than 300 terminally ill people a year taking their own lives in this country behind closed doors".[843]

The new law, proposed by Labour MP Rob Marris, would have provided "competent" adults with less than six months to live with help to end their own life on request. Both sides of the debate agree that the issue won't go away. Business magazine *The Economist* had previously commented:

some people would like to die peacefully, at a time of their choosing and with the assistance of a doctor. Their desire for a humane end should not offend liberal societies, which rest on the principle of self-determination, so long as one's actions do not harm others. This newspaper supports making assisted suicide legal. So, according to polls, do more than two-thirds of Americans and western Europeans.[844]

The debate was given added prominence by the case of Tony Nicklinson and support from the *British Medical Journal*[845] as well as individuals such as author Terry Pratchett.[846] Nicklinson, a former rugby player and skydiver, had developed locked-in syndrome (an incurable condition leaving patients aware but unable to move or talk) after a stroke. He learned to communicate by blinking his eyes. Denied a medically assisted death by the high court in 2012, he refused food and finally died of pneumonia.

Campaigners for assisted suicide say that in such cases, where there is little or no quality of life or where a terminal illness progressively reduces physical or mental capacity, people should have the right to die at a time of their choosing. Most (but not all) supporters also argue that it should apply only to those who are competent to make decisions but are terminally ill.

In February 2015, Canada's Supreme Court ruled that the country should join Belgium, Colombia, Luxembourg, the Netherlands and Switzerland in making assisted suicide legal. The decision followed the long-running legal case of Gloria Taylor, which continued after her death in 2012. A rare disease cumulatively limited her physical functions, beginning with her hands and eventually ending her ability to breathe by herself. The Supreme Court quoted her plea to spare her family needless trauma: "I live in apprehension that my death will be slow, difficult, unpleasant, painful, undignified, and inconsistent with the values and principles I have tried to live by".[847]

Most disability activists who have taken a stance are opposed to assisted dying—although 75 per cent of disabled people taking part in the 2007 British Social Attitudes Survey believed those with a terminal and painful illness should be allowed an assisted death.[848] The divisions over the issue reflect its sensitivity and complexity.

Although it can be misleading to generalise from individual cases, the focus here is on the use of different standards in relation to the lives and wishes of disabled people compared with those of others.

US background

In February 2014, a Pennsylvania court threw out a prosecution against a nurse for allegedly assisting her ailing 93-year-old father's suicide. Her decision to give him a potentially lethal bottle of morphine was treated as an attempt to help alleviate his pain. The ruling illustrated an increasing reluctance by US authorities to criminalise medical care that hastens death.[849] Since a 1997 referendum in Oregon, which voted by 60 to 40 percent to uphold a law permitting assisted suicide, five other US states have adopted their own versions.[850]

The current US debate can be traced back to the case of Larry McAfee, a 34-year-old engineer who became a quadriplegic due to a 1985 motorcycle accident. After four years spent in successive nursing homes and despite stable health, he was moved to an intensive care unit in one of Georgia's poorest hospitals. Three months later, McAfee sought the right to turn off the ventilator that kept him breathing. He said the accident had deprived him of the things that made his life worth living. A judge who came to the hospital to hear his case said the decision was brave and sensible and that, as McAfee's lawyer argued, turning off his respirator was simply "allowing the injury process to take its natural course".[851] This was four years after the original accident.

Disability activists pointed out that a non-disabled person who wasn't terminally ill or in continual pain would have received suicide-prevention counselling. A campaign eventually convinced McAfee that he could live a meaningful and self-directed life. In February 1990, he spoke at the Georgia State Senate, attacking a system "that will pay for the warehousing of the disabled but one that does not address or even consider the quality of our shattered lives".[852] McAfee and his supporters eventually convinced the authorities to properly fund his support, along with new state provision for severely disabled people to live in the community with full attendant care.[853]

In 1996, a series of controversial court decisions backed multiple suicides facilitated by physician Jack Kevorkian, who admitted that most of those he killed did not have a terminal illness. He said that his suicide device was intended for quadriplegics and that the "voluntary self-elimination of individual and mortally diseased or cripple lives taken collectively can only enhance the preservation of public health and welfare".[854] Despite support from the likes of the *New York Times*, Kevorkian was eventually found guilty of second-degree murder in one case—mainly due to him recording this killing for the national *60 Minutes* TV show and publicly challenging the law to stop him.[855]

US law professor Yale Kamisar first pointed out the link between inadequate health care for the majority and assisted suicide in 1958, stating: "It would be ironic if the judiciary selected physician-assisted suicide as the one health care right that deserves constitutional status".[856]

Quality of life

Tony Nicklinson's case may seem at first a compelling argument for changing the law, but others with locked-in syndrome continue with lives they themselves describe as happy and fulfilling.[857] The term "right to die" is sometimes applied much more broadly to those who have conditions described as "incurable" or terminal. People who are blind, unable to walk or who have learning difficulties or dementia could all be described as "incurable." Few would say (not publicly at any rate) that anyone with such impairments has such a low quality of life that they would be better off dead.

"Rolling quad" leader and pioneer of the Independent Living Movement Ed Roberts pointed out that he has been living on a respirator for nearly three decades, noting that some of the cases involved are people "just as dependent on a respirator as I am. The major difference is that they know they're going to be forced into a nursing home—or they're already there—and I'm leading a quality life. That's the only difference. It's not the respirator. It's the money".[858]

In the case of terminal illness, what may be intolerably painful for one person and must end at all costs, may for someone else be a difficult trial where every remaining moment is nevertheless precious. Kevin Yuill asks on what basis we should legalise assisted suicide:

If it is autonomy, we must allow all who feel they are suffering unbearably assisted suicides, or patronisingly tell those who do not fit the criteria that they are not really suffering. If it is compassion, how can we legislate [for] acts of kindness? Surely, euthanasia or mercy killings would be more appropriate...doctors, if legalisation takes place, will not act from compassion but will be carrying out a professional duty. If, as studies show, pain is not the reason why individuals request assisted suicides, what possible justification can there be for restricting assisted suicides to those with 6 or 12 months to live? Why are they less valuable than anyone else?[859]

Too expensive?

The UK Mental Capacity Act of 2007 legalised "living wills" which allow patients to appoint an "attorney" to tell doctors when hospital food and water should be stopped. A year later, prominent right-to-die campaigner Baroness Warnock told dementia sufferers: "you're wasting people's lives...and you're wasting the resources of the National Health Service".[860]

Taro Aso, at the time of writing still Japanese Deputy Prime Minister, argued in January 2013 that the elderly should "hurry up and die" to relieve pressure on the state. Referring to elderly patients no longer able to feed themselves as "tube people", Aso added that "it costs several tens of millions of yen" a month to treat a single patient in the final stages of life.[861]

These views may rarely be articulated in public, but many old and disabled people do die each winter from malnutrition or hypothermia because they cannot afford both food and heat. Some might well decide on assisted suicide if it were offered to them. Could their actions and decisions really be described as autonomous? Personal choice is not equally available or equally exercised across society and it can carry little real meaning for the majority of people whose lives are dominated by a constant struggle to make ends meet.

The problems that people with terminal illnesses face are problems for society as a whole: under-resourced hospitals and care homes and a lack of resources for palliative care. A system that subjects its elderly and sick to poverty, neglect and social isolation undermines their will to live.[862]

Changing the law on assisted suicide in a climate of austerity will add to the pressures on healthcare staff already forced to balance competing priorities. Hastening the death of "bed-blocking" patients could become a regular option. There are many other objections: the impossibility of providing adequate legal safeguards,[863] relatives desperate for an inheritance, courts defining when and in which circumstances life is not "worth living". It is clear that this last scenario would apply most often to elderly and disabled people, whose organisations are consistently against assisted suicide.

Two reports in early 2015 highlighted inequities in access to quality end-of-life care across the UK. The first was by a House of Commons Health Committee. A second, *Equity in the Provision of Palliative Care in the UK: Review of Evidence*, made similar findings. It highlights how such care is:

> skewed towards those receiving cancer therapy; is poorly delivered in care-home settings; and is less likely to be available for people aged older than 85 years, for those living in areas of social deprivation, and for people from ethnic minority backgrounds. Alarmingly, the report emphasises how only a fraction of hospital specialist palliative care teams are available 24 hours a day, 7 days a week.[864]

Complex issues

Surveys in the Australia, Canada, New Zealand, the UK and the US consistently show large majorities in support of legalisation. Although a majority want the right to die, however, few seem likely to use it. "Around 0.2 per cent of all deaths in Oregon are assisted suicides, comprising less than one per cent of those who request information about an assisted death".[865] The equivalent figure for the Netherlands is 3 percent of all deaths—although this number has increased by an average of 15 percent a year since 2006.[866]

Of three state referendums in the US in the 1990s, only Oregon's was successful, partly because the law's explicit prohibition of euthanasia silenced opponents: "it was a reasonable 'prescribing only' measure that barred any kind of lethal injection or other direct action on a dying patient by the physician".[867] The law in the Netherlands, however, (in effect since 2002) is not restricted to those who are terminally ill, and does not distinguish between voluntary euthanasia and assisted suicide. This has led to more concerns but not to reports of abuse. Elsewhere, support for such legislation drops significantly when it is suggested that it *could* apply beyond terminal illness or to those who lack mental capacity.[868] Oregon has issued annual Death With Dignity Act (DWDA) reports since 1999. These show that "decedents" are elderly, white and mostly well educated and also that pain is not one of the main concerns of those requesting assisted suicide.[869] The report for 2014 states: "As in previous years, the three most frequently mentioned end-of-life concerns were: loss of autonomy (91.4 percent), decreasing ability to participate in activities that made life enjoyable (86.7 percent), and loss of dignity (71.4 percent)".[870]

Most of the available evidence does not offer support for the "slippery slope" argument—namely, that introducing legislation would lead to these laws being extended and the targeting of more vulnerable groups. Neither Oregon (where the law has applied since 1997) nor Washington State has seen any attempt to extend the legislation and the detailed annual reports for each state have to date shown no evidence of abuse. Oregon's legislation requires that applicants for assisted dying are informed of all alternative options, such as palliative care or pain relief, and that their request is both voluntary and "well-informed".[871] However, as a recent article in the *Wall Street Journal* noted, the Oregon Health Plan covers the cost of assisted suicide but excludes many important services and drugs, encouraging doctors to put pressure on poorer patients to consider it.[872]

None of this is to say that euthanasia is always morally wrong or that there is no such thing as "mercy killing". The other dimension of assisted suicide—the provision of pain relief which also speeds a patient's death—rarely involves a moral judgement that life is no longer worth living, but rather a clinical one that death is imminent. Throughout history, medical practitioners and family members have acted humanely in discreetly helping people in extreme physical distress to die. It is accepted medical practice in such circumstances, where requested by "competent" dying people, that pain-killing drugs can be administered or treatment withdrawn in the knowledge this may prove fatal.

Few people, given the personal circumstances in which such decisions are made, would not support an individual's right to an assisted suicide. It is this which largely explains the lack of any successful prosecutions of an assisted suicide in England and Wales since the Suicide Act of 1961. These decisions are private, often painful and extremely difficult to legislate for in the kind of society we live in. In the meantime, most disability activists are likely to continue opposing the legalisation and institutionalisation of assisted suicide. The belief that any such law carries too much potential for abuse may have more to do with disabled people's experiences and fears in a context of protracted austerity than the relative merits of the opposing arguments.

Jim Kirk was diagnosed with Motor Neurone Disease in 2004. His obituary pointed out that he had fought the illness and its effects, both on him and those close to him, until the end: "[Jim] was angry that the media was more interested in the 'exoticism' of assisted suicide than the more mundane but essentially life-supporting issues of access to adequate resources such as wheelchairs and computer technology for people who are hugely limited, isolated and disadvantaged by illness".[873] This seems an appropriate sentiment on which to conclude.

13.
Capitalism and disability today

Previous chapters explained how disability discrimination developed with the rise of class society and with the rise of capitalist society in particular. As we have seen, the roots of disability discrimination have less to do with particular types of industry than the general nature of labour under capitalism. This chapter looks at the character of this discrimination in late capitalism and how this has been affected by the rise of neoliberalism and the attacks on welfare spending.

Late capitalism

Western interest in China's industrial expansion has increased over recent decades, but this rarely extends to its impact on the workforce. Between 1985 and 2002, China reported more than 200,000 work-related deaths—a workplace fatality rate over three times more than that of the US—and more than 400,000 cases of serious injury. Health and safety rules are often ignored:

> competition in both the domestic and international markets has pushed firms to take every available measure to reduce costs, which includes under-investing in safety equipment or training. For example, if China's coal mining industry followed safety regulations, then the cost of production would increase by four times.[874]

The speed and scale of China's rise as an economic power is unprecedented, as is the scale of its pollution problem. It is now the world's biggest source of greenhouse gases. The *New York Times* reported in 2007 that only 1 percent of the 560 million Chinese city dwellers breathe air considered safe by the European Union: toxic smog kills hundreds of thousands every year. It is estimated that roughly two thirds of China's soil is polluted and 60 percent of underground water is too contaminated to drink.[875] Environmental catastrophe is commonplace:

> industrial cities where people rarely see the sun; children killed or sickened by lead poisoning or other types of local pollution; a coastline so swamped by algal red tides that large sections of the ocean no longer sustain marine life... Sulphur dioxide and nitrogen oxides spewed by China's coal-fired power plants fall as acid rain on Seoul, South Korea, and Tokyo. Much of the particulate pollution over Los Angeles originates in China.[876]

Such descriptions bring to mind the nightmare vision of Engels' classic writings about Manchester in the 19th century. According to the International Labour Organisation's "conservative estimates", every year two million men and women die due to accidents and diseases linked to their work. Every year, there are also 270 million occupational accidents and 160 million incidences of occupational disease.[877] The capacity of modern capitalism to wreak devastation on the world and its inhabitants is many times greater than in the period in which Marx and Engels wrote their indictments of its nature as a mode of production.

Meanwhile, the deinstitutionalisation programme initiated in Western countries from the 1950s onwards has never been completed. Campaigns to shut asylums and long-stay hospitals for people with learning difficulties were often prompted by a series of high-profile scandals which exposed appalling conditions. On the 761 wards Pauline Morris visited for her 1969 book *Put Away* nearly 80 percent of inmates were kept in wards of 40 beds or more and most did not even own their own toothbrush.[878]

In the US the number of psychiatric beds available fell from 558,000 in 1955 to 53,000 in 2005, with equivalent bed numbers in Britain falling from 150,000 to 27,000 over the same period. Mental health care since then "has moved in two different and contradictory directions. One, motivated by media and public fears", is to treat all those in mental distress "as potential axe murderers" who must be locked up. "The other approach, equally exaggerated, is to understate the gravity" of those in severe and chronic mental distress, pretending that all those affected can live "in the community" without major support networks in place.[879] In 1999, the Labour government's Health Minister derided Care in the Community as "couldn't care less in the community".[880] The head of an NHS watchdog, meanwhile, said in 2013 that UK mental hospitals "are effectively becoming prisons for people suffering from schizophrenia and other severe disorders".[881]

The huge factories and child labour now found elsewhere in the world largely disappeared from the advanced economies of the West in the second half of the 20th century. The number of people working in manufacturing in Britain is now half of that in 1973. Such facts are employed in support of claims that we live in a "post-industrial" society, in some way less capitalist than before. Restructuring, however, has always been central to capitalism. In Britain in the 1840s, the typical worker was employed in a cotton mill. Fifty years later, the working class was identified with heavy industry such as mines or shipyards. In the advanced capitalist economies of the 21st century, most workers are now employed in routinised white-collar jobs in finance or service industries. These range from call centres to supermarkets where the repetitive nature of the work means those workers are as subordinated to the work process as the earlier workers in the cotton mills.

As capitalism becomes more sophisticated in its production methods, so the impairments it creates become more diverse. Workers today are as likely to develop anxiety or depression as they are repetitive strain injuries or back problems caused by operating machinery or manual labour. In every field of industry, employers push workers harder to keep pace with competitors.

International agencies use a variety of means to help these companies further entrench their power. One current UN campaign pressurises nation states to adopt a single measure of disability using questions drawn up by its "Washington Group"—drawing heavily on classifications in the American Psychiatric Association's *Diagnostic Service Manual.*[882]

Disability and work in late capitalism

Across the 28 member states of the European Union (EU) in 2011, 66.9 percent of non-disabled people of working-age had jobs compared to 47.3 percent of this group among disabled people. Disabled women and people with mental impairments are most likely to be unemployed. The employment gap is highest in Hungary and the Netherlands and lowest in France, Luxembourg and Sweden, with the UK's figures considerably worse than the EU average. The unemployment rate of disabled people of working age in the UK has remained at around 50 percent for the last 50 years.[883] Employment rates for disabled people in other countries such as the US tend to be even lower.[884] In 2010, earnings were 11 percent lower for disabled people in work in the UK than for their non-disabled counterparts with the same level of educational qualifications.[885]

In the poorest countries, up to 80 percent of the work force are in unregulated and informal areas such as subsistence farming, small shops, street trading, repairs, small services and begging. This makes it difficult to estimate employment rates for disabled people, who are likely to be among those trapped in low-income activities offering little prospect of improvement.[886]

In previous societies, discrimination did not flow directly from relations of production. As we have seen, pre-class societies enabled people with impairments to play an active and equally valued role. Agricultural modes of production allowed large groups of people to co-operate in dividing up tasks and so impairment was not necessarily a particular problem. With capitalism, the extraction of surplus value relies on the commodification of labour power, devaluing the role of impaired people's labour and leading to discrimination against them on the basis of their cost to society.

Without some form of assistance to compensate for a particular impairment or lack of function, the labour power of many disabled people is more expensive to purchase than that of their non-disabled peers. This is not, however, a sentiment which it is considered acceptable to express in public. In late 2014, the UK government's welfare reform minister Lord Freud was forced to issue a public apology after saying that some disabled people were "not worth" paying the minimum wage and could be paid as little as £2 an hour.[887] In September 2015, UK Work and Pensions Secretary Iain Duncan Smith, referring in parliament to the number of disabled people with jobs, said he wanted to increase this "up to the level of normal, non-disabled people who are back in work".[888]

The re-entry of disabled people into the workforce on a significant scale began during the First World War when those previously labelled as unemployable were recruited to work in Europe's factories in response to labour shortages. With jobs provided for war veterans in the inter-war period, many more disabled people joined the workforce in the Second World War. The US Borden-Lafollette Act of 1943 specifically provided for the employment of people classed as blind, mentally ill or "retarded",[889] while the UK 1944 Disabled Persons (Employment) Act provided for a disability employment register and a (non-enforceable) 3 percent disabled employee quota for companies with more than 20 workers.[890]

This change became more permanent during the long economic boom of the mid-20th century, with the development of white-collar work and a more complex division of labour. So employers have proved willing to accommodate more disabled workers in periods of economic expansion or when labour is in short supply, but are reluctant to risk this greater level of investment in recessions.

Even before disabled people entered open employment, inmates of the old institutions and asylums performed significant unpaid labour, sometimes performing the very same tasks as paid attendants. Patient labour reduced daily running costs associated with paid care of the site as well.[891] Today, sheltered workshops in the US provide largely unskilled work for 420,000 learning disabled workers. The "commensurate" wage is determined by comparing a disabled worker's productivity to that of a non-disabled worker, so that s/he receives as little as half the wages of the latter. The original legislation—from 1938(!)—required that disabled employees in competitive industries earn 75 percent of the minimum wage. In 1986, this restriction was removed altogether.[892] The 300,000 disabled workers in German sheltered workshops[893] are similarly not covered by the minimum wage.

Sheltered workshops are a controversial subject among disability activists. Most Remploy factories in Britain, originally built to employ disabled ex-servicemen, have been shut down in the last decade. These segregated workplaces, employing people with a range of impairments but in particular people who are learning disabled, provided largely unskilled work, but in practice their closure meant unemployment and isolation rather than any improvement in the circumstances of former employees.

The social costs of labour

As the old saying goes, if there is one thing worse than being in work, it is not having any work at all. The "reserve army of labour" are the unemployed seen as temporarily surplus to production, whose presence exerts a downward pressure on wages.

> Wages tend to fluctuate around average levels, Marx argues, [as] the ebb and flow of particular branches of production draws workers into expanding areas and expels them from those which are contracting. The threat of unemployment places limits on the average level of wages.[894]

Education, healthcare and social services comprise the main "social costs of labour"—providing the healthy and literate workforce relied on by capitalists. The concern of the latter is that much of this "social wage" is insufficiently productive, leading to constant arguments over different aspects of welfare provision, including demands for more school exams, more privatisation and for unemployment benefits to be available only to those who show they are able and willing to work. Sometimes the mask slips and this inhumanity is made explicit. In the UK, a recent Department of Work and Pensions (DWP) report declared its intention to "use credit reference agency data to cleanse the stock of fraud and error",[895] while a "Standard Definition" for someone who dies while on the DWP Work Programme is a "completer".[896]

The greatest pressure on social spending, particularly in periods of austerity, is on welfare expenditure such as old age pensioners, the long-term unemployed (who lack needed skills) and those who are chronically ill or disabled (whose labour power costs too much).

The notion that the UK welfare state is exceptionally generous, although reinforced by widespread stories about "benefit scroungers" or "welfare tourism" by migrants, is mistaken. Britain's public social spending is not much bigger as a proportion of Gross Domestic Product (GDP) than the average across OECD states; 24.1 percent against 22.1 per cent as of 2009.[897]

> For many British supporters of a smaller welfare state the role model is the US, which has a very small welfare state (considering its level of income), accounting for only 19.2 percent of GDP as of 2009. However, it has a huge level of private spending on social expenditure, especially medical insurance and private pensions, which is equivalent to 10.2 percent of GDP. This means that, at 29.4 percent, the US has total social spending that is almost as high as that of Finland, which spends 30.7 percent of GDP on it (29.4 percent public and 1.3 percent private). Moreover, if the cost is 'spiralling out of control' anywhere, it is in the largely private US healthcare system, thanks to over-treatment of patients, rising insurance premiums and soaring legal costs.[898]

There is no correlation between the size of a country's welfare state and its economic performance. Despite, for example, Finland's welfare state being 50 percent bigger than that of the US (in 2009, 29.4 percent of GDP as against 19.2 percent in the US), its average annual per capita rate of income growth rose by 3.8 times between 1960 and 2010, while that of the US rose by 2.7 times.[899]

Claims that recent increases in health spending are unsustainable should be treated with scepticism. UK spending on health increased from 5.24 percent of GDP in 1981[900] to 8.3 percent of GDP in 2006, then to 9.3 percent in 2012. These figures are in line with international trends, reflecting the greater healthcare needs of an ageing population. Growth in US health spending, the highest in the world, increased from 15.3 percent of GDP in 2006 to 16.9 percent in 2012.[901]

According to the *New York Times*, the "share of the economy devoted to health care...has been the same since 2009."[902]

Whenever capitalists believe that welfare spending is cutting into profits, however, the pressures to make cuts further intensify:

> states come under the same pressures as do big capitals when faced with sudden competition—the pressure to restructure and reorganise their operations so as to accord with the law of value. On the one side this means trying to impose work measurement and payment schemes on welfare sector employees similar to those within the most competitive industrial firms. On the other side it means cuts in welfare provision so as to restrict it as much as possible to servicing labour power that is necessary for capital accumulation—and doing so in such a way that those who provide this labour power are prepared to do so at the wages they are offered.[903]

Jobs in a range of professions previously identified as part of the middle class, from psychology and nursing to social work and teaching, have in recent years been subject to a process of "proletarianisation". Unqualified workers increasingly perform jobs done previously by qualified professionals, while other "efficiency" measures such as standardisation, performance management and productivity drives exert a downward pressure on wages and conditions.

On introducing car factories designed for assembly line production, US industrialist Henry Ford asked: "Why is it every time I ask for a pair of hands, they come with a brain attached?" The techniques Ford and others pioneered, called Taylorism or "scientific management", have been extended further into all aspects of work in late capitalist society.[904] This involves the cumulative redivision of aspects of the labour process, and intensifying the separation between mental and manual labour, thus increasing the control exerted by managers and deskilling the jobs of more workers.

Digitalised communications technology has helped intensify the measurement of work.

> Thus the work output of checkout assistants at supermarkets can be measured by collating the swipes of barcodes... Warehouse workers

and forklift drivers at Tesco, for example, alleged that radio-linked (RFID) armband tags were being used to monitor work rates and identify those staff spending too long in the toilet. In Ohio a security firm has gone one step further and implanted RFID chips in two of its employees.[905]

Alienation today

As outlined in chapter 6, the theory of alienation describes how the labour process under capitalism undermines rather than affirms our humanity. As Marx put it, workers are "at home when not working, and not at home when at work." Work in which people might otherwise take pride is increasingly depersonalised, regulated and deskilled. Human Resources departments (formerly called Personnel Services) play the role previously fulfilled by industrial psychologists, grading and monitoring to an ever-greater degree every aspect of an individual's performance.

Deprived of control in the sphere of production, workers find solace in leisure or consumption such as food, drugs and entertainment, where we feel we can exercise some degree of control. Even here, however, humans are manipulated to buy fun in the same way as we are influenced in what clothes or shoes to buy. The market creates "fantastical desires"—from extreme sports to designer labels to the newest models and latest gadgets.

Modern life is increasingly dominated by new technology. Online activities and mobile phones offer ever more ways for human beings to be in touch with each other, but the form this communication takes is increasingly disembodied and depersonalised. Adopting particular lifestyles seems to offer the only real chance of personal fulfilment, whether through cooking, gardening, computer gaming or fashion and cosmetics. Social life is stripped of every vestige of community, colonised by the priorities of the market. The lives and pastimes of stars in the entertainment industries are turned into commodities, with "cheap replicas of the clothes, makeup and lifestyles of the rich and famous"[906] marketed by the fashion industry and media for mass consumption. Women in particular are expected to be a certain size and shape in order to be sexually appealing. The bodies and minds of the "ideal" human being are also increasingly standardised.

Alienation undermines our ability to have genuinely human relationships. We are forced to seek compensation for this loss of humanity in our privatised personal lives, yet this merely reinforces our alienation from each other. Our misery is not due to a lack of autonomy, but to a mode of production that isolates us as atomised individuals. Even as new technology provides the means to bring us closer together, the greater seems "the space between us". As for the bigger social issues affecting our lives, "helplessness before the forces which govern us appears more drastically in those social catastrophes...economic depression and wars" which are denounced as "regrettable accidents" or natural disasters rather than the social phenomena they really are.[907]

Human relations in late capitalist society contrast with those of the early classless societies in which humans lived for the vast majority of our history:

> In small-scale societies...individuals are related and connected to each other in diffuse social roles and contexts... a single personal characteristic, such as a physical impairment, does not generalize to define one's total social identity. In complex societies, however, social relationships, and contexts are more impersonal and task specific... visible physical characteristics are commonly used to classify and socially denote the individual's identity. A hallmark of Western industrialized nations concerning the social status of disabled persons is that the general population has lost the traditional familiarity with disability found in many preindustrial societies.[908]

Human customs and ways of life which are recent historical creations are presented as natural and inevitable, while institutions such as the stock market take on a life of their own and are attributed with human characteristics. As every aspect of life is measured and assessed for performance, humans constantly feel pressurised to improve their productivity in these areas. As Goodley puts it: "in representing the world of market rules as a state of nature, marketization has been naturalised. And the able body has been naturalized".[909]

Until the late 1960s, it was widely believed that high levels of stress mainly affected those at the top of society. The Whitehall Studies, the first of which was carried out in 1967, showed that civil servants in lower grade jobs suffered from much poorer health and died younger than those in the most senior positions. The biggest contributory factors were job stress and people's sense of control over their work.[910]

> While acute momentary stress perks up our immune system, chronic continuing stress suppresses immunity and can lead to growth failure in children, ovulation failure in women, erectile dysfunction in men and digestive problems for all of us.[911]

In their influential book *The Spirit Level*, Richard Wilkinson and Kate Pickett show that inequality "is associated with lower life expectancy, higher rates of infant mortality, shorter height, poor self-reported health, low birth weight, AIDS and depression".[912] They also cite what Oliver James calls the "affluenza virus", which "entails placing a high value on acquiring money and possessions, looking good in the eyes of others and wanting to be famous". What one writer calls the "beauty-industrial complex" is an industry worth US$160 billion a year.[913] Such values increase the risk of mental distress, as well as drug and alcohol misuse and personality disorders,[914] and further demonstrate the effects of alienation.

Ending the systematic undermining, distortion and fragmentation of human creativity demands the transformation of society as a whole. Whatever we do with our personal lives and leisure time, we cannot individually fulfil our collective ability to shape the natural world. Lifestyles and leisure activities cannot liberate us or create islands of freedom in a sea of alienation. Only collective struggle against capitalist society carries the potential to eradicate alienation, to "bring our vast, developing powers under our conscious control and reinstitute work as the central aspect of life".[915]

Exploitation and oppression

Disabled people in work are paid about 10 percent less than non-disabled people, and are four times more likely to be out of work.

Disabled people in work are more likely to be in lower paid jobs, with the pay gap between disabled and non-disabled people widening by one third since 2010.[916] Facts like these are sometimes quoted as evidence that disabled people are more exploited than others.

Exploitation and oppression are terms that may seem interchangeable, but they are in reality very different concepts. The use of low-paid migrants or children as cheap labour, for example, may well be immoral and heartless, but their labour, which is likely to be relatively unskilled, rarely generates as much surplus value as skilled workers, who may receive what is regarded as a good wage in comparison. For Marx, exploitation was not about workers being treated worse than others, but instead was—and remains—a precise and general economic term to describe how labour produces surplus value.

Marx recognised that oppression, far from being a natural and thus a permanent feature of human society, is a historical invention. Engels traced the origins of women's oppression to the formation of the family with the rise of class society. Others explained how racism was created to justify the slave trade and imperialism. Oppression has a material basis and arises from the structures and dynamics of class society, benefitting the interests of society's rulers by dividing the majority from whose exploitation they benefit.

The nature of oppression under capitalism, however, differs from that of previous class societies. For thousands of years, most of the population were either slaves or serfs, with their societies based on a rigid and widely accepted belief that everyone's place in the hierarchy was fixed by god or nature. The bourgeois revolutions that paved the way for capitalism were fought in the name of individual freedoms—"liberty, equality and fraternity"—in the case of the French Revolution. As Marx argued in *The Communist Manifesto* and elsewhere, this was a huge step forward for humanity.

Under capitalism, workers are doubly free: liberated from production tied to the land and to individual masters. Individual freedom and equality for workers, however, means an equal right and freedom to sell their labour power on the market as the only means of survival. For the capitalist, these ideas mean an equal freedom to exploit and to compete on the market with their rivals. In this way, capitalist society holds out the promise of liberation to all, but in practice denies it to the vast majority.

As capitalism brings workers together so too it simultaneously divides them to compete for jobs, overtime, housing, even for status as deserving of welfare services. The mass media and mainstream parties encourage the view that immigrants are less deserving than the indigenous population. Migrants or disabled people welcomed into the workforce when there are plenty of jobs are then portrayed as a threat or unaffordable burden when jobs become scarce.

The common-sense idea that power is about individual relations, that everyone oppresses everyone else, is reflected in much of Disability Studies theory—and also partly reflects real life experiences. After all, it is individuals who enforce discriminatory attitudes, whether these are directed against disabled people, Muslims or gays and lesbians. Such a view, however, lets those who do have huge economic and political power off the hook.

> For Marx, by contrast, while there is a group of people in society who, directly and indirectly, wield enormous power over the lives of millions—the ruling class—the experience of the vast majority of people in contrast...is not of exercising power but rather of *powerlessness*.[917]

It is the fact that this vast majority lack any real power—meaningful control over their lives or those of other people—which often leads people to seek to try and both find and exercise it in their relations with other people who they perceive to be a threat or to be inferior to themselves. This lack of power leads to a whole series of oppressions and the violence and hatred these give rise to. Susan Faludi, in her book *Stiffed*, examined what is described as the emasculation of masculinity:

> The men had probably felt in control when they beat their wives, but their everyday experience was of being controlled—a feeling they had no way of expressing because to reveal it was less than masculine, would make each of them, in fact, 'no man at all'.[918]

Some workers feel empowered by looking down on others: this cuts across oppressed groups too. For example, second-generation immigrants might scapegoat recently arrived migrants, or a lesbian may argue that trans people are "unnatural". Studies have shown that "displaced aggression"—where people react to a provocation by someone with higher status by redirecting their aggression to someone with a lower status—applies in a range of different social circumstances:

> the man who is berated by his boss and comes home and shouts at his wife and children; the higher degree of aggression in workplaces where supervisors treat workers unfairly; the ways in which people in deprived communities react to an influx of foreign immigrants; and the ways in which prisoners who are bullied turn on others below them—particularly sex offenders—in the prison hierarchy.[919]

This applies within oppressed groups too. Disabled people might dismiss others as "not really disabled", believing that they (or members of other oppressed groups) are less deserving of benefits or services than themselves. Jane Campbell described how at her special school she was "taught to dislike people with 'learning difficulties' because we were 'better' than them... when I was a child I wouldn't be seen dead with one of them, because I was ashamed".[920]

The experience of oppression may also lead them to think that prejudice against them is in some way justified or even natural. Richard Rieser contracted polio as a young child and grew up with increasing mobility difficulties. He recalls fellow pupils at school avoiding or staring at him: "I was not often allowed to forget my body, being the butt of jokes and jostled and pushed in corridors or on the stairs. Most harmful was being told almost daily that I was an 'ugly cripple' and that I would never have a girlfriend". This treatment convinced him that he was indeed ugly and unattractive and he became disruptive and depressed. As Rieser puts it: "each disabled person has to work through the layers of internalised oppression we have accumulated inside ourselves... Our perceptions of oursel[ves] mirror the attitudes and actions towards us".[921]

One popular current argument, provided by "privilege" theory, is that sections of workers have an interest in sustaining oppression as this provides them with material benefits. These theories hold that all men benefit from women's oppression or that all whites benefit from the oppression of black people. Marx addressed this argument in relation to the main form of racism affecting British workers during his lifetime—anti-Irish racism:

> The ordinary English worker hates the Irish worker as a competitor who lowers his standard of life. In relation to the Irish worker he regards himself as a member of the ruling nation and consequently he becomes a tool of the English aristocrats and capitalists against Ireland, thus strengthening their domination over himself. He cherishes religious, social, and national prejudices against the Irish worker. His attitude towards him is much the same as that of the "poor whites" to the Negroes in the former slave states of the USA... This antagonism is artificially kept alive and intensified by the press, the pulpit, the comic papers, in short, by all the means at the disposal of the ruling classes. This antagonism is the secret of the impotence of the English working class.[922]

The fact that women in full-time work continue to earn around 15 percent less than their male counterparts makes it easier for capitalists to keep wages down overall. The best solution, a united fight for decent wages, may not seem obvious to women who are victims of sexist behaviour by male colleagues at work. Nor has it always seemed obvious to fellow male workers. In the same way, disabled workers may see their non-disabled peers as to blame for their being paid less for doing the same work or may themselves believe that many other disabled people are frauds who should lose entitlement to their benefits.

It is of course individuals rather than "capitalism" who oppress others, but it is the ruling class which benefits from such divisions among workers. However, such behaviour can be overcome precisely because it cuts against the interests of workers; it weakens the unity of the workforce as a whole. Oppression is rooted in capitalism and class society and its continuation is vital to their survival.

The cost of disability

As we have seen, the main concerns for the capitalist class as regards disability relate to social and economic costs. One of the concerns of recent UK governments has been to pass more of these additional expenses onto individual disabled people. These costs rise according to the severity of people's impairments, and increasingly exceed those provided for by benefits. Disabled people in the UK spend on average £550 a month on disability-related expenses:[923]

> Disabled people spend on average £60 a month on food or drink for special diets or allergies and around £85 a month on specialist equipment. [Other expenses include] the cost of taxis to get to work when there is no accessible transport. Products and services needed by both disabled people and nondisabled people...cost more... For example one in five of disabled people feel they pay more for insurance generally because of their impairment... [D]isabled people are twice as likely to have unsecured debt totalling more than half of their household income, are three times more likely to use door step loans, [and have] on average £108,000 fewer savings and assets than nondisabled people.[924]

Extra costs are highest for disabled pensioners.[925] Another study from 2010, taking account of these costs, suggests that half or more of all disabled people in the UK are living in poverty. Current calculations therefore significantly underestimate the extent of disability poverty.[926]

This, however, is only part of the picture. The same study, by Demos, found that the range of costs in each impairment group is so large as to make average figures almost meaningless. With the exception of specialist clothing and equipment, care and support needs were found to be wholly unrelated to disability-related costs. Disability spending "increases with available resources. Those on higher levels of Disability Living Allowance (DLA) and those employed full time spent more overall than those on lower levels of DLA and unemployed", suggesting that disability spending "is likely to be driven not by actual costs, but by ability to spend." Unemployed disabled people, on the other hand, "had higher spending in other areas, including transport and utilities." The highest disability spending is associated with difficult social circumstances, such as unsuitable and/or private rented accommodation, reliance on public transport, unemployment, lack of informal support from family or friends and financial factors such as debt, a lack of savings or bank account. In other words, disability spending is related to class.

A series of UK benefits introduced since 1971,[927] paid to disabled people in recognition of these extra costs, are currently being restricted or abolished. Some 386,000 (21 percent) DLA claimants are in work and research shows that over half of them could not work without it. The eligibility criteria for DLA's replacement benefit, Personal Independence Payment (PIP), are far more restrictive. The DWP estimates that 600,000 disabled people will drop out of the system by 2017, losing between £21 and £134.40 a week (at 2013/2014 rates). As one London claimant explained: "I use my DLA to meet the extra costs of food that I can't cook and to pay for using a car to get to work. I don't know how I will cope if I lose it at the introduction of PIP".[928]

The Demos report concludes that disability costs "are not solely generated by factors the government cannot change—such as impairment, condition or age. They are driven by a range of environmental factors which, with the right intervention, could reduce disability costs significantly". Investment in areas such as social adapted housing, public transport and employment could, therefore, significantly reduce disability poverty.[929]

Disability and identity

The international symbol of disability is the wheelchair user—a clear and immediately recognisable visual representation. Even within this impairment category, however, things are less simple. In the UK, 28 percent of wheelchair users are under 60 and a large proportion of the total use a wheelchair only some of the time. At roughly 2 percent of the UK population,[930] wheelchair users represent only a small minority of disabled people. Most impairments, however, are not so obvious or easily identified—a fact which has significant implications for disability as a form of identity.

Disability is a hugely diverse category, linked to a wide range of impairments which may not be considered disabling (either in the medical or social model sense) by those who have them. A recent UK government report pointed out that there are "over 900 separate conditions recorded" in disability benefit award statistics.[931]

Most impairment is invisible to others or, with intermittent conditions such as epilepsy, may be hidden for most or all of the time. Recent UK government research confirmed that most people who meet official classifications of disability do not see themselves as disabled:

> [The Office of National Statistics] Opinions Survey 2012 included a question asking those who came under the Equality Act definition if they thought of themselves as disabled. Only a quarter (25 per cent) did. Those least likely to think of themselves as disabled were those who were working; those who had higher levels of qualifications; and those with medium to high income. Those more likely to think of themselves as disabled were: economically inactive; those with no qualifications; and those with low income. Men were more likely than women to think of themselves as disabled. Those with vision or mobility impairments were more likely to think of themselves as disabled whereas those with dexterity impairment or with breathing, stamina or fatigue were less likely to. Those whose condition had existed at birth were more likely to think of themselves as disabled whereas those who described the cause of their health condition as being natural ageing were less likely to.[932]

Changes in the character of disability today relate to wider social and economic trends. As the prevalence rate of impairment rises with age, an ageing population means that most disabled people are likely to be elderly. The 2015 World Alzheimer Report estimates that nearly 47 million people globally are living with dementia, with the number of people projected to nearly triple to more than 130 million by 2050.[933]

Around one in 20 UK children are disabled, compared to one in five working-age adults, and almost one in two people over state pension age.[934] A government report in 2005 confirmed that increasing numbers of children are "reported as having complex needs, Autistic Spectrum disorders and mental health issues", and that "there are increasing numbers of [adults] reporting mental illness and behavioural disorders, while the number of people reporting physical impairments is decreasing".[935] More recent research estimates the number of older disabled people will increase by around 40 percent between 2002 and 2022 and the WHO has predicted that depression will be the leading cause of disability by 2020.[936]

A recent European Court ruling is likely to intensify efforts to classify obesity as a disability[937] and as a "protected characteristic" under the UK Equality Act. By the early 1990s, obesity was more common among poor compared to rich women in 26 countries surveyed and among poor men in all except five of them.[938] Projections by the WHO suggest that 74 percent of men and 64 percent of women in the UK will be overweight by 2030, up from 70 percent and 59 percent respectively in 2010.[939]

What are the implications of these facts for those who wish to organise disabled people as a social group on their own behalf?

First, the impairments underlying disability are very diverse.[940] Second, there is no stark dividing line between those classified as disabled and those who are not. Around a third of England's population (15 million people) have a long-term health condition, two-thirds of whom have "a limiting long-term condition" meeting the Equality Act definition of disability.[941]

Recent UK research shows that 8 percent of adults "with moderate or severe impairment do not experience any barriers to participating in life areas".[942] As we have seen, most disabled people are reluctant to identify themselves as such. This may be because they do not think they qualify or because they see such an identity as having only a negative impact on their lives. As Vic Finkelstein commented in 1993:

Perhaps this has to do with the general confusion of disability as a synonym for physical impairment (with negative associations) and as a term for those who suffer discrimination. The universal instinct of disabled people to separate their experience of discrimination (which should be opposed) from the experience of living with a body impairment (which has to be managed) may explain the general reservation about identifying oneself with a term which confuses both states.[943]

There is, therefore, a negative aspect to identifying as disabled which is not the same for other oppressed groups. Part of the reason that the stigma associated with being disabled is more pervasive and insidious is because without some form of social assistance or support individuals with an impairment may have considerably greater difficulty in fulfilling certain roles or functions than their non-disabled counterparts.

This raises a further difference in the nature of disability as a form of discrimination compared to other forms of oppression. There is a clear and obvious distinction, for example, between terms such as racism or sexism and the social groups whose oppression these terms describe. There is no confusion between the terms "sexism" and "woman", or "racism" and "black person" or "Muslim". However, this is not true of "disability" and "impairment". The former term is used almost everywhere when it may actually be the latter which is being referred to. This illustrates something of the nature of disability as the "last civil rights movement"; it developed later and has (so far) had less social impact than other movements of the oppressed with which it is often compared. As Kudlick put it:

> [S]o many terms for disability are negations (dis-ability, impairment, mal-formation) yet we still lack a widely used expression such as 'racism', 'misogyny' or 'homophobia' to describe the phenomenon of casting it in a negative light.[944]

Given the way in which *dis*ability is so often equated with *in*ability, it should perhaps be unsurprising that so few people are prepared to identify themselves as disabled.

As is the case for all forms of oppression, the experience of disability is highly isolating. An additional factor, however, is the huge number and diverse nature of specific impairments. Someone with chronic fatigue syndrome, for example, may find it hard to see any link with the obstacles faced by someone else with a form of attention deficit "disorder". Likewise, the difficulties experienced by a blind person may differ significantly from those of someone in mental distress. More importantly, class divisions mean that even people with the same impairment are likely to experience its social impact very differently. A wheelchair user in Britain who is unemployed and living on a run-down peripheral housing estate is unlikely to share much in common with another who works as a commodities broker and lives in an upmarket new financial district.

How disabled people experience their impairments in society also influences the extent to which they consider this as amounting to discrimination. Wealthy or successful disabled people often state that they do not consider themselves as disabled. US President Franklin D Roosevelt went to extreme lengths, for example, to avoid being seen in public in his wheelchair, describing himself as a "cured cripple".[945] The complicity of the press, as well as the number of staff at his disposal, helped him achieve this goal, at least so far as his public image was concerned. The life of someone as severely impaired as Stephen Hawking would be qualitatively more difficult (and probably far shorter) if he did not have at his disposal an even more extensive range of support, including the latest assistive technologies.

The point, however, remains that their more fragmented experiences of oppression means disabled people are less likely to identify with each other than other groups of the oppressed. The social model's assumption that disabled people can find common cause first and foremost with other disabled people is therefore problematic.

The disability movement of the 1980s and 1990s (not only in the UK) organised a fairly narrow stratum of physically impaired people, led mainly by wheelchair users. Mike Oliver acknowledged this in his history of the British disability movement, explaining that for wheelchair users (like himself), "the obstacles to political participation...are less severe than for people with other impairments".[946] As an activist with learning difficulties complained: "[we] are always asked to talk about advocacy and our impairments as though our barriers aren't disabling in the same way."[947]

The issue of disability identity is further complicated by the fact that only a small minority of disabled people (varying from 3 to 17 percent in recent UK research) are born with an impairment.[948] The vast majority of disabled people acquire their impairments later in life, increasingly and most commonly in the years after their retirement. A UK government study in 2008 found that 79 percent of disabled people in the UK aged over 65 reported that they acquired their impairment after the age of 50.[949] Living with impairment often therefore represents a new experience in people's lives which may be sudden or gradual and the impact of which can range from relatively benevolent to immensely traumatic.

Unlike oppression, the process of exploitation forces workers together, concentrating them in workplaces where they need to co-operate to produce goods or services. As we shall see in the next chapter, this provides workers with an opportunity to discover and act upon a common interest.

Rights in the age of neoliberalism

The figures above demonstrate that a large majority of disabled people, or their families and those they live with, are increasingly forced to cope with the extra costs and work associated with disability. The main contrast with the past is that official rhetoric tries to sell this as a sign of progress.

The main report in a series of documents produced by the UK Coalition government of 2010-15, entitled *Fulfilling Potential*, has "three themes: realising aspirations, individual control and changing attitudes and behaviours". Although agreeing that society "has to include disabled people on an equal basis", it immediately adds that: "With very constrained public expenditure we will need to find new and innovative ways of bringing this about".[950] The answer to what these ways might be comes a few pages later: "Reforming welfare to support disabled people to gain and maintain independence and reduce the risk of dependency".[951] Emphasising the "need to ensure support is affordable", the report begins with the claim:

> we spend 2.4 per cent of our Gross Domestic Product (GDP) on disability benefits, a fifth more than the European average, and significantly more than Germany, France, Italy and Spain, our major European competitors—and our spending grew by a third between 2005 and 2009.[952]

Lord Freud, the then Conservative Welfare Reform Minister, repeated these claims in June 2013, arguing that only two of the other

33 OECD countries spent more than the UK on disability. Esther McVey, the then Minister for Disabled People and the report's author, repeatedly claimed that OECD figures showed the UK government "are world leaders" in spending on services and benefits for disabled people. These statements and statistics are in fact grossly misleading and were used to justify cuts to spending on disability.

OECD statistics include one set of figures for spending on "disability" and another for "sickness" spending. McVey and Freud quoted the "disability" figures, ignoring those for "sickness". Once the figures are taken together, six OECD nations—Denmark, Finland, Iceland, the Netherlands, Norway and Sweden—spend more than the UK. The OECD average includes countries such as Chile, Mexico, South Korea and Turkey, whose much lower disability-related spending distorts the figures. In European terms, the UK's spending is lower than average. Where the UK spent 2.9 percent of GDP on "disability and sickness" in 2009, its nine OECD neighbours spent an average of 3.2 percent.[953]

These figures, however, may already have changed as states react to the impact of austerity and the dominant neo-liberal consensus. Since 2008, spending on disability services in the Irish Republic has been cut by 10 per cent.[954] In 2011, the Dutch government removed entitlement to healthcare budget payments from 117,000 people, with the Greek, Portuguese and Spanish governments also making major cuts in disability-related services.[955]

Governments do have an interest in preventing disability discrimination insofar as it means more disabled people are able to work instead of being forced to rely on state benefits. However, employers are also keen to avoid the additional expense associated with investing in disabled workers. So recent years have seen more legislation introduced in different countries, promoted by the UN and other international bodies, to outlaw aspects of such discrimination but which has weak or no enforcement mechanisms. So the UK Equality Act requires only "reasonable" adjustments, with cost being one of the primary factors to be considered and a similar provision in the Americans with Disabilities Act (ADA) is called "reasonable accommodation".[956] Despite being regarded as a model internationally, the ADA's impact since its introduction in 1990 (see chapter 9) has in some areas actually been negative. The proportion of disabled Americans in full or part-time work, for example, declined from 33 percent in 1986 to 31 percent in 1994.[957] This figure fell by a further 9 percent between 2008 and 2012.[958]

This book began by looking at the UN Convention on the Rights of Persons with Disabilities (UNCRPD) which came into force in 2008, just before the onset of the banking crisis. Article 4 says states must: "ensure and promote the full realization of all human rights and fundamental freedoms for all persons with disabilities... [and] take measures to the maximum of its available resources." What if states do not meet these obligations? In the words of the relevant UN committee: "any deliberately retrogressive measures...would require the most careful consideration and would need to be fully justified by reference to the totality of the rights provided for". These words are unlikely to make governments that flout the UNCRPD nervous of reprisals.[959]

Conclusion

Modern capitalist society has created the potential for disabled people to live a full and rewarding life. A bewildering range of new and assistive technologies, not least the rapid advance of computer science and the internet, has facilitated participation in the workforce and in wider society in a way that was not possible for many people during the 18th or 19th centuries. Similarly, advances in healthcare, education and social services have enabled more disabled people to live longer and to enjoy a greater degree of independence.

The problem is that the organisation of capitalist society undercuts all these possibilities; only those with the wealth and resources to afford these technologies, education and support can take full advantage of them. For the vast majority, life as a disabled person continues to mean poverty, isolation, neglect and discrimination, as well as increasingly being reminded of one's status as a burden on the state's services. The fundamental reason for all this is that production in capitalist society is not based on meeting the needs and aspirations of the many, but to provide profit for a small minority. A new form of society, therefore, is necessary if disabled people are to achieve genuine inclusion and their human potential.

14.
From rights to revolution

What kind of changes would need to occur, for example, for all human beings, disabled or not, to have access to the needs of daily life, to satisfying work or activities, to forms of culture that express and speak to all their faculties, and to a world where nature and biodiversity are preserved and cherished rather than destroyed?[960]

The higher profile of disability as a political issue in recent years is due to several inter-related factors. First, the spread of anti-discrimination legislation, itself partly a consequence of earlier disability activism; second, the debates associated with an ageing population which contains a higher proportion of disabled people; third, the existence of skill shortages in an increasingly sophisticated and hi-tech economy; and fourth, the current savage cuts in public spending—in disability-related benefits in particular—during an era of austerity.

The changes in disabled people's lives over the last century— at least in some countries—have been considerable. These gains are currently being reversed by an austerity offensive in which many disabled people's support needs are increasingly viewed as an unaffordable luxury. Opposition parties offer little hope of anything significantly different. Disability activists in Britain have fought a long struggle in defence of the Independent Living Fund, which provides £300 million of essential support to 19,000 of the country's most severely disabled people. Despite the efforts of these activists during the 2015 General Election campaign, they failed to secure a promise from the Labour Party that it would reinstate the Fund. It is hard to think of a more apt illustration of the degeneration of a party long and widely regarded as representing the interests of working people.[961]

If there are no solutions possible within capitalist society, then what alternative solutions exist? This chapter looks at whether and how a future society can dismantle disability discrimination entirely, include all people with impairments fully in its affairs and provide them with the support necessary to realise their individual potential.

Is science our saviour? From prosthetics to perfection

The Wellcome Foundation hosted an exhibition in 2012 to coincide with the Olympic and Paralympic Games in London. The title—*Superhuman: Exploring Human Enhancement from 600 BCE to 2050*—drew on the provocative title for Channel Four's TV coverage of the Games. As the accompanying booklet says: "People have long 'enhanced' their bodies and lives, compensating for some kind of loss of function, using prostheses—be they artificial limbs or new sets of teeth".[962]

Prostheses evolved from wooden sticks or crutches to the ivory, leather and rubber artificial limbs of Victorian times through to the computerised versions of today. Until the late 19th century, most devices were available only to the rich.[963] As shown in chapter 8, modern warfare, involving the large-scale loss of labour power, prompted the development of prosthetic limbs. Spectacles and dentures, however, which compensate for a lack of natural sight or teeth, are not seen as prostheses, for no apparent reason other than the ubiquity of their use. They rightly belong, however, to this first group of prostheses, which substitute for an absent or incomplete function:

> Over the past decade, prosthetic technology has advanced significantly, with computerized knees and ankles that adjust to terrain and activity. Lighter and more malleable materials have allowed amputees to wear synthetic legs longer—and even run marathons. And devices have been customized for a dizzying array of activities, from golfing and skiing to scuba diving, backpacking and even rock climbing.[964]

Such has been the success of modern prosthetic devices that future models are likely to soon exceed levels of human performance. This will lead to rather more thorny disputes than those in Paralympic sports concerning the hi-tech running blades of Oscar Pistorius, which it was argued gave him an unfair advantage over his competitors.[965]

The second group of prostheses are those designed to "normalise" and gain social acceptance for the wearer. A glass or acrylic eye, for example, does not assist sight, but is purely for aesthetic purposes. The 2012 *Superhuman* exhibition also included a silver false nose made for a syphilitic woman in the 17th or 18th century. The exhibit's caption explained that it was returned when she married and found her husband preferred her without it.

A more controversial and notorious example arose from the European thalidomide scandal. This involved babies being born with serious deformities caused by inadequately tested drugs being prescribed for symptoms of morning sickness or sleeplessness to pregnant women from 1958 to 1962. Bulky leather and metal exoskeletons were invented to replicate children's missing or foreshortened limbs:

> The complex prostheses that were developed for the children born affected by the drug thalidomide were based on this idea, attempting to replicate the 'normal' body—at the expense of functionality. Many children rejected these devices, preferring instead to adapt to their own particular bodies.[966]

This category of prostheses also includes false breasts, often offered to women after mastectomies following treatment for breast cancer. Since the invention of the first silicone implants in March 1962, however, breast enhancements became increasingly popular, along with other forms of cosmetic surgery. The pressures to achieve "normality", the original concept for such inventions, has again proved in many instances to be about being the best—the most sexually desirable or glamorous, the fittest, the employee of the month, even the "disability champion" envisaged in UK government documents.

There is clearly, however, huge potential for wider technological and scientific innovations to benefit disabled people. One recent example illustrates this well. In 2014, Darek Fidyka, a Bulgarian firefighter paralysed for four years from the waist down after receiving multiple stab wounds, began to walk again. Polish surgeons had used nerve-supporting cells from his nose to help regrow nerves in his severed spine. The 38-year-old, the first person in the world to recover from complete severing of the spinal nerves, can now walk with a frame and even drive a car.[967] The success, partly funded by UK charities, came six months after another team at the University of Louisville and the University of California confirmed that their use of electrical stimulation of the severed spinal cords of four paralysed men enabled them to move their legs for the first time in years.[968]

Ironically, this surgical breakthrough occurred ten years after the death of actor Christopher Reeve (best known for the *Superman* films). After being paralysed in a riding accident in 1995, Reeve spent the rest of his life promoting research into a medical cure for spinal cord injuries. Many disability activists were openly hostile to Reeve's efforts, believing that his highly public campaign diverted more routine and badly needed support for others who also had spinal injuries but lacked his wealth. One letter in *Forward*, the magazine of the UK Spinal Injuries Association, argued that: "Reeve...has swapped superstardom for new role of victim and super cripple... His promises of a cure suggest that it is wheelchair users, not society, that need to change. Pinning hopes on a cure is no way to live a life. You need a good quality of life now".[969] A different letter countered: "I can live now and hope for research and help with bowel, bladder, sex, arm movement, sensation, pressure sores, root pain. The sooner you accept there is a place for both approaches, the better".[970]

The latter approach is surely correct, although one of the news stories on the Fidyka case pointed out that the Polish-UK team responsible was struggling to secure the necessary funding to treat more patients.[971] The question of cost, whether in the form of private or public funding, permeates all discussion around science and technology. What might have been achieved and how much earlier had these two international teams co-operated and shared research from the outset?

Other innovations originally intended to benefit disabled people have indeed been taken up more widely.

Pellegrino Turri invented the typewriter in 1808 while trying to provide his blind friend or lover with a way to write legibly.[972] In 1886, Herman Hollerith, who had learning difficulties, designed a system to process information rapidly. His machine was used to tabulate the 1890 US census and the company he founded later became International Business Machines (IBM). E-mail was invented in 1972 by Vinton Cerf (who was hearing impaired from birth) to communicate with his Deaf wife via text messaging. Cerf developed the host level protocols for Arpanet, the first large-scale packet network and precursor to the Internet.[973] Other examples include the jacuzzi, whose inventor was looking for something to relieve his son of rheumatoid arthritic pain.[974]

As one review of the *Superhuman* exhibition concluded, however:

> Who will control and disburse these costly products of this drive towards self-enhancement? A conference of the US National Science Foundation written up on the last wall concludes with a prediction for 2025: 'robot and software agents will operate on principles compatible with human goals, awareness and personality'. It would fly in the face of history if they did.[975]

Science and technology are driven by the same imperatives as the wider economy and society. If it is not considered profitable to invest in research, it is unlikely to be funded, even though it might immensely benefit a particular impairment group. Most research and development is privately funded and much of what is sponsored by nation states is for military purposes. The emphasis on hi-tech enhancements and adaptations or costly medical interventions, however, does tend to obscure the fact that the assistance most disabled people who need it want is low-tech and labour intensive.

Revolution and oppression

Disability, as we have seen, is deeply embedded within capitalism and can be overcome only with a fundamental social and economic transformation of society. The need for such change is easily demonstrated. It has been calculated, for example, that as much as half the impairment in the majority world could be prevented by the introduction of effective policies to reduce poverty and malnutrition and improve sanitation, drinking water and working conditions.[976]

The question, here, however, is how people view their oppression in relation to wider social change. Writing in 2011, M Miles argued that:

> The vast majority of the world's people with disabilities do not read English and have never heard of any kind of [social model of disability], and probably never will… Even in [the] UK, 'recent research from the Office for Disability issues has shown that only six per cent of disabled people know about the social model of disability', a rise of three per cent since 2003.[977]

It is true that many people—disabled or non-disabled—have never heard of the social model, but many nevertheless believe that disabled people experience discrimination. Disability, as we have seen, is based on the fact that the labour of people with impairments is less profitable for capitalism. To overcome this form of oppression, workers need to break from the common sense ideas associated with this society—such as a "fair day's work for a fair day's pay" or "what's good for the boss is good for me"—which make it easier for employers to intensify exploitation. Accepting this common sense also implies acceptance of the notion that disabled people are an economic burden. On the other hand, many large workplaces now include some disabled workers and most major trade unions in Britain have policies opposing disability discrimination. There is, therefore, at least the potential to win the majority of workers to such a position, as well as to actively fight for it.

Those who suffer the greatest oppression in society have often emerged to play a central role in revolutionary movements. Irish immigrants and the children of black slaves were among those who led the great Chartist revolt in Britain during the 1830s. Jewish people in Russia, subjected over decades to violent racism including mass pogroms, saw activists such as Trotsky, Zinoviev and Sverdlov elected to the leadership of the revolutions of 1905 and 1917. More recently, gays and lesbians targeted by media hysteria over AIDS made common cause with 120,000 miners in the UK, raising money for and promoting solidarity with them during their epic year-long battle with the Thatcher government in 1984-1985. The mass entry of black people and women into the US and UK workforces has strengthened the fight against racism and women's oppression. From a situation where the early craft-based trade unions often opposed equal pay and status for black people and women in the workplace, it is now commonly expected that trade unions will resist and organise against racism, sexism and homophobia in the workplace.

The position Marx took in relation to anti-Irish racism (discussed in the previous chapter)—that it undermined the potential strength and unity of the working class movement in England—is true of all forms of oppression. A brief survey of the dominant political climate in many countries today confirms how well this applies to Islamophobia and anti-immigrant racism. It also confirms there is nothing inevitable about the labour movement (broadly conceived of as the trade unions and the political left) taking a consistent position in opposition to all forms of oppression. This is instead a matter of a clear and principled political analysis.

The Russian revolutionary Lenin, referring to Tsarist Russia as the "prison house of nations", described the need for revolutionaries to be "tribunes of the oppressed"—fighting all forms of national, religious and other forms of oppression as a matter of political principle. The decline and defeat of the 1917 Russian Revolution can be seen from the way in which its historic gains—for example, equality for women and homosexuals, as well as for national, ethnic and religious minorities—were reversed with the rise of Stalinism, which among its many other crimes, ruthlessly incorporated other countries into a new imperial "prison house".

Many people oppose capitalism because it is a system of production which exists not to meet the needs of society, but to provide profits for a tiny minority. As we have seen, it is this factor which is largely responsible for the exclusion of so many disabled people from the workforce. What part, then, could they play in a future society based first and foremost on meeting human need?

The negation of the negation

Alongside his highly effective arguments in relation to impairment and disability (discussed in chapter 2), Paul Abberley also argued that while "Marxism has provided effective tools" to explain the nature of disability discrimination in capitalist societies, its vision of a future "Utopia" presented "profound difficulties for impaired people":

> In the 1875 Critique of the Gotha Programme Marx makes the well-known statement that 'in a more advanced phase of communist society... when labour is no longer just a means of keeping alive but has itself become a vital need (we may then have) from each according to his abilities, to each according to his needs.' But this implies that impaired people are still deprived, by biology if not by society. Impairment, since it places a limit upon creative sensuous practice, is alienatory...the ability to labour in some socially recognised sense still seems a requirement of full membership of a future good society based upon Marxist theory.[978]

In Abberley's view, a small number of people with impairments in a "Marxist Utopia" would remain excluded from the system of production and as a consequence "would still occupy the essentially peripheral relationship to society we do today".

Marx in fact wrote very little on the nature of post-revolutionary society and was thoroughly dismissive of "Utopian Socialists" who spent their time imagining what such a society would look like. There is good reason, however, to reject Abberley's view that disabled people would continue to be marginalised in a socialist society. As he concedes, a socialist society based on a new and emancipatory concept of labour could and would provide work for the vast majority of people with impairments. Such a society would also have an interest in promoting the fullest possible participation of all its members, enabling each "according to their abilities" to make a contribution. Marx's meaning in the famous "from each/to each" quote differs to that attributed to it by Abberley. This is made clearer in the immediately preceding paragraphs where Marx discusses the concept of equal rights in the context of labour. They are worth quoting in full:

> But one man is superior to another physically, or mentally, and supplies more labour in the same time, or can labour for a longer time; and labour, to serve as a measure, must be defined by its duration or intensity, otherwise it ceases to be a standard of measurement.

This equal right is an unequal right for unequal labour...it tacitly recognizes unequal individual endowment, and thus productive capacity, as a natural privilege. It is, therefore, a right of inequality, in its content, like every right. Right, by its very nature, can consist only in the application of an equal standard; but unequal individuals (and they would not be different individuals if they were not unequal) are measurable only by an equal standard insofar as they are brought under an equal point of view, are taken from one definite side only—for instance, in the present case, are regarded only as workers and nothing more is seen in them, everything else being ignored. Further, one worker is married, another is not; one has more children than another, and so on and so forth. Thus, with an equal performance of labour, and hence an equal in the social consumption fund, one will in fact receive more than another, one will be richer than another, and so on. To avoid all these defects, right, instead of being equal, would have to be unequal.

But these defects are inevitable in the first phase of communist society as it is when it has just emerged after prolonged birth pangs from capitalist society. Right can never be higher than the economic structure of society and its cultural development conditioned thereby.

In a higher phase of communist society, after the enslaving subordination of the individual to the division of labour, and therewith also the antithesis between mental and physical labour, has vanished; after labour has become not only a means of life but life's prime want; after the productive forces have also increased with the all-around development of the individual, and all the springs of co-operative wealth flow more abundantly—only then can the narrow horizon of bourgeois right be crossed in its entirety and society inscribe on its banners: From each according to his ability, to each according to his needs![979]

This concept of rights is vital to any discussion of how disability would be addressed in a socialist society. Marx's recognition of differing human abilities formed the very basis of his analysis of capitalism, including how competition at every level of society divides workers. The basis for disability under capitalism is the identification of a distinct layer of people with certain impairments judged to have a substantial impact on their ability to labour. With the use of the social surplus generated by this labour also subject to all manner of disputes, rights can never be truly equal—either in how they are implemented or exercised.

In seeing impairment as a continuum, instead of as the crude "them" and "us" dichotomy of capitalism, a socialist society would take account of differing ability and levels of skill based on a form of democracy incomparably more extensive than anything experienced under capitalism.

The "negation of the negation" involves overthrowing a system of production which systematically deprives human beings of any control over the manner, nature and product of their labour, the key means through which they affirm their humanity:

> The capitalist mode of appropriation...produces capitalist private property. This is the first negation of individual private property, as founded on the labour of the proprietor. But capitalist production begets...its own negation. It is the negation of negation. This does not re-establish private property for the producer, but gives him individual property based on the acquisitions of the capitalist era: ie, on co-operation and the possession in common of the land and of the means of production.[980]

Revolution, therefore, requires not just the reorganisation of work, but reclaiming it as something workers do for themselves because they see it overwhelmingly as a social good rather than something alien and hostile to them. The concentration of workers in large workplaces and the integrated nature of production under capitalism means that this can only be achieved by collective action to seize control of the productive process and everything associated with it.

Finally, a socialist society would provide a basis to overcome and dismantle all artificial barriers between work, leisure and education, nourishing and promoting creativity and individuality. In a formulation expressive of its time but whose deeper meaning is nevertheless hugely appealing, Marx described a communist society as one:

where nobody has one exclusive sphere of activity but each can become accomplished in any branch he wishes, society regulates the general production and thus makes it possible for me to do one thing today and another tomorrow, to hunt in the morning, fish in the afternoon, rear cattle in the evening, criticize after dinner, just as I have a mind, without ever becoming hunter, fisherman, shepherd or critic.[981]

In contrast to the systematic division and competition characteristic of capitalist society, socialism would promote a collective and co-operative culture based on common interest. Democratic planning would promote the interests of teachers and students, service providers and users, doctors and patients, architects and the occupants of city and countryside as mutual, interdependent and complementary to each other. Such a society would therefore promote genuine individuality, cultivating rounded human growth in place of a one-sided and fragmented development of skills.

What force, then, has the power to achieve that change?

Agency

The austerity offensive, under whose impact social and economic inequality has hugely increased, has prompted the development of new political movements. Broadly identifying themselves as anti-capitalist, these tend to embrace some variant of autonomist ideas. Current demands for change on the left tend to be couched in terms of "social movements" centred on the vague but powerful notion of unity against the "one per cent" who rule the world. In terms of understanding the current economic crisis, Marxism itself has seen something of a renaissance. The idea of revolution, once seen as the preserve of those on the far left, has become commonly discussed— even if the return of dictatorship in Egypt dampened the optimism of the Arab Spring of 2011.

Increased awareness of a predatory and ruthless international ruling class, however, has also been accompanied by a widespread common sense view that identifies the working class as a spent force, its power fragmented under the impact of globalisation and restructuring.

As ubiquitous as such ideas are, they are also demonstrably false. As we have seen, capitalism involves a continual reshaping of the working class. The proportion of workers engaged in manufacturing in the advanced countries, for example, has declined significantly for the last two generations. In Britain in the 1970s, workers' power was epitomised by strikes of tens of thousands of car workers. Today's workforce in the car industry is a fraction of what it was then, but investment in automation and robotics has led to hugely improved productivity:

> Overall auto production in the UK has not fallen. The UK remains home to over 30 manufacturers building more than 70 models. Similarly the volume of autos produced in the UK is set to reach an all time high in 2017. Restructuring has enabled increases in productivity to compensate for labour shedding.[982]

This pattern can be shown in every other area of the economy. The power of collective action also extends beyond the manufacturing sector, as demonstrated by the impact of strikes by, for example, oil tanker drivers or transport workers. Prior to the turn of the 20th century, dockers and textile workers were seen as temporary and disposable sections of the workforce—but their militancy inspired the subsequent rapid spread of trade unions in the period known as New Unionism. The "precarious workers" often identified as typical of today's economy can similarly be inspired by modern examples of "new unionism". Walmart is the world's biggest corporation, with US$160 billion in assets and an annual turnover similar in size to the GDP of Norway.[983] In September 2012, 38 workers at its largest US distribution centre in Elwood, Illinois, won a three-week strike against their employer, a temping agency subcontractor. Despite the absence of union recognition, they not only won their key demand—reinstatement of all those sacked or suspended for trade union activity—but also full back pay for everyone who participated in the action.[984]

The problem is not that the social and economic power of workers has declined. Rather, it is that an historically low level of strike action has led to a corresponding decline in the belief that workers have or are able to exercise that power.

Conclusion

Oxfam reported in January 2014 that 85 billionaires have the same wealth as the bottom half of the world's population. Its website predicts that the wealth of the 1 percent will overtake that of the other 99 percent in 2016. This inequality is an inevitable consequence of an entirely unnatural and maddening society. There is nothing natural about oppression, war and environmental destruction; it is all part of "a very capitalist condition".

Throughout their history, human beings have shown immense adaptability—in the diversity of their living and working environments, in their occupations, social beliefs and customs and even in their more biological functions, such as sleeping or eating. This is also true of living with impairment.

In one of his fascinating books, Oliver Sacks discusses achromatopsia, or colour blindness. Most people with this very rare condition grow up without knowing (or even knowing of) anyone else who also has it. Sacks tells the story of Knut and his brother and sister, who by a rare genetic chance, were all achromatopic and have reacted and adapted to this in very different ways. Knut, the firstborn, was diagnosed as an infant. As it was felt that he would never see well enough to learn to read, he (and later his siblings) were sent to the local school for the blind:

> Knut rebelled at being regarded as disabled, and refused to learn Braille by touch, instead using his sight to read the raised dots, which cast tiny shadows on the page. He was severely punished for this and forced to wear a blindfold in classes. Soon after, Knut ran away from the school, but, determined to read normal print, taught himself to read at home. Finally, having convinced the school administrators that he would never make a willing student, Knut was allowed to return to regular school.
>
> Knut's sister, Britt...flourished at the school for the blind as much as Knut hated it, becoming fluent in Braille; and she has spent her professional life as an intermediary between the blind and sighted worlds, supervising the transcription and production of books into Braille at the Norwegian Library for the Blind. Like Knut, Britt

is intensely musical and auditory and loves to close her eyes and surrender herself to the nonvisual domain of music; but equally, she relaxes by doing needlework, using a jeweller's loupe attached to her glasses, to keep her hands free.[985]

This kind of individual choice—whether to embrace or reject a "disability identity"—is distorted in current society by discrimination. In a society where such oppression is absent, both of these decisions would be equally valid and unremarkable, informed wholly by individual preference. While this story illustrates how individuals can adapt differently to the presence of a particular impairment, another more celebrated example shows how this can also happen on a social level.

The island of Martha's Vineyard, off the eastern coast of the US, is today known as a retreat for the rich. For over 250 years beforehand, however, it was a relatively isolated fishing community with an unusual distinction—a strikingly high incidence of hereditary deafness. This originated with families from The Weald, a remote part of Kent in England, who had emigrated and settled there in the 1630s. A recessive deafness gene spread through inbreeding, both in The Weald and on the Vineyard. The probability of an island inhabitant having more than one Kentish ancestor rose with each new generation, with the number of deaf people reaching a peak in the 1840s (after which it rapidly declined).[986]

Nora Ellen Groce, in her classic 1980s study *Everyone Here Spoke Sign Language*, shows how the presence of deaf people on the Vineyard was taken for granted, with most hearing people fluent in sign language. One older man remarked to her: "I didn't think about the deaf any more than you'd think about somebody with a different voice". When Groce asked another woman in her eighties about those "handicapped" by deafness, she replied emphatically: "these people weren't handicapped. They were just deaf".[987]

As the gene was recessive, deafness could skip one or more generations. Its seemingly random appearance in the population led to deafness being viewed as something that could happen to any family—which it usually did at some point. Hearing people often used sign language even when deaf people were not present and never perceived deafness as an impairment. As another islander said to Groce: "You know, we didn't think anything special about them. They were just like anyone else. When you think about it, the Island was an awfully nice place to live".[988]

This striking—and rather beautiful—example shows that it is entirely possible to create a society where disability is unknown and genuine individuality can flourish. A society which harnessed the latest scientific and technological knowledge to the creative capacities of its citizens, who would debate and decide what is produced and how and for what purpose, would be far more likely to nourish and promote true human potential.

As capitalism compels its rulers to push for ever-greater profits, so workers are similarly compelled to resist. It is in the course of this resistance that people can discover new truths about themselves and their comrades in struggle and discard the common sense notions of capitalism. Ever since the French Revolution of 1789, apologists for the status quo have associated the spontaneity and intensity of revolt with crazed mobs and irrationality. In words that bring to mind the counter-revolution in Egypt, Laure Murat asks a pertinent question:

> Whether pilloried or tacitly praised, why is the violence of insurrection always associated with madness, whereas the violence of repression never is? Blanqui was a madman who should be 'put away', whereas Louis Eugène Cavaignac, who turned the events of June 1848 into a bloodbath, was hailed as the savior of the nation. It is singularly crazy to castigate popular uprisings but reward massacres; this weird rule systematically relegates revolution to insanity but attributes to reaction all the virtues of common sense.[989]

This approach has been adopted in the case of other more modest threats to our rulers' interests. Shortly after his election as leader of the Labour Party in autumn 2015, the *Daily Mail* awarded members of Jeremy Corbyn's new shadow cabinet with a "looney left rating".[990] This was an attempt to revive the press campaigns of the 1980s which sought to represent left wing individuals and ideas "as so deranged and psychotic that they represented a danger to society".[991]

As Marx put it, socialists must prove the "this-sidedness" of their thinking in practice. In other words, the truth or otherwise of the idea that the working class is a force which can transform the world can only be demonstrated by real events. The Russian Revolution of October 1917 provided a unique, if all too brief, example of what a successful workers' revolution could achieve. The preamble of its Education Act of 1918 expressed its spirit and ideals:

> The personality shall remain as the highest value in the socialist culture. This personality however can develop its inclinations in all possible luxury only in a harmonious society of equals. We do not forget the right of an individual to his own peculiar development. It is not necessary for us to cut short a personality, to cheat it, to cast it into iron moulds, because the stability of the socialist community is based not on the uniformity of the barracks, not on artificial drill, not on religious and aesthetic deceptions, but on an actual solidarity of interests.[992]

Tragically, despite inspiring huge struggles across Europe, that revolution did not spread. There is good reason, however, to believe that next time we can win. The sense of a single global enemy is widely shared. On a single day on 15 February 2003, 30 million people around the world marched against imperialist war, sparking a chain of events that led to the Arab Spring and the end of the Mubarak dictatorship in Egypt—an event itself celebrated around the world within minutes.[993] In today's more interconnected and globalised economy there is no question that a workers' revolution would have a rapid and inspiring impact.

This is not an academic question. Capitalism continues its relentless pillage of global resources, hurtling humanity toward self-destruction. An appeal made by Jules Vallès after his participation in the Paris Commune in 1871 needs little amending almost 150 years later:

> We must begin pulling together, and not wait to go mad before storming the fortresses. Then perhaps one day we shall overturn them all, royal households and mental homes alike.[994]

Notes to the 2024 introduction

1   Kahl and Wright (2012), quoted in Alex Callinicos, *The New Age of Catastrophe* (Polity, 2023), p114.

2   World Health Organisation (2022), "Global report on health equity for persons with disabilities", https://www.who.int/publications/i/item/9789240063600 p3. This represents a rise of 0.3 billion on the figure for 2011 (see p24).

3   WHO (2022), p5.

4   WHO (2022), p5.

5   United Nations (2023), "Factsheet on Persons with Disabilities", UN Department of Economic and Social Affairs, www.un.org/development/desa/disabilities/resources/factsheet-on-persons-with-disabilities.html

6   Missing Billion Initiative (2022), "Reimagining health systems that expect, accept and connect 1 billion people with disabilities", www.themissingbillion.org/the-reports

7   A Health Handbook for Women with Disabilities (2020), https://en.hesperian.org/hhg/A_Health_Handbook_for_Women_with_Disabilities:Causes_of_disability, pp10-14.

8   *The Economist* (2021), "Campaigners in China struggle to improve the lot of the disabled", 18 March, www.economist.com/china/2021/03/18/campaigners-in-china-struggle-to-improve-the-lot-of-the-disabled

9   The average percentage for those classified as disabled across the EU is 24 percent. See European Council (2022), "Disability in the EU: facts and figures", 4 July, www.consilium.europa.eu/en/infographics/disability-eu-facts-figures/

10 A survey by the charity Sense found that one in four of the UK public became more interested in Deaf issues after the victory of Rose Ayling-Ellis in BBC One's "Strictly Come Dancing". A third of the respondents, however, felt there was not enough representation of disabled people on TV. Sense, 13 (2021), "Call for more disability representation on television", www.sense.org.uk/media/latest-press-releases/impact-of-strictly-finalist-rose-ayling-allis/

11 John Elflein (2023), Statista, 17 April. See www.statista.com/statistics/979003/disability-poverty-rate-us/

12 Rebecca Leppert and Katherine Schaeffer (2023), "8 facts about Americans with disabilities", Pew Research, 24 July, www.pewresearch.org/short-reads/2023/07/24/8-facts-about-americans-with-disabilities/

13 US Department of Labor n.d., "Section 14(c) of the Fair Labor Standards Act", www.dol.gov/sites/dolgov/files/WHD/legacy/files/RightsForWorkersWithDisabilities.pdf

14 Mark Betancourt (2022), "Inside the Kafkaesque process for determining who gets Federal

Disability Benefits", *Mother Jones*, September and October issue, www.motherjones.com/politics/2022/08/inside-the-kafkaesque-process-for-determining-who-gets-federal-disability-benefits/; Atticus Advice Center (2022), "Your chances of winning a Social Security Disability Appeal", www.atticus.com/advice/general/your-chances-of-winning-a-social-security-disability-appeal-your-odds-change

15   The figure given is $12,140 annually. See US Social Security Administration, n.d. www.ssa.gov/disabilityfacts/facts.html

16   The figures given are for the fiscal years 2021 and 2022. Lisa Rein (2023), "Judges rebuke Social Security for errors as disability denials stack up", *Washington Post*, 25 May, www.washingtonpost.com/politics/2023/05/25/social-security-disability-denials-court-remands/

17   Heather Gautney and Eric Blanc (2020), "Students with disabilities deserve a quality education - Bernie's new Disability Rights Platform would give them one", *Jacobin*, 2 July, https://jacobin.com/2020/02/disability-special-education-bernie-sanders

18   BBC News (2022), "Sackler family to pay $6bn for role in US opioid crisis", 3 March, www.bbc.co.uk/news/world-us-canada-60610707

19   *Socialist Worker* (2020), "Opioids in the US – a crisis prescribed by profit", 2 January, https://socialistworker.co.uk/features/opioids-in-the-us-a-crisis-prescribed-by-profit/

20   Department for Work and Pensions (2022), "National Disability Strategy: Foreword from the Prime Minister", 2 December, www.gov.uk/government/publications/national-disability-strategy/forewords-about-this-strategy-action-across-the-uk-executive-summary-acknowledgements#foreword-from-the-prime-minister

21   John Pring (2021), "Peers criticise government for 'objectionable' Equality Act failure", Disability News Service, 9 September, https://www.disabilitynewsservice.com/peers-criticise-government-for-objectionable-equality-act-failure/

22   Ellen Clifford (2020), *The War on Disabled People*, Zed Books. My review of this excellent book is at https://isj.org.uk/disability-class-agency/

23   House of Commons Library (2022), "The UN Convention on the Rights of Persons with Disabilities: UK Implementation", Research Briefing, 10 November, https://commonslibrary.parliament.uk/research-briefings/cbp-7367/

24   Inclusion London (2023), "Alternative report from civil society", 25 August, www.inclusionlondon.org.uk/campaigns-and-policy/uncrdp/crdp23/crdp23/

25   Scope (2023a), "Disability Price Tag 2023: the extra cost of disability", 26 April.
     Scope's "previous Disability Price Tag research found an average extra cost of £583 (a person) a month. However, our 2023 figure is non-comparable as we have developed and revised our modelling. If we recalculate our previous figure using our new approach, our new baseline average extra cost was £645, suggesting a rise of £330 over three years to our current figure of £975 for 2019/2020." See www.scope.org.uk/campaigns/extra-costs/disability-price-tag-2023/#:~:text=reach%20their%20potential-,What%20are%20extra%20costs%3F,pay%20more%20for%20the%20basics

26   Scope (2023a).

27   Patrick Butler (2023), "Hunt's

disability plans put 1 million people at risk of losing £350 a month, IFS says", *The Guardian*, 15 March, www.theguardian.com/society/2023/mar/15/hunts-disability-plans-put-1m-at-risk-of-losing-350-a-month-ifs-says

28 See https://news.railbusinessdaily.com/transport-watchdog-objects-to-proposed-ticket-office-closures/

29 Joshua Nevett (2023), "Ministers skip UN meeting on disability rights", BBC News, 30 August, www.bbc.co.uk/news/uk-politics-66648764

30 Nabil Ahmed and others (2022), "Inequality kills: the unparalleled action needed to combat unprecedented inequality in the wake of COVID-19", Oxfam, 17 January, www.oxfam.org/en/research/inequality-kills

31 Callinicos (2023), p45.

32 Waasila Jassat and others (2023), "Long COVID in low-income and middle-income countries: the hidden public health crisis", *The Lancet*, volume 402, issue 10408, 30 September, www.thelancet.com/journals/lancet/article/PIIS0140-6736(23)01685-9/fulltext

33 Callinicos (2023), p58.

34 The King's Fund (2022), "Deaths from Covid-19 (coronavirus): how are they counted and what do they show?", 23 August, www.kingsfund.org.uk/publications/deaths-covid-19

35 Sarah Neville and Federica Cocco (2021), "'Horrifying' death toll prompts calls to prioritise jabs for disabled people", *Financial Times*, 18 February, www.ft.com/content/bc616b88-0368-43e9-94b7-a715ef456685

36 Ian Sample (2021), "People with learning disabilities in England 'have eight times Covid death rate'", *The Guardian*, 15 July, www.theguardian.com/society/2021/jul/15/

people-with-learning-disabilities-in-england-have-eight-times-covid-death-rate. The report added that people with Down's syndrome may have additional biological risks such as underlying heart conditions and immune system dysfunction.

37 BBC News (2022), "Covid: Discharging untested patients to care homes 'unlawful'", 27 April, www.bbc.co.uk/news/uk-england-61227709

38 Haroon Siddique (2021), "Downing Street Covid briefings excluded deaf BSL users, judge finds", *The Guardian*, 28 July, www.theguardian.com/law/2021/jul/28/downing-street-covid-briefings-excluded-deaf-bsl-users-judge-finds

39 June Kelly (2021), "Coronavirus: Domestic abuse an 'epidemic beneath a pandemic'", BBC News, 23 March, www.bbc.co.uk/news/uk-56491643

40 UK Parliament (2022), "£4 billion of unusable PPE bought in first year of pandemic will be burnt 'to generate power'", 10 June, https://committees.parliament.uk/committee/127/public-accounts-committee/news/171306/4-billion-of-unusable-ppe-bought-in-first-year-of-pandemic-will-be-burnt-to-generate-power/

41 Transparency International (2021), "Concern over corruption red flags in 20% of UK's PPE procurement", UK Press release, 21 April, www.transparency.org.uk/track-and-trace-uk-PPE-procurement-corruption-risk-VIP-lane

42 United Nations High Commissioner for Human Rights (2021), "Disability, Displacement and Climate Change", April, www.unhcr.org/uk/media/disability-displacement-and-climate-change

43 The UN estimates that "9.7 million people with disabilities

are forcibly displaced as a result of conflict and persecution and are victims of human rights violations and conflict-related violence." Human Rights Watch, 2018, "UN: War's Impact on People with Disabilities", 3 December, www.hrw.org/news/2018/12/03/un-wars-impact-people-disabilities

44 Shada Islam (2023), "The taboos are falling fast as the EU embraces the far-right racist approach to migration", *The Guardian*, 15 February, www.theguardian.com/world/commentisfree/2023/feb/15/eu-far-right-migration-fortress-europe

45 World Bank Group (2022), "Mental Health in the West Bank and Gaza", 22 November, https://bit.ly/47xqcc4

46 United Nations High Commissioner for Human Rights (2020), "Analytical study on the promotion and protection of the rights of persons with disabilities in the context of climate change", 22 April, www.ohchr.org/en/documents/thematic-reports/analytical-study-promotion-and-protection-rights-persons-disabilities

47 UNHCR (2020).

48 United Nations (2021), "Human Rights Council panel discussion on the rights of persons with disabilities in the context of climate change", www.ohchr.org/en/climate-change/impact-climate-change-rights-persons-disabilities

49 State of Nature Partnership (2023), State of Nature 2019, https://nbn.org.uk/stateofnature2019/

50 Rodrigo Menegat Schuinski (2023), "Air pollution: Nearly everyone in Europe breathing bad air", *Deutsche Welle*, 9 July, www.dw.com/en/air-pollution-nearly-everyone-in-europe-breathing-bad-air/a-66657048

51 Gary Fuller, Stav Friedman and Ian Mudway (2023), "Impacts of air pollution across the life course – evidence highlight note", Environmental Research Group, Imperial College London, April 2023, https://bit.ly/49S8NMs

52 Emma Lawrance and others (2021), "The impact of climate change on mental health and emotional wellbeing: current evidence and implications for policy and practice", Imperial College London, May 2021.

For an up-to-date analysis of issues relating to mental health, see the new edition of Iain Ferguson's excellent book, *The Politics of the Mind: Marxism and Mental Distress* (Bookmarks, 2023)

53 See for example, Steve Silberman's (2015) bestselling book *Neurotribes*, the subtitle of which is *The Legacy of Autism and How to Think Smarter about People who Think Differently* (Allen & Unwin).

54 The difficulty here is less with the term "neurodiverse" – which expresses the range of characteristics within the autistic spectrum but also within ADHD, dyslexia and dyspraxia – than with its converse "neurotypical". Nick Chown and others have suggested that the latter be replaced with the term "predominant neurotype". See Nick Chown (2017), *Understanding and Evaluating Autism Theory* (Jessica Kingsley), p25. While this term is more accurate, it is perhaps unsurprising that it has so far gained little popular traction.

55 Lydia Brown (2013), "How 'differently abled' marginalizes disabled people", 29 August, www.autistichoya.com/2013/08/differently-abled.html

56 Lydia Brown (2013).

57 Scope (2023b), "How to be a disability ally", 21 March, https://business.scope.org.uk/article/how-to-be-a-disability-ally

58 For an excellent critique of privilege theory, see Esme

Choonara and Yuri Prasad (2014), "What's wrong with privilege theory?", *International Socialism*, Issue 142, https://isj.org.uk/whats-wrong-with-privilege-theory/

59   Yuri Prasad (2022), "Is 'allyship' an effective tool to fight racism?", *Socialist Worker*, 23 July, https://socialistworker.co.uk/features/is-allyship-an-effective-tool-to-fight-racism/

60   *The Economist* (2020), "The power of protest and the legacy of George Floyd", 11 June, www.economist.com/leaders/2020/06/11/the-power-of-protest-and-the-legacy-of-george-floyd

61   Thanks to Esme Choonara for some of these points, made in her talk "Can identity politics help end oppression?" at Marxism Festival 2023, London, July.

62   Cited in Tom Shakespeare, (2019), keynote speech, British Psychological Society Division of Clinical Psychology Annual Conference, 11 March, www.youtube.com/watch?v=QMPb_554c50

63   Emma Yeomans (2019), "Journal editors quit in protest over 'transphobic' academic", *The Times*, 26 June, www.thetimes.co.uk/article/journal-editors-quit-in-protest-over-transphobic-academic-6tvq3cwfv

64   Scope (2023c), "Disability facts and figures", www.scope.org.uk/media/disability-facts-figures/

65   Frances Ryan (2020), *Crippled: Austerity and the Demonisation of Disabled People* (Verso), p54.

66   Charlie McCurdy (2022), "Labour Market Outlook Q3 2022", Resolution Foundation, 6 October, www.resolutionfoundation.org/publications/labour-market-outlook-q3-2022/

67   Department of Work and Pensions (2022), "The employment of disabled people 2021", updated 11 February, www.gov.uk/government/statistics/the-employment-of-disabled-people-2021/the-employment-of-disabled-people-2021

68   Robert Joyce (2019), "Benefits spending: five charts on the UK's £100bn bill", BBC News, 22 March, www.bbc.co.uk/news/business-47623277

Joyce shows that in 2016-17, 58 percent of working age benefits in the UK were paid to households with at least someone in paid work – a rise of 18 percent from the equivalent figure in 1994-95.

69   David Matthews (2021), "Disability and welfare under monopoly capitalism", *Monthly Review*, 1 January, https://monthlyreview.org/2021/01/01/disability-and-welfare-under-monopoly-capitalism/

Matthews cites several other writers, such as the recently deceased US writer Marta Russell, who also take this view.

70   Amounting to well over 40 percent of all disabled workers in the UK. See Figure 14, Department of Work and Pensions (2022), "The employment of disabled people 2021".

71   Higher Education Statistics Authority (2023), "Who's studying in HE?", 31 January, www.hesa.ac.uk/data-and-analysis/students/whos-in-he

72   House of Commons Library (2023), "Disabled people in employment: briefing paper number 7540", 19 June, https://researchbriefings.files.parliament.uk/documents/CBP-7540/CBP-7540.pdf

73   David Blunkett (2018), "Employers, give yourselves a chance to find hidden talents", *Financial Times*, 10 May, www.ft.com/content/a4c1aace-4870-11e8-8ae9-4b5ddcca99b3

74   Ellen Halliday and Luke Gbedemah

(2021), "FTSE silent on disability", Tortoise Media, 18 May, www.tortoisemedia.com/2021/05/18/sensemaker-210518

The *Financial Times* Stock Exchange 100 Index is a share index of the 100 companies listed on the London Stock Exchange with the highest market capitalisation.

75 Interview in Gary Younge (2023), *Dispatches from the Diaspora: From Nelson Mandela to Black Lives Matter* (Faber and Faber), p234.

76 Chris Jay (2022), "Why 'hidden' disabilities shouldn't also mean hiding disability", *Personnel Today*, 25 January, https://bit.ly/3RakRBB

77 National Union of Journalists (2022), "TUC Disabled Workers' Conference 2022", 24 May, www.nuj.org.uk/resource/tuc-disabled-workers-conference-2022.html

78 Melanie Jones (2023), "Disability and trade union membership in the UK", British Journal of Industrial Relations, 8 August, https://onlinelibrary.wiley.com/doi/full/10.1111/bjir.12767

79 Laura William and Ian Cunningham (2018), "Evaluating the Role of Trade Unions and Civil Society Organisations in Supporting Graduate Educated Disabled Workers", *Economic and Industrial Democracy*, volume 42, issue 3, pp2-3.

80 John Pring (2023), "Report for Labour rules out early end to care charges", *Disability News Service*, 8 June, www.disabilitynewsservice.com/report-for-labour-rules-out-early-end-to-care-charges/

81 Sir Keir Starmer (2023), "Some say we should not talk about immigration. Others want Britain to shut up shop. Both are wrong", *The Sun*, 13 September, www.thesun.co.uk/news/23945317/not-talk-about-immigration-britain-shut-shop-both-wrong/

82 "58% of Americans support the first-ever simultaneous strike by the United Auto Workers union against Ford Motor, General Motors and Chrysler parent Stellantis to win better pay and benefits", and "60% of Americans support the dual strikes by screenwriters and actors to win better pay and protections". Andy Sullivan (2023), "Americans broadly support auto, Hollywood strikes", Reuters/Ipsos poll shows, *Reuters*, 21 September, www.reuters.com/world/us/americans-broadly-support-auto-hollywood-strikes-reutersipsos-poll-2023-09-21/

83 Personal communication with the author, 12 November 2023.

Notes

1   Diane Driedger, *The Last Civil Rights Movement* (St Martin's Press, 1989).

2   See http://apps.who.int/gb/ebwha/pdf_files/EB130/B130_9-en.pdf.

3   Global South is an inexact and problematic term, but is nevertheless preferable to more misleading ones such as the Third or Developing World. I use it in this book to refer to societies distinct from the main advanced economies (principally Northern America, Western Europe and parts of the Far East). Some societies occupy a place somewhere in between, or share elements of both, combining huge swathes of economic backwardness with the world's most advanced industries.

4   See, for example, the influential collections *Disability and Culture* and *Disability in Local and Global Worlds*, edited by Benedicte Ingstad and Susan Reynolds Whyte (University of California Press, 1995 and 2007).

5   US Equal Employment Opportunity Commission. As this website notes, corporations have sought in successive lawsuits to make these definitions as restrictive as possible so that individuals cannot meet the necessary criteria to qualify as disabled. See http://www.eeoc.gov/laws/statutes/adaaa.cfm.

6   "The definition of disability: what is in a name?", *The Lancet*, vol 368, issue 9543, 7-13 October 2006, pp1219-1221. See http://www.sciencedirect.com/science/article/pii/S0140673606694981.

7   See http://www.who.int/topics/disabilities/en/.

8   Frances Ryan, "Don't forget the word 'disability', but don't pity it either", Independent, 11 September 2012 http://www.independent.co.uk/voices/comment/dont-forget-the-word-disability-but-dont-pity-it-either-8125961.html?origin=internalSearch.

9   Elements of this section appeared previously in Slorach, "Marxism and disability", *International Socialism* 129. See http://www.isj.org.uk/?id=702

10 Tom Shakespeare, *Disability Rights and Wrongs* (Routledge, 2006).

11 A further complication here is that (in the UK at least) this group of hearing impaired people legally qualify as disabled, although this group of visually impaired people do not.

12 Vic Finkelstein in John Swain and Vic Finkelstein, *Disabling Barriers—Enabling Environments* (Open University, 1992)

13 Mark Deal, "Disabled People's Attitudes Toward Other Impairment Groups", quoted in *The Guardian*, 21 March 2007. See http://www.theguardian.com/society/2007/mar/21/disability.socialcare.

14 *Fulfilling Potential: Building a Deeper Understanding of Disability in the UK Today* (DWP, February 2013). See

https://www.gov.uk/government/uploads/system/uploads/attachment_data/file/320509/building-understanding-main-report.pdf. Research in 2006 found this was true of "around half of those covered by the Disability Discrimination Act." Quoted in "Time to drop the 'disabled' label?" p28, Disability Now, November 2006. The UK's Disability Discrimination Act (1995) was replaced by the Equality Act (2010)

15 Jane Campbell and Michael Oliver, *Disability Politics: Understanding Our Past, Changing Our Future* (Routledge, 1996) p120. As we shall see, it is perfectly possible to see deaf people as a linguistic minority while still seeing their social and economic exclusion as amounting to disability discrimination.

16 UPIAS, *Fundamental Principles of Disability*, 1975.

17 Michael Oliver, *The Politics of Disablement* (Palgrave Macmillan, 1990), p2.

18 *The Economist*, 14 December 2013. See http://www.economist.com/news/international/21591615-defining-disability-trickyand-measuring-it-even-harder-who-counts.

19 Karen McVeigh, "One billion people disabled, first global report finds", *The Guardian*, 9 September 2011.

20 Extract from WHO *World Report on Disability*, 2011.

21 http://web.worldbank.org/WBSITE/EXTERNAL/TOPICS/EXTSOCIALPROTECTION/EXTDISABILITY/0,,contentMDK:21150847~menuPK:420476~pagePK:210058~piPK:210062~theSitePK:282699,00.html#HowMany (last updated 19 November 2009).

22 See http://www.who.int/violence_injury_prevention/disability/en/

23 The *DSM* is published by the American Psychiatric Association. For more on the *DSM*, see

chapter 10.

24 Jonathan Cole, *Still Lives: Narratives of Spinal Cord Injury* (Bradford Books, 2004), p21.

25 "Mencap celebrates as derogatory wording is removed from electoral law", *The Guardian*, 23 May 2006.

26 "How offensive is the word 'lunatic'?", BBC News Magazine, Washington, 9 May 2012. See http://www.bbc.co.uk/news/magazine-17997413.

27 Clare Allan, "On mental health, it's wise to choose your words carefully", *The Guardian*, 6 September 2011. See http://www.guardian.co.uk/society/2011/sep/06/mental-health-choose-your-words-carefully

28 According to Keith Armstrong, e-mail correspondence, 5 Apr 2012. See https://www.jiscmail.ac.uk/cgi-bin/webadmin?A2=DISABILITY-RESEARCH;31e69f54.1204.

29 This term was first coined by the US disability activist and writer Marta Russell.

30 Andrew Lansley speech, 16 July 2010. See http://webarchive.nationalarchives.gov.uk/20130107105354/http://www.dh.gov.uk/en/MediaCentre/Speeches/DH_117366.

31 The phrase is from the song by The Clash, *White Man in Hammersmith Palais*.

32 https://www.bps.org.uk/system/files/user-files/Division percent20of percent20Clinical percent20Psychology/public/understanding_psychosis_-_final_19th_nov_2014.pdf.

33 Jeffrey A Brune and Daniel J Wilson (eds), *Disability and Passing* (Temple University Press, 2013), p46.

34 Paul Hunt (ed), "A Critical Condition" in *Stigma: The Experience of Disability* (Geoffrey Chapman, 1966). See http://disability-studies.leeds.ac.uk/files/library/Hunt-a-critical-condition.pdf. The book's title was

inspired by Erving Goffmann's book, *Stigma*, itself a survey of the suffering and humiliations meted out to "handicapped" people in modern society.

35 Hunt's story is told in a BBC4 documentary, *Disowned and Disabled*, broadcast on 29 October 2013.

36 See http://disability-studies.leeds.ac.uk/files/library/Hunt-Hunt-1.pdf

37 Vic Finkelstein, "A Personal Journey into Disability Politics" (2001) http://disability-studies.leeds.ac.uk/files/library/finkelstein-presentn.pdf

38 Finkelstein (2001)

39 Finkelstein (2001)

40 UPIAS, *Fundamental Principles of Disability* (1975), p4. See http://disability-studies.leeds.ac.uk/files/library/UPIAS-fundamental-principles.pdf

41 UPIAS (1975), pp14-15.

42 UPIAS (1975), p4.

43 Mike Oliver, *Capitalism, Disability and Ideology: A Materialist Critique of the Normalization Principle* (1999). See http://disability-studies.leeds.ac.uk/files/library/Oliver-cap-dis-ideol.pdf

44 Cole (2004), p279.

45 Cole (2004), p279.

46 Mike Oliver, *Exploring the Divide* (1996), chapter 3. See http://disability-studies.leeds.ac.uk/files/library/Oliver-ex-div-ch3.pdf.

47 C Barnes and G Mercer (eds), "Theorising & Researching Disability from a Social Model Perspective", in *Implementing the Social Model of Disability* (2004). See http://disability-studies.leeds.ac.uk/files/library/Barnes-implementing-the-social-model-chapter-1.pdf.

48 Michael Oliver and Colin Barnes, *The New Politics of Disablement* (Palgrave Macmillan 2012), p165.

49 The quote is one of the key points in a report for a conference called Reclaiming the Social Model of Disability organised by Greater London Action on Disability in February 2000.

50 Vic Finkelstein, *The Social Model of Disability and the Disability Movement* (2007).

51 Tom Shakespeare, *Disability Rights and Wrongs* (2007), p34. Shakespeare, formerly a passionate advocate of the social model, became one of its main critics, especially in this nevertheless interesting book which was highly influential in Disability Studies circles. Routledge published an updated edition, entitled *Disability Rights and Wrongs Revisited*, in 2014.

52 Shakespeare (2007), p41.

53 Shakespeare (2014), p46.

54 Oliver and Barnes (2012), p23.

55 Oliver, chapter 3 in Barnes and Mercer (1996)

56 Paul Abberley, "Work, Utopia and Impairment", in L Barton, *Disability and Society: Emerging Issues and Insights* (Longman, 1996), p64.

57 Dorothy Dinnerstein, *The Mermaid and the Minotaur* (1976), quoted in Abberley (1996).

58 Paul Abberley, *The Concept of Oppression and the Development of a Social Theory of Disability* (1987). See http://disability-studies.leeds.ac.uk/files/library/Abberley-chapter10.pdf.

59 Mike Oliver, "Defining Impairment and Disability", in Colin Barnes and Geof Mercer (eds), *Exploring the Divide: Illness and Disability* (1996). See http://disability-studies.leeds.ac.uk/files/library/Oliver-ex-div-ch3.pdf.

60 Abberley (1987).

61 Thanks to Gareth Jenkins for this example.

62 http://www.hse.gov.uk/Statistics/causdis/index.htm

63 http://www.hse.gov.uk/Statistics/history/index.htm

64 Paul K Longmore, *Why I Burned My Book and Other Essays on*

Disability (Temple University Press, 2003), p205.

65 Susan Wendell, *The Rejected Body: Feminist Philosophical Reflections on Disability* (Routledge 1996), pp124 and 130.

66 Shakespeare (2007), p109.

67 For an excellent account of the biopsychosocial model, see Debbie Jolly, "A Tale of two Models: Disabled People vs Unum, Atos, Government and the Disability Charities" (DPAC, April 2012), http://dpac.uk.net/2012/04/a-tale-of-two-models-disabled-people-vs-unum-atos-government-and-disability-charities-debbie-jolly/.

68 Oliver and Barnes (2012), p23.

69 *Fulfilling Potential: Next Steps* (DWP, 2012), p15. See https://www.gov.uk/government/uploads/system/uploads/attachment_data/file/321046/fulfilling-potential-next-steps.pdf.

70 Mike Oliver, Disability Now, June 2013, http://www.disabilitynow.org.uk/article/social-model-victim-criticism.

71 Robert Garland, *The Eye of the Beholder: Deformity and Disability in the Graeco-Roman World* (Bristol Classical Press, 2010), p178. The book's title reflects Garland's view that disability is less a historical matter than a cultural or subjective one.

72 Katherine Quarmby, *Scapegoat: Why we Are Failing Disabled People* (Portobello Books, 2011), p16.

73 P A Spikins, H E Rutherford and A P Needham, *The Prehistory of Compassion* (2010), p10. See http://www.york.ac.uk/media/archaeology/documents/staff/staffpersonalfiles/Compassion7.pdf.

74 Spikins, Rutherford and Needham (2010), pp.11-13.

75 "Elderly for a Neanderthal man". See http://humanorigins.si.edu/evidence/human-fossils/fossils/shanidar-1.

76 See, for example, http://evoanth.wordpress.com/2012/04/26/caring-neanderthals/.

77 "Ancient Bones That Tell a Story of Compassion", *New York Times*, 17 December 2012, http://www.nytimes.com/2012/12/18/science/ancient-bones-that-tell-a-story-of-compassion.html?_r=0

78 Lorna Tilley and Marc F Oxenham, "Survival against the odds: Modeling the social implications of care provision to seriously disabled individuals", *International Journal of Paleopathology*, vol 1, issue 1, March 2011, pp35-42 http://www.sciencedirect.com/science/article/pii/S1879981711000064.

79 Kim E Nielsen, *A Disability History of the United States* (Beacon Press, 2012), p3.

80 Neilsen (2012), p11.

81 For a detailed account of the role of women in pre-class societies, see Judith Orr, *Marxism and Women's Liberation* (Bookmarks, 2015) and Eleanor Burke Leacock's classic study, *Myths of Male Dominance* (New York: Monthly Review Press, 1981).

82 Aud Talle, "A Child Is a Child; Disability and Equality among the Kenya Maasai" in Ingstad and Whyte (1995), p71.

83 Hanks & Hanks (1980) quoted in Oliver and Barnes (2012) pp33 and 36.

84 Oliver and Barnes (2012), p33.

85 Jared Diamond, *Why Is Sex Fun?* (Orion Books, 1997), pp162-163.

86 Colin Barnes, "A Legacy of Oppression: A History of Disability in Western Culture", pp3-24, in Len Barton and Mike Oliver (eds), *Disability Studies: Past Present and Future* (Leeds: The Disability Press 1997). Available at http://disability-studies.leeds.ac.uk/files/library/Barnes-chap1.pdf.

87 Barnes (1997).

88 Achondroplastic dwarfism refers

to people with disproportionately short legs and arms compared to their trunk (body), with shortness most prominent in the upper parts of the arms and legs.

89 Chahira Kozma, "Dwarfs in ancient Egypt", *American Journal of Medical Genetics Part a*, vol 140A, issue 4 (2006).

90 Sonia Zakrzewski, "Paleopathology, disability and bodily impairments", pp59-60, in Metcalfe et al (eds), *Paleopathology in Egypt and Nubia* (Archaeopress Egyptology 6, 2014).

91 Martha L Rose, *The Staff of Oedipus: Transforming Disability in Ancient Greece* (University of Michigan Press, 2003). In this otherwise excellent book, Rose repeatedly applies the term "disability" to ancient Greek society in a manner which confuses her argument.

92 Rose (2003), p14.

93 Garland (2010), pp19-20.

94 Rose (2003), p3.

95 Rose (2003), p11.

96 Rose (2003), p43.

97 One scholar argues that Plato did not advocate exposure in *The Republic* at all, but rather the casting out of children of "inferior" parents from a "guardian class". See G van N Viljoen, *Plato and Aristotle on the Exposure of Children at Athens* (University of South Africa, 1954), at http://www.casa-kvsa.org. za/1959/AC02-06-Viljoen.pdf.

98 (2003), pp36 and 48.

99 Yasmine Maher, *Exposure of Children* (undated) http:// www.academia.edu/3429478/ child_exposure_in_roman_empire.

100 Mary Beard, "The real Romans", *The Guardian Review*, 3 October 2015, http://www.theguardian.com/ books/2015/oct/02/mary-beard-why-ancient-rome-matters.

101 Rose (2003), p40.

102 Rose (2003), p44.

103 W V Harris, "Child Exposure in the Roman Empire", *Journal of Roman Studies*, vol 84 (1994).

104 Harris (1994).

105 W G Armer, *In the Shadow of Genetics* (2005). Available at http:// disability-studies.leeds.ac.uk/files/ library/armer-Bill.pdf

106 Gevaert in Rupert Breitweiser (ed), Behinderungen und Beeinträchtigungen, *Disability and Impairment in Antiquity* (BAR International Series 2359, 2012), p88.

107 C Laes, C F Goodey and M Lynn Rose, *Disabilities in Roman Antiquity: Disparate Bodies* (Brill, 2013), p213. For an interesting (if rather speculative) discussion of the terms monstrum and mirabilium, see Laura Conroy, *Monstrum or Mirabilium: Status and Fate of Human Monsters in Ancient Rome* (undated) at https:// www.academia.edu/11357834/ Monstrum_or_Mirabilium_Status_ and_Fate_of_Human_Monsters_ in_Ancient_Rome.

108 Laura Conroy (undated).

109 Rose (2003), p3.

110 Ian Jenkins, *Defining Beauty: The Body in Ancient Greek Art* (The British Museum, 2015), p94.

111 Breitweiser, in Breitweiser (2012), p1.

112 Irina Metzler, *Disability in Medieval Europe* (Routledge, 2006), p5.

113 Quoted in Metzler (2006), p13.

114 Disability in the medieval period 1050-1485, http:// www.english-heritage.org.uk/ discover/people-and-places/ disability-history/1050-1485/.

115 Irina Metzler, *A Social History of Disability in the Middle Ages* (Routledge, 2013), p57.

116 One entertaining and informative source on the role of the Church as a library as well as a battleground of ideas is Umberto Eco's historical novel *The Name of The Rose*, also made into an excellent film.

117 Metzler, quoted in "Episode 2: Miracle Cures", Radio 4 series *Disability: A New History*,

28 May 2013.

118 Metzler, *Disability: A New History*, 28 May 2013.

119 Metzler (2013), p38.

120 Henri-Jacques Stiker, *A History of Disability* (University of Michigan Press, 1982), p79.

121 http://www.english-heritage.org. uk/discover/people-and-places/ disability-history/1050-1485/.

122 Metzler (2006), p63.

123 Catherine Slater, "Idiots, Imbeciles and Intellectual Impairment", at http://langdondownmuseum. org.uk/the-history-of-learning-disability/idiots-imbeciles-and-intellectual-impairment/

124 Slater, "Idiots, Imbeciles and Intellectual Impairment".

125 Quote from a museum plaque in Rothesay Castle on the Isle of Bute, Scotland

126 Contrary to myth, the practice of footbinding was ended by the Chinese themselves. For more on its history, see http://www.theguardian.com/ artanddesign/2015/jun/15/the-last-women-in-china-with-bound-feet.

127 Stiker (1982), pp65 and 69.

128 M Miles, "Disability in an Eastern Religious Context: historical perspectives", *Disability and Society*, vol 10 (1), (1995)

129 M Miles, "Can Formal Disability Services be Developed with South Asian Historical and Conceptual Foundations?" (1999). See http:// disability-studies.leeds.ac.uk/files/ library/stone-chapter-14.pdf.

130 The climate change which is a cumulative consequence of capitalism was not apparent 200 years ago.

131 Metzler (2013), p78.

132 Chris Harman, *A People's History of the World* (Bookmarks 1999), p145.

133 Stiker (1982), p84.

134 Metzler (2013), p77.

135 Metzler (2013), p74.

136 Harald Kleinschmidt, quoted in Metzler (2013), p72.

137 Metzler (2013), p72.

138 Harman (1999), p247.

139 Metzler (2013), p76.

140 C F Goodey, *A History of Intelligence and 'Intellectual Disability'* (Ashgate, 2011), pp22 and 51.

141 Goodey (2011), p126.

142 Metzler (2013), p85.

143 Goodey (2011), p221.

144 Metzler (2013), p86.

145 Brian Logan, "All the King's Fools", *The Guardian*, 24 February 2011.

146 Goodey (2011), p220.

147 Ruth von Bernuth, "From Marvels of Nature to Inmates of Asylums: Imaginations of Natural Folly", *Disability Studies Quarterly*, Spring 2006, vol 26, no 2. See http://dsq-sds.org/article/view/697/874

148 Goodey (2011), pp201-203.

149 C F Goodey, "Exclusion from the Eucharist: A Formative Moment in the seventeenth-Century Creation of "Intellectually" Disabled People" pp.107-120 in Hans S. Reinders (ed) *Authenticity and Community: Essays in Honor of Herman P Meininger* (Garant Publishers, 2012)

150 Goodey, *Exclusion from the Eucharist* (2012).

151 Harman (1999), p204.

152 Harman (1999), p175.

153 http://www.english-heritage.org. uk/discover/people-and-places/ disability-history/1485-1660/.

154 Stiker (1982), p86.

155 Stiker (1982), pp99-100.

156 Notoriously, sightseers were allowed to view the inmates at Bethlem until the practice was banned in 1770. See http:// www.english-heritage.org.uk/ discover/people-and-places/ disability-history/1485-1660/

157 Andrew Scull, *Madness: A Very Short Introduction* (Oxford University Press 2011), pp22-25.

158 Metzler (2013), p51.

159 Metzler (2013), p60.

160 Metzler (2013), p70.

161 See, for example pp37-38, Brian Stratford, *Down's Syndrome: Past, Present and Future* (Penguin, 1989). Chris Goodey addresses the matter as follows: "The passage in which he says 'if I were prince of that country, so I would venture homicidum thereon and he would throw it [the changeling child] into the River Moldau' [was] not his own published text, but assembled from reported conversations by a disciple who seems to reflect the second-generation Reformers' increasing focus on the Devil and witchcraft." Goodey (2011), p265.

162 Peter Sedgwick, *Psychopolitics* (Pluto Press, 1982), p129.

163 Harman (1999), pp239-244.

164 Scull (2011), pp36-37.

165 Harman (1999), p318.

166 Karl Marx, *Capital*, vol 3, quoted in Lewis Siegelbaum, "Industrial Accidents and Their Prevention in the Interwar Period", in Stephen P Dunn and Ethel Dunn, *The Disabled in the Soviet Union* (University of Pittsburgh Press, 1989) p.85.

167 Elements of this chapter first appeared in R Slorach, "Marxism and disability", *International Socialism* 129 (2011) http://www.isj.org.uk/?id=702.

168 E J Hobsbawm, *The Age of Capital* (Abacus, 1985), p70.

169 Hobsbawm (1985), p49.

170 Neilsen (2012), p125.

171 USA http://www.encyclopedia.com/doc/1G2-3406401046.html.

172 Karl Marx and Frederick Engels, *The Communist Manifesto* (1848).

173 Vic Finkelstein, "Disability and the helper/helped relationship" (1981). Available at http://disability-studies.leeds.ac.uk/files/library/finkelstein-Helper-Helped-Relationship.pdf.

174 Eric Hobsbawm, *Industry and Empire* (Penguin 1977), p134.

175 Hobsbawm (1977), p27.

176 Harman (1999), p319.

177 Quoted in Alan Roulstone, "Disabling Pasts, Enabling Futures?", *Disability and Society*, vol 17, no 6 (2002).

178 Ann Rogers, "Back To The Workhouse?", *International Socialism* 59 (1993).

179 From the preface to the English edition (1892). See http://www.marxists.org/archive/marx/works/1892/01/11.htm.

180 Anne Borsay, *Disability and Social Policy in Britain since 1750: A History of Exclusion* (Palgrave Macmillan, 2005), p126.

181 Karl Marx, *Capital*, vol 1 (Lawrence & Wishart, 2003) p355.

182 See http://omf.ucsc.edu/london-1865/victorian-city/sanitary-report.html.

183 David Turner and Kevin Stagg, *Social Histories of Disability and Deformity* (Routledge, 2006) p107.

184 For more detail on these categories, see Colin Barnes, chapter 2 in "Disabled People in Britain and Discrimination: A case for anti-discrimination legislation" (1991), http://disability-studies.leeds.ac.uk/files/library/Barnes-disabled-people-and-discrim-ch2.pdf.

185 Barnes (1991).

186 Borsay (2005), p22.

187 Borsay (2005), p30. This is portrayed well in the 1994 film *The Madness of King George*.

188 Quoted in Alex Callinicos, *The Revolutionary Ideas of Karl Marx* (Bookmarks, 1996) p150. Collective action by workers forced capitalists to accept the Factory Acts, imposing limits on working hours. It eventually became clear that to constantly increase them was self-defeating, exhausting and even killing workers prematurely.

189 Marx (2003), p398.

190 Marx (2003), p79.

191 What is deemed socially necessary, such as "the going rate" for the job in the labour market, is of course

determined by class struggle.

192 Marx (2003), pp329-330.

193 Karl Marx, *Economic and Philosophical Manuscripts*, *Early Writings* (1844) (Penguin, 1975), p326.

194 Marx (1975), p329.

195 Marx (1975), p359.

196 Marx, quoted in Joseph Choonara, *Unravelling Capitalism* (Bookmarks, 2009), pp15-16.

197 John Rees, *The Algebra of Revolution* (Routledge, 1998) provides a useful comparison of Marx's theory of alienation with that of others, particularly Hegel, from whom Marx derived his own distinctive account.

198 Borsay (2005), p67.

199 Scull (2011), p35. Such practices were largely established in the ancient Roman period (see chapter 10).

200 Scull (2011), p40. As Scull notes, such figures, replicated in other European countries as well as in the US, contradict Michel Foucault's claim in *Madness and Civilisation* that the 17th century signalled the beginning of "The Great Confinement".

201 Laure Murat, *The Man Who Thought He Was Napoleon: Toward a Political History of Madness* (University of Chicago Press, 2014), p36.

202 Murat (2014), p34.

203 Non-violent methods, including the removal of patients' chains, were in fact an innovation of Jean-Baptiste Pussin, Governor at Bicêtre, whose methods Pinel learned from and generalised. See Murat (2014), pp43-45.

204 Murat (2014), p45.

205 Murat (2014), p105.

206 The York retreat, founded by William Tuke and based on Pinel and Pussin's ideas of moral therapy, was originally run by and for Quakers but gradually opened its doors to others. The Retreat's practices, widely derided at first, were gradually adopted more widely. See http://en.wikipedia.org/wiki/The_Retreat.

207 Andrew Scull (ed), *Madhouses, Mad-Doctors and Madmen* (University of Pennsylvania Press, 1981), p6.

208 Scull (2011), p49.

209 Purnell Barnsby Purnell, quoted pxviii, Sarah Wise, *Inconvenient People* (The Bodley Head, 2012)

210 Scull (2011), p52.

211 Peter McCandless, "Liberty and Lunacy: The Victorians and Wrongful Confinement" in Melling and Forsythe (eds), *Insanity, Institutions and Society* (Routledge, 1999) p343.

212 Borsay (2005), p66.

213 Scull (2011), p55.

214 Scull (2011), pp55-56. In the Russian Empire, also undergoing industrialisation, the number of asylums nearly quadrupled between 1860 and 1912, with 160 institutions housing 42,489 people. See Sarah D Phillips, "There Are No Invalids in the USSR!", *Disability Studies Quarterly*, 29(3), (2009) http://dsq-sds.org/article/view/936/1111

215 Scull (2011), p55.

216 Scull (2011), p57.

217 Borsay (2005), p70.

218 Andrew Scull, *Hysteria: The Biography* (Oxford University Press, 2009), pp47-55.

219 Scull (2009), pp76-83.

220 Scull (2009), pp88-91.

221 Scull (2009), p96.

222 Scull (2009), p94.

223 Scull (2009), pp113-114. An 1887 painting by André Brouillet captures Charcot presenting Blanche Wittman, his pet hysteric. "She swoons over the outstretched arm of his assistant…her pelvis thrust forward, her breasts barely covered by her blouse and pointing suggestively toward the professor, her head twisted to the side and her face contorted in what looks like the throes of orgasm." As

Scull notes, Sigmund Freud kept a copy of this painting in his study in Vienna and in London.

224 Scull (2009), p126.

225 Elaine Showalter, *The Female Malady: Women, Madness, and English Culture, 1830-1980* (Virago, 1985). According to Showalter, depression is the modern equivalent of hysteria.

226 Elaine Showalter, "Victorian Women and Insanity" in Scull (1981), p319. For a wide-ranging and detailed but also accessible account of women's oppression, see Judith Orr, *Marxism and Women's Liberation* (Bookmarks, 2015).

227 Joseph Melling, "Accommodating Madness", in Melling and Forsythe (1999), p17.

228 Elaine Showalter in Scull (1981), p330.

229 Scull (2011), p61.

230 As Joseph Melling puts it, Foucault's "grand narrative of the history of madness…obscure[s] the fierce debates over asylum reform… His emphasis on the surgical division of space and the manufacture of the modern patient in the hands of the professional physician… marginalis[ed] the agency of social classes, kinship networks and political movements in the shaping of the treatments offered for insanity… Foucault's work often implies that the rule of Reason determined the terms on which resistance could be mounted." Melling and Forsythe (1999), p2.

231 Finkelstein (1981).

232 Although a reformer, Langdon Down's views were shaped by Victorian prejudices—referring to people with Down's Syndrome as "Mongolians", a supposed racial group considered to be "degenerate".

233 An exhibition in Britain in 2011, "Reframing Disability", profiled a number of particularly successful "freak" exhibitors from this period. See www.rcplondon.ac.uk/museum-and-garden/whats/re-framing-disability-portraits-royal-college-physicians.

234 David Gerber, "Pornography or Entertainment? The Rise and Fall of the Freak Show", Reviews in American History, vol 18, no 1 (1990), pp15-21.

235 Nadja Durbach, *Spectacle of Deformity* (University of California Press, 2010) p167.

236 Durbach (2010), p116.

237 Durbach (2010), p24.

238 Robert Bogdan, *Freak Show* (University of Chicago Press, 1988) p26.

239 Nadja Durbach, "The Missing Link and the Hairy Belle" in Marlene Tromp (ed), *Victorian Freaks* (Ohio State University Press, 2008), p136.

240 Durbach in Tromp (2008), p136.

241 Durbach, in Tromp (2008), pp142-147.

242 Durbach (2010), p174.

243 Several million customers were reputed to have paid the 25 cents admission to attend the museum between 1841 and 1865. Its attractions included the famous dwarf Tom Thumb and the "Fejee Mermaid" (supposedly a mummified maiden, but actually the desiccated head of a monkey and the body of an orang-utan attached to the back of a fish). See http://www.nytimes.com/2000/07/01/nyregion/a-museum-to-visit-from-an-armchair.html.

244 Bogdan (1988), p56. Dreamland burned down in 1911.

245 Christine C Ferguson, "Elephant Talk", in Tromp (2008), p120.

246 Durbach (2010), p34.

247 Durbach (2010), p53.

248 Durbach (2010), p56.

249 Durbach (2010), p177.

250 *Daily Mail*, 4 December 2013,

http://www.dailymail.co.uk/news/
article-2517373/Boris-Johnson-
tackled-controversial-IQ-speech-
FAILS-intelligence-tests-live-radio.
html.

251 See http://liberalconspiracy.
org/2010/11/25/
eugenics-and-the-tory-right/

252 Lennard Davis, *Enforcing Normalcy:
Disability, Deafness and the Body*
(Verso, 1995), p26.

253 The ideas and careers of Morel and
Lombroso are discussed at length
in Daniel Pick's excellent book,
*Faces of Degeneration: A European
Disorder, c1848-c1918* (Cambridge
University Press, 1989).

254 Davis (1995) p25.

255 Davis (1995), pp32-33. For an
effective and entertaining
demolition of the science behind
IQ tests, see *The Mismeasure of
Man*, Stephen Jay Gould (1996).

256 Quoted in Pick (1989), pp197-198.

257 Pick (1989), pp203-216.

258 Henry Maudsley, *Body and Will*
(1883), p292, quoted in Pick
(1989), p211.

259 The same fact was also observed in
1939 when it was discovered that
the cause had nothing to do with
hereditary factors but was simply
the result of poor diet leading to the
bone-deforming disease rickets.

260 Victoria Brignell, "The eugenics
movement Britain wants to forget",
New Statesman, 9 December 2010.
See http://www.newstatesman.
com/society/2010/12/
british-eugenics-disabled.

261 R C Elmslie, *The Care of Invalid and
Crippled Children in School* (London:
School Hygiene Publishing 1911), p7.

262 See http://www.secondspring.
co.uk/articles/sparkes.htm.

263 "The Churchill you didn't know",
The Guardian, 28 November
2002 http://www.theguardian.
com/theguardian/2002/nov/28/
features11.g21.

264 Anne Kerr and Tom Shakespeare,
Genetic Politics (Clarion Press, 2003).

265 See http://www.secondspring.
co.uk/articles/sparkes.htm.

266 Brignell (2010).

267 Brignell (2010).

268 Pick (1989), p232.

269 Kerr and Shakespeare (2003), p17.

270 The title of Chesterton's book was
Eugenics and Other Evils, quoted in
Quarmby (2011), p60.

271 Interview for the book *Twentieth
Century Authors* (1950). See
http://en.wikipedia.org/wiki/
Lancelot_Hogben.

272 Alexandra Minna Stern and Tony
Platt, "California's Dark History
of Eugenics and Compulsory
Sterilization". See http://hnn.us/
article/152733.

273 Susan M Schweik, *The Ugly Laws*
(NYU Press, 2009), pp2 and 26.

274 Schweik (2009), p1.

275 Schweik (2009), p167.

276 Schweik (2009), p5. The existence
of the laws was only rediscovered
in 1974 when an Omaha policeman
scoured the city code to find a
legal basis on which to detain a
homeless man.

277 Neilsen (2012), p107.

278 Neilsen (2012), p103.

279 Neilsen (2012), p102.

280 Dr William Spratling, *An Ideal
Colony for Epileptics and the
Necessity for the Broader Treatment
of Epilepsy, American Medicine*,
24 August 1901, quoted in Neilsen
(2012), p118.

281 Kerr and Shakespeare (2003), p19.

282 Edwin Black, "The Horrifying
American Roots of Nazi Eugenics"
(2003) http://hnn.us/article/1796.

283 Transcript of judgement at
http://www.houseofrussell.
com/legalhistory/alh/docs/
buckvbell.html.

284 Denis R Alexander and Robert
L Numbers (eds), *Biology and
Ideology from Descartes to Dawkins*
(University of Chicago Press, 2010),
pp180-182.

285 Kerr and Shakespeare (2003), p11.

286 Black (2003).

287 Edwin Black, "Hitler's debt to America", *The Guardian*, 6 February 2004, http://www.theguardian.com/uk/2004/feb/06/race.usa.

288 Black (2003).

289 Quoted in Pick (1989), p237. Pick notes that this entry disappeared in post-war editions of the encyclopaedia.

290 Ernst Haeckel, *The Riddle of the Universe* (1899) and Karl Binding and Alfred Hoche, *The Permission to Destroy Life Unworthy of Life* (1920). See Kerr & Shakespeare (2003), pp22-23.

291 Carole Poore, *Disability in Twentieth Century German Culture* (University of Michigan Press, 2007), p67.

292 For more on disabled veterans under the Nazis, see the next chapter.

293 Poore (2007), pp67-68.

294 Kerr & Shakespeare (2003), pp27-28.

295 Poore (2007), p97.

296 Poore (2007), p98.

297 Poore (2007), p115.

298 Kerr and Shakespeare (2003), pp29-30.

299 Kerr and Shakespeare (2003), p31.

300 Kerr and Shakespeare (2003), p32

301 Kerr and Shakespeare (2003), p37.

302 Kerr and Shakespeare (2003), p43.

303 Disability Rights Advocates, 2001. See http://www.dralegal.org/downloads/pubs/forgotten_crimes.pdf.

304 Kerr and Shakespeare (2003), p45.

305 Marta Russell and Ravi Malhotra, "Capitalism and Disability", *Socialist Register*, vol 38 (2002). Sweden's sterilisation programme was only ended in 1975.

306 See separate sources itemised at http://en.wikipedia.org/wiki/Compulsory_sterilization.

307 http://www.errc.org/article/czech-prime-minister-apologises-to-victims-of-coercive-sterilisation/3056.

308 Jonathan Freedland, "Eugenics: the skeleton that rattles loudest in the left's closet", *The Guardian*, 17 February 2012, http://www.theguardian.com/commentisfree/2012/feb/17/eugenics-skeleton-rattles-loudest-closet-left.

309 Hilary Rose and Steven Rose, *Genes, Cells and Brains* (Verso, 2012), p134.

310 Rose and Rose (2012), p129.

311 See http://www.genomicsengland.co.uk/about-genomics-england/.

312 John Parrington, *The Deeper Genome* (Oxford University Press, 2015).

313 Isser Woloch, "A Sacred Debt": Veterans and the State in Revolutionary and Napoleonic France, in David A Gerber, *Disabled Veterans in History* (University of Michigan Press, 2012), p159.

314 This history—of the central role of the military in a revolutionary war against slavery, which led directly to the formation of the US—is one reason for the influence of ex-servicemen who fought in the Vietnam War and then joined the movement against it.

315 US National Library of Medicine, http://www.nlm.nih.gov/exhibition/lifeandlimb/maimedmen.html.

316 http://www.encyclopedia.com/topic/United_States_Department_of_Veterans_Affairs.aspx.

317 Quoted in Dave Sherry, *Empire and Revolution: A Socialist History of the First World War* (Bookmarks, 2014), p83.

318 Edgar Jones et al, "Shell Shock and Mild Traumatic Brain Injury: A Historical Review", *American Journal of Psychiatry* 2007; 164.

319 Edgar Jones, "Shell shocked" https://www.apa.org/monitor/2012/06/shell-shocked.aspx.

320 Fiona Reid, *Broken Men: Shell Shock, Treatment and Recovery in Britain* (Continuum, 2010), p12.

321 Reid (2010), p43.

322 Ben Shephard, *A War of Nerves* (Jonathan Cape, 2000), p29.

323 Elizabeth Speller, "Firing squads: Cruel fate of the 'cowards'", *Daily Express*, 24 February 2010, http://www.express.co.uk/expressyourself/160138/Firing-squads-Cruel-fate-of-the-cowards

324 *Daily Express*, 24 February 2010. After a long campaign by their relatives, the 306 executed men were granted a collective pardon by the Labour government in 2008. Their names, however, still don't appear on official war memorials.

325 Shephard (2000), p70.

326 http://www.pcs.org.uk/en/equality/news/news-items/disability-in-the-world-wars.cfm.

327 Both British veterans' organisations sponsored candidates in the 1918 UK general election, but after 1919 rapidly became more conservative. In 1921, they merged with the Officers' Association to form the Royal British Legion. This grew to 100,000 members within a year and to 300,000 by the 1930s. See https://en.wikipedia.org/wiki/The_Royal_British_Legion.

328 Reid (2010), p94.

329 Reid (2010), p79.

330 Reid (2010), p76.

331 We now know "shell shock" is likely to have been applied to a range of different conditions or responses to war trauma. Surgeons in Napoleon's Grande Armée identified a "narrow escape syndrome" in which the whistle of a cannonball could paralyse infantrymen. See Laure Murat, *The Man Who Thought He Was Napoleon: Toward a Political History of Madness* (University of Chicago Press, 2014), p201. A study of UK troops returning from Iraq showed an association between mild traumatic brain injury and post-traumatic stress disorder, with a range of symptoms often meeting the criteria for both diagnoses. See Jones et al (2007).

332 Robert Whalen, *Bitter Wounds* (Cornell University Press, 1984), pp121-127.

333 Whalen (1984), p116.

334 Shephard (2000), p134.

335 Shephard (2000), p134.

336 Poore (2007), p17.

337 Whalen (1984), p125.

338 For a short introduction to her politics and the German revolution, see Sally Campbell, *A Rebel's Guide to Rosa Luxemburg* (Bookmarks 2011). For a longer history, see Chris Harman, *The Lost Revolution* (Bookmarks, 1983).

339 Whalen (1984), pp118 and 115.

340 Whalen (1984), p127.

341 Whalen (1984), pp131 and 141

342 Whalen (1984), p169.

343 Whalen (1984), p174.

344 This was the suicidal policy of the Communist International, by then completely under the control of Stalin. See Trotsky's prophetic writings of the period, particularly "What next for the German proletariat?" in Leon Trotsky, *Fascism, Stalinism and the United Front* (Bookmarks, 1989).

345 Whalen (1984), p176.

346 M Rassell and E Iarskaia-Smirnova (eds), *Disability in Eastern Europe and the Former Soviet Union* (Routledge, 2014), p21.

347 Rassell and Iarskaia-Smirnova (eds) (2014), p17.

348 Rassell and Iarskaia-Smirnova (eds) (2014), p19.

349 Rassell and Iarskaia-Smirnova (eds) (2014), p5.

350 Phillips (2009).

351 Phillips (2009).

352 Phillips (2009).

353 Dunn and Dunn (1989), pp181 and 187-188.

354 Phillips (2009).

355 Phillips (2009).

356 http://www.encyclopedia.com/topic/

United_States_Department_of_Veterans_Affairs.aspx.

357 The contrasting fortunes of the two veterans' organisations are examined in Stephen R Ortiz, "Rethinking the Bonus March: Federal Bonus Policy, the Veterans of Foreign Wars, and the Origins of a Protest Movement", *The Journal of Policy History*, vol 18, no 3 (2006).

358 The Florida hurricane was in August 1935. Roosevelt's objections to paying the bonus were not unsophisticated. He cited the millions of civilians disabled by wartime work in munitions factories or by the 1918 flu epidemic and the millions of veterans who did not go to war—none of whom would be entitled to any bonus payment. Any notion that they too should be paid was clearly considered so absurd as not worthy of consideration. See Paul and Thomas B Allen, *The Bonus Army* (Walker and Company, 2006), p229.

359 http://www.encyclopedia.com/topic/United_States_Department_of_Veterans_Affairs.aspx.

360 Shephard (2000), p348.

361 Shephard (2000), pp347-348.

362 Ron Kovic, *Born on the Fourth of July* (Akashic Books, 2005), pp27-29.

363 David A Gerber, *Disabled Veterans in History* (University of Michigan Press, 2012), p352.

364 Shephard (2000), p344.

365 Shephard (2000), p351.

366 Shephard (2000), p340.

367 *Daily Mail*, 28 May 2012, http://www.dailymail.co.uk/news/article-2150933/The-shocking-cost-war-Afghanistan-Iraq-veterans-damaged-generation-HALF-seeking-disability-benefits.html.

368 Gerber (2012), pp352-356.

369 Ewen MacAskill, "Fort Hood shooting raises questions over high suicide rate among veterans", *The Guardian*, 3 April 2014, http://www.theguardian.com/world/2014/apr/03/fort-hood-shooting-questions-high-suicide-rates-veterans-mental-illness.

370 In 1866, for example, the State of Mississippi spent more than half its yearly budget providing veterans with artificial limbs. Hunter Oatman-Stanford, "War and Prosthetics: How Veterans Fought for the Perfect Artificial Limb", *Collectors Weekly*, 29 October 2012. See http://www.collectorsweekly.com/articles/war-and-prosthetics/

371 Carol Flascha, *Prosthetics Under Trial of War* (2011). See http://prospectjournal.org/2011/09/15/prosthetics-under-trials-of-war/.

372 Katherine Ott, David Serlin and Stephen Mihm (eds), *Artificial Parts, Practical Lives* (New York University Press, 2002), p93.

373 Ott et al (2002), p155.

374 Gary L Albrecht, *The Disability Business* (Sage Publications, 1992), p102.

375 See http://en.wikipedia.org/wiki/Physical_therapy.

376 Albrecht (1992), p204.

377 Albrecht (1992), p207.

378 James Dao, "War and Sports Shape Better Artificial Limbs", *New York Times*, 17 April 2013.

379 Editorial comment, *London Evening Standard*, 8 July 2014.

380 For US troops, at any rate. See Dao, *New York Times*, 17 April 2013

381 "Paralympics offers life after trauma for wounded soldiers", *The Guardian*, 23 August 2012. See http://www.guardian.co.uk/sport/2012/aug/23/paralympians-british-military-rehabilitation.

382 "The Paralympic effect on amputees' legal claims for prosthetics", editorial, *British Medical Journal*, 28 February 2013. See http://www.bmj.com/content/346/bmj.f1165. As Peter Walker has noted: "some less developed nations' success in Paralympic events has come directly from war.

Sitting volleyball is enormously popular in Iran—the country won five out of six gold medals since 1988—and has long been popular with injured veterans from the brutal war with Iraq. Iran's main rivals, Bosnia and Herzegovina, who won the 2004 title, are captained by Sabahudin Delalic, who lost a leg in 1992 in the Balkan conflict." He adds that Cambodia, one of the world's poorest countries, also has one of the "highest ratios of amputees due to landmine blasts, but managed to send only one of them to compete at London 2012." Quoted in Michael Lavalette (ed), *Capitalism and Sport* (Bookmarks, 2013), p139.

383 Ethan Watters, *Crazy Like Us: The Globalisation of the American Psyche* (Free Press, 2010), p101.

384 *Daily Mail*, 28 May 2012.

385 *The Guardian*, 3 April 2014 http://www.theguardian.com/world/2014/apr/03/fort-hood-shooting-questions-high-suicide-rates-veterans-mental-illness.

386 L N Indolev, "A Brief Historical Account of the Disability Movement in Russia", http://www.disabilityworld.org/June-July2000/IL/Russia.html.

387 S Humphries and P Gordon, *Out of Sight: The Experience of Disability 1900-1950* (Northcote House, 1992), p133.

388 Vic Finkelstein, "Disability and the helper/helped relationship. An historical view" (1981) http://disability-studies.leeds.ac.uk/files/library/finkelstein-Helper-Helped-Relationship.pdf.

389 Initially by professionals themselves—notably Erving Goffmann in *Stigma* (1963).

390 See chapter 8.

391 See the excellent chapter on the League in Longmore (2003).

392 See https://libcom.org/history/workers-employers-unions-sitdown-strike-wave-1933-1937-jeremy-brecher.

393 Quoted in Joseph Shapiro, "The New Civil Rights", http://www.disabilityculture.org/course/article3.htm.

394 "A Brief History of the Disability Rights Movement". See http://iipdigital.usembassy.gov/st/english/article/2005/06/20050614105615liameruoy0.1511499.html#axzz3N5nIrr7X

395 In 1976, Ed Roberts was appointed Director of the California Department of Vocational Rehabilitation which had 15 years earlier told him it was "unfeasible" that he would ever find work. See Joseph Shapiro, *No Pity: People with Disabilities Forging a New Civil Rights Movement* (Three Rivers Press, 1994), p54.

396 Shapiro (1994), p57. The headline refers to the fact that the New Deal President, Franklin D Roosevelt, had polio. Famously, however, Roosevelt ensured that he was never seen or photographed in public using his wheelchair, fearing that this would lead to him being perceived as weak.

397 Longmore (2003), p105.

398 Ravi Malhotra, "The Politics of the Disability Rights Movements", *New Politics*, vol 8, no 3 (new series), no 31, (2001).

399 Longmore (2003), p107.

400 In what was to prove a fateful decision, HEW secretary Joseph Califano sent a low-ranking assistant to defend changes to the draft regulations in a live TV debate. These included exemptions for hospitals and schools from access requirements such as ramps and plans to place some disabled schoolchildren in what he called "separate but equal" facilities. When Judy Heumann angrily denounced this as segregation, he "retreated into an office and locked the door. The incensed [local Democrat

Representative] Burton, demanding that Califano's representative listen to the disabled activists, ran to the office and began kicking the door". Longmore (2003), p108.

401 Malhotra (2001).

402 Malhotra (2001).

403 Shapiro (1994), p130. This protest took place at ADAPT's national Wheels of Justice March at the White House. The latter, according to Shapiro, was attended by 725 people. After the ADA's implementation, ADAPT changed its name to American Disabled for Attendant Programs Today, and switched the target of its direct actions to the for-profit nursing home industry. See Shapiro (1994), p251.

404 Mary Johnson, *Make Them Go Away* (Advocado Press, 2003), p187.

405 Marta Russell, *Beyond Ramps: Disability at the End of the Social Contract* (Common Courage Press, 1998).

406 Johnson (2003), p44.

407 Historian Edward Berkovitz, quoted in Shapiro (1994), pp70-71.

408 Johnson (2003), p196.

409 Johnson (2003), p141.

410 For the figures, see the concluding sections of chapter 13.

411 Johnson (2003), p261.

412 The Allied occupation of West Germany continued until 1949, leaving behind permanent US military bases.

413 Poore (2007), pp174-175.

414 The US government controlling these trials also imported leading Nazi scientists to occupy central roles in its space programme.

415 Poore (2007), pp184-185. Poore also notes that the reinstatement of former Nazi judges contributed to the light sentences and acquittals in subsequent "euthanasia" trials into the 1960s.

416 Poore (2007), p191.

417 Poore (2007), p260. Trade union demands that employment quotas reserved for war veterans should apply to all disabled people were finally granted in 1974 (p179). Unemployment in West Germany in 1981 was 72 percent for all disabled people.

418 Poore (2007), p253.

419 Poore (2007), p271.

420 Poore (2007), pp274-275.

421 Poore (2007), p277.

422 Poore (2007), p279.

423 Poore (2007), p271.

424 Poore (2007), p286.

425 The controversial bioethicist, who advocates euthanasia for disabled babies, was invited to visit Germany twice in 1989, prompting major protests and a wider debate about his views. See, for example, the speech by Horst Frehe at http://www.independentliving.org/25yearsfrehe.

426 Poore (2007), p302.

427 Poore (2007), p287.

428 For Independent Living, Equal Rights, Accessibility and Inclusion! BRK-Allianz (Alliance of German NGOs Regarding the UN CRPD) (BRK-Allianz (2013), p6. See http://www.brk-allianz.de/attachments/article/93/Alternative_Report_German_CRPD_Alliance_final.pdf.

429 M Jahnukainen, "Book review of Justin J W Powell, Special education in the United States and Germany: barriers to inclusion (2011)", *Disability and Society*, vol 28, no 3 (2013), pp435-437.

430 Nicole Eggers and Yaak Pabst, "Ein versteckes Sparpaket?", *Marx21*, issue 3 (2013).

431 Eggers and Pabst (2013).

432 BRK-Allianz, pp73-74.

433 Matthew Kohrman, *Bodies of Difference* (University of California Press, 2005), p71.

434 Kohrman (2005), p81.

435 Kohrman (2005), pp101 and 107.

436 Kohrman (2005), p97.

437 J Pierini et al, "Glorious Work",

Disability and Society, vol 16, no 2 (2001).

438 http://www.cdpf.org.cn/english/ laws1documents/200804/ t20080410_267460.html.

439 See http://www.cdpf.org.cn/ english/aboutus/aboutus.htm.

440 See http://censusindia.gov.in/ Census_And_You/disabled_ population.aspx.

441 *The Indian Express*, 12 September 2014. See http://indianexpress.com/ article/india/india-others/3-quota-must-have-for-disabled-in-all-govt-jobs-including-ias-supreme-court/.

442 Tadashi Kudo, "Japan's Employment Rate of Persons with Disabilities and Outcome of Employment Quota System", *Japan Labor Review*, vol 7, no 2 (Spring 2010).

443 According to *The Japan Times*, 27 August 2006. See http://www. japantimes.co.jp/life/2006/08/27/ to-be-sorted/is-disability-still-a-dirty-word-in-japan/.

444 Rassell and Iarskaia-Smirnova (2014), p6.

445 Indolev (2000).

446 Indolev (2000).

447 Elena Tarasenko, "Problems and Perspectives of Disability Policy in Russia: The Move from Paternalism towards Disability Rights?" (2004). See http://www. lancaster.ac.uk/fass/events/ disabilityconference_archive/2004/ papers/tarasenko2004.pdf.

448 "End 'Orphanage' System; Support Family Care", 15 September 2014. See http://www.bearr.org/hrw-on-disabled-children-in-russia/.

449 Rassell and Iarskaia-Smirnova (2014), p240.

450 Rassell and Iarskaia-Smirnova (2014), p239.

451 *Russia: On the Path to Equal Opportunities* (UN Office in the Russian Federation, 2009), p10, http://www.unrussia. ru/sites/default/files/doc/ russia_on_the_pat_en.pdf.

452 Tarasenko (2004).

453 Ingstad and Whyte (1995), pp10 and 277.

454 (UNESCO 1995: 9-14), quoted in Barnes (2009), p7.

455 "Figures from India are from Ghia" (2001), adapted from Barnes, C and Colin Barnes and Geof Mercer (eds), *The Social Model of Disability and the Majority World* (The Disability Press, 2005), pp1-16.

456 "Billions affected daily by water and sanitation crisis", http://water.org/ water-crisis/one-billion-affected/.

457 See Killugudi Jayaraman, "Bhopal returns to haunt former Union Carbide chief, 5 August 2009", http://www.rsc.org/ chemistryworld/News/2009/ August/05080901.asp.

458 WHO, "7 million premature deaths annually linked to air pollution", http://www.who.int/ mediacentre/news/releases/2014/ air-pollution/en/.

459 "Respiratory illness in asbestos contaminated sites: the role of environmental exposure", *European Respiratory Journal*, 1 August 2011, vol 38, no 2. See http://erj. ersjournals.com/content/38/2/ 248.full.

460 *Foreign Correspondent* (ABC1 Melbourne), TV documentary, 8 November 2011.

461 Ingstad and Whyte (1995), p277.

462 Ingstad and Whyte (1995), p241.

463 Ingstad and Whyte (2007), pp251-252.

464 Ingstad and Whyte (1995), pp17-18.

465 James Staples, "Culture and carelessness: constituting disability in South India" (2012) http://bura.brunel.ac.uk/ bitstream/2438/8775/2/Fulltext.pdf.

466 Ingstad and Whyte (1995), p15.

467 Mansharparven Q Mirza, "War and peace in the global village: Bio-politics of disability in Kandahar and beyond", *Critical Disability Discourse*, vol 1 (2009) See http://

pi.library.yorku.ca/ojs/index.php/cdd/article/viewFile/23384/21574.

468 Barnes (2009), pp8-9.

469 Ingstad and Whyte (1995), pp23-24.

470 *Disability Scoping Study* (commissioned by DFID Uganda, February, 2009) See https://www.ucl.ac.uk/lc-ccr/downloads/240709_Disability_Executive_Summary__2_Uganda.pdf

471 Ingstad and Whyte (2007), pp23-24.

472 See, for example, http://disability-uganda.blogspot.co.uk/2008/05/ugandan-disability-movement-political.html.

473 *Disability Scoping Study* (2009).

474 Ingstad and Whyte (2007), pp293-294.

475 Barnes (2009), pp20-21.

476 Ingstad and Whyte (2007), p260.

477 Ingstad and Whyte (1995), p285.

478 Much of the material in this section previously appeared in a longer article about the UK disability movement: Roddy Slorach, "Out of the Shadows", *Critical and Radical Social Work*, vol 2, no 2, August 2014 (Policy Press, 2014). See http://www.ingentaconnect.com/content/tpp/crsw.

479 Finkelstein quoted in Campbell and Oliver (1996), p67. This is easily the best and most detailed history of the UK disability movement of the 1980s and early 1990s.

480 UPIAS, *Fundamental Principles of Disability*, http://disability-studies.leeds.ac.uk/files/library/UPIAS-fundamental-principles.pdf.

481 Anne Borsay in *Disowned and Disabled*, BBC4 documentary, 29 October 2013.

482 Campbell and Oliver (1996), p144.

483 Campbell and Oliver (1996), pp129-136.

484 Driedger (1989), p89.

485 Campbell and Oliver (1996), p79.

486 Jane Campbell in Campbell and Oliver (1996), p182.

487 *Independent*, 08 July 1992 http://www.independent.co.uk/news/media/media-another-telethon-what-help-is-that-if-youre-disabled-itvs-fundraising-marathon-does-more-harm-than-good-say-critics-lisa-okelly-reports-1531897.html.

488 According to one organiser, Alan Holdsworth, quoted in "Spitting on Charity", *Independent on Sunday*, 9 April 1995, http://www.independent.co.uk/arts-entertainment/spitting-on-charity-1614885.html.

489 Alan Holdsworth, "Our Allies Within", *Coalition*, July 1993.

490 http://hansard.millbanksystems.com/commons/1994/may/20/disability-rights-commission.

491 Caroline Gooding, *Disabling Laws, Enabling Acts: Disability Rights in Britain and America* (Pluto Press, 1994), pp129, 162 and 163.

492 Mike Oliver and Colin Barnes, "Disability Politics & the Disability Movement in Britain: Where Did It All Go Wrong?" (2006) http://www.leeds.ac.uk/disability-studies/archiveuk/Barnes/Coalition percent2odisability percent2opolitics percent2opaper.pdf.

493 Finkelstein (2007), quoting from his own earlier article "GMCDP" in *Coalition* (April 1996).

494 Jenny Morris, *Rethinking Disability Policy* (Joseph Rowntree Foundation, posted on 15 November 2011). Available at https://www.jrf.org.uk/report/rethinking-disability-policy.

495 *The Guardian*, 9 June 2011 http://www.theguardian.com/society/2011/jun/09/axe-sheltered-workshops-says-report.

496 The phrase is Gary Younge's. See "Black presidents and women MPs do not alone mean equality and justice", *The Guardian*, http://www.theguardian.com/commentisfree/cifamerica/2010/mar/14/america-race-gender-obama-diversity and

also Gary Younge, *Who Are We?* (Viking, 2010).

497 Atos are a French multinational IT services company who were first brought in to assess eligibility for the Employment and Support Allowance (ESA) under a pilot project in 2008 by the then Labour government. Its defeat was despite the outsourcing of more than £3 billion of public services to Atos by the last two UK governments. See Slorach (2014).

498 "Atos quits £500m work capability assessment contract early", *The Guardian*, 27 March 2014. See http://www.theguardian.com/society/2014/mar/27/atos-quite-work-capability-assessment-contract-early.

499 From "About DPAC" at http://dpac.uk.net/about/.

500 See, for example, http://www.theguardian.com/society/2013/dec/27/uk-anti-muslim-hate-crime-soars, http://www.channel4.com/news/is-the-uk-a-racist-country, http://www.unison.org.uk/news/cuts-to-health-and-housing-services-push-lgbt-people-to-margins-of-society, http://www.independent.co.uk/news/uk/home-news/more-than-half-of-women-are-discriminated-against-at-work-9029535.html.

501 Jo Verrent, "Disability and the arts: the best of times, the worst of times", *The Guardian*, 23 March 2015, http://www.theguardian.com/culture-professionals-network/2015/mar/23/disability-arts-best-worst-of-times. For more about disability arts, see http://www.disabilityartsonline.org.uk/What-is-Disability-Arts-Online.

502 "Access All Areas: putting disability centre stage", *The Guardian*, 7 March 2011. See http://www.guardian.co.uk/stage/theatreblog/2011/mar/07/access-all-areas-disability-live-art.

503 For a review of the series, see http://socialistworker.co.uk/art/27612/The+Undateables percent3A+a+look+at+disabled+lives+beyond+the+stereotypes.

504 Clare Allan, "No joke, being a psychiatric patient has its funny side", The Guardian, 4 August 2010.

505 Hannah Ellis-Petersen, *The Guardian*, 13 August 2015, http://www.theguardian.com/stage/2015/aug/13/edinburgh-festival-fringe-disability-if-platform-stopgap-venue-access-disabled-performers.

506 Verrent, *The Guardian*, 23 March 2015.

507 Cole (2004), pp61-62.

508 Tom Shakespeare, *The Genius of Disability* (Episode 4 of 5, BBC Radio 3), 8 January 2015.

509 By 2005, for example, Tom Shakespeare could note that Scope had a majority of disabled people on its ruling council. See http://www.bbc.co.uk/ouch/features/sweet_charity_1385.shtml.

510 See http://inclusionnorth.org/uploads/attachment/307/leadership-in-transitions-disability-history-timeline.pdf.

511 Campbell and Oliver (1996), p79.

512 For the Scope campaign, see http://www.scope.org.uk/awkward and the comment on DPAC's website at http://dpac.uk.net/2015/09/oh-give-me-a-break-you-rattle-your-tins-for-this-disabled-people-deserve-better/.

513 BBC News http://www.bbc.co.uk/news/uk-25273024.

514 Finkelstein (2001).

515 For a good outline of the consequent tensions see Campbell and Oliver (1996), pp131-136.

516 Quoted in Richard Wilkinson and Kate Pickett, *The Spirit Level* (Penguin, 2010), p157.

517 As explained in chapter 2, I have chosen to use the term "mental distress" in preference to others such as "mental illness", "mental

disorder" or "madness". The use of such terms varies widely, due to the number and diversity of mental health "conditions", the existence of which in many cases is disputed, and related tensions between "objective" diagnosis and subjective experience. In addition, many of the sources quoted here use different terms, making consistency difficult. While none of these terms are acceptable to all, mental distress seems to be the least controversial or judgemental and so is used wherever possible or appropriate.

518 See Mark Deal, "Disabled People's Attitudes Towards Other Disabled People: a hierarchy of impairments", *Disability and Society*, vol 18, no 7 (Routledge, 2003). Deal quotes research from 1970, repeated in 2000, showing mental illness, "mental retardation" and alcoholism to be the impairments "least preferred" by the non-disabled participants.

519 See *Papworth Trust Disability Facts and Figures* (2010).

520 Larry Elliott, *The Guardian*, 10 February 2014. See http://www.theguardian.com/society/2014/feb/10/mental-health-issues-uk-cost-70bn-oecd.

521 Note that this figure includes only those employers who were willing to admit that they would discriminate. *Working our Way to Better Mental Health: A Framework for Action* (Department for Work and Pensions / Department of Health, 2009).

522 Attitudes to mental illness, NHS Information Centre, 2011. See http://www.hscic.gov.uk/catalogue/PUB00292/atti-ment-illn-2011-sur-rep.pdf

523 See *Bad News for Disabled People: How the Newspapers are Reporting Disability* (GU Media Group, October 2011) http://www.gla.ac.uk/media/media_214917_en.pdf.

524 One notorious example was the front-page headline of the British tabloid newspaper *The Sun* of 7 October 2013, with its entirely fictitious and inflammatory claim, "1200 Killed by Mental Patients".

525 Centre for Economic Performance/LSE, *How Mental Illness Loses Out in the NHS*, June 2012.

526 "Antidepressant use on the rise in rich countries, OECD finds", *The Guardian*, 20 November 2013, http://www.theguardian.com/society/2013/nov/20/antidepressant-use-rise-world-oecd.

527 Robert Whitaker, *Anatomy of an Epidemic* (Crown Publishers, 2010), pp7-8.

528 In 2009, a survey in *The Lancet* placed China second in the world league table. David Cyranoski, "China tackles surge in mental illness", *Nature* 468, 145 (November 2010), http://www.nature.com/news/2010/101110/full/468145a.html.

529 Andrew Scull, "Madness in civilisation", *The Lancet*, 21 March 2015, vol 385, no 9973, pp1066—1067, http://www.thelancet.com/journals/lancet/article/PIIS0140-6736(15)60591-8/fulltext.

530 *Long-term Conditions and Mental Health: The Cost of Co-morbidities* (The Kings Fund/The Centre for Mental Health, February 2012). See http://www.kingsfund.org.uk/sites/files/kf/field/field_publication_file/long-term-conditions-mental-health-cost-comorbidities-naylor-feb12.pdf.

531 Centre for Economic Performance/LSE (June 2012)

532 Whitaker (2010), p211.

533 Report for Time to Change, 2 November 2011, http://www.time-to-change.org.uk/news/your-experiences-stigma-percentE2 percent80 percent93-what-you-told-us.

534 Hadley Freeman, "I didn't have anorexia because I wanted

to look like a fashion model",
The Guardian, 19 March 2015,
http://www.theguardian.com/
commentisfree/2015/mar/19/eating-
model-french-skinny-anorexia.

535 Centre for Economic Performance/
LSE (June 2012).

536 "Black and minority ethnic mental
health patients 'marginalised'
under coalition", *The Guardian*,
17 April 2012. See http://www.
guardian.co.uk/society/2012/apr/17/
bme-mental-health-patients-
marginalised.

537 http://www.patient.co.uk/doctor/
Poverty-and-Mental-Health.htm

538 "Ohio transgender teen's suicide
note: 'Fix society. Please.'", *The
Guardian*, 5 January 2015. See
http://www.theguardian.com/
world/2015/jan/05/sp-leelah-
alcorn-transgender-teen-suicide-
conversion-therapy. Aversion
therapy was used to "treat"
homosexuality in the UK until the
mid-1970s. See Tommy Dickinson,
*"Curing Queers": Mental Nurses and
Their Patients, 1935-74* (Manchester
University Press, 2015).

539 WHO, Social Determinants of Mental
Health (WHO, 2014). See http://
www.instituteofhealthequity.org/
projects/social-determinants-of-
mental-health.

540 Wilkinson and Pickett
(Penguin, 2010).

541 Gomm (1996), quoted in Gerry
Mooney and Michael Lavalette
(eds), *Class Struggle and Social
Welfare* (Routledge, 2000), pp238-
239. See also *Better Or Worse: A
Longitudinal Study Of The Mental
Health Of Adults In Great Britain*
(National Statistics, 2003).

542 Mooney and Lavalette (2000), p239.

543 Scull (2011), pp11-12.

544 Sedgwick (1982), pp135-137.

545 Richard P Bentall, *Doctoring the
Mind* (Penguin, 2009), pp36-40.

546 H Kutchins and S Kirk, *Making us
Crazy: DSM: The Psychiatric Bible*

and the Creation of Mental Disorders
(The Free Press, 1997), p39.

547 Robert H Felix (Director, NIMH),
"What is Mental Illness", *Pastoral
Psychology*, May 1957, vol 8, issue 4.

548 Kutchins and Kirk (1997), p72. This
reflected the greater influence
of psychoanalysis at the time; it
remained the dominant form of
psychiatry in the US until the late
1970s.

549 Since its inclusion in the *DSM* in
1980, PTSD has become one of the
most frequent diagnoses, "a catch-
all category used to identify an
increasingly wide pool of problems
that originate in traumatic life
events" such as child abuse, rape
and family violence or persistent
racial or sexual harassment.
Kutchins and Kirk (1997), pp112
and 116-118.

550 Scull (2011), p111.

551 http://www.psychologytoday.
com/blog/rethinking-
psychology/201307/
the-new-definition-mental-disorder.

552 Two-thirds of the *DSM-5* taskforce
responsible for revising the manual
had direct links to pharmaceutical
companies. See http://www.nhs.
uk/news/2013/08august/pages/
controversy-mental-health-
diagnosis-and-treatment-
dsm5.aspx.

553 Kutchins and Kirk (1997), p14.

554 "By the book (*DSM-5*)", *The
Economist*, 18 May 2013. See http://
www.economist.com/news/
science-and-technology/21578024-
american-psychiatric-associations-
latest-diagnostic-manual-
remains-flawed.

555 Ian Hacking, "Lost in the forest",
London Review of Books, vol 35,
no 15, 8 August 2013. See http://
www.lrb.co.uk/v35/n15/ian-hacking/
lost-in-the-forest.

556 "From neurosis to neurons", *The
Economist*, 11 July 2015. See http://
www.economist.com/news/

special-report/21657024-mapping-brain-may-eventually-yield-new-treatments-prevention-better.

557 Andre Deutsch, quoted in Whitaker (2010), p44.

558 Foucault's writings combined sharp insights about the history and practice of mental health treatment with flamboyant and almost impenetrable prose, two characteristics which enhanced his popularity among later structuralist and postmodernist writers.

559 Szasz went on to found the Libertarian Party in 1971, which condemned what it saw as a conspiracy of government and psychiatry mind control operations. His political values are best summarised by his statement, quoted in Sedgwick (1982), p158: "Man is a predator; everyone knows that."

560 Quoted in Jon Ronson, The Psychopath Test (Picador, 2011), p54.

561 Bentall (2009), p71.

562 Sedgwick (1982), p38. Sedgwick's influential book contains a detailed assessment of the work of all the main figures associated with anti-psychiatry. The book was the subject of a special conference organised by the UK's Social Work Action Network in April 2015.

563 David Rosenhan, "On Being Sane in Insane Places", Science, vol 179 (January 1973). Available online at http://psychrights.org/articles/rosenham.htm.

564 Rosenhan (1973).

565 Scull (2011), p101.

566 For an account of Basaglia's work, see John Foot, The Man Who Closed The Asylums (Verso, 2015).

567 Whitaker (2010), p268.

568 Whitaker (2010), p266.

569 Ben Goldacre, Bad Pharma (Fourth Estate, 2013), p39.

570 Goldacre (2013), p182.

571 Goldacre (2013), p80.

572 New York Times, 3 July 2012.

See http://www.nytimes.com/2012/07/03/business/glaxosmithkline-agrees-to-pay-3-billion-in-fraud-settlement.html?_r=0.

573 Goldacre (2013), pp58-61.

574 Doris Zames Fleischer and Frieda Zames, The Disability Rights Movement (Temple University Press, 2011), p227.

575 WHO. See http://www.who.int/trade/glossary/story073/en/.

576 Bentall (2009), pp202-203.

577 Gary Greenberg, The Book of Woe (Scribe Publications, 2013), p13.

578 Whitaker (2010), pp54-60.

579 Whitaker (2010), p126.

580 Whitaker (2010), p320.

581 Richard Warner, Recovery from Schizophrenia. See Whitaker (2010), p16.

582 Whitaker (2010), p177.

583 Whitaker (2010), p84.

584 Whitaker (2010), p116.

585 Watters (2010), pp137-138.

586 Mark Rice-Oxley, The Guardian, 8 November 2013. See http://www.theguardian.com/society/datablog/2013/nov/08/where-world-people-most-depressed.

587 As, for example, a Guardian editorial argued in August 2010: "There are reasons to think that depression is a disease of affluence, or a consequence of the way modern urban life is lived." See http://www.theguardian.com/commentisfree/2010/aug/04/editorial-depression-mental-health.

588 British Psychological Society, Understanding Psychosis and Schizophrenia (2014), p38.

589 Quoted in Greenberg (2013), p351.

590 Mikkel Borch-Jacobsen, "Psychotropicana", London Review of Books, 11 July 2002.

591 Watters (2010), pp214-218.

592 Watters (2010), pp223-227.

593 Watters (2010), p245.

594 Watters (2010), pp135-6.

595 Laurence Kirmayer quoted in

Watters (2010), p.195.

596 All discussed at length in Watters (2010).

597 See for example Simon McCarthy-Jones, *Hearing Voices: The Histories, Causes and Meanings of Auditory Verbal Hallucinations* (Cambridge University Press, 2012), pp156-158.

598 British Psychological Society (2014), p13.

599 Sedgwick (1982), pp216-217.

600 Sedgwick (1982), p210.

601 Sedgwick (1982), pp193-194.

602 Sir Roy Griffiths, quoted Scull (2011), in p115.

603 Scull (2011), p115.

604 See Sedgwick (1982) especially pp201-205.

605 Jenny Diski, "I haven't been nearly mad enough", *London Review of Books*, vol 36, no 3, 6 February 2014. See http://www.lrb.co.uk/v36/no3/jenny-diski/i-havent-been-nearly-mad-enough.

606 Quoted in British Psychological Society (2014), p23.

607 British Psychological Society (2014), p42.

608 British Psychological Society (2014), p114.

609 Wilkinson and Pickett (2010), pp176 and 66-70.

610 Hilary Osborne, *The Guardian*, 20 May 2013. See http://www.theguardian.com/money/2013/may/20/british-workers-less-secure-more-stressed.

611 Sedgwick (1982), p146.

612 Peter Beresford, *A Straight Talking Introduction to Being a Mental Health User* (PCCS Books, 2010), p61.

613 Beresford et al, *Towards a Social Model of Madness and Distress? Exploring What Service Users Say* (Joseph Rowntree Foundation, November 2010). See https://www.jrf.org.uk/report/towards-social-model-madness-and-distress-exploring-what-service-users-say.

614 The NUS originally launched this campaign on 3 December 2013. For the latest updates, see http://www.nusconnect.org.uk/articles/coming-out-as-disabled-the-identities-and-experiences-in-our-movement.

615 Nicola Field, *Over the Rainbow* (Pluto Press, 1995), quoted in Ferguson and Mooney (2000), p243.

616 "Mad pride and prejudices", *The Guardian*, 3 September 2008. See http://www.theguardian.com/society/2008/sep/03/mentalhealth.

617 A crusade for dignity, *The Guardian*, 3 September 2008. See http://www.theguardian.com/society/2008/sep/03/mentalhealth.health

618 http://www.theguardian.com/society/2008/sep/03/mentalhealth.

619 Sedgwick (1982), p183.

620 Sedgwick (1982), p224-226.

621 Peadar O'Grady, "Stop Making Sense: Alienation and Mental Health", *Irish Marxist Review* (Nov 2014).

622 British Psychological Society (2014), p71.

623 British Psychological Society (2014), p68.

624 H Spandler, J Anderson, B Sapey (eds), *Madness, Distress and the Politics of Disablement* (Policy Press, 2015).

625 Fleischer and Zames (2011), p226.

626 Ben Goldacre, *The Guardian*, 5 January 2014. See http://www.theguardian.com/commentisfree/2014/jan/05/scandal-drugs-trials-withheld-doctors-tamiflu.

627 For an account of some recent campaigns, see R Moth, J Greener and T Stoll, "Crisis and resistance in mental health services in England", *Critical and Radical Social Work*, 3 (1), March 2015, and also http://www.unison-scotland.org.uk/news/2014/novdec/1211.htm.

628 For Social Work Action Network, see http://www.socialworkfuture.org/; for Psychologists Against Austerity, see https://psychagainstausterity.wordpress.com/ and for

Psychotherapists and Counsellors for Social Responsibility, see http://pcsr-uk.ning.com/.

629 Georgina Littlejohn, *Daily Mail*. See http://www.dailymail.co.uk/health/article-201226/Priory-Clinic-waste-money.html.

630 *The Guardian*, 21 November 2013. See http://www.theguardian.com/society/2013/nov/21/prescribing-culture-blame-rise-antidepressants.

631 BBC News, 24 June 2014. See http://www.bbc.co.uk/news/health-27980677.

632 BBC News, 18 June 2012. See http://www.bbc.co.uk/news/uk-18481943.

633 "The future of mental health in the UK: an election manifesto", *The Lancet*, vol 385, no 9970, 28 February 2015. See http://www.thelancet.com/journals/lancet/article/PIIS0140-6736(15)60315-4/fulltext.

634 British Psychological Society (2014), p41.

635 Others include humanistic therapies such as person-centred, existential, gestalt and transactional analysis.

636 Richard Layard and David M Clark, *Thrive* (Penguin, 2014).

637 This is known as the "dodo bird verdict"; that is, it is factors common to all therapies which account for changes observed. CBT researchers dispute this evidence, but CBT methods are more amenable to standardisation and measurement than other therapies. It is therefore easier to claim that it is "evidence based" than other methods where comparison of outcomes is intrinsically more subjective and anecdotal. See Mick Cooper, *Essential Research Findings in Counselling and Psychotherapy* (Sage, London, 2008)

638 British Psychological Society (2014), p93.

639 British Psychological Society (2014), p103.

640 *Guardian* letters, 12 March 2015. See http://www.theguardian.com/society/2015/mar/12/open-dialogue-approach-mental-healthcare

641 Sedgwick (1982), p218.

642 Hadley Freeman, *The Guardian*, 19 March 2015. See http://www.theguardian.com/commentisfree/2015/mar/19/eating-model-french-skinny-anorexia.

643 Beresford (PCCS Books, 2010), p124.

644 Ferguson and Mooney (2000), p242.

645 Alienation is discussed further in chapter 13.

646 As indicated earlier, this chapter uses the capitalised term "Deaf" when referring to the modern Deaf community. I have opted not to do so in discussing events prior to the 20th century, because it was only from this point that Deaf people began to consciously define themselves in this way.

647 Lip-reading requires intense concentration and is hugely laborious. It is estimated that even the best lip readers understand only 25-35 percent of what is being said. Many mouth movements appear similar and may look the same to a deaf person. See http://www.hearinglosshelp.com/articles/speechreading.htm.

648 Paddy Ladd, *Understanding Deaf Culture* (Multilingual Matters Ltd, 2003), p168.

649 Report by the World Federation of the Deaf, quoted in Ladd (2003), p44.

650 Ladd (2003), p27.

651 Intriguingly, a recent consultation on new sign language legislation for the Scottish Parliament estimates that the real figure could be considerably larger—almost 155,000 as opposed to just over 63,000, based on the results of a recent Scottish census. See British Sign Language (Scotland) Bill, Scottish Parliament Information

Centre briefing (SPICe, 15 January 2015), p9.

652 Ladd (2003), p33.

653 Nora Ellen Groce, *Everyone Here Spoke Sign Language* (Harvard University Press, 1985), pp68-70.

654 Ladd (2003), pp90-101. Downing was a friend of the diarist Samuel Pepys, who tells of a dinner in 1666 when one of Downing's servants, who was deaf, conversed in sign with him about the Great Fire of London.

655 "Medieval monks used sign language", *Prague Post*, 22 January 2015, http://www.praguepost.com/education/43943-medieval-monks-used-sign-language.

656 Harlan Lane, *When The Mind Hears* (Random House 1984), pp75-91.

657 Epée, quoted in Oliver Sacks, *Seeing Voices* (Picador, 1990) p15.

658 Sacks (1990), p18.

659 The new school was opened under the name National Institution for Deaf-Mutes. See Lane (1984), p38.

660 Ladd (2003), pp107-108. For more on Desloges, see http://gupress.gallaudet.edu/excerpts/DISIfive3.html.

661 Lane (1984), p160. Gallaudet's version of this particular history has largely been accepted. However, despite his claims that the Braidwood schools refused to reveal their teaching methods to him, he may well have baulked at serving the three-year apprenticeship they expected of all aspiring teachers of the deaf. See Ian Branson and Don Miller, *Damned for Their Difference* (Gallaudet University, 2002), p134.

662 Lane (1984), p182.

663 Lane (1984), pp222-224.

664 Sacks (1990), p21.

665 Lane (1984), p343.

666 Ladd (2003), p365.

667 Ladd (2003), p341.

668 Bell's views on heredity were contradicted by the then little known Mendelian concept of recessively inherited traits. See Groce (1988), p48.

669 Branson and Miller (2002), p155.

670 British opposition to the system of methodological signs, Branson and Miller argue, resulted in British Sign Language remaining far more "natural" than modern US and French versions of sign language. Branson and Miller (2002), p157.

671 Ladd (2003), pp382-385.

672 Richard Elliott was the English delegate who voted against. He refused, however, to sign the US delegation's statement of protest against the conference proceedings. Branson and Miller (2002), p171.

673 The US delegates represented 51 schools and 6000 pupils. Ladd (2003), pp390-394.

674 Ladd (2003), pp122-124.

675 Ladd (2003), p115.

676 Ernest Abraham, *The Limitations of the Pure Oral Method* (1899), quoted in Branson and Miller (2002), p168 .

677 Ladd (2003), pp130-132.

678 Michael Ignatieff, quoted in Carol Padden and Tom Humphries, *Inside Deaf Culture* (Harvard University Press, 2005), p19.

679 Marnie Holborow, *The Politics of English* (Sage Publications, 1999), pp63-64.

680 Given the racist claims of the eugenicists, it should be pointed out that: "The making of English was a ragbag affair which underwent as many changes—wars, settlement, peace, raids, different systems of social organisation—as its speakers encountered. The Germanic tribes of the Angles, Saxons and Jutes, early Christians with knowledge of Latin and Greek, the Danes and French-speaking Normans all contributed freely to what, with a smattering of Celtic influence, became known as English." Holborow (1999), p69.

681 Bell, quoted in Lane (1984), p356.
682 Douglas Baynton, "A Silent Exile On This Earth" in Lennard Davis (ed), *The Disability Studies Reader* (Routledge 1997), p138.
683 Padden and Humphries (2005), pp38-47.
684 Padden and Humphries (2005), p73
685 Padden and Humphries (2005), p54.
686 Ladd (2003), p62. Elsewhere, there were separate black and white deaf schools. As Ladd notes, this led to very distinct "Black ASL" dialects, further entrenching racial division.
687 Carol A Padden, "The Expansion of Sign Language Education" (2013). See https://quote.ucsd.edu/padden/files/2013/01/the_expansion_of_sign_language.pdf
688 Veditz was filmed in 1913 giving a remarkable lecture "The Preservation of Sign Language" containing his famous biblical warning: "A new race of Pharaohs that knew not Joseph are taking over the land and many of our American schools". His speech, however, "most likely struck the 'progressive' oralist educators as quaint and excessively emotional, even desperate." Padden and Humphries (2005), pp58-73.
689 Padden and Humphries (2005), p49.
690 Oralism was never made the formal education policy of the UK, as explained in Branson and Miller (2002).
691 Ladd (2003), p135.
692 Ladd (2003), p140.
693 Padden and Humphries (2005), pp78-90.
694 Ladd (2003), pp46-47.
695 Padden and Humphries (2005), p95.
696 Padden (2013).
697 Stokoe's key works were *Sign Language Structure* (1960) and (with two deaf colleagues) *A Dictionary of American Sign Language* (1965). He had earlier learned the rare Lallans Scots dialect in Edinburgh (see Padden, 2013) and applied this experience to his discovery of ASL. His work was widely derided at the time precisely because it did compare sign to other languages. However, it was an outsider's perspective (Stokoe arrived at Gallaudet new to sign language) that paved the way for further insights. See Sacks (1990).
698 Sacks (1990), p108.
699 Many deaf people in the US, it should be stressed, resent the amount of influence enjoyed by Gallaudet graduates and alumni and their perceived attitude of superiority. See Ladd (2003), p58.
700 See Ladd (2003). The book's subtitle, "In Search of Deafhood", gives a flavour of the author's approach.
701 The plans were finally abandoned in 2006. See http://www.deafweekly.com/backissues/laurent.htm.
702 Ladd (2003), p112.
703 Ladd (2003), p46.
704 Ladd (2003), p159.
705 According to the US National Institute of Health. See http://en.wikipedia.org/wiki/Cochlear_implant.
706 A US study in 2009 found that a three-year-old child who receives CIs could save up to US$50,000 in education costs as they are more likely to be mainstreamed in school and thus use fewer support services than similarly deaf children. See http://en.wikipedia.org/wiki/Cochlear_implant#cite_note-60.
707 Fleischer and Zames (2011), p31.
708 *New York Times*, 8 December 2010. See http://www.nytimes.com/2010/12/08/education/08language.html.
709 Padden (2013).
710 Sacks (1990), p26.
711 See http://wfdeaf.org/wp-content/uploads/2014/04/WFD-letter-to-OHCHR-deaf-education.pdf.
712 See http://www.signhealth.org.uk/about-deafness/mental-health/.

713 "Deaf Children slip further behind as latest figures show drop in GCSE pass rates", 29 January 2015. See http://www.ndcs.org.uk/for_the_media/press_releases/deaf_children_slip.html.

714 Gregory et al (1995), quoted in https://www.thecommunicationtrust.org.uk/media/18934/communicating_phonics_deaf.pdf

715 BSL interpreters working with deaf children in schools tend to have low-level BSL qualifications, rather than the highest.

716 See http://www.signhealth.org.uk/about-deafness/mental-health/.

717 See http://www.signhealth.org.uk/health-information/sick-of-it-report/sick-of-it-in-english/sick-of-it-report-bad-access/.

718 National Institutes of Child Health and Human Development (2000). See http://www.education.com/magazine/article/Sign_Language/.

719 Samantha Melvin, *The Effects of Learning American Sign Language on College Students' Spatial Cognition* (2013). See http://wesscholar.wesleyan.edu/cgi/viewcontent.cgi?article=2047&context=etd_hon_theses.

720 Sacks (1990), p23. Ironically, Gallaudet's support for the "combined method" actually helped to establish oral education in deaf schools in the US. Having argued in 1871 that sign language was being used excessively, Gallaudet felt forced to defend its use in 1887 against the rising tide of pure oralism. Branson and Miller (2002), p183.

721 Lane (1984), p369.

722 The RNID changed its name to Action on Hearing Loss in June 2011.

723 See http://www.bbc.co.uk/ouch/opinion/bsl_goes_mainstream_the_logical_end.shtml.

724 Executive Summary, SPICe (2015).

725 Each country has its own national sign language and some have more than one. Spain has Catalonian and Galician Sign Languages. Belgium has Flemish-Belgian, Belgian-French and German Sign Language. In Finland, there is Finnish and Finnish-Swedish Sign Language. See SPICe (2015)

726 Branson and Miller (2002), pp.239-247.

727 *New York Times*, 21 October 2006. See http://www.nytimes.com/2006/10/21/education/21gallaudet.html.

728 Nadina LaSpina, Fleischer and Zames (2011), quoted in p27.

729 UK government figures, 2013. See http://www.parliament.uk/briefing-papers/POST-PN-450/special-educational-needs. The equivalent official term in Scotland, additional support needs, covers a broader range of children, including those who need support because of bullying or bereavement.

730 "Special needs pupils account for seven in 10 permanent exclusions from school", *Observer*, 19 December 2010. See http://www.theguardian.com/education/2010/dec/19/special-needs-permanent-exclusions-school.

731 "Academies' refusal to admit pupils with special needs prompts legal battles", *The Guardian*, 24 May 2012. See http://www.guardian.co.uk/education/2012/may/24/academies-refusal-pupils-special-needs.

732 In 2012-2013, 18,763 maintained schools excluded 2,700 pupils; 2,390 academies excluded 1,930 pupils (770 less than all maintained schools). Presentation by Gus John at the Disability Equality in the Classroom 25 Years On conference, 21 March 2015. Statistics at https://www.gov.uk/government/collections/statistics-exclusions.

733 *Conservative Party Manifesto* 2010, p53. See https://www.

conservatives.com/~/media/files/
activist percent2ocentre/press
percent2oand percent2opolicy/
manifestos/manifesto2010.

734 *Commission on Special Needs
in Education, The Second
Report*, chapter 5. See http://
conservativehome.blogs.com/
torydiary/files/special_needs_in_
education.pdf.

735 John Pring, "Inclusive education
'just a lottery for disabled children',
says report", Disability News
Service, 28 March 2014. See http://
www.disabilitynewsservice.com/
inclusive-education-just-a-lottery-
for-disabled-children-says-report/

736 "Special-needs education: Does
mainstream inclusion work?", *The
Independent*, 23 March 2006. See
http://www.independent.co.uk/
news/education/education-
news/special-needs-education-
does-mainstream-inclusion-
work-6105916.html.

737 "Seven Year Sentence", Sam
Harris, in Micheline Mason and
Richard Reiser, *Altogether Better*,
(Comic Relief, 1992). See http://
www.worldofinclusion.com/res/
altogether/AltogetherBetter.pdf.

738 Sally Tomlinson, "Why Johnny can't
read: Critical theory and special
education", *European Journal of
Special Needs Education*, vol 3, no 1,
45-58 (1988), p54

739 *The Independent*, 11 April 2010. See
http://www.independent.co.uk/
news/education/schools/the-boy-
in-the-corner-why-do-children-
with-special-needs-still-get-such-a-
raw-educational-deal-1938286.html.

740 "Disabled workers and students in
education: the negative impacts of
austerity and 'reform'", TUC, *Equality
& Employment Rights*, March 2015.

741 Tomlinson (1988), pp46-49.

742 Tomlinson (1988), pp50-53.

743 Sally Tomlinson *A Sociology of
Special Education* (Routledge and
Kegan Paul, 1982), p70.

744 Tomlinson (1982), p36.

745 *Times Educational Supplement*,
8 August, 1980, quoted in
Tomlinson (1988), p57.

746 *Russia: On the Path to Equal
Opportunities* (UN, 2009). See http://
www.unrussia.ru/sites/default/files/
doc/russia_on_the_pat_en.pdf.

747 *Russia: On the Path to Equal
Opportunities* (United Nations,
2009), p28.

748 Tomlinson (1988), p54.

749 Quoted in Jacqui Freeman, "A
vision for education", *Socialist
Review*, issue 401, April 2015. See
http://socialistreview.org.uk/401/
vision-education.

750 Disability History Month, National
Union of Teachers website. See
https://www.teachers.org.uk/
node/13799.

751 Thanks to Shirley Franklin for
allowing me to borrow heavily
from her unpublished manuscript
on Vygotsky.

752 Vygotsky (1993), quoted in
Peter Smagorinsky, "Vygotsky,
'Defectology', and the Inclusion
of People of Difference in the
Broader Cultural Stream", *Journal of
Language and Literary Education*, 8
(1), Spring 2012. See http://files.eric.
ed.gov/fulltext/EJ1008098.pdf.

753 The Collected Works of L S Vygotsky,
vol 2: The fundamentals of
defectology (abnormal psychology
and learning disabilities) (Springer,
1993), p93.

754 Vygotsky (1993), p64.

755 Vygotsky (1993), pp62-63.

756 Quoted in p.112, Dan Goodley,
Dis/ability Studies (Routledge, 2014).

757 Education: Learning to Dream,
Michael Rosen, *Socialist Review*,
issue 282, February 2004. See
http://socialistreview.org.uk/28 2/
education-learning-dream.

758 Steven Graby, "Neurodiversity:
bridging the gap between the
disabled people's movement
and the mental health survivors

movement", in Spandler et al (2015).

759 The first medical paper on what became classified as ADHD was written in 1798 in the UK.

760 The more formal name for dyspraxia, as defined in the *DSM*, is developmental co-ordination disorder.

761 See for example, Julian G Elliott and Elena L Grigorenko, *The Dyslexia Debate* (Cambridge University Press, 2014).

762 Grant (2010), p52.

763 See Ellen Morgan and Cynthia Klein, *The Dyslexic Adult* (Whurr Publishers, 2000), pp54-57.

764 Morgan and Klein (2000), p85.

765 For some of the difficulties in dyslexia diagnosis, see Morgan and Klein (2000), chapter 2.

766 Morgan and Klein (2000), p58.

767 Morgan and Klein (2000), p33.

768 "Dyslexic spies", *The Independent*, 23 September 2014. See http://www.independent.co.uk/life-style/health-and-families/features/dyslexia-there-are-benefits-worth-waiting-for-9749607.html.

769 C Singleton (ed), *Dyslexia in Higher Education: Policy, Provision and Practice: Report of the National Working Party on Dyslexia in Higher Education* (University of Hull, 1999). See also C Leather and B Kirwan, "Achieving success in the workplace", in N Brunswick (ed), *Supporting Dyslexic Adults in Higher Education and the Workplace* (Wiley-Blackwell, 2012). Thanks to David Pollak for these references.

770 Grant (2010), pp105-107.

771 Grant (2010), pp111-112.

772 More recent research suggests that dyslexia may be associated with different parts of the brain among users of alphabetic scripts such as English and of logographic ones such as Chinese. See "Disability of a different character", *The Economist*, 8 September 2014, http://www.economist.com/blogs/analects/2014/09/dyslexia-chinese.

773 Grant (2010), pp122-124.

774 Research in 2007 found that the long-term benefits of medication were found to be "no better than children who were treated with behavior therapy." See http://www.telegraph.co.uk/news/7307972/BBC-must-broadcast-apology-over-inaccurate-Panorama-programme.html.

775 The full name of attention deficit hyperactive disorder was coined by the compilers of the *DSM* in 1987.

776 "Youthful Folly", *The Economist*, 11 July 2015. See http://www.economist.com/news/special-report/21657021-childhood-conditions-such-autism-and-adhd-are-now-widespread-youthful-folly.

777 Steve Silberman, *The Forgotten History of Autism* (March 2015). See http://www.ted.com/talks/steve_silberman_the_forgotten_history_of_autism/transcript?language=en.

778 Mitzi Waltz, *Autism: A Social and Medical History* (Palgrave Macmillan, 2013), pp68-70.

779 Wing's daughter was profoundly autistic. Wing and Gould's original intention in carrying out the research was to pressurise the NHS to provide more resources for autistic children and their families. See Silberman (2015).

780 According to Silberman, Kanner was aware of Asperger's theories, but chose to ignore them. See Silberman (2015).

781 Kanner must have known about Asperger's work, because Georg Frankl, the chief diagnostician in Asperger's clinic in 1938, came to Johns Hopkins University to work in Kanner's clinic later that year. See Steve Silberman, *NeuroTribes* (Allen & Unwin, 2015)

782 Waltz (2013), p52. Asperger did not support Nazi rule and in fact was twice almost arrested by the

Gestapo due to his views. See Siberman (2015), p138.

783 "In praise of misfits", *The Economist*, 2 June 2012. See http://www.economist.com/node/21556230.

784 Waltz (2013), p144.

785 Waltz (2013), p144.

786 Waltz (2013), p131.

787 *Medical News Today*, 17 October 2013. See http://www.medicalnewstoday.com/releases/267529.php.

788 Ronson (2011), pp256-257.

789 Greenberg (2013), p202: Chapter 13 comprises an interesting discussion about the controversy over the *DSM-5* and autism and Asperger's Syndrome.

790 Greenberg (2013), p196.

791 David Mitchell, *The Guardian*, 29 June 2013, http://www.guardian.co.uk/society/2013/jun/29/david-mitchell-my-sons-autism.

792 Waltz (2013), pp129-131.

793 Laura Tisoncik, "Circle of Moms blog. See http://www.autismmind.com/Blog_Entry_srk/Eliminate_Labels_High_Functioning___Low_Functioning_bek/

794 Grant (2010), pp156-157.

795 Levi Asher, in the online Literary Kicks, quoted in Waltz (2013), p156

796 *Transition and Identity* (NADP, 2011), p53. See http://nadp-uk.org/uploads/JIPFHE/JIPFHE.ISSUE percent203.2.pdf.

797 Independent Living Institute, Sweden, http://www.independentliving.org/.

798 See the section on the US in chapter 8.

799 Longmore (2003), p111-112.

800 Fleischer and Zames, (2011), p42.

801 Ruth Townsley et al, *The Implementation of Policies Supporting Independent Living for Disabled People in Europe* (November 2009, amended January 2010). Available at http://www.disability-europe.net/content/aned/media/ANED-Task

percent205 percent20Independent percent20Living percent20 Synthesis percent20Report percent2014.01.10.pdf.

802 Shakespeare (2006), pp140-141.

803 Shakespeare (2006), p142.

804 Shakespeare (2014), p178.

805 Shakespeare (2006), p142.

806 Shakespeare (2014), p193.

807 *Improving the Life Chances of Disabled People*, Prime Minister's Strategy Unit, January 2005. See http://webarchive.nationalarchives.gov.uk/+/http:/www.cabinetoffice.gov.uk/media/cabinetoffice/strategy/assets/disability.pdf, p13.

808 *Improving the Life Chances of Disabled People* (2005), p18,

809 Jenny Morris, *Independent Living: A Review of Progress* (2013?). See http://disabilityrightsuk.org/sites/default/files/pdf/IndependentLivingStrategy-A percent20review percent20of percent20progress.pdf.

810 T Burchardt, M Evans and H Holder, *Public Policy and Inequalities of Choice and Autonomy*, London School of Economics (2013). See http://eprints.lse.ac.uk/51267/1/__Libfile_repository_Content_Burchardt, percent20T_Burchardt_Public_ percent20policy_inequalities_2013.pdf, quoted in Morris (2013).

811 See the section on the UK in chapter 8, Shakespeare (2014).

812 *Daily Express*, 11 January 2015, http://www.express.co.uk/news/uk/551327/EXCLUSIVE-Hate-crimes-on-disabled-rise-by-213.

813 *The Guardian*, 14 August 2012, http://www.theguardian.com/news/datablog/2012/aug/14/disability-hate-crime-increase-reported-incidents-data.

814 Disability hate crime has been recognized since 1979 in the US, but there is insufficient space to discuss it further here, although the issues seem to be very similar.

815 A more detailed account of Raymond Atherton's story can be found in Quarmby (2011), pp97-103.

816 Scope, *Disability Now and UK Disabled People's Council, Getting Away With Murder* (August 2008), p59.

817 Scope (2008), pp33 and 26.

818 Quoted in Alan Roulstone and Hannah Mason-Bish, *Disability, Hate Crime and Violence* (Routledge, 2013), p31.

819 See https://www.gov.uk/ government/uploads/system/ uploads/attachment_data/ file/215717/dh_125065.pdf.

820 Scope (2008), pp34-35.

821 Pam Thomas, chapter 11 in Roulstone and Mason-Bish (2013), p135.

822 Hannah Mason-Bish, chapter 1 in Roulstone and Mason-Bish (2013), pp15-16 and 17.

823 Erin Pritchard, "The notion of vulnerability in relation to disability hate crimes and the experiences of dwarfs", *Journal of Inclusive Practice in Further and Higher Education*, issue 6, Summer 2015.

824 Thomas in Roulstone and Mason-Bish (2013), pp141-143.

825 *Hate Crimes, England and Wales, 2013/14*. See http://www.report-it. org.uk/files/home_office_hate_ crime_data_201314.pdf.

826 "Crime motivated by hate accounts for around four per cent of all crimes…(a figure that has not changed much over the last six years), and disability hate crime for about one sixth of that." *Crime and Disabled People*, EHRC (2103), p79, http://www.equalityhumanrights. com/publication/research-report- 90-crime-and-disabled-people- baseline-statistical-analysis- measures-formal-legal. See also http://www.scottishlegal. com/2015/06/16/disability-hate- crime-network-describes-statistics- on-increased-crime-against-

disabled-people-as-misleading/.

827 EHRC (2013), p8.

828 See EHRC (2013), p17.

829 Chih Hoong Sin, chapter 12 in Roulstone and Mason-Bish (2013), p152-158.

830 See EHRC (2013), p28.

831 Mencap, *Don't Stand By* (June 2010). See http://www.opm.co.uk/ wp-content/uploads/2014/02/ Stand-by-me-research-report.pdf.

832 Hoong Sin in Roulstone and Mason-Bish (2013), p.159. In another terrible case, that of Fiona Pilkington and her daughter Frankie, Fiona complained to the police about constant harassment 33 times over several years before finally killing herself and her daughter in 2007. See Quarmby (2011), pp152-161.

833 Mark Sherry, chapter 6 in Roulstone and Mason-Bish (2013), p87.

834 Scope (2008), p37.

835 GU Media Group (2011).

836 For some of the main public misconceptions about benefits, see for example, one article by Owen Jones in *The Independent*, 8 January 2014, at http://www.independent. co.uk/voices/comment/benefits- street-a-healthy-media-would- stand-up-to-the-powerful-and- wealthy-ours-targets-the-poor- and-voiceless-9046773.html.

837 See http://www.thesun.co.uk/sol/ homepage/features/3091717/The- Sun-declares-war-on-Britains- benefits-culture.html.

838 Quoted in Quarmby (2011), p179.

839 Joanna Perry, chapter 3 in Roulstone and Mason-Bish (2013), p49.

840 "The MacPherson report (1999) found that a culture of institutional racism in the Metropolitan Police had impeded the investigation into Stephen Lawrence's death in 1993, and made a series of recommendations for improvements. In 1993…a black

person was five times more likely to be stopped and searched on the street…black people are now seven times more likely to be stopped and searched than white. In London, the gap is actually getting worse." *The Guardian*, 22 April 2013, http://www.theguardian.com/uk/2013/apr/22/stephen-lawrence-murder-changed-legal-landscape.

841 Susie Balderston, chapter 14 in Roulstone and Mason-Bish (2013), p183.

842 Yuill, *Assisted Suicide: The Liberal, Humanist Case Against Legalization* (Palgrave Macmillan 2013), pp14-16.

843 *The Guardian*, 9 June 2015. See http://www.theguardian.com/society/2015/jun/09/assisted-dying-mps-debate-legislation-lord-falconer-bill-terminally-ill-right-to-die.

844 "Easeful death", *The Economist*, 19 July 2014. See http://www.economist.com/news/leaders/21607854-most-people-western-world-favour-assisted-suicide-law-should-reflect-their.

845 Giles Fraser, *The Guardian*, 4 July 2014. See http://www.theguardian.com/commentisfree/belief/2014/jul/04/assisted-dying-triumph-market-capitalism.

846 Pratchett joined the legalisation campaign after being diagnosed with Alzheimer's Disease in December 2007. He died in March 2015.

847 "Canada to legalise physician-assisted dying", *The Lancet*, 16 February 2015. See http://www.thelancet.com/journals/lancet/article/PIIS0140-6736(15)60177-5/fulltext.

848 E Clery, S McLean, M Phillips (2007) "Quickening death: the euthanasia debate", in A Parks, J Curtice, K Thomson, M Phillips and M Johnson (eds), *British Social Attitudes: The 23rd Report—Perspectives on a Changing Society* (Sage, 2007).

849 See http://www.npr.org/blogs/health/2014/02/12/275913772/judge-dismisses-assisted-suicide-case-against-pennsylvania-nurse.

850 The Oregon law was first supported by a referendum in 1994, but faced a series of legal challenges, coming into effect after a second referendum in November 1997. Other US states with assisted suicide laws are Montana, New Mexico, Vermont and Washington. California became the latest in September 2015, adopting a law similar to Oregon's.

851 Joseph P Shapiro, *No Pity* (Three Rivers Press, 1994), p269.

852 Shapiro (1994), p285.

853 Shapiro (1994), p288. The term attendant is used in the US in preference to that of "personal assistant".

854 Fleischer and Zames (2011), p232.

855 *New York Times*, 14 April 1999. See http://www.nytimes.com/1999/04/14/us/kevorkian-sentenced-to-10-to-25-years-in-prison.html.

856 Fleischer and Zames (2011), p134.

857 See, for example, http://www.huffingtonpost.com/2015/01/15/locked-in-syndrome_n_6474274.html, or http://www.ncbi.nlm.nih.gov/pubmed/22897205.

858 Fleischer and Zames (2011), p146.

859 Yuill (2013), p7. As Brendan O'Neill comments in the introduction to Yuill's book: "contrary to the arguments of those who support assisted suicide, to put the final decision about someone's life in the hands of the courts or an end-of-life panel [a suggestion made by Terry Pratchett] would actually diminish autonomy."

860 *Daily Telegraph*, 18 Sep 2008. See http://www.telegraph.co.uk/news/uknews/2983652/Baroness-Warnock-Dementia-sufferers-may-

have-a-duty-to-die.html.

861 *The Guardian*, 22 January 2013. See http://www.guardian. co.uk/world/2013/jan/22/ elderly-hurry-up-die-japanese.

862 Simon Basketter, "Should we support assisted suicide?", *Socialist Worker*, 4 August 2009. See http://socialistworker.co.uk/art/18378/Shou   ld+we+support+assisted+suicide percent3F.

863 One doctor asked of the UK Assisted Dying Bill, for example, how a "clear and settled intention" to end one's life can be legally defined. See Fiona M A MacCormick, *British Medical Journal*, 5 August 2014 BMJ 2014;349:g4965.

864 Editorial, *The Lancet*, vol 385, no 9977, p1478, 18 April 2015. See http://www.thelancet. com/journals/lancet/article/ PIIS0140-6736(15)60736-X/fulltext.

865 Yuill (2013), pp26-27.

866 Yuill notes that the Dutch organisation Out of Free Will is campaigning to allow assisted suicide to all Dutch people over 70 who feel tired of life. Yuill (2013), p24.

867 Yuill (2013), p29.

868 In the 2007 British Social Attitudes Survey, for example, support for assisted suicide dropped from 60 percent in cases of terminal illness to 40 percent for cases of "incurable" but not terminal illness. See http://www. commissiononassisteddying.co.uk/ wp-content/uploads/2011/10/ Evidence-from-the-British-Social-Attitudes-23rd-report-Quickening-death-the-euthanasia-debate.pdf.

869 Yuill (2013), pp36 and 39.

870 https://public.health.oregon. gov/ProviderPartnerResources/ EvaluationResearch/ DeathwithDignityAct/Documents/ year17.pdf.

871 *Dignity in Dying* report for the Trades Union Congress, February 2011, in *The Debate on Assisted Suicide*, briefing paper commissioned by the TUC Disability Committee.

872 Quoted in "Is Oregon's assisted suicide law rife with problems?", *Portland Business Journal*, 21 August 2015, http://www.bizjournals. com/portland/blog/health-care-inc/2015/08/ohsu-doc-doctor-assisted-suicide-law-rife-with.html

873 Obituary for Jim Kirk by Judy Rathbone (Jim's wife), *Socialist Worker*, 8 August 2009.

874 Hongbin Li, Lingsheng Meng and Wenqing Pan, "The human cost of China's industrial growth", *China Economic Review* 22 (2011).

875 "China vows to fight pollution 'with all our might'", *The Guardian*, 5 March 2015. See http://www.theguardian.com/ environment/2015/mar/05/china-vows-to-fight-pollution-with-all-our-might.

876 "As China Roars, Pollution Reaches Deadly Extremes", *New York Times*, 26 August 2007. See http://www. nytimes.com/2007/08/26/world/ asia/26china.html.

877 International Labour Organization, *Safety in Numbers* (Geneva, 2003). See http://www.ilo.org/ public/english/region/eurpro/ moscow/areas/safety/docs/ safety_in_numbers_en.pdf.

878 Quarmby (2011), p76.

879 Patrick Cockburn, "The demise of the asylum and the rise of care in the community", *The Independent*, 26 November 2012. See http:// www.independent.co.uk/life-style/health-and-families/health-news/the-demise-of-the-asylum-and-the-rise-of-care-in-the-community-8352927.html.

880 Alan Milburn. See http://www. theguardian.com/uk/1999/nov/17/ davidbrindle.

881 David Behan, chief executive of the Care Quality Commission. See http://www.independent.co.uk/

news/uk/home-news/mental-hospitals-treat-patients-like-prisoners-8471807.html.

882 See http://unstats.un.org/unsd/methods/citygroup/washington.htm.

883 See, for example, Alan Roulstone and Colin Barnes, *Working Futures* (Policy Press, 2005), p108.

884 US figures are particularly contested. See, for example, http://www.disabilitystatistics.org/faq.cfm#Q6.

885 *Papworth Trust Disability Facts and Figures* (2010). UK employment rates for disabled people are lowest for those with learning disabilities (less than one in five) and those with mental health problems (just over one in ten).

886 Roulstone and Barnes (2005), p176.

887 "PM ordered Lord Freud to apologise for remarks on disabled people's pay", *The Guardian*, 15 October 2014. See http://www.theguardian.com/politics/2014/oct/15/prime-minister-david-cameron-lord-freud-apologise-disabled-people-minimum-wage.

888 *Hansard*, 7 September 2015. See http://www.publications.parliament.uk/pa/cm201516/cmhansrd/cm150907/debtext/150907-0001.htm.

889 Albrecht (1992), p117.

890 See http://inclusionnorth.org/uploads/attachment/307/leadership-in-transitions-disability-history-timeline.pdf.

891 Jihan Abbas, "A Legacy of Exploitation: Intellectual disability, unpaid labor, & disability services", *New Politics* vol xiv, no 1, Whole Number 53, Summer 2012. See http://newpol.org/content/legacy-exploitation-intellectual-disability-unpaid-labor-disability-services.

892 Claire Zillman, "Disabled workers left in the cold on minimum wage", *Fortune*, 12 February 2014. See http://fortune.com/2014/02/12/disabled-workers-left-in-the-cold-on-minimum-wage/.

893 For more on sheltered workshops in Germany, see the (English language) website http://www.bagwfbm.eu/page/disability.

894 Choonara (2009), p50.

895 As reported in *The Guardian* by George Monbiot, 21 October 2014. DWP Delivery Plan, 2012-13, at https://www.gov.uk/government/uploads/system/uploads/attachment_data/file/214342/dwp-delivery-plan-2012-2013.pdf, p8.

896 Quoted in Monbiot, *The Guardian*, 21 October 2014. Standard Definitions for the Work Programme, https://www.gov.uk/government/uploads/system/uploads/attachment_data/file/394689/wp-pg-chapter-15.pdf, p3.

897 The OECD includes relatively poor economies such as Chile, Estonia, Mexico, Slovakia and Turkey where the welfare state is much smaller.

898 "Think welfare spending is spiralling out of control? You're wrong", *The Guardian*, 28 March 2014. See http://www.theguardian.com/commentisfree/2014/mar/28/welfare-spending-spiralling-out-of-control-wrong.

899 *The Guardian*, 28 March 2014.

900 See http://www.ukpublicspending.co.uk/past_spending.

901 http://www.oecd-ilibrary.org/social-issues-migration-health/total-expenditure-on-health_20758480-table1.

902 http://www.nytimes.com/2014/12/04/us/pace-of-health-care-cost-increases-falls-to-a-54-year-low.html.

903 Harman (2009), p138.

904 The seminal analysis of this process is Harry Braverman's *Labour and Monopoly Capital* (1974).

905 Martin Upchurch, "The internet, social media and the workplace", *International Socialism*, issue 141. See http://isj.org.uk/

the-internet-social-media-and-the-workplace/ posted on 9th January 2014.

906 Rees (1998), p213.

907 Erich Fromm, "Alienation under Capitalism" in Eric and Mary Josephson (eds), *Man Alone: Alienation in Modern Society* (Dell, 1962), p67.

908 Jessica Scheer and Nora Groce, "Impairment as a Human Constant", *Journal of Social Issues*, vol 44, no 1 (1988).

909 Dan Goodley, *Dis/ability Studies* (Routledge, 2014), p29.

910 Wilkinson and Pickett (2010), p75.

911 Wilkinson and Pickett (2010), p86.

912 Wilkinson and Pickett (2010), p81.

913 Quoted in Orr (2015), p170.

914 Wilkinson and Pickett (2010), p69.

915 Judy Cox, "An Introduction to Marx's Theory of Alienation", *International Socialism* 2:79, July 1998. See https://www.marxists.org/history/etol/newspape/isj2/1998/isj2-079/cox.htm.

916 See http://www.papworthtrust.org.uk/campaigns/disability-facts-and-figures.

917 Iain Ferguson and Michael Lavalette, "Beyond Power Discourses: Alienation and Social Work", *British Journal of Social Work*, 2004.

918 Ferguson and Lavalette (2004)

919 Wilkinson and Pickett (2010), pp166-167.

920 Quoted in Quarmby (2011), p86.

921 Richard Rieser, "Internalised Oppression: How it seems to me", *Disability Equality in the Classroom* (1992), pp29-32. See http://worldofinclusion.com/res/deinclass/text_only.pdf.

922 Karl Marx, letter to Sigfrid Meyer and August Vogt, 9 April 1870. See https://www.marxists.org/archive/marx/works/1870/letters/70_04_09.htm.

923 Some disability-related costs are particularly high, such as a £4,000 stair lift, a £5,000 mobility scooter or an electric wheelchair, costing between £900 and £6,000.

924 *Priced Out: Ending the Financial Penalty of Disability by 2020*, Scope (2014). See http://www.scope.org.uk/Scope/media/Documents/Publication percent20Directory/Extra-Costs-Report.pdf?ext=.pdf.

925 Asghar Zaidi and Tania Burchardt, "Comparing incomes when needs differ: equivalization for the extra costs of disability in the UK", *Review of Income and Wealth* series 51, no 1, March 2005.

926 *Counting the Cost*, Demos (2010). See http://www.demos.co.uk/files/Counting_the_Cost_-_web.pdf?1292598960.

927 Attendance Allowance, for personal care costs, was introduced in 1971, followed by Mobility Allowance in 1976. These were combined to form Disability Living Allowance in 1992.

928 Scope (2014), pp13-15.

929 Demos (2010).

930 *Disability in the United Kingdom 2014: Facts and Figures* (Papworth Trust). See http://www.papworthtrust.org.uk/sites/default/files/UK percent20Disability percent20facts percent20and percent20figures percent20report percent202014.pdf, p16.

931 *Fulfilling Potential: Next Steps* (DWP, 2012), p54. See https://www.gov.uk/government/uploads/system/uploads/attachment_data/file/321046/fulfilling-potential-next-steps.pdf.

932 *Fulfilling Potential: Building a Deeper Understanding of Disability in the UK Today* (DWP, February 2013). See https://www.gov.uk/government/uploads/system/uploads/attachment_data/file/320509/building-understanding-main-report.pdf. Interestingly, when asked the same question during earlier UK research in 2001, a far higher proportion—48

percent—said they saw themselves as disabled. As with the 2012 research, the answers given also varied according to the type of impairment. (DWP, 2001)

933 "A global assessment of dementia, now and in the future", editorial, *The Lancet*, vol 386, no 9997, 5 September 2015. See http://www.thelancet.com/journals/lancet/article/PIIS0140-6736(15)00117-8/fulltext.

934 Office for Disability Issues, updated DWP estimates based on Family Resources survey 2009/10

935 *Improving the Life Chances of Disabled People*, Prime Minister's Strategy Unit (January 2005), p9. See http://webarchive.nationalarchives.gov.uk/+/http:/www.cabinetoffice.gov.uk/media/cabinetoffice/strategy/assets/disability.pdf.

936 *Disability in the United Kingdom 2014: Facts and Figures* (Papworth Trust), p7. See http://www.papworthtrust.org.uk/sites/default/files/UK percent20Disability percent20facts percent20and percent20figures percent20report percent202014.pdf.

937 See http://www.theguardian.com/society/2014/dec/18/obesity-can-be-disability-eu-court-rules.

938 Wilkinson and Pickett (2010), p91.

939 *The Guardian*, 6 May 2015. See http://www.theguardian.com/society/2015/may/05/obesity-crisis-projections-uk-2030-men-women.

940 *Fulfilling Potential: Making it Happen* (DWP, July 2013). See https://www.gov.uk/government/uploads/system/uploads/attachment_data/file/320745/making-it-happen.pdf, p54.

941 *Fulfilling Potential* (DWP, February 2013), p56.

942 Quoted in *Fulfilling Potential* (DWP, February 2013).

943 Vic Finkelstein, "The Commonality of Disability", in Swain, Finkelstein, French and Oliver, *Disabling Barriers, Enabling Environments* (Sage, 1993). See http://disability-studies.leeds.ac.uk/files/library/finkelstein-Commonality-of-Disability.pdf.

944 Catherine Kudlick, "Disability History: Why We Need Another 'Other'", *The American Historical Review*, vol 108, no 3 (June 2003), pp763-793.

945 See, for example, "Passing in the Shadow of FDR", in Jeffrey A Brune and Daniel J Wilson (eds), *Disability and Passing* (Temple University Press, 2013).

946 See Campbell and Oliver (1996), p96.

947 Campbell and Oliver (1996), p97.

948 Quoted in Papworth Trust (2010).

949 Office of Disability issues, 2008, quoted in *Fulfilling Potential* (DWP, February 2013).

950 Fulfilling Potential (DWP, 2012), p18.

951 Fulfilling Potential (DWP, 2012), p35.

952 Fulfilling Potential (DWP, July 2013), p3.

953 OECD statistics at http://stats.oecd.org/Index.aspx?datasetcode=SOCX_AGG, quoted in *Disability News Service*, 16 August 2013. See http://www.disabilitynewsservice.com/ministers-misuse-figures-to-show-uk-is-world-leader-on-disability-spending/.

954 *The Journal*, 15 September 2015. See http://www.thejournal.ie/vigil-dail-protest-anger-disability-2331523-Sep2015/?utm_source=shortlink.

955 I B Portero, "Are there rights in a time of crisis?", *Disability and Society*, vol 27, no 4 (2012).

956 The UN Convention on the Rights of Persons with Disabilities defines reasonable accommodation as "necessary and appropriate modification and adjustments not imposing a disproportionate or undue burden, where needed in a particular case, to ensure

to persons with disabilities the enjoyment or exercise on an equal basis with others of all human rights and fundamental freedoms." See http://www.un.org/disabilities/default.asp?id=262.

957 PLen Barton (ed), *Disability, Politics and the Struggle for Change* (David Fulton Publishers, 2001), p15.

958 Portero (2012).

959 Portero (2012).

960 Poore (2007), p348.

961 Rachel Reeves, the then Shadow Work and Pensions Secretary, announced in March 2015 that Labour was "not the party of people on benefits", pledging also to be tougher than the Conservatives in cutting benefits. *The Guardian*, 17 March 2015. See http://www.theguardian.com/society/2015/mar/17/labour-vows-to-reduce-reliance-on-food-banks-if-it-comes-to-power.

962 *Superhuman: Exploring Human Enhancement from 600BCE to 2050* (The Wellcome Collection, 2012), p10.

963 The most famous of these is perhaps the Berlichingen arm, named after a German knight who lost his right arm in battle in 1508. He was fitted with an iron arm and hand that was capable of moving at the joints. See, for example, Hunter Oatman-Stanford, "War and Prosthetics: How Veterans Fought for the Perfect Artificial Limb", *Collectors Weekly*, 29 October 2012. See http://www.collectorsweekly.com/articles/war-and-prosthetics/.

964 Dao, *New York Times*, 17 April 2013.

965 Ironically, after his defeat in the T43 200 metres final at the London 2012 Paralympics, Pistorius himself complained that winner Alan Oliveira had cheated by switching to longer running blades before the Games.

966 *Superhuman* (2012), p10. The use of the thalidomide drug, which had not been tested on pregnant women, led to thousands of miscarriages and stillbirths and babies born with severely disfiguring impairments.

967 "Paralysed man Darek Fidyka walks again after pioneering surgery", *The Guardian*, 21 October 2014. See http://www.theguardian.com/science/2014/oct/21/paralysed-darek-fidyka-pioneering-surgery. When asked in a subsequent radio interview if he would be paid for pioneering this technique, the surgeon responsible responded: "what money could ever compare for the feeling I have?" He also confirmed that the patient had regained some sexual and bladder function.

968 "Paralysed men move again with spinal stimulation", BBC News, 8 April 2014. See http://m.bbc.co.uk/news/health-26920521.

969 Cole (2004), pp283-284. Michael Oliver argued in 1996 that "the aim of research should not be to make the legless normal, whatever that may mean, but to create a social environment where to be legless is irrelevant."

970 Cole (2004), p284.

971 *The Guardian*, 21 October 2014.

972 See http://site.xavier.edu/polt/typewriters/tw-history.html.

973 Disability History Timeline is a fascinating compilation of disability-related historical facts and events. See http://inclusionnorth.org/uploads/attachment/307/leadership-in-transitions-disability-history-timeline.pdf

974 Shapiro (1994), p233.

975 Adrian Hamilton, "An exhibition inspired by the Paralympics looks at the quest to improve the body", *The Independent*, 23 July 2012. See http://www.independent.co.uk/hei-fi/entertainment/the-quest-to-replace-lost-parts-7965542.html.

976 J I Charlton, *Nothing About Us Without Us: Disability Oppression and Empowerment* (University of California Press, 1988) quoted in Colin Barnes and Geof Mercer (eds) *The Social Model of Disability and the Majority World* (The Disability Press, 2005). See http://disability-studies.leeds.ac.uk/files/library/Barnes-EMW-Chapter-1.pdf, p4.

977 M Miles, "The Social Model of Disability Met a Narrative of (In) Credulity: A Review", in *Disability, CBR and Inclusive Development*, vol 22, no 1, 2011.

978 Paul Abberley, "Work, Utopia and Impairment", in L Barton (ed), *Disability and Society: Emerging Issues and Insights* (Longman, 1996).

979 Karl Marx, *Critique of the Gotha Programme* (1875). See https://www.marxists.org/archive/marx/works/download/Marx_Critque_of_the_Gotha_Programme.pdf.

980 Karl Marx, *Capital*, vol 1 (1867), (Lawrence & Wishart, 2003), p715.

981 Karl Marx, *The German Ideology* (1845). See https://www.marxists.org/archive/marx/works/1845/german-ideology/ch01a.htm.

982 Martin Upchurch, "The end of the 'safe space' for unions? A response to Simon Joyce", *International Socialism* issue 146, posted 12 April 2015. See http://isj.org.uk/the-end-of-the-safe-space-for-unions/.

983 Choonara (2009), p92.

984 "Walmart Warehouse Strikers Return to Work with Full Back Pay", 9 October, 2012, http://www.labornotes.org/2012/10/walmart-warehouse-strikers-return-work-full-back-pay.

985 Oliver Sacks, *The Island of the Color Blind* (Vintage Books, 1996), pp71-72.

986 Groce (1985), pp40-43.

987 Groce (1985), p5.

988 Groce (1985), p109.

989 Murat (2014), p181. Louis August Blanqui was a socialist and contemporary of Marx who rejected mass democracy and believed that revolution had to be carried out by a small group who would establish a temporary dictatorship by force. See http://en.wikipedia.org/wiki/Louis_Auguste_Blanqui.

990 *Daily Mail*, 14 September 2015. See http://www.dailymail.co.uk/news/article-3233981/Jeremy-Corbyn-s-shadow-Cabinet.html

991 Julian Petley in James Curran, Julian Petley and Ivor Gaber (eds), *Culture Wars: The Media and the British Left*, (Edinburgh University Press, 2005), p85.

992 Chanie Rosenberg, *Education Under Capitalism and Socialism* (Socialist Workers Party, 1991), p53.

993 As shown, for example, in the film *We Are Many* (Amir Amirani, 2015).

994 Murat (2014), p221.

Index